Voyage of No Return

Voyage of No Return

A Novel

❋ INSPIRED BY TRUE EVENTS ❋

Dorian Clay

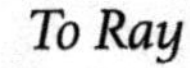

To Ray

Acknowledgments

My special thanks to my wife, Marie, for her undaunted support for so many years in the making of this novel.

And to my two sons, Justin and Jason, who have stood with me since day one.

And to my bonus daughter and most brilliant and gifted editor, Alicia. Without her this book would never have happened.

Part I

Chapter 1

Clay Family Vineyard, Hesse, Germany

1852

Thomas Clay was standing beside his mother at the edge of the vineyards. She was tall for a woman and quite slender from much hard work. She wiped a lock of flaming-red hair from her eyes with the back of her hand, then touching Thomas's shoulder, she commented, "Life was much easier when we were living in Denmark and Sweden, where your father and I first met." Then turning to take study of the produce and baskets of grapes neatly stacked at the edge of the vineyard, she sighed. "This cart is not going to load itself." Shrugging, she winked at her son with one of those blue eyes that was totally captivating. "Let's get started loading these baskets into that rickety old cart."

This cart, in spite of its condition, was the only one they had left and was harnessed to their only horse—weary and patient—his reins dropping to the ground, certainly no need to be tied. It would take a clap of very loud thunder or a stick of dynamite to provoke him into movement. The horse was nineteen years old but still able to get their harvest, meager as it was, to the town of Darmstadt no more than a few miles to the north of their home and vineyards in the central part of Germany. For certain, he was the only horse left from the many teams that had once supported the very profitable business when Thomas's father was still alive.

Most of the horses had been stolen, probably by the same group roaming the area that had killed Thomas's father. It was a difficult time in their history. The not-so-old oak wooden railroad system that his father had built and used to pull the once heavily laden wagons of grapes and other farm produce up the track with the teams of horses to Darmstadt were still in very good repair, and they hoped to use them again in the future. That endeavor, however, would require the use of the many teams of horses that they no longer had.

Thomas's father was slain on his return trip from one of these short hauls by a group made up to look like common thieves that roved the surrounding wooded countryside. However, many thought they were no common thieves and their motives had something to do with his successful business dealings. Possibly they originally intended to kidnap him and collect a hefty ransom from a distraught wife.

On that day he had collected the entire summer's revenue from one of the warehouses in town and had a considerable amount of cash that was, Thomas was quite sure, a surprise to the would-be kidnappers so they just killed him and took the money, not bothering with the ransom idea.

His death was a devastating loss to the family, as well as the robbery, presenting a staggering financial blow they would quite possibly not recover from. The local authorities said he had been attacked in a heavily wooded area near the toe of the mountainous range between the family's farm and town, then murdered and robbed of the considerable fortune he carried. It appeared to have been a severe battle to the end. Thomas knew his father was a master with the sword, and he was not surprised to hear he had left four from the group lying dead in the road before he was ultimately brought down by the much larger crowd. The consequent investigation by the local authorities suggested that there were approximately ten people against his father that day.

His mother's feelings were to the effect that there were no real investigations of this horrible crime—the authorities knew exactly what had happened and were perhaps a part of it, and the assassination and robbery of his father was clearly at the hands of a corrupt band of slave traders embedded subtly and deeply in the local government.

The family had had devastating dealings with them—the corsairs, or Ottoman slave traders—in Denmark before they left there for safety reasons and resettled in Germany. Thomas's grandparents, an uncle, an aunt, and three cousins as well as several other village residents had been kidnapped. Most of the time, they knew, prisoners were taken by privateer ships to the Barbary Coast of Algiers and Tunis on the shores of the Mediterranean Sea for the slave markets or held for ransom but usually never seen or heard from again.

Thomas and his father and mother and sister had narrowly missed that raid, as they were away visiting his mother's kin in Sweden. Every child in Europe had been warned of the dangers of falling into the hands of these corsairs, a fate worse than death, it was said. Thomas still missed his father deeply, and his mind lingered there despite the task in front of him.

"Thomas," his mother said, raising her voice with some degree of urgency. "Stop daydreaming and help me to finish loading this old cart with this day's goods and see if you can get to town and back before dark."

It had been three years since his father's death, and he was now sometimes allowed to make the trip alone. Usually his mother and his sister, Anne, and he would make the trip together with their goods, and they never followed the same backwoods route that his father had taken, where the wooden railroad still lay, but he was starting to make the trip alone more and more. Thomas was, after all, twelve years old and nearly a man, large and strong for his age and a hard worker, even by his mother's standards, but she still worried about him being alone and out of her sight. His father's death had such a horrifying impact on their family and all those around, reminding them how vulnerable they all still were to the daily hardships they faced and the corrupt political system.

They finished loading the old cart, and Thomas thought even without the constant concern of bandits, foul weather, and bad roads, he would be lucky to get to the bustling city of Darmstadt, unload at the warehouse, and return in a week, let alone before dark, which was only three hours away. Climbing into the cart amongst its considerable goods, he waved and reassured his mother he would return before dark.

Riding along at a snail's pace but the fastest pace the old horse could travel gave Thomas more than adequate time to ponder a fate at the hands of the corsairs. His mother had spoken to him of them many times since his father's death, but he still didn't comprehend the full meaning of the group or the vast area of their influence. The Barbary Coast slave traders from Algiers, Tunis, and Tripoli that had once haunted portions of the Mediterranean, England, and most of the countries bordering the North Sea had been responsible for over a million poor souls kidnapped and sent to the slave markets. Ultimately, but not entirely, they had been driven out by the English and American navies. However, in being forced from their quarters along the Barbary Coast, they had simply moved to other areas of Europe and were still quite active in their barbaric practices.

In spite of the many dangers and constant threats, Thomas loved these weekly trips to the city with their goods. His father, with all his political and business influence, had managed to obtain an 1847 Colt Walker revolving six-shot pistol prior to his death. He had personally met Samuel Walker, the inventor of this pistol, on a trading trip he had made to America. Thomas's father and Mr. Walker had remained friends until his father's death. The Colt Walker was a formidable weapon, but unfortunately Thomas's father had not been carrying it at the time of his death and robbery or, Thomas was quite certain, neither would have happened. Father had taught him to shoot it, load it, and clean it.

Chapter 2

Darmstadt Road,
Hesse, Germany

1852

In the past two years, Thomas had nearly been robbed twice. The first occasion was by a single bandit that was armed only with a sword and walking stick. He was shabbily clothed and carried a small flea-ridden bundle on his back. He shouted at Thomas sitting on the wagon to toss down his purse with coins.

"Not likely," Thomas replied with a certain degree of confidence and a lot of cynicism. "And you don't have to shout. You're only an arm's length from me, and I can hear perfectly well."

This took the robber by surprise, and he once more demanded in a milder tone, "Hand over the purse."

Being large for his age, Thomas looked him over carefully and felt he could fairly flay him with his sword—however, he did not have it, so Thomas casually bent over as to pick up the purse handily stashed by his seat and pulled up the shiny Colt Walker instead. The pistol was as long as the distance between the end of his fingers and elbow, looking more like a small cannon. Pulling the hammer back and pointing it directly at the robber's midsection, wondering if he could really shoot someone, Thomas stared and casually said, "Should necessity dictate such action, I can and will shoot you. We have too little to share with the likes of a bony thief. I would suggest that you turn the other way and start walking very fast."

The robber smiled nervously, ſtaring at the huge piſtol, the likes of which he had surely never seen before, and said, "I think I will do juſt that," as he turned and ran as if being chased by the hounds of hell.

The city was always so busy with activities and people dressed in fine clothes, filled with never-ending laughter, a conſtant babble of gossip, and the feeling of being safe. The ſtreets were crowded with people and coaches and wagons loaded with an array of goods—some wandering aimlessly through the ſtreets and others progressing orderly on the wooden rails acting as a track syſtem for moving freight and passenger cars. The buildings were ancient three- and four-ſtory buildings of an architecture that defied consiſtency. During Thomas's limited time now of being the man of the house and tending to some of the financing and bartering in delivering goods to the city, he'd managed to inveſtigate moſt of the city's capacities and was quite familiar with its bland charm. It lacked the colorful attitude of other cities that Thomas's mother had read to him and Anne about and shown pictures of, but it did hold a certain attraction.

The ſtench at times was hardly bearable, though. The hundreds of carts and coaches that lined the busy ſtreets were horse drawn, with horses leaving tremendous amount of residual residue in the form of tons of horse manure. Thomas was quite fascinated by the city but, once there, could hardly wait to return home again to the peace and quiet of the countryside. Their farm was of considerable size, taking up much of the surrounding countryside with vineyards, orchards, and vegetable gardens full of such root crops as potatoes, carrots, turnips, radishes, onions, and garlic as well as lettuce and fields of hay and grains, barleys, and such. Even though their farm was only a short diſtance from Darmſtadt, it was very secluded with no really close neighbors. They seldom had company, and it was a lonely setting with only his mother, Anne, and himself.

Creaking along at a slow pace, Thomas thought much of the dangers they faced at that time in Germany. He thought much of the lonely life they lived and the hard work handed to their family after Father's death. They no longer could afford the many attendants his father had managed, nor could they put out the harveſts he had so successfully kept.

Their once-comfortable lifestyle was gone. Their modest prosperity was gone, and with this their abundant friends seemed to be gone. Of these facts Thomas did not have to think much on—it was the way things were. They were barely able to hold on to what they had. He knew he was young and of little experience, but he had many conversations with his mother about the pending fate of the farm. It was slowly deteriorating in front of their very eyes, but there was little they could do but survive from day to day.

Their home, typical for the time in rural Germany, was of the Quereinhaus design. It was a long, two-story building of which their living quarters were in one half with a hallway that ran front to back, splitting the building in halves. The kitchen was the focal point of the home where they ate, rested, and spent their family time. The upstairs had three small bedrooms, each with a window and shutters. The kitchen also had a window with shutters on each side and a huge fireplace with hanging steel arms to hang cooking pots from. The other side of the same building on the upper level had shocks of hay and quantities of grain stored for the animals. The lower level—across the hall from their living quarters—held stalls for the milk cows and horses as well as a small hard and level surface on which grains were threshed with a flail. When Father was alive, it had been a cheerful place with so much room for Thomas and Anne to run, hide, and play. The stone cellar was attached to the back of the house opening into the kitchen and was crammed with necessary foodstuffs, mainly common staples but always enough for family and friends who'd often frequented them in those times.

Now the days of summer were passing too quickly. Mother and Thomas would start work at daylight and would only stop for a short noon dinner and then back at it until dark and supper. No matter how hard the day, Mother would still always sit down after supper for special time with Anne and Thomas, storytelling or reading out of the many books in their well-stocked library. Father had been a very well-versed man who'd read and collected books on every subject available. Books were very hard to come by, but he had managed to amass a considerable library of most of the ol' classics as well as some newer books on advanced mathematical theories, current politics, and others Thomas could not understand.

Although he missed their old lifestyle, Thomas was grateful for all they still had.

Chapter 3

Clay Family Vineyard, Hesse, Germany

1855

This was now the third fall since Thomas's father's death, and he was fifteen years old. The years had dragged by with the time spent doing only work and studies, and they had no time for social activities nor the financial ability for such and received only a very rare visitor. The days now were noticeably shortening, much to Thomas's delight, and the leaves had turned to their beautiful colors that dominated the countryside in Germany in fall. On that day, those stunning leaves were still very evident, but overnight it had turned viciously cold. The wind was gusting, and it had started to sleet.

After supper on this particular chilly fall night, Mother said, "Thomas, get out your quill and some paper. From the looks of the weather, I think it's time to start your lessons again."

"What about her?" Thomas said. "Doesn't Anne have to study too?"

Mother blew a curly lock of her fire-red hair from over one eye, gave him that look, and pointed a finger, which started him in the right direction for the necessary items. "Don't worry about her." She smiled. "She can already knit and crochet better than you, and if you don't want to perfect those skills, I would suggest you get busy on things more to your tastes."

After Father's death, Mother's smiles were very rare but when they came, they would radiate the entire room. Thomas knew she was only joking with him and was delighted for these rare moments. Due to his mother's insistence on their continual education, Thomas and Anne both had learned to read and write at a very young age, and the other related academic skills just fell into place despite not having the benefit of a formal school with other children of their age, thanks to their father's willingness to teach and their mother's continual persistence of education. Thomas had to give them credit that he had read such fine works of art as Daniel Defoe's *Robinson Crusoe* and *Moll Flanders*—though that one was not to his liking—and Jonathan Swift's *Gulliver's Travels*, Charles Dickens's *The Adventures of Oliver Twist*, and many more of that nature, most of them interesting and enjoyable. Also to his credit were some of his father's books on politics, philosophy, science, astronomy, and geology—not so interesting—and one other he'd found buried behind the other books that he dared not mention, and he most certainly did not tell his mother about. As yet he had no knowledge of any of the pleasures described in this manuscript or seen any other images as in that volume so had no opinion of these things other than mild curiosity. However, in giving this a bit more thought, he could not imagine his mother and father indulged in these activities and cared not to ponder this further.

Mathematics and the study of different languages were by far his favorite subjects. His father had started him on the basics at a very young age, and he had an inherent aptitude for these subjects. Now he was not only fluent in German but also English, French, and Spanish. Father had taught him well, and he'd continued his studies. At fifteen years old, Thomas was also well-versed in the studies of algebra, geometry, physics, and astromancy. Mother had indicated on several occasions that Thomas and Anne had the same level of education as college students. Thomas had by far surpassed his mother's mathematical skills, and they were both aware of that.

One evening while deeply involved in one of Father's books on physics by Aristotle, Thomas took another leap of faith trying to gain one of his mother's rare smiles. He asked for some advice on a physics problem. She gave him that head tilt with the red hair falling into her eye again and then the smile but made no comment on the matter of physics. He left it at that, satisfied with the smile.

The winter was becoming very harsh. Over the summer and fall, they had prepared well for this winter, cutting and stacking many cords of wood. The fireplace in the kitchen kept the whole house comfortable, but they were consuming alarming amounts of wood. It was in this warm and comfortable atmosphere that Mother spent hours lecturing them on the subjects she was so familiar with, everything except mathematics and physics. She would talk to them of what little she knew of issues in Denmark prior to moving to Germany. She would talk relentlessly of Father's pursuit of knowledge and wealth in the shipping industry in Denmark, which could have been somewhat accountable for the loss of so many poor family members to the corsairs. Knowing that the family had some wealth, the corsairs would kidnap them then demand ransom money prior to sending them to the auction block. In their case, they were never obliged with the ransom notice and did not have the opportunity to negotiate their loved ones' release—they never again heard from those poor souls. After fleeing Denmark for Darmstadt, Germany, Father had once again set himself up as a merchant, renting some space in the warehouse on the quayside in Nierstein on the Rhine River only a few miles from Darmstadt. He had invested heavily in the ship cargoes from the Americas, primarily tobacco from the Virginias and coffee from wherever he could get it. At that time there were no dependable sources for that commodity.

With Anne and Thomas sitting in front of the warm fire in the kitchen, the wind and hail rattling the shutters, Mother spent many evenings telling them of the many wonders of America, often still referred to as the New World. She still had such a fear of the distant Ottoman corsairs and the local bandits—perhaps some were the same—wandering the surrounding countryside and was constantly on the watch for anything of a suspicious nature. She would never forget the experience of losing so many of her relatives.

On one evening, Mother told Thomas and Anne of the great American fleets helping the English to rid the Barbary Coast of the privateers and slave traders. She lived in hope that even after this many years, they may hear from some of her own who had been captured by Barbary Coast corsairs and that they would still have an opportunity to ransom their release should they have funds to do so. There were stories of this kind of thing happening, and she lived in hope—and still harbored great anxiety toward the group that had been principally responsible for her family's exodus from their beautiful home in Denmark.

They talked often of the vast wildernesses in America, about the abundance of wild game, the clean rivers and streams, and the great wild buffalo herds. Other times she would tell stories of the gold found in the Oregon Territory and California, of the beautiful cities of New York, Philadelphia, and San Francisco. Thomas had heard many of these details of the great America from talk at the marketplace, from the people he was associated with in delivering their goods around the warehouse districts in Darmstadt, and from the occasional trip to his father's old haunts in Nierstein over on the Rhine River. Everywhere that people gathered, the talk was of the opportunities of the great Americas. The hardships of the pioneers on the Oregon Trail, the fur trappers, and the mountain men. This was the time of the prodigious migration of Germans to America. Thousands were leaving Germany for the Americas.

One evening after supper when Mother was assisting the children in their lessons, Thomas said to her, "I'm going to go to America."

She looked at him with a steady gaze from those piercing blue eyes, making him somewhat uncomfortable, and he looked down. One eyebrow still cocked at an alarming slant, she replied, "I have no uncertainty that you will one day go to America, but you will take your sister and me with you."

That was not a request that required an answer, so he did not reply. He did want always to be with his family, but this did bring a flood of uncertain feelings to his mind. They were all getting very tired of this long, hard, and very unfriendly winter. They had an uncharacteristic amount of snow, which had stacked to a height of over three feet, and he was ready for spring. Even though his duties during the winter were simple—only tending to the one old horse, milking the cow, and gathering a few eggs, and of course the never-ending studies—he was ready for spring and the extra workload of the long, hard days ahead.

He was ready to put the books away and face the challenges of whatever the new season may bring.

Mother would get an occasional newspaper, typically heavily censored of local German news but containing much about matters in other parts of Europe and especially America. The great America was always on their minds, and Thomas was quite certain they would one day visit there and very possibly make the move.

During his trips to town, he rarely missed the opportunity to stop at the workshop of Mr. Hollenbeck. He was a gunsmith and had been a very trusted friend of his father's. They would converse tirelessly, sometimes for hours, about the finer points of gunsmithing, current events, political turmoil in Germany, and what was known about life in America. Mr. Hollenbeck and his wife, Cattie, had two children, a son and a daughter, who had emigrated to America two years prior. They were always speaking of them kindly but missed them dearly. In a small way, Thomas's visits helped fill the void of that loneliness. He was quite fond of Mr. Hollenbeck—or Raymond, as Thomas was informed would be quite adequate. Mrs. Hollenbeck, however, would never escape the formal term of Mrs. Hollenbeck. Thomas had no grandparents, having lost them to the corsairs when he was only a small child. He treasured the Hollenbecks' company profoundly.

When it was time for him to leave for home, Mrs. Hollenbeck would sometimes send a basket of freshly baked pastries to share with his family. The first time he had returned home with these delicacies, his mother had commented, "Lovely, and where did you get these, young Thomas?"

"From Father's old friends the Hollenbecks. You know—he is the gunsmith on the outskirts of Darmstadt."

She sighed, staring at him with a frown. "Your father knew how I disliked violent weapons and failed to tell me about that old friend. But I am happy that you have maintained that relationship. Hollenbeck—a different name, certainly not German. I wonder, what is the origin of their background?"

Looking up and grinning, Thomas said, "Well, probably Yorkshire in northern England or perhaps Derbyshire in its central part."

"Oh my God," Mother said in mock frustration, hands on hips staring at Thomas. "Is there no end to your limitless knowledge of trivia?"

"Not likely," he replied with a crooked smile. "You are responsible for holding my feet to the fire, insisting I read everything available and study all the scholarly issues at hand, since I was born I think."

Rolling her eyes and raising her hands in the air, she gave one of her rare smiles and left him to his studies.

Chapter 4

Clay Family Vineyard,
Hesse, Germany

1856

Thomas's father had been an admirable man with the sword—few better in all Germany, Thomas had heard—and had started his only son in that art at a very early age. Thomas had trained with Father from the time he could walk by means of only a stick to swing and jab. By the time Thomas was five years old, with Father's constant coaching, he had become quite proficient with the blade. His father was moderately proud of this achievement, and friends were totally amazed. While accompanying Father on short trips to the wharfs in Erfelden—not much of a wharf, as it sat on the Alter Rhein, just an oxbow of the Rhine—Thomas was forever asked to exercise with friends of his father. They all took tremendous delight in facing such a small and quite excellent foe. Each had a slightly different style, and Thomas's abilities soon advanced to a point that totally astonished his father, the master of the art. He continued to practice when occasion presented itself, and he would one day soon be as good as his father had been.

During the summer months in delivering his family's goods to the warehouses in the city, Thomas would still take the time to visit and spar with some of his father's old friends. He achieved a tremendous degree of finesse. He was older, taller, heavier, and much stronger from his constant practice with the sword and hard work at the farm. None of the old friends were better than him now, but the practice was in keeping his skills as sharp as the sword.

Of this, Thomas talked little to his mother about and never showed the blade in their home. It was tucked away in a corner of the barn where his mother never visited. It was right beside the Colt Walker .44 and the other articles that went with it. She hated violence of any nature with a passion that was unwavering. However, she did not speak to Thomas of quitting the practice or giving up the Colt. She knew the sword was something for which he had a great passion, and it was a small remembrance of one of his father's favorite pursuits. The Colt Walker .44 was something entirely different—there was not another firearm in the country like it, and it was strictly for protection.

The winter finally lessened, and spring with all its magnificence was about. The daffodils and tulips were always the first to raise their delicate heads from the small patches of ground appearing where the snow had melted first. The trees were starting to bud, and it was—according to Mother—a splendid time of year. Thomas was excited about the pending spring, but the reality of long, hard workdays ahead was starting to set in.

During the winter months, they discussed a systematic plan to revive the orchards for better crops and tend the vineyards to increase grape production. They slowly brought themselves to accept the tragedy of Father's death and try to get the farm back to a producing manner before it was too late for such efforts to matter. Mother reasoned that if they could possibly once again afford some support, they could get the farm back on its feet and shoes back on their feet. They had no money left from Father's account, and it was time for a fresh start.

Mother was busier than ever, if that were imaginable. She came to Thomas when he had the cart ready for his first trip to town with spring crops from the garden. "Keep an eye out for somebody we may hire for the season," she said. "We need a hardy lad who can prune the trees and vineyard as well as help in removing the winter's residue of cow manure from the barns to be used as fertilizer on the gardens and vineyards."

"That I will do," Thomas replied. He reminded her of their severely decrepit old horse hitched to the cart. "It would be good to have some help and another horse, a young and healthy one."

"Good luck with the horse part." She shrugged. "We may be able to hire a temporary helper, but new horses—as bad as we need some—are out of the question for this year."

Thomas no longer measured himself a young boy, and his mother did not treat him as one either. He had been carrying a man's burdens for some time and could converse with some of the warehouse district's finest scholars with never a foul word. And he had become a favorite visitor with many of his father's old friends, who still worked with him tirelessly in practice with the sword. Still being young in years and hardly more than just a boy, he was very good. Thomas felt he was, at this early age, as good or better than some of them, and possibly better than most, and perhaps even better than his father had been. He thought of this with a smile knowing Father would be very proud.

On the trip back from the market, Thomas had a second and very serious encounter with a group that wished to relieve him of his proceeds. Thomas was always very conscious of his surroundings on the slightly used road going to and from the market area in Darmstadt. His practiced eye picked many unusual tracks in the dusty road and a slight disturbance in the heavy brush along the side. Suddenly the brush exploded with riders, sullen and menacing in appearance. On this occasion, there were six of them, mounted and all armed with blades and clubs.

To say the least, Thomas was truly afraid, sitting alone on the cart quivering like a fall leaf in a hefty breeze. His father had always cautioned him that the worst thing to do in an emergency was to panic. *Easier said than done*, he thought, but with that verdict, a bit of his courage returned.

The outlaws were no better dressed than the first lonely bandit he had met two years before, and they were making very little noise due to their proximity to Darmstadt. It was a very eerie scene, and the hair was standing up on the back of Thomas's neck. These hostiles were riding beautiful horses, four of them he recognized as most likely some that had belonged to his father. He was sure that these reprobates had had something to do with Father's robbery and death. Thomas felt such a flood of emotion at now facing some of the group that he threw all caution to the wind. This had been a long time coming, and Thomas was ready for this conflict.

The rider in the lead was staring at Thomas, totally emotionless. "Hand over your purse of coins, boy."

Thomas being severely rankled at the word *boy* made no reply but casually bent over as to pick up the purse but instead pulled up the Colt and fired, making no attempt to aim.

It was like flock shooting a tightly knit group of geese. The thunderous roar of that pistol with smoke and flame belching from its barrel and the echo from the surrounding hillside created total mayhem amongst horses and riders. Thomas's own poor old nag was also—for the first time in ten years, he was quite sure—dancing on her hind legs, swinging the cart in a circle, causing even more confusion. With one shot, Thomas had emptied three horses of their riders, now thrashing on the ground and trying to make some sense of what had just happened, but three horses were still with riders attempting to gain some mark of control of their mounts, so he fired again. And with the same results. Two more horses were bucking, rearing, and snorting. Neither horse nor rider had ever witnessed a weapon like this that bellowed smoke and carried the impact of a cannonball.

Thomas's old horse jolted once more in a circle, causing more confusion and making his aim more unpredictable. On his third shot he hit one of the horses squarely in the arse, and the heavy bullet came out his side and embedded in the leg of that rider. Thomas was truly sorry for hurting that animal. He hadn't just injured him—he had surely killed him dead and only wounded the rider.

As some degree of order returned to this agonizing scene, Thomas noticed only one horse still with rider, though that rider had blood running down his cheek and was missing one ear. Noting this, Thomas was somewhat disappointed, as he thought he had aimed for his middle and only got an ear. He had held the pistol with both hands at arm's length as his father had instructed, but with each roar of belching flame and smoke, his arms would fly upward from the kick of the pistol, demanding time to bring it back down and once again take proper aim. The other five figures flailed on the ground.

Gaining control of his own old nag, Thomas stood in the wagon shouting, "You there, on the horse, dismount!"

The man rapidly did so, holding the side of his head with blood spurting between his fingers from his missing ear. Not a one of them could fathom what a fifteen-year-old boy with such a magnificent pistol had done.

Thomas kept the pistol trained on the men huddled on the ground and ordered the man who had so obligingly dismounted to gather up and secure all five of the remaining horses to a nearby tree. He didn't notice in the disorder that he had fully run over two of the men with his cart as they were scrambling around on the ground, and now they each appeared to have a broken leg.

With the pistol still pointing into their midst, Thomas calmly ordered them to pick up their belongings, including the swords they had dropped higgledy-piggledy over the immediate area—he had no need for six swords of varying degrees of quality—and ordered them to leave the country of Germany. They all stared at him, disbelieving what had just happened and the manner of the order a fifteen-year-old boy had just delivered. Thomas still had three shots in the heavy revolver but hesitated to shoot again, not knowing what further chaos would result from such a deafening, smoking roar of the pistol and definitely not wanting to be forced to attempt to reload if necessary.

Even though this formidable weapon held six shots, it was not necessarily easy to reload and did take considerable time, at least for him. Each of the six holes in the cylinder had to be recharged with powder, then wad, then bullet, all properly measured and fitted or it could blow up in his face. This was not something he wanted to do in a hurry.

The badly shaken leader of the group said, "You can't just expect us to walk away without our mounts, some of us severely wounded and in need of a doctor."

Surprised at this statement, Thomas was quite certain no man blasted with such a cannon as his would require the services of a doctor—he would have met his untimely demise and would require the services of the undertaker.

So Thomas yelled, "Your mounts? These belonged to my father! Your group robbed and murdered him. I do not expect you to walk away. I demand you run and make due the best you can, or it will not be some of you wounded—it will be all of you with blood spurting from missing appendages."

Sudden comprehension came to the man's eyes, and knowing what charges they would face—if they lived long enough to face charges before the ruling classes—they begrudgingly started making an attempt to gather their belongings and bandage their bloodied and wounded group. Thomas watched them stumble out of sight around the next corner, then hurriedly tied the five horses to the cart. If he could get them home without further incident, it would greatly improve the family's chances of once again having an industrious and rewarding farm.

Upon arriving home with horses in tow, Thomas had to relate the tale to his mother. She was first struck with total panic, then awe, then anger, and then she gained some degree of understanding of the event, knowing what the horses meant and the fact that some retribution had come to her husband's wrongdoers. After Thomas related the events to her in detail, his mother once again waved the red curl of hair from her face and said, "I hope you never run out of powder for that thing," and flounced off shakily to the house, where she sat down and consumed a very large cup of wine from their own vineyards.

It was only a few days later after a very severe lecture from her concerning the dangers on the road to and from the Darmstadt markets and the fact that they didn't need more horses bad enough to shoot bandits for, Thomas was scheduled to make another trip. It was one of these first spring journeys and a stunning morning that he met Fredrick C. Burgdorf, "a strapping young man," his mother would later say.

Chapter 5

Darmstadt Road,
Hesse, Germany

1856

Ahead, Thomas could see a man was walking toward town only a mile or so from his terminus going the same course as him. He stopped the cart beside the man, totally astonished to see anyone along this stretch of road. He had only seen one or two other vagrants here in several years. He was nearly at a loss for words but not quite. With some degree of concern and not wanting another bandit encounter, he casually unfolded the coat he had lain over his pistol.

"Who are you?" Thomas asked, turning sideways in the wagon seat and looking down at the man with a somewhat puzzled frown.

"Well, who are you?" the young man snapped back. He was somewhat bigger and older than Thomas, but Thomas felt no real peril.

"I asked first," Thomas replied, regaining some of his wit.

He tilted his ragged hat back to expose more of his face and a nearly yellow shock of hair, then said with an amount of arrogance, "I am Fredrick C. Burgdorf, and that's how I prefer to be addressed."

"What are you doing here, and where are you from, Fredrick C. Burgdorf?" Thomas asked. He only knew a few people in Darmstadt and Nierstein over on the Rhine, mostly of his father's friends, but he knew he had never seen this one before.

The stranger looked at Thomas shiftily and replied, "Why are you asking?" some of his defensiveness now lacking.

Thomas's younger years dealing with the dock work and merchants in town had taught him a certain amount about character, and he thought this one may have a lot of it. Without revealing too much of his family condition, not sure if Fredrick C. Burgdorf's intentions were to take advantage of Thomas or not, and still not knowing where the man was from, Thomas retorted, "I'm looking to hire someone to work at our farm for the summer."

He took a better look at Thomas—worn clothes, beaten shoes, and shabby coat—and hooted. "You look no better off than I. How much and how will I be compensated, if I was looking for work?"

Thomas hastily reviewed his attire and noticed he also looked like a vagrant, having not troubled to change clothes this morning before leaving for town, a mistake he would not make again. He did have decent clothes, even though handmade, and some left by his father that he hadn't quite grown into but nevertheless would have been better than what he was wearing now. "Well," said Thomas with some awkwardness, "we can pay you thirty thaler per month and a small portion in advance. From the looks of your unkempt being, you could use it just to get in a condition to work."

At this, Fredrick C. Burgdorf grinned and said, "Who is *we* and who are *you*?"

Their verbal sparring was now put aside, and Thomas replied. "I am now Thomas Clay. My mother, Frida, and sister, Anne, live on a small farm close by, and we are severely in need of help getting our farmstead back in order after my father's death a few years ago."

Fredrick studied him for a few moments trying to decide if his offer was worthy of consideration. Then with a smile, he stuck out his hand and said, "I humbly accept your offer and expect no wage till I have earned it. As to where I'm from and why I am here, we can discuss at a more fitting time. I will assure you that I am neither a thief nor a murderer. However, I may have a few other small vices that may be somewhat dubious."

Unbeknownst to Thomas, Fredrick was now considering his own question with wry humor. Who was he? A fair question, but a difficult one. He was nobody. He was a young man without a name of his own, born of parents somewhere, somehow, but with no heritage of reputation or love. *I am nobody. I'm nobody at all. And soon if I don't get employment and something to eat, I'll even be less than that—a skeleton lying in the woods in a secret place under a tree.*

Chuckling, something Thomas had rarely done for years, he said, "This cart will hold another person if you care to ride."

Fredrick C. Burgdorf took him up on the offer, piled his very few possessions in the back of the cart, clambered in himself, and together they accomplished the trip to town with the scanty load, and homeward bound they were. Thomas said to Fredrick, "My mother will be happy to make your acquaintance, I'm sure." The conversation on their return trip was steady but was lacking any degree of importance—the weather, the colors, animals, and such. Thomas had not felt contented to inform his new friend yet of the trouble he'd had on previous trips or of the true solemn nature of the farm. He thought Fredrick also seemed somewhat hesitant in enlightening him more of his past or reason for being there at that place at that time.

When they came within sight of the farm, Thomas could see his mother and Anne in front of the house watching their approach. They had surely noticed Thomas's approach before but had never observed another person riding with him. The women both were gazing with some uneasiness the closer the boys got.

"Well, what do we have here?" Thomas's mother asked as he pulled up alongside her.

"This is Fredrick C. Burgdorf, our new associate," he said. Thomas used the man's name in its entirety, as he had been informed earlier about the preference. *A bit eccentric*, Thomas thought, *but if that is what he wants and he can turn a decent day's work, it is okay with me.*

"Well, Fredrick, wel—" Frida started but was also immediately informed the man favored to be called the full Fredrick C. Burgdorf. Smiling, she started again, "Well, Fredrick C. Burgdorf, welcome to the farm."

"Thank you," he replied.

"Thomas," she said, "gather Mr. Burgdorf's belongings"—then corrected herself—"please gather Fredrick C. Burgdorf's belongings and show him to a comfortable spot in the barn. Supper is nearly ready, and I'm sure you're both famished." Looking at Anne, she said, "Could you bid Fredrick C. Burgdorf good evening?"

Unlike Thomas, Anne was small for her age, rather shy, and would not attempt that name for some time.

"Come," Thomas told the man, "we shall find you a place to rest your weary head and clean up for supper."

"My head is rather weary as well as the rest of me," Fredrick admitted. "I have been walking steadily with little to eat for weeks." He gathered his worldly belongings in one hand and followed Thomas into the barn and upstairs to the hay loft just across the hall from his room. Fredrick picked a spot upstairs in the loft with the comfort of hay for a cushion and a blanket that Frida had furnished. The spring weather was mild, and the new farmhand would be most comfortable until fall when he probably was to move on.

Thomas's mother had put on a meal that would have impressed royalty, so Fredrick's eyes fairly bulged from his head as he cast an eye on the first real meal he had had in months. His behaviors were soon forgotten as he ate not sparingly of the many dishes Frida had arranged. Anne and Thomas both sat in total amazement at the measures of food this fellow could eat. Their mother just smiled. They had had no company for a considerable time, and she did relish his enjoyment in her skills with the food.

Dawn came early the next morning, and Thomas was totally astonished to find Fredrick up before him and out in the vineyard pruning. "These vines look as though they haven't been tended to for years," he commented.

"They haven't. Now let's go for breakfast," Thomas said. "Mother has put on another spread, and I'm hungry." Apparently so was Fredrick. As soon as all the piles of waffles, eggs, and ham had vanished from the table, they were hard at work in the vineyards.

During the following days, Fredrick and Thomas worked untiringly patching fences, fertilizing the small fields, and working the vast vineyards as well as doing repairs to the house and other out structures. Fredrick attacked the work handed to him with a vengeance and would never stop. It was the start of a pleasing spring. The boys talked limitlessly of everything that came to their minds, although no matter how craftily Thomas tried to encourage Fredrick to reveal more of his mysterious past, he never budged and would always turn the discussion in another direction.

"Fredrick C. Burgdorf," Thomas would say, "you once told me you would reveal where you were from and what you were doing here."

Looking him straight in the eyes and holding the gaze, Fredrick replied, "When we first met, you said your name was now Thomas Clay. What did you mean by *now*, inferring that it once may have been something else?"

Thomas had forgotten about that possibly fatal slip of the tongue. He broke the eye contact first, and it was his turn to change the course of conversation. He did not bring up Fredrick's past again for a lengthy time, realizing what might unfold with explaining each of their pasts.

Chapter 6

Clay Family Vineyard,
Hesse, Germany

1856

When Thomas and Anne had been babies, their mother and father had made the decision to move from Denmark after the tragic kidnapping of the children's grandfather, grandmother, uncles, aunts, and cousins by the Barbary corsairs. When they arrived in Germany, they changed their name from Klaus to Clay. They felt they were very lucky in escaping, though they talked little of this tragic and painful event to Anne and Thomas as the children grew up, so in any case Thomas knew little about that time and learned more only after his father's death. Fearing the possibility of still another attack even after all these years, Frida had related the story in its entirety. She spared no details as to what had happened or the probable consequences. Both Anne and Thomas had occasionally quizzed their mother about their grandparents to no gain, and it wasn't until now that they learned the true and horrible nature of the tragedy that had robbed them all. Thomas read expansively from his father's books on European culture, events, and politics, but his death was too recent an event to show in any of the books in the family's considerable library.

Thomas did not know Fredrick well enough to discuss family secrets, especially not ones as sensitive as this, although they had spent much time together over the last months since their first meeting. Thomas now measured him a dear friend and ally—the two were nearly insep-arable. Frida had taken an immediate liking to him as well, and Anne would now pester him doggedly.

The day finally came when Anne could say "Fredrick C. Burgdorf" clearly. She was in the garden alone and stepped on a snake, only a harmless garden snake, as that was the only kind they had in that part of Germany. Even though small and harmless, to her it was horrifying, and she clearly screeched, "Fredrick C. Burgdorf, please help me!" and he did so, severing the snake's head from its body with a shovel before her very eyes. If ever there was a question of loyalty to the family, it was now settled, and he was a part of them.

In the pasture they now had five horses that Thomas had retrieved from the bandits months earlier. They had had little time to work with them or repair the wagons that sat on the abandoned wooden track that Father once used to haul the vast quantities of grapes to the mar-ketplace in Darmstadt. Due to the excessive help from Fredrick, who had not only pruned the fruit trees but also had brought the extensive acres of grapes back to a producing crop, they would now need the large horse-drawn wagons that still sat behind the barn on the tracks. Thomas was still using the old cart but hauling much larger loads of goods several trips a week. It was now time to think on the repairs of the larger wagons, the harnesses, and other related burdens that went with this long-forgotten endeavor.

Mother came out to Fredrick and Thomas's area of work and casu-ally mentioned, "Perhaps you need to revisit some of your father's old business connections and friends in the wineries." She approached the matter very tactfully, but Thomas was still a bit self-conscious of the fact he had not thought of that himself. The family once not so long ago had some of the finest vineyards in the country, it was said, and Thomas wanted that standing again. Fredrick had not attended Thomas to town once since coming to work many months ago. Thomas had not insisted on his company even though he thoroughly enjoyed it. It was settled that due to dubious activities in the recent past, Fredrick should remain behind to assist Frida and Anne in case of an emergency of any kind. Fredrick was nearly two years older than Thomas, but not once did Thomas feel threatened by his presence, and Fredrick likewise was never uneasy with taking instructions from any of them. Thomas knew Fredrick was in all likelihood more experienced at the daily work routine than him, but Fredrick never reminded Thomas of that one time—and somehow always remained cheerful, hardworking, and completely at ease with this lifestyle. Thomas was more relaxed with him there to help look after things while he was away, and his mother and sister were obviously more at ease.

It was only two days later that Fredrick said to Thomas while working on the wagons behind the barn, "Don't stare, but there are people standing in the woods off to our left about a hundred yards out. They have been vigilantly watching us from a concealed position for more than an hour," he said.

Thomas had seen the same on various occasions over the past months but had not mentioned it to his mother, as she was still very sensitive about his father's death and his recent encounters with bandits. One of those now missing an ear, two with a broken leg, one with a bullet in his knee, and all with severely damaged egos. Thomas shared this with Fredrick now and speculated on whether the ones in the trees now were of the same group or another roving gang.

Fredrick frowned at Thomas for the first time since their first meeting on the road near Darmstadt months ago. "Thomas, lad, you should have told me of this. We must keep more ready."

Again Thomas was self-conscious, knowing Fredrick was right, and now told him of other incidents of the same nature. Fredrick listened intently, deep in thought. Thomas had a strong feeling that Fredrick's perceptive awareness now had much to do with the past he was so elusive about. Fredrick never called Thomas's mother by her first name—it was always Mrs. Clay. He had been with the family now for four months, but he always addressed her with that respect. Anne, he referred to as "the little one" unless talking directly to her, and even then at times he would call her "Little One." She took much delight in this. Now, he said, "Thomas, we should inform Mrs. Clay as to the presence of those we have sporadically spotted in the woods."

"I think you're right, and we shall do so tonight at supper."

Fredrick nodded in agreement, and no more was said of it for the rest of the day. They were both much more watchful from this moment on, and Fredrick was not quite his usual easygoing self. Supper was placed on the table in its normal abundance that evening, and Fredrick attacked it like the hungry man he always seemed to be. All the food he could eat had taken a startling toll on Fredrick—he had gained much weight, considerable width and thickness to his chest, and had actually become the strapping young man Frida referred to him as. The same applied to Thomas—he was no longer a gangly boy but one of tremendous strength and even a little more height than Fredrick, though two years younger.

At supper that night, Thomas was uneasy. He couldn't stop fidgeting and had hardly any appetite. He didn't quite know how to address the issue Fredrick and he had witnessed in the woods earlier in the day or the other occasions when he had seen people. Fredrick came to his rescue.

"Mrs. Clay," he said, getting her undivided attention. Then he casually reconstructed the events of the day's sighting of men hidden in the surrounding woods with little input from Thomas.

Frida was plainly shaken and sat for a few moments in complete silence. "I was afraid of something like this happening." She shivered even though the evening was warm. "I always have a deep-seated fear of those who nearly ruined our life in Denmark showing here in Germany, especially after we have reached some degree of success again." She said, "In the few months since Fredrick has been here to help, we have been able to get the farm on its feet and productive. We will show substantial profit this year," she said. "There were those who would have liked to see us completely fail and lose it all in its entirety to one of your father's enemies. He had few enemies, but those few were formidable. He was a very successful businessman again since coming to Germany, but that came with a very high price. His death."

That slip of "since coming to Germany" did not pass Fredrick's keen ears, but he respectfully did not mention it.

It was now rapidly approaching fall. Fredrick, Frida, Anne, and Thomas had been working tirelessly long days week after week gathering grapes for market. They were of varying types and fortunately did not all ripen and require picking at the same time. Fredrick and Thomas had accomplished the most needed repairs on wagons, wooden rails, tack, and other items required to get the immense amounts of grapes and other produce to the marketplace.

Much to Frida's apprehension, Thomas would ride the teams down the track pulling the heavily laden wagons alone the few miles to the marketplace. Fredrick would stay in watch of the farm and continue in the harvest while Thomas was away. Now Thomas always carried the pistol hidden in his coat, although it was hard to hide something of that magnitude, and he had started to carry his sword in scabbard plainly visible too. It would not be long now before the harvest would be complete and he would be carrying home a considerable amount of wealth, as his father had been doing when he was murdered. Thomas was considering asking Fredrick to accompany him on that upcoming trip.

It was on one of these last trips to a notable winery warehouse Thomas delivered to that he happened to meet the owner and one of his father's old associates, Horst, one who Thomas had practiced with the sword several years prior, but to no great extent, as he hardly ever had time to humor a mere boy.

"Always beware of this one," Thomas's father had warned on one occasion. "I trust him not a bit. In years past I have had some less than pleasant dealings with him. It is reported that he was chased from Hamburg a few years ago for his crooked transactions and foul temper."

Horst called out to Thomas while approaching his establishment that afternoon. He knew Thomas would be inquiring as to the considerable amount he owed the Clays for the summer's deliveries. "Thomas," he said smirking, "there is much talk concerning the success you and your family have experienced this season." Grinning through his crooked and broken teeth, he continued, "The talk, of course, is by some seedy thugs hanging around the docks at Nierstein. I'm quite sure they are more interested in your pending wealth than the success of the farm and vineyards."

His attitude was somewhat hostile, and Thomas was immediately uncomfortable with his approach to the subject. A good portion of the family's pending wealth was owed by this man, Horst.

"You must be very careful now," Horst nonchalantly said. Glancing at the sword hanging at the boy's side, he leered. "Would you care to spend a minute in action with me? It has been a while, and you seemed quite good as a youngster."

Thomas had continued to practice techniques at home and with others of his father's old friends and was sharper and stronger than ever. But he noticed a blaze to this man's eyes that he had never seen before. Thomas was sure Horst thought he could best him in a minute, and Thomas also suspicioned that Horst had other motives than practice, like pinning him to a post then blaming the deed on some waterfront worker that may have passed by and was now long gone. His family would never see any of the money owed to them, and Horst would be that much richer. Looking the man over and noting he was very stocky and appeared very strong, but as Thomas remembered, he had no real finesse with the blade. He was slightly taller than Thomas and had a certain arrogance, seemingly because the boy was young and with little real experience. The observations were correct—Thomas was young and with no real experience with the blade in a genuinely do-or-die situation.

Thomas was starting to feel his abilities were perhaps not as sharp as he had believed and was wishing that Fredrick was there at least for moral support. It was not a good time to be alone, and it was now the time to make the decision: face Horst here and now or worry about a more stealthy attack from him in an isolated part of the woods? With his father on his mind, Thomas smiled and nodded with a confidence that he did not feel. Inwardly, he felt his chances of escaping with his hide were as good as a hen surviving at a hobo picnic.

Horst only grumbled, "What a pity, to die so young."

"Young? I do not consider you so young, Horst."

Then they moved into the darkness of the warehouse with no one around. Thomas watched Horst warily, knowing he would be up to any trick to divert his attention from the pending duel. Thomas stood away from him, lay down his heavy-laden jacket with the enclosed pistol tucked inside where he could easily reach it, and extracted his sword before him.

"If we must fight, let us do so. Your breath is as foul as your manners, and the sooner we are done, the better."

"You little creep," Horst said. "I have never liked you and always loathed your father. He had all the things I should have had—a thriving, successful farm, the stunning wife, and family and wealth."

Thomas said to him, "And you too indolent to work for any of it and only wanting what others have."

Horst looked at Thomas crookedly then went after him with a lunge, grunting and spouting profanity that would put any sailor to shame. Using only the edge of his saber with reckless moves and overhead slashes, he made a daunting foe. Thomas stepped back, knowing he was outmatched in height, reach, and strength by the larger and well-conditioned Horst. For the next few minutes, Thomas was on his own. He could count on no help from anyone, as no one knew his whereabouts. His manhood would have its full test this afternoon, or he could die here on the dirty and stained floors of this old building. He was afraid but not unmanned by his fear. Rather it gave power to his awareness, his wrist, and his sword arm. He found within him an inner strength that he had never felt before this moment.

Thomas positioned himself inherently into the natural fighting stance that his father had instilled in him through the many years of boyhood training. He felt the strength of the saber in his hand as he grasped it. The brute he faced was a brawler and not a refined swords-man. Although the power of Horst's swinging blade was tremendous, Thomas did not make the mistake of trying to match it. Instead he anticipated each wild, wavering stroke before it was launched. There was no subtlety in the way Horst signaled his intentions with his glaring eyes and contorted, sweat-smeared face or in how he moved his feet and opened his shoulders to make the next move.

As each stroke came whistling down at Thomas's head, he reached out and touched it with his own blade, never attempting to stop it in the air, lightly deflecting so that it flew harmlessly an inch past his head. Each time Thomas did this, Horst's rage swelled until it overwhelmed him. Throwing all caution to the wind, he held his sword high above his head with both hands and rushed straight at Thomas, roaring at him like a bull elephant. He made no attempt to cover himself from any countermove, leaving his body wide open.

Thomas, standing full in the path of the towering Horst, was as pale as the whitewashed walls of their confines. His face was set and hard with determination, his eyes bright and intent without the slightest glimmer of fear as he sighted over the weaving point of his saber. Horst had expected Thomas to back down before his charge on him. The set of Thomas's shoulders and the balance of his lean but hardened body signaled just that intention.

But suddenly, his left foot swung forward, and he launched himself like an arrow straight at Horst's throat. The big man had no time to bring down his guard or turn aside from the thrust. Thomas's thrust caught Horst precisely in the hollow at the base of his neck, and there he hung precariously for just the blink of an eye. Thomas had never killed another person before and hesitated to do so now. Instead of completing the lunge and thrusting the saber through Horst's throat, he flipped the sword and used its butt to smash him between the eyes. Horst dropped like a big elephant turd, spreading out unconscious on the floor.

There was just a moment that Thomas froze staring down at the grotesque form of the man lying there. Horst groaned, rolled over, sat up, and gave him a look of confused hatred. As a mere boy, Thomas had made a fool of him and knew he would never forget this. He would only be that much more threatening and dangerous in the future. Thomas had the foreboding feeling that he should have made the final lunge to pierce Horst's throat and end this madness once and for all. Turning slightly so as not to turn his back on his foe, Thomas picked up his jacket and pistol, then backed out of the warehouse door, letting it slam loudly on his departure. He ran madly to his horse and wagon tied just outside.

Jumping into the seat of the wagon, he made as hasty a retreat as the old nag could handle for the return trip home. Moving through the side streets and alleys of the warehouse district, he noticed no one seemed to be paying any attention to him. For this he was thankful—he did not want to be scrutinized for the huge lump on the forehead of the semiconscious man lying against the wall in the warehouse.

Chapter 7

Clay Family Vineyard, Hesse, Germany

1856

Once again Thomas had to return home and make an attempt of explaining the day's events. Upon his return he related the story in the presence of his mother, Fredrick, and Anne. Frida sat listening, quite troubled and angry. She was not angry at Thomas but at the situation created by the ugly thug Horst.

"I would prefer you never go to town alone again," she said firmly. She did not blame Thomas for the violent behavior of those involved in the two robbery attempts nor for the match with Horst, but she seemed to think trouble was riding his heels.

Fredrick C. Burgdorf sat there not saying a word. Thomas thought it unusual for Fredrick to sit back and have no comment—he usually had something to say about everything. They also discussed the issue of getting paid for the outstanding balance Horst owed from their last few deliveries. They had done well for the summer but could not afford this kind of a loss.

The entire day's events were told again and again, with Frida quiet and very distressed, Anne thinking her brother was a hero, and Fredrick still making few comments. After lengthy deliberations, of which Fredrick did contribute some input regarding their payments from Horst and the likelihood of another attack, everyone retired for the evening. It was much later than usual, and Thomas was somewhat disturbed at Fredrick's sullenness in the matter.

Sometime during that night, Thomas awoke thinking he heard some noise with the animals. He lay quietly, not hearing another sound, so eventually went back to sleep. The morning breakfast brought only Frida, Anne, and Thomas to the table. No Fredrick. This caused much apprehension and confusion. They all began talking at once. The little one, as Fredrick often called her, was panic-stricken, and Frida was immensely concerned, as she was as fond of Fredrick as she was of Anne and Thomas.

Thomas ran directly to the corrals and immediately noted their big gray horse was missing. Back inside he ran to the table and finished a hearty breakfast, knowing it may be the last one for a while. He would find Fredrick. He had no sensible thought as to what may have happened or where he may have gone, but Thomas reasoned it had something to do with the predicament he faced with Horst. Walking to the corral and catching a horse, Thomas bridled him then threw on one of the saddles.

Reviewing the contents of the barn once again, he noticed one very puzzling aspect. All the saddles were there—only the horse and Fredrick were missing. This must have been what he had heard last night, Fredrick hastily and silently slipping away with the horse. *But why?* So many thoughts were racing through Thomas's mind when his mother joined him in the barn. After all, how well did they know him? He had been the most hardy of workers, loyal beyond belief to the family, and Thomas's best friend—as a matter of fact, his only friend except for Mr. Hollenbeck, the gunsmith in Darmstadt.

Thomas checked for tracks around the house and barn, but there were far too many to make any sense of. His mother had packed a small bundled of food for him in a blanket, which he tied behind his saddle. He led the horse to the front of the house, with his mother giving him final instructions on which way to start the search. He had the pistol concealed in his coat and the sword hanging from his saddle. It was with much trepidation that Thomas placed his foot into the stirrup to mount and start what could be a long and tedious search for Fredrick.

Thomas had barely seated himself in the saddle when there was a clattering of hooves running on the gravel road on the other side of the trees. Sitting there in bewilderment, not knowing what to expect of the disorder, Thomas finally saw Fredrick come tearing through the trees at a full charge, riding the big gray horse with no saddle. He slid to a halt in front of them.

From the looks of the foam-covered horse, he had been running for some time, the horse and Fredrick both pitiful sights. Fredrick's light-colored hair was windblown, and he was missing the ragged hat he always wore. He had a badly cut lip, an eye entirely swollen closed, hands cut and bleeding with little skin on his knuckles, and in general he looked as if he had been dragged behind the big gray for some distance. He hadn't been dragged behind the horse, but as his tale unfolded later, someone else had that dubious pleasure for at least a slight distance.

Frida and Anne had heard the commotion and now stood on the porch in total shock, all eyes turned on Fredrick. They were all waiting for some enlightenment, and for once Fredrick was having a difficult time, not knowing where to commence.

"Well," he started, "I was running hard trying to get here before you noticed my lack of presence for breakfast, and I nearly made it." He slid from the lathery horse and handed Frida a sizable bag of coins. "At least," he said, "one of our problems has been solved. Here is the payment from Horst for Thomas's last few deliveries to his warehouse. I seem to have encountered him alone in the warehouse last night, and he was persuaded to pay in full. I doubt if he will give us any further trouble. It seems that in our discussion over payment, he suffered several broken ribs, a broken jaw, and will require dentures if such are available. One arm also seemed to be broken, and he will not see from either eye for some time until his facial swelling lessens. May I please have some breakfast now?"

Due to their routine there on the farm and vineyard, Fredrick had become accustomed to eating at dawn—it was well past that now, and he had worked up an appetite of heroic proportion. Fredrick cleaned up from the bucket of water near the kitchen door then joined the family at the table for another breakfast and, Thomas was sure, a much more complete and detailed blow-by-blow account of his experiences with Horst.

Frida sat across the table from Fredrick with her chin cupped in both hands staring at Fredrick. "We will forever be grateful for the success of your trip to collect from Horst, but why did you go alone, Fredrick? And in the middle of the night and without the benefit of a saddle?" she added. She did not use his full name, and he for once did not correct her.

"I knew Horst from another place and time, before either of us came to Darmstadt. He had a bad reputation while in Hamburg. Many people turned up maimed or missing as a result of him. I felt it safer to approach him alone—I knew his habits and did not want any harm to come to Thomas or anyone else, and I did not want you to lose any of the summer's profits as a result of that thug. One of the merchants I worked with on the docks taught me, 'Do good to all men, but at the end remember to collect your fee,' so that I did. I'm not sure if what I did to persuade Horst was all good, but I did ask him politely for the funds prior to mopping the warehouse with his miserable body."

I felt quite capable in dealing with him, Thomas thought, but remembering the punishing duel he had with Horst and the man's strength, he was grateful for the help Fredrick had offered. This was the first time that Fredrick had ever stepped in to relieve Thomas of any physical confrontations, but he certainly took no offense to that and in fact was quite grateful.

Fredrick continued, "I've not shared any of my past with you since coming to work with you months ago. My life was a bit brutal in those years of living in Hamburg." He went on, "I grew up not knowing my father, and my mother raised me as well as she could. She died of the black plague when I was at a young age, and somehow I miraculously escaped that horrible death sentence. I have been fending for myself since. I lived in one dirty closet after another and ultimately took a job with some of the ruthless shipping merchants on the wharf when I was seven or eight years old, at first as a messenger runner then later as I learned more of the business, I was a debt collector using every available resource to fulfill my profession. I was strong and learned the art of wrestling from others of my type and also practiced the fine art of bare-knuckle boxing. Something you get very good at very fast or get killed."

As Fredrick went on about his lean, hard years growing up on the waterfront, the little one sat next to him in total awe, just staring at Fredrick, the one that the Clays had all truly respected and trusted with their lives since his onset with them. Fredrick was opening up about his life, feelings, and experiences during the years prior to their meeting. He had studied as widely as Thomas, or more, first using the libraries of the merchants he worked for then later more expansively with some of the merchant clientele he had befriended. As a result of the diverse background of his associates at the time, he had also become fluent in the languages of English, Spanish, and French. Fredrick also had wide-ranging skills with the sword and had proved to be a very intelligent young man and a true survivor.

Frida sat across the table from Fredrick in total alertness and not saying a word, for a change, for she was as opinionated as Fredrick and usually had a comment on most conversations that came up. After they had all regained their self-possession from the story he related between mouthfuls of food, they sat there looking at him then at one another, each with their dazed thoughts trying to come to grips with what they had just heard. How could the mild-mannered Fredrick C. Burgdorf have lived such a harsh and severe life? Even the little one, who usually rambled on and on over the beautiful butterflies, birds, horses, or whatever, just sat there staring at Fredrick.

"That's about it for now," he said. "Let's get to work."

They did just that.

Chapter 8

Clay Family Vineyard, Hesse, Germany

1856

Autumn was far advanced, and the weather appeared ready to cast its net of white across the landscape. At supper one evening Frida glanced at Fredrick. "It's getting colder, Fredrick C. Burgdorf, and I think you should move from your not-so-comfortable space in the hayloft to our spare bedroom."

It wasn't a big move, as it was just across the hall. Fredrick accepted graciously without comment. They now thought of him as a member of the family, and so he was treated as such. Fredrick now joined them each evening after supper while Frida read or related tales of her and Thomas's father's experiences while living in Denmark and in dealing with the Barbary pirates.

"Fredrick," she asked one night, "why did you leave your life on the docks of Hamburg, and how did you come to be here in Darmstadt?"

Fredrick sat with his arms folded across his thick chest for a moment in deep thought then replied, "My whole life had been one of tremendous turmoil and much danger and hardship. Some of the merchants I worked for were changing in attitude with new and perhaps less violent methods of doing business, and my skills were becoming less in need. It was time for a change before I was phased out in the middle of the night with an unknown bullet or a knock on the head and dumped in the harbor."

"But why here to Darmstadt?"

"It was a matter of fate, I guess. I just packed my meager belongings and left without notice with a possible destination of, perhaps Austria or Switzerland. Someplace I would never be recognized and could get a fresh start. By chance I met Thomas on the road near Darmstadt, and the rest, as they say, is history."

They worked tirelessly day in and day out trying to finish up last-minute chores before the onset of winter. Thomas had become a formidable foe to a block of wood with an ax. He and Fredrick would have countless challenges as to who could better the other in chopping wood and every other task—numerous in the day-to-day activities of getting ready for winter. Sometimes Thomas would best Fredrick, and other times it was quite the opposite. When they were not busy with work or studies, which Frida made sure they were never to neglect, they would exercise with the blade, something Thomas's mother did not approve of but never forbid.

"Come with me," Fredrick said one evening, "and we will start some lessons in wrestling," and to the hayloft they went. "We need to further your skills in self-defense. I fear that with both of us besting Horst and ruining his delicate appearance a few months ago, that will have far-reaching consequences. I'm quite sure he has somewhat recovered and will be seeking revenge against you and your family as well as myself. We will practice and be as prepared as possible for whatever his hired brutes send our way. I'm sure he will not be capable of doing much himself, but he does have friends in low places, as they say."

Fredrick taught Thomas well, and they practiced relentlessly. Thomas was very strong for his age and a good student, and Fredrick was an excellent teacher. It was not so long until Thomas was nearly as good as Fredrick, who was by his account one of the best on the wharfs in Hamburg.

"You are an excellent wrestler," Fredrick commented. "You have learned much and seem to have an inherent technique. I doubt there is much more I can teach you. We will start the boxing lessons soon."

Chapter 9

Clay Family Vineyard, Hesse, Germany

1860

Several years passed like this, with Thomas and Fredrick working side by side in the vineyards and sparring in any spare moment, Frida and Anne managing the household, and the vineyard steadily regaining the production and stature it had once been known for. Horst continued to glower at all of them anytime they were in Darmstadt, but his attacks seemed to have subsided—at least for now.

This winter was upon them with full-blown fury. The landscape outside of the snug warm house was covered with a white blanket with only the trees and the haystack offering any obvious relief in the terrain. One evening at supper, Frida acknowledged this fact and announced, "We have done well with crops and harvests this year, and we can afford another hired hand next summer." None of them looked at Fredrick as just a hired hand—he was now a member of the family. And they all looked forward to more help for the next season.

Christmas was just around the corner, and Anne and Frida were busy every day and evening planning and completely rearranging the household furnishings for that occasion. Thomas did not know at the time that Germany was the founder of the Christmas holiday, and other countries did not practice the event like they had. Mother and the little one had hung gaily colored materials around the windows and set the table with a new red cloth.

Two days before Christmas early in the morning, Thomas yelled at Fredrick, "Come, let's now get the tree from the forest for decorating."

"I shall beat you to the forest," Fredrick said with his usual challenge.

It was less than a mile to the trees that surrounded the farm, and Thomas beat him there soundly. Fredrick was a gracious loser and never commented or complained at being second best. Sometimes Thomas thought his defeats were intentional and that he was certainly more competent than he led him to believe. It seemed Fredrick had a very healthy ego. They accomplished the task with little difficulty. The forest in this particular area was dense with full-bodied fir and spruce, and in no time they had found the perfect tree. It was about seven feet tall, well-rounded, and had the perfect spot on top for the tiny star that mother had made just for this occasion.

Even on this carefree jaunt into the woods, they were always watchful for any sign of another's presence. Horst was always on everyone's mind, and with good reason. Returning home, the boys were both ever on the lookout for anything of a suspicious nature, as they remembered so well the activities of the unknown characters in the forest's edge they had seen the previous summer. As the young men were approaching the house, Anne and Frida were there to greet them.

"What a beautiful tree," Anne yelled with delight.

The trail in the snow was very obvious, and Frida frowned with noticeable concern, also remembering the incidents with strangers spying on them.

"Take the tree into the house," she suggested, "and we will prepare it with all of the tiny candles and ornaments that Anne and I have made. This will be a very special event this year. Fredrick is here with us to help, we had a good year financially, and we have a substantial stock of food and wood for the winter. Since your father's death and the less than favorable success with the vineyard in the years after, we barely observed Christmas. Soon enough it will be spring and all the laborious tasks will begin, so let's enjoy this great time while we can."

The season was spectacular. Frida and Anne spent laborious hours preparing, baking, cooking, and doing all the other tasks required in preparation of the first real Christmas they'd had since Thomas's father's untimely demise. The dinner was one never to be forgotten— they had wild turkey taken from the forest, fish they had traded for and smoked last summer, smoked ham from their own smokehouse, various types of berries they had dried from their own gardens as well as dressings, gravy, potatoes, and all the trimmings one could hope for. Fredrick had never been involved in a real Christmas and had only observed one occasionally from the lonely streets outside, looking through a window here and then another window there during his meager existence while living in Hamburg. Even Thomas could not remember such a wonderful time in their lives for many years.

Chapter 10

Horst Warehouse, Darmstadt, Hesse, Germany

1860

Horst was in his sparsely furnished room in the warehouse in Darmstadt. He had somewhat recovered from the beating that Fredrick had given him one evening last summer when he had refused to pay for the goods the Clays had delivered.

Looking at him through a veil of cigarette smoke, a man said, "I know something of the matter. You should have just paid the illiterate Clays for their crops delivered and you would not be in this painful situation."

Horst snorted in anger. "What would you know? You're no brighter than them that put me in so much discomfort."

"Discomfort? Ha, you can still hardly walk, your mouth is as crooked as your bitter soul, and you are asking me to eliminate the lot of them in any matter. I may be as despicable as you, but I don't take to killing women—I have a far better use for them. And I've never harmed a child. I'll not do the job for you, Horst. Not my style."

Horst shrieked at him with rage. "You have done worse deeds than this before."

The man stood up and walked to the door, turned, and said, "Not this time, Horst. Get another of your worthless muggers for this one." Never taking his eyes from Horst, he stepped out the door and into the bitter night air. Shifting rapidly he turned to an alley running parallel to the warehouse and vanished into the oncoming snowstorm. He knew full well the fury of Horst and knew he was readily capable of shooting him in the back even now as he hastily retreated to a nearby tavern to wash the taste of this event from his mouth. The area was noted for its fine ale, and he was about to indulge in several mugs.

Horst sat in the dimly lit room seething with rage at being turned down from this unworthy character. Ultimately simmering down, he thought, *I will take care of him, then the Clays, myself*, knowing full well that he could do neither at this time—or maybe ever.

Even though he was still recovering from Fredrick's beating, he knew he would never be the same. His arm had healed crooked, and his jaw that had been broken was dislocated, and he found it difficult to eat without tremendous pain. *I am wasting away to nothing*, he thought. He would never handle a sword again and had great difficulty just trying to load a gun, let alone steadily aim and fire. How did that hired hand of theirs come to be here of all places? Horst had known Fredrick a few years prior as a brutal debt collector for some of the merchants on the docks of Hamburg and had had some minor disagreements with him before but never expected to run into him again. *What else could go wrong?* he thought. *There are lots of others*, he thought. *These are hard times, and many of the waterfront bums from Nierstein on the Rhine River would jump at this chance.*

Horst sat tilted back in his dilapidated chair in his warehouse apartment, smoldering in silence for a moment then tilted the nearby bottle to his disfigured lips and drank heavily. *Someway I will get them all*, he thought then drifted into an alcohol-induced slumber. This had become the routine as of late. The embarrassment of his failed attempt to swindle the Clays and his severe beating was something someone like Horst would never recover from.

Chapter 11

Clay Family Vineyard, Hesse, Germany

1860

"Anne, would you please do the honors of passing out the Christmas gifts?" Mother said.

"I would be delighted to do so," she said, grinning from ear to ear. Anne had become quite the charming young lady. Maturing charmingly over the last few years, especially since Fredrick's arrival.

Gift-giving was yet another custom that Fredrick was unfamiliar with, and he very humbly accepted the gift Anne had passed. She gave one to her mother then Thomas then took one for herself.

"You first, Mother."

So she did, and opening her present, she stared totally shaken. "Where did you ever find something like this?" she questioned. "I have never seen anything of this beauty since the old days with your father in Denmark."

"I traded for them on one of my last trips to market. Fredrick, Sis, and I have had a very hard time keeping this a secret." Thomas had started calling Anne "Sis" some time ago—it just seemed natural. "We all were involved in the procurement of this but just didn't know how we were going to give it to you. Christmas seemed just the perfect occasion."

Mother held up the necklace made of pearls, looking at each of them with gratefulness that she would never be able to express in words.

Still trembling with her emotions of receiving something of this beauty especially during these times, and with tears gently rolling down both cheeks, making no attempt to control them, she said, "You next, Anne."

Anne had achieved a tremendous degree of maturity and other feminine attributes as of late, but patience was not one of them. She had sat fidgeting while her mother had unwrapped her present, but now it was her turn. She gasped as she tore the paper from the set of paints, small easel, and hard-to-find cloth used to paint on. This was also something Fredrick had asked Thomas to try to find on a trip to the city last summer. They both knew what this would mean to Anne, but neither knew when nor how to present her with it, so they waited until Christmas. Anne was as stunned as Frida but did not cry, only beamed, hardly able to control herself.

Next was Fredrick's turn. He opened the heavy package, folding the paper back to expose the beautiful new LeMat revolver. Fredrick shook his head and stuttered then tried again, totally without words. After several attempts, he was able to gasp, "I have never seen anything of this quality before. I have never even held anything like this before and certainly never owned anything like this." He then slowly rose from the chair he was sitting in and embraced each person in the room. Fredrick was a rough individual and had always survived a hard life, but underneath that tough veneer was a young man with a heart of gold and a true and dedicated friend.

Next was Thomas's turn. His gift was smaller than any of the others, and he stared at it curiously. It was hardly more than a folded paper to form a small box that rattled some with mild movement. Cautiously and slowly opening the box, he stared at the contents and read the note carefully. He was given a tidy sum of currency and instructed that on his next visit to Darmstadt, he was to purchase a real barber haircut, which he had never had before. He was instructed to attend one of the finer men's clothing stores and get a new wardrobe of pants, shirts, overcoat, and hat popular at the time. He had never owned store-bought clothes before—his mother had always hand-made them, and she always "sheared" his hair too, as she referred to it. That experience only happened once or maybe twice a year. He was also instructed to get new work boots and a new pair of shoes to be worn only for dress occasions.

"Thomas, you are now twenty years old, a delightful and charming, well-educated young man as well as steadily maturing. I'm sure that one day soon, you will be approached by an equally delightful and charming young lady, and you should be prepared for such an occasion."

Not likely, he thought about his mother's idea of the delightful young lady, but he was enthusiastic at the prospect of the store-bought clothes.

Thomas had a hefty sum and was now ever more impatient with the waning winter. That winter was a cold one but probably no more severe than usual. They had spoken many evenings during the winter months about how to approach the coming season. The Clays were once famous for the excellence of grapes from this region and were desperately going to try to achieve that standard again and even surpass it.

"How many workhands are we going to be able to manage to pay for this coming season?" Thomas asked his mother one evening.

Leaning forward in her chair with elbows resting on the table she looked up and smiled. She had taken a keen interest in Thomas's awareness of the responsibilities of running the farm and vineyards.

"We are going to have to think on this some more," she replied. "We will definitely get more workers this spring but perhaps not as many as we previously discussed. I for one have had my fill of this pedestrian life your sister and I have been leading and would like a small horse-drawn carriage of some quality to go to and from town. Your sister and I have made but few trips a year to Darmstadt and that was at times on foot. With God's good grace, we will have another good season with the vineyards and hopefully can afford this small luxury."

Meeting her eyes innocently, Thomas joked, "What is more important? Your fancy carriage and no sore feet or another rail wagon to haul more produce to market?"

She looked at him not wavering those icy-blue eyes and flatly stated, "My poor feet." Then came the smile.

Thomas was older now and at times pressed his mother to her tolerable limits but always knew that he was not skating on thin ice when he got the smile.

Chapter 12

Clay Family Vineyard,
Hesse, Germany

1861

Fredrick and Thomas were once again very busy with the routine of repairing the harnesses, feeding the animals, and other daily chores. This was Thomas's first winter of having so many horses and the consequent repairs of the harnesses, but with Fredrick's unwavering support and help, it went smoothly.

They spent every hour that was not involved in work, studies, or the never-ending talk of the great America working to improve Thomas's fighting skills. He practiced tirelessly and relentlessly boxing, wrestling, and sword fighting, with which he usually always won. His fractured confidence with the sword due to the encounter with Horst was overcome, and once again he knew he had his father's inherent talents. He was very good and was quite confident there would never be another outcome such as his shabby attempt as with Horst, even though he did best him.

On every trip to town with the farm and vineyard goods the last summer, Thomas had also improved his skills by fencing with any man he could find who wished to cross blades. They were usually and most often old friends and former acquaintances of his father's and were more than willing to accommodate him. Some of them were uncommonly good. One in particular was an older gentleman named

Alan Slichter, an apprentice brick layer. Many a good bout they had. Alan had a technique like none other Thomas had ever practiced with, and it sharpened his skills to a fine point. He had no doubt the time would soon come when he would have need of them, knowing full well that he would have to test his skills against one of the louts that Horst would most likely send his way.

Chapter 13

Clay Family Vineyard, Hesse, Germany

1861

One morning was more cold and miserable than usual, with fog and blowing ice crystals. Fredrick's mood was somewhat subdued, not like the usually charming positive individual that he had become. In his small but comfortable room, he had pulled on his shirt and pants and stomped his feet into his worn boots but saw no reason to put on his hat and jacket before he had someplace to go. He was up earlier than usual and just finished dressing.

Breakfast was not ready, and Fredrick soon realized no one else in the house was even up yet. Not wanting to disturb the others, he strode around the small room then casually glanced out the window. From the corner of his eye, he glimpsed an unfamiliar movement near one of the haystacks. In the early morning freezing mist, the stack was only barely visible. He stared then slightly turned his head to look out the corner of his eye. This trick would sometimes make clear an object not clearly visible looking straight on. There was a figure there scarcely visible and a slight glowing, like a cigarette.

Sudden comprehension came to Fredrick: someone was trying to burn the haystack. Shouting at the top of his lungs, rousing everyone in the house, he rushed down the stairs clutching only his blade as he ran out the door for the hay pile.

It took only a moment for Thomas to jump into his clothes, and he was right behind him with the Walker Colt in his hand. Since the last sightings of visitors hiding in the fringe of the surrounding forests, it had rarely left his side. He was directly at Fredrick's side, quickly pulling the heavy coat from his back to flail at the fire while Fredrick tore at the growing flame with the hay fork. Gradually, with the aid of the freezing mist, they gained control and the fire was snuffed.

Now sweating and not wanting to get chilled, Thomas replaced the smokey fleece with a few blackened holes, and they took stock of this event. Speaking as one they both voiced, "Horst."

Thomas made a quick survey of the surrounding snow-covered field for tracks. They looked to have originated from the forest and then returned the same way. Fredrick paced a few steps in each direction looking at the foul weather and reluctantly tossed aside the hay fork.

"We will not follow at this time," Thomas said. "Who knows what waits on us out there in the blurred light and blinding snow? Whoever it is can see better from their hidden position in the trees than we could." He noted wolf tracks too and thought, *We have to keep a closer watch for these creatures.* So far they had not harmed any of their livestock, but as the winter developed they would likely become more aggressive. "I think that next spring we will get a dog, not only because of the wolves but to also hopefully warn us of other possible intruders."

Knowing full well that Horst was in some way accountable for the morning's events, Thomas and Fredrick returned to the house. Frida and Anne were starting out the door to help as the boys went in.

"What in heaven's name just happened?"

The inquiries and responses were flying, and soon order was restored over breakfast. It was generally decided Horst was accountable for the attempted fire. Fredrick reiterated as to the horrible reputation he had and to all the apparent foul play he had been involved in at Hamburg before hastily leaving in front of the blood-craving mob that had exposed his deceitful actions.

"But his reputation could be overinflated when you consider the other local businesses do not seem to have much concern of his actions." Thomas shrugged. Then looking at Fredrick, Thomas leaned closer to the fireplace to warm his hands and turned his attention to the dimming coals. "In Darmstadt he seems to have kept a low profile and has only focused his unfavorable attention toward us. I hardly think we can expect any help from the authorities with no more proof of his ill behavior than we have."

In light of the recent events, Fredrick and Thomas took turns standing watch. Thomas would prowl the surroundings from nightfall until midnight, and then Fredrick would take over for a few hours, then Thomas again until daylight. They kept this up for the next month watching for anything suspicious, and eventually as the days grew longer, they eased into spring with no problems. However, they were always watchful for anything of a suspicious nature. Even with the severe weather hounding them uncompromisingly, it was February, and the days were getting longer and less severe. It would not be long until spring and the busy timetable of crops and marketing, and of course Thomas was impatiently awaiting the opportunity to spend time in Darmstadt shopping for those new clothes and a real haircut from a real barber. He had scoffed at his mother about a pretty young lady seeking his attention, but with each passing month, he thought more on the subject with less disapproval and found the idea to be somewhat interesting. Fredrick had touched lightly on the topic of delightful young women before, but Thomas had always disregarded it as an uninteresting subject.

Thomas's thoughts now turned once again to the attempted fire to their haystacks and the never-ending issue of the winter chores. Along with the next summer's additional field workers, they probably should get a dog. They had not done so in years past, as they could hardly keep food on the table for the humans let alone a hungry dog. Thomas knew it would take some convincing to get his mother to agree, but he would work on it.

"The temperature is progressively improving, and the snow is melting some, and flowers will soon be out," Frida commented one morning. "It is time to think about getting more help and increasing our acreage under cultivation as well as adding to the vineyards substantially if we are going to afford the lifestyle I would like to become accustomed to." She laughed.

"We can do that," Thomas answered smiling, relieved that her humor was warming along with the spring days. Taking another leap of faith, hoping for another smile, he commented on how much healthier she looked with the few pounds she appeared to have gained during the winter months. The humor instantly disappeared, no smile, and the piercing ice-blue eyes did seem to smolder a bit. *No more of that kind of compliment*, he thought and gracefully sought an easy exit from the conversation and the room.

Chapter 14

Clay Family Vineyard, Hesse, Germany

1861

The Clays had meticulously prepared for this spring and had passed the word with an occasional traveler that they were of need of additional help for the coming season's crops and the never-ending maintenance of the vineyards. The unemployment rate in Germany was atrocious, but it seemed the only people seeking work were transients looking for a meal and were certainly not stayers.

With the absence of most of the snow and the weather improving, it was time for their first trip with the wagon to Darmstadt. Early morning after tending to some mundane tasks, totally bored and impatient for no particular reason, and observing his mother through the kitchen window, Thomas approached the house and announced, "I'm taking the team and a wagon to the city today for supplies and to buy some clothes, get a new hat, get a haircut, and buy a dog."

Frida cocked an eyebrow, flipped a lock of red hair from her face, and stared at Thomas incredulously. "You are going to town to buy clothes having never been in a real clothing store and get a haircut never before being in a real barber shop, and you're going to buy a dog?"

Not knowing exactly how he was going to answer that, he was rescued by Anne. She smiled and innocently invited herself, Mother, and Fredrick to accompany him for some similar shopping. It had been years since his mother and Anne had accompanied him to town. Occasionally Fredrick had made the trip to town alone but rarely had joined Thomas. He thought Fredrick's sporadic trips were more of a nature of pleasure than business. But his exploits, conquests, or whatever one wished to refer to them as, were increasingly interesting in his retelling of them to Thomas on a later occasion. Thomas was now also taking an interest in some of the girls met at the marketplaces in town as well the warehouse districts and found his friend's tales most interesting.

Fredrick had heard this exchange. "Mrs. Clay, with all due respect, I'll stay behind and tend the farm while you are away for the day with Thomas and Anne. I'm somewhat concerned of leaving things unattended with the threat of Horst still hanging over our head."

That was a graceful exit, Thomas thought but had to chuckle as to Fredrick's slyness and to his own social absence in managing this affair. *Wow*, Thomas thought, *in days gone by, I was the man of the house doing most business affairs, conveying goods to market and storerooms, engaging in sword fights and a gun fight with bandits, accidentally shooting the bandits' horse that was perhaps mine to begin with stolen from my father on that fatal day, and have now become a chaperone for my mother and sister to the city.* Inwardly smiling to himself, he was enjoying this moment.

Anne was turning into the most delightful of young ladies, and of course Thomas saw his mother as the forever mentor and his life blood. He was proud to have this occasion with them and would continually enjoy these special times. The three of them piled into the old wagon and were soon in town. Frida now as bubbly as Anne at the thought of a lively day in the city and of other female company, she shook her head of dense, luxurious hair, which seemed to be one of her prized attributes, and asked, "Where would you like to start first, Thomas? Perhaps a haircut."

"Sounds good to me. Let's find a barber."

And find one they did. She guided them around a corner from the main street onto a side alleyway with the striped barber pole hanging out front. Thomas had a fleeting feeling of apprehension. This was very close to the warehouse area that housed Horst's shady business. Though the feeling soon faded with the jovial attitude of his mother and Anne.

"How did that striped red-and-white pole come to be associated with a barber?" Thomas asked, being new to this.

"It comes from the age-old practice of bleeding people," his mother replied. "When people were sick, the barber would cut them and bleed them into a bowl. Apparently it was thought bleeding was a medicinal practice, a miracle cure."

Thomas did remember something of this nature in one of his father's books at home. Anne did not say a word but looked as if she was going to relieve her stomach of a very hearty breakfast. Into the shop they went without further discussion on the matter. Women were seldom seen in barbershops, and here were two of them, one beautiful woman and one beautiful young lady. One on each side of Thomas.

"Good afternoon, Heinrich," Frida said without hesitation.

"And good afternoon to you, Mrs. Clay," he replied. "Be with you in just a minute as soon as I finish with this young fellow in the chair."

"How do you know him?" Thomas whispered to his mother in total skepticism—to his knowledge they had never had another male in the house since his father's demise, except Fredrick and perhaps an occasional traveler just passing through.

"Heinrich was an old friend of your father's as well as his barber."

Totally amazed and not knowing what to say, Thomas said nothing and just followed the conversation between two old friends as they talked about old times, and then it was his turn in the chair. Heinrich guided him gracefully to the seat, knowing full well he had never been in a barber chair before and wanting to make the first visit as graceful and relaxed as possible. However, that good intention did not stop him from a good laugh at Thomas's expense. He lightly wrapped the sheet around the boy's neck and ran his fingers and a comb through his thick mat of coal-black hair. Unlike his parents and sister, who had blond and red hair, Thomas's was very black.

"Oh my, who was your previous barber?"

Thomas stared at Heinrich somewhat defensively. "Why is that important?"

"Well, from the looks of your last haircut, I just wanted to make sure I never went to that one." Heinrich knew Thomas's mother had cut his hair all his life, and they both had a good laugh again at the boy's expense.

Anne had gotten over her initial surprise of the original purpose of a barber and also snickered quietly. Heinrich was a rare individual that one couldn't help but like on first meeting. In the times to come, Thomas and Heinrich would become very good friends and have lengthy conversations about Thomas's father and his untimely death. Heinrich also was well-acquainted with Horst and had heard of some discreet threats passed around by some of Horst's acquaintances—at very best only acquaintances, as Horst had no real friends. He had literally burned all of his ties and relied on money and not relationships to get anything done.

"The haircut makes you look so distinguished," Anne commented. "And you look slightly older, like a refined gentleman."

Where did that come from? Thomas wondered. *What does she know about older and refined gentlemen?*

Now his mother said, "We shall see to new pants and underwear."

At this Thomas felt totally confused. Underwear was something he had read about but never had the opportunity to indulge in. They had little money and only bothered in the bare necessities. And pondering on this now Thomas realized his necessities were indeed nearly bare. He was starting to realize that there was a lot more than academics involved in becoming a well-rounded person that was a bit older looking and with a certain quality of refinement, as Anne had put it. True, he had successfully debated with some of the most learned in the streets and warehouse districts in Darmstadt, but never had he discussed the bare essentials of underwear. Even Fredrick C. Burgdorf never broached that subject. However, when he returned home, Thomas would certainly get his friend's favored opinion on the subject.

Frida was also friends with this shop owner, and they chatted at length about some local politics and the migration of the masses of Germans to America. This was a subject Thomas found most interesting. He was measured and fitted, and now had several sets of new trousers, tailored shirts, top coat, and of course underwear, some of which were full length for warmth during the next wintertime cold. Still needing boots and a hat for him, they next visited the shoe shop. The owner of this shop also addressed Frida as Mrs. Clay as they entered, and Thomas was not the least bit surprised. His father had been a very well-dressed and respected business man in Darmstadt.

The realization of how he now looked in his new attire was amazing. Thomas had been transformed from a well-educated but socially inept, rough expert in the physical arts of the sword, wrestling, and boxing to a strikingly handsome young man. His mother opined, "But you could still use some social refinement."

Other than the possible acquaintances of a charming young lady, he wondered what the purpose of all this refinement was, and he asked his mother just that.

"We will talk of that on the way home," she said.

True, Thomas was first excited about the thought of all the new store-bought items, but he now wondered. Anne had been sitting by inattentively through this achievement, and Thomas also questioned this. She usually pursued the center of attention, but on this juncture she sat back and let it be entirely her brother's day. They were up to something, of this Thomas was sure. The amount he'd thought was a modest fortune to carry in coming to town for his new wardrobe had soon dwindled to nothing, and his mother was called upon for more finances for the remaining purchases.

"What now, just for fun?" she asked. "I know it has been a bit more of a trial than you believed in getting this done, but there is a purpose, and we will talk of that soon. What would you like that is just a fun thing not related to the new clothes?" Although a dog crossed his mind, he felt perhaps this not to be the time.

Thinking a moment, he simply responded, "A new novel. I have read all that father had many times over and would like something new to read." So it was soon to be.

Their next stop was the finest bookstore in all of Darmstadt. The bookstore was well supplied for the time, and Thomas didn't know where to start. He had only read books that belonged to his father, the ones that ostensibly were of specific interest to his father, and in reading them, the deceased patriarch became a part of the son. They had a strong bond through the literary arts. Thomas learned he had the same subjects, the same interests, and the same habits, and he was soon to learn a lot more about what his mother had in mind. He did purchase *The Wealth of Nations* by Adam Smith, an author and philosopher from his mother's country of Scotland. Also *The Lady of the Lake* by Sir Walter Scott, another Scottish historical novelist. He knew little about either novel, but his father had talked a lot about both authors and had read *Ivanhoe* to the family in the cold winter evenings in front of the fireplace, some of Thomas's most unforgettable times—his mother, Anne, and him sitting mesmerized by the story and his father's voice hypnotizing them into the total deepness of the tale.

With this shopping done, Thomas was ready to be homeward bound. His feet hurt, and he was more tired than if he had done a full day's work on the farm. He was very grateful for all the new things he had acquired but was ready to call it a day. "Shall we go now?" he suggested to his mother, grinning. It had taken most of the day, and it would soon be dark. He did not mind the trip from the city home in the dark alone after taking goods to the marketplace but certainly did not want to expose his mother and Anne to that risk if not necessary. There was always the threat of the robbers, and of course a possible revenge attack from Horst was always on his mind.

"One more stop," Frida said. "Anne and I both would like some of the latest London perfume I have read so much about recently."

"Perfume?" Thomas gasped. "What would you do with perfume?"

Another social blunder, he soon realized by the look from those ice-blue eyes. At least her hair was up in braids wrapped around her head and she didn't have to whisk it from her face before giving him that look. Hastily retreating to Anne's side and escorting her out the door of the bookstore, Thomas smiled and asked, "Where is this store with perfume?"

They casually walked farther down the boardwalk, his mother smiling again and making no comment on that last blunder but chatting about nothing in particular and everything in general, just happy to be away from the farm and enjoying the city. Thomas was learning some social graces the hard way without the benefit of books. But where would this lead? They turned the corner of the next street and approached a storefront with huge letters: *Perfumeries Douglas.*

Chapter 15

Perfumeries Douglas, Darmstadt, Hesse, Germany

1861

Thomas's reflection in the large glass storefront was a very different-looking person than the one who had come to town that morning. Maybe there was some truth to Anne's assessment of him in his new wardrobe. Upon entering this store, Thomas gasped out loud. It was unlike anything he had ever seen, and he was totally unprepared for this exhibition of women's personal items. It was somewhat thought provoking that his mother and little sister knew of its exact location and its contents and, he was quite sure, were well-acquainted with the personnel.

Anne was also totally thrilled to be here and indeed seemed to know all of the personnel. *How could this happen?* Thomas thought. It confirmed what little he really knew of his mother or Anne, or any other girl in fact. He had made many trips to the city during the season for several years but was not aware of their most obvious visits also. No wonder she wanted a new carriage with a graceful horse. The one they had would look very out of place in front of this store.

There were beautiful dresses that seemed to be stuffed with something that made them stand at attention—*mannequins*, he was later to find out was the proper term. Hundreds of hats of the latest style, parasols, beautiful gloves, and form-fitting dresses similar to what Thomas's mother and sister wore surrounded him in the well-lit space.

"Thomas," Anne said, "I would like to introduce my dear friend Elizabeth Klein. Elizabeth, my only and older brother, Thomas."

She was such a beautiful young lady, Thomas momentarily stood in amazement and then forgot his shyness. Stepping up to her with what he thought to be his most delightful smile, removing his new hat gracefully with his left hand in a manner that would suggest that he was totally accustomed to such an act, and bowing very slightly, he said, "This chance meeting is of my total pleasure."

From where this grand spiel came from, he knew not—probably from one of his father's books—but Elizabeth loved it. It was Frida's turn to look shocked, and Anne watched the performance happily. Both young people looked like they were thinking, *Who is this charming well-dressed new young person?* With some humor in her brown eyes, Elizabeth graciously offered her hand, and Thomas accepted it without haste.

Now smiling, she said, "No, Thomas, it is my total pleasure," with an ever-so-slight curtsy. It was complete acceptance at first sight. They were both enchanted with the company of the other.

Both were eloquently dressed, due to Thomas's recent shopping session, and obviously well-schooled with what would appear to be the same degree of interests and intelligence. They stood there talking of so many little things, nothing of real interest, but the topic of conversation seemed not to matter. They enjoyed each other's company, totally oblivious of all things around.

Realizing she was still holding his hand, Elizabeth slowly removed it and once again addressed Anne and Frida. "Please forgive me, but I have a meeting to attend with the store's owners in a few moments." Then she walked to the door at the edge of the room, turning to look back at Thomas with a smile. Frida and Anne both stared at Thomas, who had a slight smile and the most wonderful feeling he'd had in the years since his father died. His sister and mother diverted their attention elsewhere with slightly concealed smiles, trying not to betray their total approval of this not-by-chance meeting—Frida with the thoughts of a new daughter-in-law and Anne in hopes of a new sister-in-law.

Thomas gently took his mother by the elbow, gave Elizabeth a slight bow with hat in hand, and led his mother and Anne to the door. "Shall we go now?"

His mother looked at him in a totally different way, perhaps a new-found respect. Thomas had never treated her in such a gentlemanly and adult manner. It was probably clear that he had not only lost his head but his heart as well. They casually walked back to the cart. It was but a few blocks away where they had left it that morning near one of the warehouses, in the hands of a small boy by the name of Josh. He had watched over the horse and cart for a small fee and, according to Frida, had done so many times before when she visited town. He was a shabbily dressed young lad with the knowing look of an old man in his eyes. Thomas had a tremendous sympathy for this boy, and it disturbed him much to leave him standing there.

The Clays had spoken little since leaving the ladies shop, and Frida kept casting Thomas curious glances. He was subtly smiling, walking with a light bounce, and not saying a word.

"Thomas, what's come over you? I've not seen you act this way before."

After helping his mother and Anne into the cart with all the packages they had accumulated during the day's shopping, Thomas climbed in beside them. "I'm in love," he said.

She gasped. "Good lord, one trip to town, some new clothes, an introduction to one of his sister's friends, and he's in love."

Anne smirked, knowing this was not a chance meeting. "Elizabeth had seen Thomas around town before and asked me to arrange a meeting with him. It seems she was as taken with him as he with her."

"Good lord." Their mother gasped, trying to carry on the charade of being totally surprised.

Turning the cart and starting for home, Thomas noticed Horst and two of his followers covertly watching from the shadows of a nearby building.

"The tall well-dressed lad driving the wagon with those two beautiful women," Horst whispered from the shadows. "I want him gone forever. He is to be disposed of in any manner you see fit but just get rid of him. The sooner the better."

"Seeing what you are paying us, you can consider it done," one of them said and scowled before they hastily made their way back inside to make further plans.

Chapter 16

Darmstadt Road,
Hesse, Germany

1861

Riding in the old wagon with his mother on one side and Anne on the other and nearing the outskirts of town, Thomas nonchalantly looked at Anne sitting next to him so prim and proper, "Well, little sister, tell me about your part in this not-by-chance meeting with Elizabeth." He chuckled. Thomas looked and was acting much older and more mature than ever before. It seemed as though he had somehow gone through some miraculous transition from a rough-and-tough but very competent boy to a delightful and most handsome young gentleman during the last few hours of this day.

"Not-so-secret, huh?" she said in a serious tone. "I have known Elizabeth for a few years. We first met on one of the trips to town with Mother when you were working the vineyards. It was before Fredrick came to stay, and Mother had taken me with her for supplies. Elizabeth was then working in the stable not far from the Perfumeries Douglas, tending to horses, cleaning stalls, and such. It was the one Mother and I sometimes left the horse and wagon at for some attention. When I talked with her, she was obviously well-educated and totally out of place in that environment. Her clothes had patches on patches, and she was skinny as could be. A sight for tender eyes, she had a very threatening and tough existence but was very proud. She once laughed about this to Mother saying, 'Not only do I have patches on patches, but also my hands have callouses on callouses.' She always had that certain look of eloquence even while shoveling the stables and maintaining the animals.

"On one occasion, she told me that this too was just a stepping stone in life and she was quite certain it would not be a long-lasting career, only a temporary setback. She was happy to be able to help as best she could in keeping her family together. She and her two sisters, one older and one younger, are all now living in a very small apartment with their mother and father not far from downtown Darmstadt. Her father was once a professor at the university, and they had lived lavishly in one of the most luxuriously appointed neighborhoods on the west side. Somehow he was persuaded to leave that position for a commission in the revolution. Elizabeth thinks he was forced to do so and consequently was seriously injured in that upheaval.

"Upon returning home, he could not go back to his previous position at the university and was unable to contribute amply to the family's maintenance. Falling from political favor due to his failed role in the uprising, they were now unable to afford the beautiful home they had lived in and were forced to take up their very meager existence in the small apartment. Her mother became quite ill and was just barely hanging on to life. With her unable to work, their meager existence was supported only by Elizabeth and her two sisters. The older one, Mary, worked in a popular tavern, and the younger one, with the same name as me, worked in a local fabric store, and Elizabeth at the stable.

"You can thank Mother for Elizabeth's position with the Perfumeries Douglas. Our mother was immediately taken by Elizabeth and eventually persuaded Mrs. Hoogendyk, the owner, to hire her. Mother and I assisted Elizabeth in getting a suitable wardrobe to start her new career. As you can see, she has become a very worthy and most competent employee. She has since, with the assistance of Mrs. Hoogendyk, been able to finish her education at the university, a different one than the one her father had taught in, however."

Thomas, listening intently, said not a word and let Anne continue on for the next quarter hour. Finally he interjected with, "How are her father and mother now?"

Going on, but frowning at Thomas for interrupting her, Anne said, "Her father is much better and will soon be able to seek gainful employment. Her mother is continuing to recover from the dreaded fever, though, still very sick. Her father, Manfred, is very concerned about the possibilities of work now due to the extreme unemployment rate here and his misgivings in the political field. He will have to keep a very low public profile, I'm told, and will probably never be able to work in the education field again."

Thomas sat in silence for several minutes, deep in thought about this day's proceedings, the intellectual response from Anne, and his introduction to Elizabeth. Anne, he knew, was very well-educated especially for her young age, but nevertheless he had never had an in-depth conversation with her like this before. He had always thought of her as the little one. Their mother sat in total and thoughtful silence as they rode slowly toward home. Somehow she knew this day would alter their lives forever.

After a few moments without a word, everyone deep in their own private thoughts, Thomas broke the silence. "I am going to marry Elizabeth one day."

Anne, once again her usual carefree self, cheeped, "The sooner, the better. Can I be in the wedding?"

"Yes, you may be in the wedding. Maybe it will be in the great *America*." Noticing the look of discomfort in his mother's eyes, Thomas stopped the wagon at a wide-open space along the road with no trees or brush nearby—a place they could stop and talk with no chance of hostile visitors approaching unseen. "Something is severely bothering you," he said.

She sat there in silence in all her true splendor for only a moment, never one to avoid speaking her mind no matter the consequences. "I'm sure you recall on the trip into town this morning I mentioned I had a reason for nudging you toward the idea of new clothing items and there was more to the trip than just a new shirt and pants?"

"Yes, I do remember, and I thought it peculiar." The setting there in the open space along the road with the beautiful sky above and the snowcapped mountains in the background was something to behold.

Frida then continued on, "The vineyards have been doing very well, even better than you know. Thanks to you, we have many new accounts from several wineries here in the Rhine Valley, and the Clay vineyard grapes are once again a sought-after crop that will continue to prosper, I'm sure, as it is highly unlikely that Europeans will stop drinking good wine. And we do produce some of the finest grapes in the Rhine River Valley and will continue to do so. But this is all of our eggs in one basket, so to speak. We live in extremely troubled times both politically and socially. Should our very unstable government weaken more and take over more of the profitable industries, as is talked about in some circles, we could have nothing. Your father, before we left Denmark, made two trips to the great America—once scouting out the coffee plantations of Central America where he made some lasting friends, of which I still keep in contact with the Tribaldos family with the coffee plantations, and secondly trading in the tobacco products and making friends there too, as well as a modest fortune that was lost to the corsairs, forcing us to move from Denmark. That was how he came to have that Walker Colt pistol you are so proud of carrying most of the time. Mr. Walker, who made that thing, was a good friend of your father's, and they kept in touch until your father's death. And thank you for not having it today, as you know how I feel about firearms."

Sheepishly, he reached under the seat, pulling it out of its hiding spot. "I know you are not comfortable with this, but I would never take the chance of something happening to you or Anne. As you just mentioned, these are troubled times we live in."

A slight frown crossed her face. Then she smiled. "Thank you, Thomas. You have become quite the young gentleman. With this being said," she continued, "we will need to diversify our occupation if we expect to continue doing business and reap the modest rewards we now enjoy. And I would like you to make a trip to America next spring and possibly find a place for a tobacco plantation or to purchase an existing plantation, then continue on to South America and rekindle the relationship with the Tribaldos family coffee plantations there. The trip should take less than six months. Two of the biggest imported items in Europe are coffee and tobacco. No matter what the situation here may become, people will always require coffee, tobacco, and wine—the third of which you know quite well, as we already have a hand in that business if we are fortunate enough to continue with the vineyards. It may seem a bit untimely with your new romance with Elizabeth, of which I am proud to have had a hand in, but it is something I wish you to consider."

Still sitting in the wagon and still parked alongside the road fidgeting with the reins to the horse, Thomas sat not saying a word for what seemed like several minutes then choosing his words very carefully before responding to his mother's request. "Untimely, yes, but still a brilliant idea. I have thought often as of late about at least a trip to America to look for a new place to live but never took into consideration the tobacco or coffee markets. In your opinion, my dear mother, what are the chances of selling the vineyards now while we still have considerable influence in the area and it is still ours to sell?"

"Not good—we are doing very well, but due to the masses from the area migrating to America, the available labor force has been severely reduced. Most businessmen know this, and it would be impossible to replace this family's knowledge and experience in this industry. For the vineyards to continue as successfully as they are now, we would have to stay and manage them at least for a while. We are gambling on a more stable and less corrupt government in the future. My proposal is for you to make the trip to America scouting the tobacco markets and then on to South America for the coffee businesses with the Tribaldos family. If you find a place in America to your liking that we could move to, we will deal with that."

Deep in thought, Thomas clucked at the horse, slapped the reins across its rump, and they continued the journey toward home without further conversation. Rounding the bend in the road and looking through the trees, they saw Fredrick standing in the grass by the house. It was a soothing sight, as it had been a very rich but emotional day with meeting Elizabeth, hearing of her family's turbulent life, and learning about Frida's thoughts for Thomas to go to America.

Fredrick directly loaded his arms with packages and started helping carry things into the kitchen, the main room of the big old house. "What is this order?" He sniffed. "It smells of vanilla, lavender, and roses all in one."

Frida and Anne both laughed and dove into the story of the events of the day. Thomas tended the horse and wagon as Fredrick listened to Anne relate the day's events, highlighting her horror at the barber profession before telling about the ladies store and Thomas meeting Elizabeth and his proclamations of marrying her someday. Frida was cautiously festive, as was her way, while she fixed supper. She was very intuitive and had the deep-seated feeling again that their lives could soon be altered forever.

Was it the introduction of Elizabeth into their midst, the contentious talk of America, or the ongoing threat of shady events that had taken place over the past many months? Those were possibly plotted by Horst but could have been some of her deceased husband's enemies amongst the corsairs. She hardly noticed when Thomas came in, let alone when Fredrick took the string of red onions down from their hook on the wall and hesitantly asked, "Mrs. Clay, could you please fix the favorite German onion dish for us tonight?"

To Thomas's knowledge, it was the first time Fredrick had ever asked for a favor of any kind from anyone. He thought the tears running from his mother's eyes were from the onions—they were in fact tears of deeply enjoying this moment, this meal together, and most of all this time with her family, Fredrick included.

Chapter 17

Horst Warehouse, Darmstadt, Hesse, Germany

1861

The disfigured Horst and the two would-be assassins were now sitting at a table deep in the interior of the warehouse district plotting for the disappearance of Thomas—and Fredrick too, if possible. The deep-seated hate Horst had developed for the Clay family had flooded to also encompass Fredrick. He strove to destroy the Clay vineyards and to have his way with the women.

Again one of the collaborators asked, "Begging your pardon, and it is not any of my business, Horst, but why do you harbor such a deep-seated hate for that family?"

"You're right," he hissed through his broken teeth and crooked jaw. "It is none of your business. I just want this done. We will wait in ambush along the road about halfway between their farm and town. The place I have in mind has an uprooted old tree, and the brush is very dense. He will not see you if you remain well concealed and wait for him to pass. That will be the time to rise and shoot that brat, Thomas. Each of you will be carrying two pistols in case one is to misfire. He will be close, and you better not miss. It will be far enough from town that the shooting will not be noticed, and it will make no difference if those at the vineyard hear or not. You will be long gone before any help can arrive."

"What if he takes the other road—the high one that his father used frequently and the one he at times uses?" one of the thugs asked. "We have scouted him before, and he seldom uses the same route twice in a row now."

"You figure it out," snapped Horst. "He is only one, and the two of you should be able to handle the job. If he does not use the ambush route one time, he will the next."

"How will we know when he is to be on either road again? We can't just sit out there for a week in the sun, rain, wind, or whatever."

"You can if you expect to get paid such a healthy sum," Horst snapped again.

Chapter 18

Clay Family Vineyards, Hesse, Germany

1861

The morning brought forth a stunning day. All the trees and shrubbery were in full bloom, the thin misty fog had risen from the valley floor, and the sun was softly shining through. It was fresh with that earthy smell that occasionally accompanied the meeting of light moisture to the bare ground. Thomas and Fredrick had tended the animals and returned to the house for breakfast. Anne was doing most of the food preparation now. She loved being a tomboy and would probably never outgrow that, but she also enjoyed her mother's company in the kitchen and was happy with her newfound role in family matters.

Fredrick and Thomas lingered over breakfast to the point that Frida appraisingly stated, "Well, what brings on this occasion of your continued presence here at the table when there is so much work to do outside?"

Fredrick and Thomas just smiled, both thoroughly enjoying her company. "Let's talk some of hired help," Thomas started. "We discussed this some on the way home from Darmstadt yesterday, but we may at least have a temporary solution. Fredrick knows some lads out of work and says he would swear to their integrity and willingness to participate in some hard labor." Thomas had addressed his mother and had her full attention. Knowing full well that Fredrick and Anne would remain silent for only a moment, Thomas continued hastily, "Also, I would like to approach Elizabeth's father, Manfred, for one of the positions we will have to fill if I am to make a trip to the Americas. He could fill in for me. He has considerable influence in the business world of Darmstadt as well as other European influences."

Finally Frida stammered, "When do you propose to make this venture?"

"Today," Thomas replied.

"But you don't even know this man, Thomas."

"I gave it much thought last night, and I have a feeling we will all get to know this man very well very soon. The sooner we can get more supervision in the fields, the better. We have added substantially to the size and quality of the vineyards the last several years and are now reaping the harvest, so to speak. I have talked to several new wineries and have a market for everything we can produce. There are now new shipping lines to the Americas and other ports in Europe to distribute the Rhine River wines. The Clay vineyards are once again noted as one of the finest in all the Rhine Valley influence, and with more help, we will be ready for the challenge."

Frida sat there shaking her head so the red ringlets danced, then looking under those locks with huge blue eyes staring at him, she said, "My, what ambitions. You remind me so of your father. Fredrick, what is your opinion on this matter?"

Thomas thought it was smart of her to ask of Fredrick's opinion directly, knowing full well that Anne would jump in with hers soon without being asked.

"Mrs. Clay, we will need much help to continue this ambitious endeavor, and I am certainly up for that challenge or any other that may present itself in the future."

Anne sat quietly with a slight smirk. "I was hoping for this day of development to arrive. Thomas, Fredrick, and all of us as a matter fact have worked tirelessly for the last few years without a complaint, and we are ready for another move forward. Elizabeth's father, Manfred, is a brilliant man and will be a positive stimulus on our business."

She spoke with a conviction and determination strange for one so young, but Thomas was now learning this was the new Anne. "And you all know I would love Elizabeth's company," she continued, eyes twinkling.

Thomas only smiled. He was looking for any excuse to return to Darmstadt as soon as possible to speak with Elizabeth but was busy with Fredrick, his mother, and Anne working on a plan to get Fredrick's acquaintances hired and in place. The days flew by, and it was a week before he had an opportunity to take the next load of produce to town with the intention of seeing Elizabeth. Wearing new clothes but not his best, he and Fredrick loaded the new wagon, hitched the horses, and he climbed into the seat to start the journey to the warehouse district in Darmstadt.

Fredrick had returned to the barn to harness another team to take to the fields. Thomas usually made the trip alone and would have done so this time, as he wanted to see Elizabeth. *It has been some time since we have had any threat from Horst*, Thomas thought. *We have seen no prowlers on the perimeter of the vineyards, and things seemed to be going well. Too well for comfort*, he thought. "Fredrick C. Burgdorf," he shouted, hoping to get his attention before

Fredrick left for the fields. Fredrick returned from the barn at a trot. "What? Is something wrong?"

"Probably not, but I have an uneasy feeling about this trip today. Would you like to go along? It may prove interesting and/or dangerous, so bring along that pistol of yours." It was similar in size and as formidable as the one that Thomas carried hidden under the seat of the wagon.

Fetching the pistol, Fredrick jumped into the seat next to Thomas. "What are you thinking?" he said. "It has been very quiet for some time now with no sight of Horst or any of his group."

"I just have that old feeling of something not quite right and thought it would be good to have some company on the trip today. We have all been very lucky lately in avoiding Horst's threats or presence."

"Let's go, then," Fredrick stated. "Just keep a lookout for anything suspicious and make sure of what you may be shooting at if necessity dictates such."

Thomas slapped the reins on the team's rump, and they lurched forward. They were now using the big wagons that had been updated throughout the last winter with newly repaired harnesses and seats much more comfortable to ride in. "I don't expect any trouble until we get away from the house and probably no trouble at all. More than likely just a false feeling—a false alarm, I hope."

The horses walked at a comfortable steady gate, one that would lend itself well to watching for any trouble along the roadside or the not-so-distant hilly country. The road this day was dust-free due to a heavy morning mist. The sun shone overhead with only an occasional billowed cloud. Thomas and Fredrick talked but watched carefully, not appearing to be totally observant to anyone who may be watching them. They had been traveling for about an hour when Fredrick noticed something out of the corner of his eye a short way off in the green undergrowth beside the road. The tops of the bushes were moving, but there was no wind. He nudged Thomas's arm and pointed his chin in the direction of the disturbance, and they both immediately picked out the two figures lying in the brush. Each figure with a pistol pointed in their direction. *This is going to be real ugly, real fast*, Thomas thought.

"They have us in their sights and nowhere for us to go," he whispered. "Hold on—we're going for a ride."

Without hesitation he yelled as loud as he could, slapping the reins hard on the horses and pulling them left toward the undergrowth. Startled then frightened, the horses jumped forward, careening into the underbrush on the left with the wagon bouncing over the downfall, rocks, and two prone figures that had no place to go. The two men lying on the ground were taken totally by surprise and had no time to move from the suddenly altered path of the wagon bearing down on them. The team of horses was now out of control running frantically but had crashed back out onto the road, where Thomas soon got them under control. Not a shot had been fired, but it was quite possible there were two dead would-be assassins lying back there, either trampled to death by the horses or run over by the wagon, likely both.

Stopping the team and getting down from the wagon, Thomas said, "Let's take a look at the carnage, Fredrick. Just be prepared in case they escaped death and are still able to use those pistols." Examining the area, they found nothing but a lot of blood, two hats, and four pistols. "Well, with no bodies to explain, we will have little trouble with the authorities," Thomas stated.

The two had apparently been in good enough shape to get to their horses, concealed farther back in the undergrowth, and had made a hasty but apparently painful retreat, judging by the amount of blood left behind. Leaving the hats but gathering up the pistols, Thomas and Fredrick walked back to the wagon to examine their own damages. The cart appeared to be in good enough shape to get them to the livery stable in Darmstadt for the repairs that would be required. Climbing back into the seat, they took stock of what was left of its contents—very little, as most of the produce was scattered along the road and in the brush, along with the would-be killers' blood.

What will Horst try now? And what have I actually accomplished but frustrate him one more time, bringing the issue no nearer to a conclusion? His two brutes tried to ambush us but have been severely trampled by the horses and run over by the wagon but have escaped even though I was sure they would not be in any condition to bother us further. Horst will have further schemes against us.

Thomas picked up the reins, nudged the horses into action, and they and the wagon limped into town. "Let's take this wagon to the livery and have Mr. Dryden to take a look at it and, if possible, do the necessary repair."

Fredrick chuckled and reminded Thomas that Elizabeth would probably be at work at the Perfumeries Douglas located down one block and across the street from the livery.

Shuffling his feet and grinning, Thomas said, "I'm aware of that, but first things first. Mother and Anne do need a more fashionable carriage to get back and forth to town to do their shopping. I noticed one sitting in front of Mr. Dryden's livery that they would look very fashionable driving about. We will investigate that first."

Thomas and the livery owner, Mr. Dryden, had met on many occasions, and the man was quite fond of the Clay family. He offered Thomas a very appealing price on the stunning carriage and a fine-looking horse to go with it. Thomas then suggested, "Fredrick, you can take the horse and carriage home, and I will follow later with our team. I can ride one and lead the other. I would love to be there to see Mother and Anne's reaction when they see their new mode of transport, but I think I will pass that opportunity to see the reaction of another young lady's face, Elizabeth, whom you have so pleasantly reminded me will be working across the street at the Perfumeries Douglas."

Mr. Dryden helped harness the pony and hook it to the new carriage, and then Fredrick jumped in, tipping his battered old hat somewhat and looking down at Thomas. "Do be careful, my young friend Thomas. You are now skating on very thin ice with Horst, especially after his once-again failed attempt at our murder earlier today." Slapping the reins on the horse, Fredrick moved at a pleasant gait down the street and out of town toward the vineyards and home.

Chapter 19

Perfumeries Douglas, Darmstadt, Hesse, Germany

1861

Thomas dusted himself off as best he could while he crossed the street. *What will Elizabeth think of me walking in unannounced dusty and in my work clothes? I must be an alarming sight.* Taking these thoughts into consideration did not slow him down in the least. He was smitten after his first encounter with her two weeks earlier and wanted to see her again. Walking down the boardwalk to the Perfumeries Douglas, he stopped in front of the glass-fronted building looking at his reflection to appraise his appearance.

Elizabeth, inside and unseen, observed his attempts to make himself more presentable through the window before his entrance. She had a deep intuitive consideration for Thomas's efforts and would do nothing that would cause him any discomfort. She had been anxiously looking forward to seeing him again. She had observed him from a distance over the last year when he was in town and was quite possibly as enamored with him as he with her. It was totally by chance that her very dear friend Anne was his sister. And that his mother, Frida, had helped her in getting this job after her time spent working in the stable shoveling horse manure and tending to the various livestock housed there. The very stable that Thomas had just vacated.

Elizabeth looked fashionable and delicate in nature, which in fact she was but with incredible wisdom way beyond her young age. She was a very competent and extremely intelligent young lady. Staring at him through the huge glass window, she marveled at his now more rustic appearance. Unlike his last visit when he was escorting Anne and their mother, he was now very rugged with disheveled coal-black hair and a hint of dust around where his hat had perched. *He's broad across the shoulders and fills out those trousers quite nicely*, she thought. Watching him through the window, waiting for him to come in, she had a profound feeling, *He just may be a part of my life forever.*

Finally satisfying himself with his appearance and reasoning that she had seen him previously at his finest, he walked through the door. Elizabeth had stepped out into full view to position herself right in front of him.

"Thomas, what a wonderful surprise," she said and could not help but give him a slight hug. She did not want him to be the least bit uncomfortable in her presence no matter the circumstances. She inquired of her dear friends, his sister, Anne, and mother, Frida. Thomas was instantly at ease, quickly forgetting his appearance, and they talked comfortably about current events in Darmstadt and news of the constant flow of Germans migrating to America. And about Elizabeth's family, for which she was quite worried. Her mother was still quite ill with very little improvement to her condition, and her father's health had nearly totally restored, and he would soon be able to work again.

With the conversation slowing, Thomas took this opportunity to mention, "We are looking to hire more help at the vineyards. There will be a position that your father would fit perfectly if he would consider it. Our family has discussed it and would be flattered if he were to take it into consideration."

Elizabeth listened attentively. She had never suspected this development for employment for her father. "This is a major obligation you are proposing, Thomas. You really don't know anything about him or his qualifications."

"Oh, but I do. Mother and Anne have told me much, and please pardon me, but I have made several discreet inquiries in the business district about your father. Please believe me when I say I know enough about him to propose a working relationship."

Studying him for a moment, she replied, "Of course this is something you are going to discuss with him."

"Yes, of course, and will do so immediately with your approval."

"Please do what you and your family think best."

Ultimately Thomas told her about the day's events with the roadside intruders, which he suspected to have been set up by Horst. He also told her of the other unfavorable events in and around his home and the vineyards, including his fight previously with Horst and then of Fredrick's battle with him over money owed to the vineyard.

Listening carefully and with much attention and consideration, Elizabeth finally replied, "He is a nasty one. I have seen him about, and he is an evil individual. While I was working at the stables, he constantly stalked me, and I was always very wary in his presence. He is not to be taken lightly, Thomas. I never liked him from the first time I met him," she said. "He reminded me of a serpent, cold and poisonous. From now on, you should take much care. From what I have heard of him, he will not stop in his quest to destroy you and your family."

"I hope this news will not discourage your father's decision to work with us."

"So do I." She smiled. "So do I. When are you going to approach him with this proposal?"

"Now is as good a time as any. If he is home and you feel he is up to it, I mean to walk you home, and we can discuss the matter."

Giving this only a few moments' consideration and being the type to make quick, decisive, and accurate decisions, she responded, "Of course. It is time for the store to close, and I'm sure my father will be anxious to discuss this venture with you, Mr. Clay. You certainly set the wheels in motion rapidly."

"Indeed I do," Thomas said, looking directly into her eyes. "Indeed I do."

Closing the store took but a few minutes, and they were soon strolling toward Elizabeth and her family's small apartment only a few blocks away.

"I forgot to tell you how undeniably wonderful you look this afternoon," Thomas said.

Elizabeth dimpled and, with the slightest curtsy, took his arm, and they moved along down the boardwalk slowly, absolutely enjoying the well-being of each other's company, their tête-à-tête being of small, nonimportant matters, just casual and pleasant talk. Behind them somewhere, there was music flowing softly from one of the taverns. They spoke quietly of matter-of-fact things, the little details of their lives falling into place to leave way for what was to come. Reaching their destination too soon, she disengaged her arm from his, and without hesitancy, Elizabeth opened the door and stepped into the cozy atmosphere of their apartment. Her father was sitting at a table reading, her mother resting in the bedroom.

Manfred looked up from his book and saw Thomas standing behind Elizabeth, not the least bit alarmed by this tall young gentleman with the black wavy hair and unusual green eyes. *A striking person*, he thought and casually asked, "Well what do we have here?"

Elizabeth answered, "I would like you to meet Thomas Clay of the Clay family vineyards." She beamed with somewhat of an impish attitude. "Thomas, this is my father, Manfred."

Stepping to one side of Elizabeth and moving his hands unconsciously across his rankled trousers Thomas smiled and said, "I am very pleased to meet you, sir. I have heard much about you."

"That could be dangerous." Manfred smiled. "But I am also pleased to meet you. Likewise I have also heard much of you. It seems you have made quite a name for yourself in the business world. You seem to be a very talented and gifted young man." He put emphasis on the term *young*.

Slightly moving around to Elizabeth's side and facing her father, Thomas said, "And I have never been older."

Manfred gave him a surprised look. "An intelligent, charming, and handsome young man with a sense of humor. Certainly an improvement from those other ruffians you have drug home from time to time," joked Manfred.

Elizabeth, being extremely close to her father, only laughed as he too had a strong, healthy sense of humor, something that Thomas would come to enjoy. Elizabeth had in fact never brought a young gentleman friend home before, but her father was quite pleased with this one. After appraising each other for but a moment, Manfred asked his daughter, "Well, to what do I owe the honor of the presence of this young man?" Elizabeth took a step back and then extended her arms to full length with palms up pointing to Thomas and said, "Have at it, Mr. Clay."

Not being in the least bit intimidated and instantly liking this man, Thomas began to speak. "Sir, we are doing a major expansion on the farm and vineyard and will very soon need much more help. We would like to have you assist us in the future expansion of the farm. We would like you to consider working with us as soon as possible. The vineyards will be increased by twofold, and the garden produce segment will also be expanded considerably. With this comes the added responsibility of marketing and logistics of transportation of products to market. We plan on expanding our workforce by double if we can find the workers."

Manfred sat with his elbows on his knees and his chin cradled in his hands listening intently to Thomas. *This young man is one who should be heard out*, he thought with his interest in the conversation rising.

Thomas then went on to reiterate their plans in initiating a market for the tobaccos from the Carolinas in America and possibly coffee from South America. He went on for over an hour explaining his intent to expand the farm and vineyards and his ideas on how to accomplish this ambitious effort. Elizabeth sat in awed silence staring from Thomas to her father as the very intense conversation went back and forth.

Chapter 20

Darmstadt Road, Hesse, Germany

1861

Fredrick had had no problems taking the very attractive new buggy and prancing pony out of Darmstadt on the back streets. He knew Horst would not have had enough time to plot another attack yet but was still cautious. Once out of town and continuing on the little-used road toward home, he had to pass the spot where Thomas and he had been the victims of the attempted ambush earlier that morning. Slowing and surveying the area again, Fredrick had the chilling feeling that this battle with Horst was just going to worsen. It was time for him and Thomas to take the confrontation to Horst and get it over with once and for all.

Two hours later, when Fredrick trotted toward the house with the new carriage, Frida and Anne were in the front yard staring in disbelief at the approaching extravagant carriage and pony. When he stopped the carriage in front of them, Frida flipped the red hair from her eyes and gasped. "Fredrick C. Burgdorf, what is this?"

Anne just climbed up beside him, grabbing the reins from Fredrick, and they trotted further down the road laughing. "This is splendid! How did we come about this?" she inquired.

"Well, let's turn back and talk to your mother. It's a long story, and I don't want to have to tell it twice."

Anne turned the carriage around, and they returned to where her mother stood with hands on sharp hips grinning. Getting down from the seat, Fredrick gently took Frida by the arm and guided her to the first step on the carriage.

"A gift for you from your young Thomas." He smiled.

Clutching her dress skirt and pulling the hem around and up, she placed her foot on the step and sat on the padded and spring-mounted seat. Having a playful look on her face, she scooped up the reins, raising them high then slapping them hard on the startled pony's rump. The results were remarkable. Fredrick had to jump back to keep from getting run over, and Anne shrieked in startled shock as the carriage carrying her mother went careening down the driveway and slid out onto the road. It took Frida only a minute to gain full control, turn around, and come riding casually back into the yard again.

"Had to see what this thing would do." She chuckled. "Now, Fredrick, tell me what has transpired to warrant this unbelievable gift. I usually only get something new when one or the other of you or both have been in serious trouble."

"Well, it's like this," Fredrick started but, noting the frown coming to her face, he picked up the pace of the conversation and filled Frida in on the day's events—all except for Thomas's whereabouts. This took some considerable time with his flamboyant and sometimes embellishing way of relating such a story.

When he had completed, Frida's frown was only deeper. "Where are Thomas and our team of horses?"

"Well," Fredrick hastily continued, "Thomas will be bringing the team home. He was going to ride one of the horses and lead the other."

"Where is Thomas? He should have been here by now, Fredrick."

"Well," he started again, "Thomas was going to stop and see Elizabeth then her father to talk about work."

She stood there now somewhat relieved knowing of Thomas's whereabouts but still worried about her son's return trip, probably long after dark. She was very fond of Elizabeth and hoped things would work out between the two of them, but she was still worried. Fredrick was very much aware of what may happen to a lone traveler in this area after dark. During the day it was often risky, but at night it could prove fatal. There were many transients camped on the outskirts of Darmstadt not willing to work but looking for a fast coin by unscrupulous methods.

"I am going to walk a ways down the road and watch for Thomas. I can help him get the horses home and keep a watch out for any possible trouble. I'm quite sure he will be along soon."

Frida and Anne unhooked the horse from the buggy moving toward the barn. "We will tend to this delightful new animal so you can go now."

"Be careful, Fredrick," Frida said as he turned and walked from the fading light toward town.

Fredrick was still armed with his LeMat pistol, the likes of which few bandits would like to meet up with.

Chapter 21

Klein Apartment, Darmstadt, Hesse, Germany

1861

Thomas went on explaining his thoughts and ideas for another few minutes then, hardly giving Elizabeth's father a moment to think or speak, he asked, "How do you feel about all this, Mr. Klein?"

During the progression of the conversation, Manfred and Thomas had moved to the kitchen table. Elizabeth had busied herself about the kitchen and had fixed her father and Thomas a light meal of cold cuts and fresh baked bread, which they had eaten during the intense conversation. Her mother had eaten a light meal earlier and retired for the evening. She was still very weak and in failing health. Manfred sat in silence for only a moment but deep in thought. He now had his face buried in his hands with his elbows on the table. Then he lifted his head and smiled faintly. Manfred still tired easily from his previous injuries but was excited about this proposal.

"Of course I will give this thoughtful deliberation and am pleased with this proposal. It has been long since I have been productive in the work area, but I still have to give consideration to the health of my wife and her care." With an amused grin, he added, "We will discuss this further when you visit Elizabeth next. And that will be soon, I hope."

Thomas, sensing no more need be discussed at this time, at least about work, rose from his chair. "That will in fact be soon, sir—with your permission, of course."

"Permission granted."

Having heard the entire conversation, Elizabeth stood and stepped forward from where she had been seated next to her father and lightly touched Thomas's arm, gracefully guiding him to the door, stepping out with him onto the small covered entryway, and lightly closing the door behind them. "What a pleasing evening, Thomas. This will bring my father to a more rapid recovery, and I am rather sure he is serious about your offer." With a very light smile and her hand still on his arm, she asked, "When will I see you again?"

"Tomorrow," he said, turning and giving her a caring hug. Then he stepped into the now-dark street.

She turned to blow him a kiss as she stepped back to the door. "Thomas, be very careful. You know what Horst and his group are capable of."

"That, I will." He walked down the street to the stable to get his wagon team and be homeward bound.

When Elizabeth stepped back into the lighted room with her father, she was frowning.

Meeting his eyes, he perceived her worried expression. "Why the worried look? Is something wrong? He seemed to be a wonderful young man."

"He is a most wonderful young man, and I am very worried for his safekeeping." She sat down beside her father and leaned her head against his shoulder, relating Thomas's ventures for the day and all his past problems with the terrible man Horst. "I think this is something to bear in mind while you are considering Thomas's proposal."

"Indeed, it is, little darling. Indeed it is. Horst is a genuine troublemaker and always has been since I've known him. He loathed Thomas's father, and there was some speculation that he was somehow responsible for his death. He has always gone for the easy and quick dishonest gain over a genuine day's work. As you are well aware, he is a treacherous and volatile monster. I don't think Thomas has the total perception of the danger Horst presents. It is unbelievable to me that someone has not done away with him by now. I too am most worried for the safety of your Thomas as well as our family's safety. You, your two sisters, and your mother are all at risk. He has troubled you all previously, and if he becomes aware of our involvement with young Thomas, there will be more real trouble, I'm thinking."

There was a lightness to Thomas's step. He was totally pleased with the outcome of the conversation with Manfred and was now certain he was in love with Elizabeth. As starry-eyed and lighthearted as he was, Thomas still had the good sense of being very cautious and surveyed the darkened barn carefully before entering. Dryden, the stable owner left the horses with harnesses in place on their backs so he only had to lead them out, jump onto one, and lead the other. He did so and silently and warily left town.

Chapter 22

Darmstadt Road,
Hesse, Germany

1861

In the darkness Fredrick quietly walked down the road toward Darmstadt and was only another shadow in a maze of shadows cast by the trees and undergrowth. The only sounds came from the night birds, crickets, and the occasional whisper of a limb brushing another in the light breeze. His senses isolated these vague sounds from others less familiar, leaving a vacant place in his mind where strange sounds could register.

He knew Thomas was in constant danger and would be until something permanent was done with Horst's persistent threat. Standing there in silence, he felt as well as heard the movement of horses approaching from the north, the direction of the city. Patiently and quietly, he waited in the shadows until he was sure it was Thomas, then spoke in a low tone, "It is only I, Fredrick." He spoke in such a way and tone as not to alarm Thomas and get shot for his efforts.

Thomas turned the horses toward his concealed spot in the trees and jokingly retorted, "I knew you were there for the last five minutes. You need a bath." They both chuckled, and Fredrick climbed onto the second horse Thomas had in tow.

"It is not I who needs to worry about a bath. You are the one entertaining that charming young lady. Tell me about it, Thomas. How was your time with Elizabeth this evening?"

"I was the perfect gentleman."

They rode on for a time then Fredrick broke the silence. "A true gentleman is at a disadvantage in dealing with women, you know. Women are realists. And their tactics are realistic, so no man should be a gentleman where women are concerned unless the women are very, very old or very, very young. Women do admire gentlemen, but they sleep with the cads."

Thomas, having very little experience in those matters, said nothing for a few moments, not knowing if Fredrick was serious or just pulling his leg again. Deciding it was the latter, he laughed and replied, "Are you not the forever philosopher?" Amused with Fredrick's remarks, he added, "How would you know this? I have never seen you in the company of a very, very old lady or a very, very young girl or in fact in the presence of any lady we should discuss."

It was Fredrick's turn to laugh, and they continued on the short journey toward home. Quickly recovering from Fredrick's comment, Thomas said, "Thank you, Fredrick, for always being there in time of need and all the kindness you have shown the family over the last few years. A dear friend for sure."

It was too dark for Thomas to notice the light color change in Fredrick's face. Fredrick was a very tough and hardened individual due to the turbulent life he had experienced prior to meeting up with the Clays, but he was deeply humbled at Thomas's comment and had nothing else to say concerning the matter. "When are you going to Darmstadt again?" Fredrick inquired. "We still have the threat of Horst's devious disposition hanging over us."

"Probably tomorrow. I want to talk to Manfred again soon, and of course," Thomas added hastily before Fredrick could, "see Elizabeth."

But in fact he spent the next few days with Fredrick and the new fieldhands revamping equipment and procedures for the coming fall's harvest. Thomas did, however, send a note that next morning to Elizabeth and her father explaining his delayed return. He had effectively made more efficient arrangements for the buyers of grapes from his vineyards to furnish their own transportation to the wineries. The other fruits and produce were also picked up regularly, relieving the necessity of the frequent trips to Darmstadt. The once-isolated little farm was now a hustling hub of much traffic. Frida and Anne worked tirelessly day in and day out on tracking finances, keeping the general business end running smoothly and helping in any way possible. Every evening at suppertime the discussion was of how the new process would be initiated when Thomas was away on his trip to the Americas and would have no immediate influence on the function of the farm and vineyards.

They hardly had time now for any of the other favorable occasions they once enjoyed. Thomas barely had time for further studies and sorely missed his time with the books. He and Fredrick started work before daylight and ended well after dark each day. They only occasionally had lessons in the boxing and wrestling techniques, as now they were nearly identical in skill. On one occasion Fredrick commented, "My young friend, Thomas, you are one of the best I have seen with these physical skills, and your technique with the blade is masterful. Do not become complacent with these skills—I fear and have a deep feeling your future will require the necessity of them all to survive."

There were many projects still needing attention, and Thomas was anxious to get back to town to see Elizabeth and further discuss these work-related issues with her father. If Manfred chose to accept the job offer at the vineyard, there would be much to keep every man on the farm busy during the months when they waited for Thomas to return from his trip to the Americas—constant upkeep on the wagons, the horse tack, harvesting and pruning of the vines, fertilizing the fields. It was a never-ending job. He had no reservations of making the trip, but he had not had an opportunity to discuss in detail this upcoming event with Elizabeth or Manfred, and that did bother him.

Chapter 23

Horst Warehouse, Darmstadt, Hesse, Germany

1861

Horst sat alone drinking from a bottle of gin in a grimy room in the warehouse in Darmstadt, the failed attempt on Thomas's and Fredrick's lives over a week ago still exasperating him nearly to a snapping point. The two toughs he had hired to attend to Fredrick and Thomas's roadside murder had failed miserably, and he had heard nothing from either of them. He had heard from second-hand sources, though, that they had skipped the country in a very broken, beat up, and miserable condition, fearing retribution from Horst. He sat in a dreadful mood.

Horst now knew of the relationship between Thomas and that old stable girl Elizabeth he had unsuccessfully stalked. This only added fuel to his already insufferable mood. Picking up the half-empty bottle of gin, he hurled it at the wall, shattering glass and the bottle's contents over the room. Getting up, he stumbled outside, shouting at the stable boy he kept employed to run errands and tend to his horse and buggy. Horst—himself as a result of the previous fight with Thomas then the subsequent beating he had suffered from Fredrick while trying to cheat them out of moneys owed—was in no condition to ride a horse. He had to depend on a wagon or carriage for transportation.

"Come here, boy," he said in a somewhat more normal tone. "I want you to run down to the district across the tracks on the outskirts of town. You will find a big man there named Cedrick. He appears to be a fat and sloppy man with a shaved head and full beard. Be careful when approaching him—his fat appearance is deceiving. It is all muscle, and he has an unpredictable temper. Ask him to come at once. Just tell him Horst wants to see him."

Horst had known Cedrick for years but had hesitated to involve him in this matter. He was totally unpredictable, with a temper that would flare at the slightest annoyance, and his services, though always successful, were extremely expensive.

Horst continued, "You will not have trouble finding him. Just ask around. He is well-known, and you can smell him from a block away," he added sarcastically. "And do not mention this to anyone. Now be gone with you and hurry back with some positive news for a change."

The boy darted out the back entrance hastily, knowing that Horst would hurl anything in reach at him if he lingered. It was only an hour before he had located the seemingly giant Cedrick and delivered the message.

True to form, Cedrick was a foul man with no manners or patience. He grabbed the boy by the shirt front, lifting him from the ground and holding him at eye level. "You're that little Alkire brat, Josh, aren't you? Tell Horst I may come see him if and when I feel up to it." Then he dropped the boy to the ground.

Josh quickly got up, not bothering to dust himself off, knowing he was lucky to get away without a slap or a kick, and ran around a building out of sight before slowly walking back to report the message to Horst. He was an orphan of maybe seven years old and had only the meager existence that Horst provided. He did not want to deliver the message from Cedrick. He knew it was not what Horst would want to hear, and he was afraid. He slowly walked back on the now-dark street toward the warehouse with tear-streaked cheeks. All too soon, he was standing in front of the warehouse entrance. He tried to dust himself off and shake his dread of the anticipated reaction from Horst, and then he bravely marched up to the door and stepped inside the dimly lit room.

The room smelled every bit as harsh as the giant man he had just left. Horst was sitting and nursing a fresh bottle of gin.

"Well?" Horst shouted with an intoxicated slur.

Josh quickly repeated the message, "He said he would come if and when he felt like it," then quickly stepped back out the door into the darkness before Horst could get up and strike him or throw something. He made his way around the warehouse to another door and entered an area where he knew Horst would not find him, and he curled up in a nest of old burlap bags. There would be no food or drink for him tonight, but he would stay warm.

Horst had a few dealings with Cedrick in the past and paid dearly for them, but they did get done. He knew Cedrick would come probably the next day. He was a greedy man and knew Horst would pay well for whatever dishonorable deed he had in mind. He had done many fraudulent jobs for Horst in the past, but there were limits to what even Cedric would do, and Horst had a deep-down gut feeling that this may be one he would never consider. Horst was afraid of him, and Cedrick knew it—Horst knew he would have to pay well for Cedrick's services without a doubt.

True to form, the next afternoon Cedrick arrived at the shabby room in the warehouse Horst called home, and without the formalities of small talk, the negotiations concerning the permanent demise of the Clay family, including Fredrick, began.

"Not only are Thomas and Fredrick to be eliminated without a trace, but I also want his mother and sister and that Elizabeth girl brought here for me to determine their fate. I want all of this to happen very soon, and I prefer it to be done here. I have had several failed attempts on their lives in the countryside outside of town. It cannot happen again. We will somehow get them all together here and be done with it."

Cedrick looked at him incredulously. "Since when have you started telling me how to do your nasty work?" he said threateningly. "As usual, I can get it done, but it will be done on my terms and time as I see fit. Got it, Horst?"

Horst sat there in silence brooding. One more failed attempt, and he knew they would be coming for him. He had heard some talk around town that Thomas and Fredrick knew or at least suspected the previous attempts were directly related to him, and he was frightened. Fredrick had previously whipped him soundly, leaving him in the miserable physical condition he was now in, and Thomas had thoroughly made a fool of him with the sword prior to that. "However you see fit," he replied. "Just get it done in a hurry and without any slipups." Then he added, "While you're at it, get rid of Elizabeth's father, Manfred, also."

Cedrick just looked at him. "You want Thomas; his mother, Frida; his sister, Anne; his friend Fredrick; and as I hear it Thomas's soon-to-be bride, Elizabeth; and her father, Manfred, all killed. How about we also get rid of Manfred's wife, two other daughters, and their friend the barber and the gunsmith Hollenbeck? There is not a wagon in Darmstadt big enough to haul away all the bodies, and I'm sure that a massacre of that magnitude would arouse no suspicions. You are not only crazy, Horst—you're insane, and *you* belong dead in a box six feet under but not half the town." With that being said, Cedrick got up and walked out, leaving Horst sitting there alone in the semidark, stinking room, fuming with his bottle of gin.

Chapter 24

Clay Family Vineyard, Hesse, Germany

1861

Anne and her mother had occasion to go to Darmstadt twice before Thomas was able to leave the vineyard for another visit with Elizabeth. Frida and Anne had informed Elizabeth for the reason of Thomas's untimely return, as he had informed her a week ago he would be back the very next day. Elizabeth was disappointed in not seeing Thomas sooner but was sympathetic and understanding.

Finishing their rounds in the fields, Thomas and Fredrick both arrived at the house at the same time, washed up, and went into the dining room for the well-prepared supper that Anne and her mother had hurriedly fixed. They had just returned from a shopping trip to town, which had included a visit to the Perfumeries Douglas as usual. As of late, if anyone was to go hungry around there, it was their own fault. Frida once announced, "We are fortunate to have an abundance of good food, good manners, and good company."

"I am going to town tomorrow," Thomas announced. "I want to see Elizabeth. Can I borrow your dainty little horse and frilly buggy to go?" he inquired of his mother.

"Wouldn't that be a sight—a big, black-haired, well-built, charming young man like yourself carrying himself to town in my buggy?" She laughed.

After breakfast the next morning, Fredrick helped Thomas catch and saddle one of the horses. "Be very watchful, Thomas. We know it is only a matter of time until we have the final confrontation with Horst."

Thomas was worried more for his mother and Anne than himself, as they had made frequent trips to town unaccompanied by him or Fredrick. "I will be very watchful not only on the road but also in town. I do want to see Elizabeth, though."

"Understood," Fredrick replied, smiling, then jokingly reminded him he was also to discuss Manfred's decision on helping run the fields and vineyards. When Thomas was to make his trip to the Americas, Manfred's help would be paramount. "We also have to consider the possible added threat to Elizabeth and her family should Manfred decide to join us," Fredrick added. "But I do have some thoughts on that. Over the past few months some of my old acquaintances from Hamburg have been filtering into Darmstadt. Hamburg, as you know, is the place of my origin and is some five hundred kilometers from here to the northeast. Seems things are getting a little heated with the gangs and dock workers up there, and this far into the interior will be a safe temporary retreat. They may be a seedy, rough group but would prove useful and loyal, asking for no more than a smile and a handshake. I knew them all well, and they are worthy of mention. They will be here in Darmstadt for only a few months until the somewhat unpredictable political situation in Hamburg stabilizes again, and I'm quite sure they would be more than willing to keep an eye on the Klein family while waiting in Darmstadt for conditions to return to normal in Hamburg. They may just be the answer in dealing with Horst also."

After some discussion as to the character of these friends, Thomas agreed to the idea. Fredrick would meet with each over the following days and enlighten them to the situation, knowing they would take delight in such a clandestine challenge with little else to do.

Thomas took the longer route to Darmstadt, the route that the old wooden railroad followed along the base of the mountain—also the one that his father had been killed on. He had time to spare, as Elizabeth wouldn't get off work until late afternoon, and he wanted some alone time to regroup his thoughts. He had been very busy for the last few days and needed time to think undisturbed. Not wanting to wander thoughtlessly across the dangerous mountainside, he stopped amongst a well-protected wall of boulders and trees. Dismounting and sitting where he had a good view of the surrounding area, he tried to clear his mind and think about what was ahead for him—his budding relationship with Elizabeth and his meeting with her this afternoon, his marketing trip to America, Manfred's possible employment at the vineyards, and the never-ending threat of Horst. And now the possible help from Fredrick's acquaintances from Hamburg. Were they even slightly trustworthy? Fredrick seemed to think so and was in hopes they would even keep an eye on the Klein family. It was a heavy load, and he knew that all of their lives could very possibly be changed forever depending on the outcome of the following days. After much thought sitting there in the semishaded afternoon sun, he felt more relaxed and much more at ease.

He came to the conclusion that the only real unpredictable issue was Horst. All else would be as it should. Remounting his restless horse, he continued his journey into town. There, he stabled his horse with Dryden and walked across the street to the Perfumeries Douglas where Elizabeth worked, hoping she would be there.

She saw him outside through the large store windows and met him at the door. Extending her hands, she took Thomas's in hers, beaming. "It's wonderful to see you again."

"And you too," he replied.

Giving him a light hug, Elizabeth then turned to help a customer who had followed Thomas into the store. When she returned, she asked, "Will you have supper with us this evening?"

"I will, and I would like to further discuss employment with your father."

Stepping back and frowning a bit, she said, "Well, I thought you were here just to see me." They both laughed.

Mrs. Hoogendyk, the store owner, noticed them in deep conversation and stepped around the corner. By now she knew and was very fond of Thomas and had a long relationship with his mother and sister, so she heartily approved of his relationship with Miss Elizabeth. "Why don't you two get out of here?" She smiled. "She is not going to get anything done the rest of the day anyway with you around."

"Thank you, Mrs. Hoogendyk. We will do just that," Elizabeth said, leading Thomas to the door.

They stepped out into the late afternoon shade and strolled casually down one of the busy streets deep in conversation. The conversation of two young people in love. It had been a short time since their first meeting, but neither had any doubts as to the other's true feelings. Finally steering him toward the apartment she shared with her family, Elizabeth once again gave Thomas a light hug at the doorstep before entering.

Manfred and his other two daughters sat in conversation and looked up when the couple came in, both of her sisters staring in fascination at the tall, broad-shouldered, black-haired young man with those piercing green eyes their sister had just brought in.

Rising from his chair and extending his hand, Manfred acknowledged Thomas's presence with "Welcome, young Thomas. I have been wondering what was keeping you." With the faintest of smiles, he continued, "I thought she may have said something to offend you and scare you off. However, she needn't worry about that—I usually do a good job of that."

Not knowing exactly what to say, Thomas stuttered, "Sh-she is quite beautiful." Then he added, "And very sensitive, and intelligent. And I'm also sure you could frighten me off, but I truly hope you will not do that."

Manfred chuckled suddenly, and Thomas did not know why, but the older man glanced at him slyly. "It is not often I hear a young man comment on a stunning young woman's mind."

"Oh, but it is worthy of comment, and her beauty also," Thomas replied, and Manfred only chuckled.

"You will stay for supper, will you not?"

"Yes, sir, I will and hungry, I am."

Elizabeth's mother, who had been resting in another room, feebly entered. "I have to meet this charming young man I have heard so much about."

Thomas turned, giving her one of his most gracious smiles. Elizabeth had told him of her mother's failing health, and he was as delighted to meet her as she him. She walked to him extending both hands, which he gracefully accepted.

"I can certainly now see what my daughter is so infatuated with."

Neither Thomas nor Elizabeth revealed any embarrassment over the comment.

"I heard Manfred invite you for supper. The girls will put on a feast, I'm sure. But now if you will excuse me, I must lie down." She was very weak and did not want to miss this delightful young man's company but could stand no longer.

"Please sit and we will talk of much while the ladies fix something to eat," Manfred said, gesturing to a chair on the opposite side of the small table.

Frowning at her father's dismissal, Elizabeth followed her siblings to the kitchen.

"Have you given thought to our offer of work?" Thomas started.

"I have. I have thought of little else." Manfred then went on to recap his thoughts and concerns. "I know Horst, and with this joint venture, we will all be at more risk of his cowardly but deadly actions."

Discussing this at great length, Thomas finally mentioned to Manfred, "We may have a solution that will help with the threat of Horst," then went into great detail reiterating his earlier conversation with Fredrick and the arrival of his friends from Hamburg, finally concluding, "They will not be here forever but might just add a comforting level of security for the time being. Maybe something will become of Horst in the meantime to eliminate his threat forever."

Manfred sat in deep concentration for but a few moments then said, "Let us get on with this. I am anxious to go to work, young man."

Supper was now being placed on the table, and the girls sat to join them, with Elizabeth discreetly beating her two sisters to the seat next to Thomas. The conversation was unusually light, each one at the table more involved with their personal thoughts than the meal in front of them. It had been an intense evening, and the conversation between Thomas and Elizabeth's father would have a far-reaching effect, far beyond what any of them would realize at this moment.

Slightly turning to face Elizabeth's two sisters, Thomas crossed his arms over his chest and said, "My mother has extended an invitation for you all to come visit the vineyard and get acquainted with our business as soon as possible. We all would like to know your family better. Mother and Anne will of course have lunch for all, and Manfred will have the opportunity to review firsthand the new duties involved in managing the marketing and logistics of the vineyard."

"If Father is to going to have such a responsible role in the business as you have suggested, what is your role to be, young Thomas?" Elizabeth had come to refer to him as her father had.

"Well, I'm going to—" He drew out the last word as he realized he had never really discussed the timing of his pending trip to the Americas with Elizabeth. He closed his mouth, and he sat in silence. He thought this was certainly not the time for this discussion, so Thomas changed the subject, distracting her with other more pleasant memories, and soon they were all laughing again.

"Could I interest you in but a very small glass of after-dinner wine, Thomas?" Manfred asked. "If I'm going to be a part of one of the more noted vineyards in all of the Rhine Valley, we should toast the occasion appropriately, don't you think?"

"Yes, of course. We often sample a glass at home from some of the finer wineries we supply grapes to," Thomas said. "My father and mother would have a glass of it from time to time, and I have learned the fine art of wine tasting."

"I hope I do not disappoint you with this then, but it's all we have."

"The wine is excellent, as is the fabulous dinner and company," Thomas said looking directly at Elizabeth. "However, I am afraid it is getting late and I should be on my way before I cause too much worry on the home front." He reiterated the invitation of the Klein family to the farm, and they heartily accepted, hoping it to be soon. With that, he rose, collected his coat, bid his farewells, and agreed to meet with Manfred again the next day to finalize the details of his new work role. Manfred knew the location of the vineyards and was to ride out the following morning.

Elizabeth walked him to the door, and they stepped out onto the covered patio facing the street. "It was a wonderful evening," she commented, not pressuring for more conversation as badly as she wanted to. There was still so much she did not know about young Thomas.

With a parting embrace and a promise to return soon, Thomas walked across the street and down a block to where his horse was stabled. It was nearly dark, and he approached it with much caution as he noticed a slight movement from the corner of one eye. Stopping in the shadow of the open door, he stood, not making a move.

Slowly, a small figure stepped out and curiously looked around. *Where did he go?* the young boy thought. *He was just here.*

Observing the boy's very slight stature, Thomas stepped from the shadow. He did not want to scare the wits from this small boy but did wonder why he was following him. "Can I help you?" he quietly asked.

For just a moment, the boy stood facing Thomas frozen in fear. Most of his associations with adults had not been pleasant, and he did not want to suffer another cuff to the head for just being there. Hastily he stammered, "Please pardon me, sir. My name is Josh, and I work around the warehouse district as I can. I run errands for Mr. Horst and some of the others there. I have most recently overheard Mr. Horst making serious threats on your life. I have tended to Mrs. Clay's horse and carriage occasionally when she is in town. She has always been very kind and very generous to me, and I would like no harm to befall her or any of you."

Thomas stood still, judging the boy. *Could this be a misleading trap set by Horst to divert my attention?* He saw the boy was shaking badly with fright and was in no apparent haste to leave. "Where do you live? Do your parents know you are out at this time of night?"

"I have no parents," the boy replied, "and I sleep in a corner of one of the warehouses out of the way where I am not to be found."

Still suspicious, Thomas questioned him more about his seemingly meager existence. The city was abundant with beggars, vagabonds, and the likes. It was a very difficult time for many, but this was just a mere boy and he had asked for nothing, just voiced a warning for Thomas's well-being. "How old are you, Josh?"

"I'm not sure. Maybe close to seven."

Still wary of the situation, Thomas gently guided the boy around the corner to a more lit area of the street for a closer look. The sight before him was alarming. The boy wore rags that barely covered his skinny, frail body. He was dirty with unkempt hair and wore no shoes. "Josh," he addressed the boy, "you have shown an excessive consideration in warning me about Horst's harmful intentions for me and my family, and I think he would be very angry with you if he were to find out about this. Would you consider allowing me to repay some of the thoughtful kindness you have shown? We just may have a need for a stable boy at our farm, and I am quite sure there would be something to eat on a more regular basis than what you are apparently accustomed to."

The boy thought for only a moment and decided, *Why not?* Thomas had not hit him yet, and there was mention of food. Anything would be better than his bare survival there in Darmstadt. "I will give it consideration."

"Well, how much time do you need for consideration?" Thomas smiled.

"About a minute."

"Then let's grab your things, and I will take you to the farm with me."

"I have no things to grab and am ready now."

Cautiously bringing his horse from the barn, still wary of some wrongdoing from Horst, Thomas mounted and extended his hand for the boy to grasp and swing up behind him. Then they started the journey home. *Mother of God*, Thomas thought, *how am I going to explain this one when I get home?*

The lantern hanging on its wrought-iron arm extended from the front of the house was still lit, casting faint shadows on the lawn and walkway. Fredrick, Frida, and Anne were anxiously awaiting Thomas's return due to the never-ending threat of Horst. They were deep in conversation of the pending transition, the adjustment of the work force that would take place upon Thomas's departure to America, and the expected arrival of Elizabeth's father, Manfred, to the farm in the immediate future. Now hearing the arrival of Thomas's horse in front of the house, Fredrick and Frida both strode to the door, opening it to offer help with the horse and the few items he would be returning with after his meeting with the Klein family. Enough light reflected from the hanging lantern to light up the faces of not only Thomas but that of a small, ragged little boy sitting behind him on the horse. Thomas's horse had turned slightly to the side, giving full exposure to the two sitting on its back.

Frida immediately recognized Josh's small unkempt frame sitting behind Thomas. He had on many occasions tended her horse and carriage while she was on business in town, and she had always felt a deep fondness for him. She had constantly given him an extra coin and regularly tried to bring him some little treat before returning home. Waiting for no explanations, she stepped further into the light. "Well, what do we have here? Looks like someone needing a meal and perhaps even some shelter for the night."

Fredrick quickly stepped up to the horse and helped Josh down. He was frightened, tired, and very hungry. He did not remember when he had last eaten. Not knowing what reception he would receive here amongst these people, he stood ready to take whatever the punishment was to be or collapse from hunger and fatigue.

Perceiving Josh's wariness and apprehension, Frida gently took him by the shoulder and guided him into the kitchen. "Sit down, young man," she said gently. "Could I fix you something to eat?" He only nodded his head. Frida prepared him a ham sandwich with all the trimmings. The trimmings coming fresh from the garden that day.

Gazing at the sandwich, Josh sat in bafflement. Having never seen anything like it before, he had no idea where to start.

"Go ahead. Eat," she said. "You certainly look as if you could use it."

Josh picked up the sandwich with his dirty little hands, and soon he'd devoured it, along with two glasses of milk. Having said nothing until he had finished, now he timidly offered, "Thank you. It has been long since I have eaten."

"Come, let's get you cleaned up and a place for the night." Frida stoked the fire and hung a bucket of water over the flame to heat. Placing a small tub, soap, and a towel behind a makeshift curtain, she dumped hot water into the tub and suggested he strip his clothes and climb in. Then stepping outside the curtained area, she added, "And don't forget to wash your hair."

While the boy was bathing, she went quickly to a closet and dragged out some old clothes that Thomas had outgrown years prior and discreetly slid them under the curtain for Josh. Fredrick and Thomas had left the comfort of the little boy to Frida's care and had tended the animals, then sat in front of the barn while Thomas related the day's events, including the appearance of Josh.

Fredrick, true to his nature, listened in deep concentration, silently digesting everything Thomas said with care. Then he stood to stretch his arms and legs from sitting too long. "Now that you have finalized the position with Manfred, I will go to town early tomorrow morning and arrange their family's discreet protection with my friends visiting from Hamburg. They will not be here long but long enough—I hope—to cope with Horst. Now let's go in and see how Mrs. Clay is doing with little master Josh."

"Hmmm, I'm not sure I'm looking forward to that." Thomas shrugged.

Inside, Josh was standing in front of the fireplace, freshly bathed in clean clothes, and Frida had prepared him a cup of hot chocolate, a rare delicacy the likes of which he had never had. Frida was sitting next to him, still taller than him even while she sat. Being a mother with all of its intuitive natures, she had managed to coax out most of his life story and the events leading to his presence here with Thomas. As the men came in, she stood and gently touched Josh's shoulder. "Let's find Josh a place to lay his head—he is exhausted."

"He can sleep on the extra pallet in my room," Fredrick suggested, and so it was.

When Fredrick had returned to the kitchen after showing Josh his bed, Thomas and his mother were sitting at the kitchen table deep in conversation recapping the day's events. Fredrick had also known of Josh previously around town and had occasionally contributed to his meager existence when opportunity presented itself.

Frida stood and stomped her foot in disgust and anger. "That bastard," she hissed. "How could he treat such a small boy like that? And his continual harassment to our family—and now probably Elizabeth's family—is totally deplorable."

Thomas had never heard his mother swear before, but he knew exactly who she had directed the derogatory remarks toward.

"I have changed my attitude toward firearms and wish you to find me one. A small one that I can easily conceal, and I shall shoot that man myself if given the chance."

Chapter 25

Clay Family Vineyard, Hesse, Germany

1861

The next few days were extremely busy. Anne had taken little Josh under her protective wing and was as delighted with his company as he with hers. He had not been assigned any chores and had no responsibilities. Josh was free to roam the farm and vineyards and just play and enjoy life as a very young boy should. Everyone totally enjoyed his presence, as he was a delightful boy and proving to be a witty young man.

One morning catching Thomas alone, Frida complimented him. "You know, that was a brave and very generous move on your part to bring little Josh home with you that night. You have incredible compassion, Thomas. I doubt if the others here have noticed it like I have, but you are kind and thoughtful, son. In spite of the gunfights, sword fights, and brawls," she added with her arms folded across her chest and that lock of fiery-red hair hanging in her face.

Manfred had made his first appearance at the vineyards earlier in the summer and was adjusting into his new role as the professional he was. Fredrick had made arrangements with his friends in town to keep a watch out for any suspicious behavior directed toward the family, and Thomas still made his frequent business trips to town, which always included a visit with Elizabeth. They set up a family picnic at the vineyards for the following Sunday, a day that Elizabeth and her sisters had off from work. Thomas's mother and Anne were busily preparing for that event. It would soon be harvest time, and Manfred was adjusting into his role quite well, allowing Thomas more time for preparation for his trip to the Americas.

The day of the much-awaited social event and family gathering finally arrived. It was not only to familiarize the Klein family in its entirety to the now very successful business but also for the Clays to rekindle their standing with some of their old acquaintances. Something they had not done since the death of Thomas's father. The gunsmith Raymond Hollenbeck and his wife, Cattie, as well as the barber Heinrich and his wife were amongst the many invited guests. Mrs. Jenifer Hoogendyk, the owner of the Perfumeries Douglas where Elizabeth worked, was also to attend. Many other members of the business community were arriving and milling around, anxiously anticipating the banquet. It was the first such occasion on the Clay family vineyards in years. The preparation for the event had required the assistance of many of the field workers in setting up makeshift tables, chairs, and other decorations, as meager and short supply as they were at the time. It was a very impressive arrangement, and Frida and Anne were taking full advantage of it. Little master Josh was at his best. He helped here, completed minor tasks there, and was a delightful help in every way.

Thomas had rented a large carriage from Mr. Dryden at the livery to pick up and bring Elizabeth's family to this lavish affair. After stopping in front of their door, he jumped down and knocked. There was a long pause before Elizabeth finally came to the door.

"Oh, Thomas, I am so worried. Mother has taken a turn for the worse, and I'm afraid we will not make it."

Thomas stepped into the solemn room and was greeted by Manfred. "Her spells are becoming more frequent and prolonged," he said. "I am afraid we cannot attend the event today. I know how you were so counting on this. I must stay here with my wife, but it will be quite okay for Elizabeth and her two sisters to go. Please extend our regrets to Mrs. Clay for not being there, but there will be another time."

"I am sure there will be many more socials," Thomas replied sympathetically, "and we will expect you all to attend."

Elizabeth's older sister, Mary, and her soon-to-be husband as well as her younger sister, also named Anne—the same as Thomas's younger sister— and Elizabeth wished their mother a quick recovery, and the five of them climbed into the splendid carriage Thomas had rented.

The social at the farm was now in full swing. Frida and Anne were the forever generous hosts while nervously awaiting the arrival of Thomas and Elizabeth's family. Most of the people were friends from Darmstadt, and others were neighbors from the surrounding area, and all were busily indulging in conversation entertaining themselves. But Thomas's presence was in demand, and Frida was becoming worried. *Where is he? Why is he so late?* Seeing the carriage arrive without Manfred and Mrs. Klein, she became alarmed and rushed to its side as Thomas pulled into the yard.

He tried to hide the apprehensive look on his face as he quietly explained the condition of Mrs. Klein to his mother and helped the others from the wagon. "I'm afraid her condition is much worse than we believed," he said. "Let us join the party now, and we shall talk of this later." Thomas extended an elbow to each side, with his mother taking one and Elizabeth the other, and they strolled amongst the guests exchanging greetings and other pleasantries.

It was a lavish social gathering with a grand meal to follow. With the help of others now employed on the farm, Fredrick had barbecued three whole pigs, picked dozens of roasting ears fresh from their own fields, and roasted ten wild geese hunted from the nearby river. All any person could expect or want. Because they were one of the finer vineyards in the valley, there was wine with the feast but no other alcohol. Thomas's mother did not like liquor, so there was none. The crowd sat and enjoyed the meal, mingling occasionally, and soon a fiddle started on a small elevated area of the lawn, followed by other instruments as other musical guests joined in, and the crowd transitioned from casual chatter to laughter and dancing.

Thomas strolled up to Elizabeth and asked her to dance. She looked right into his eyes and gratefully accepted. And then for a few minutes, they danced together without saying a word, enjoying each other's presence immensely.

"I could dance like this forever...with you."

She looked at him, her eyes sparkling a little. "I think you would get very hungry and have very sore feet."

After the song, Thomas was beholden to greet some late-arriving guests. He chatted with them and poured them wine, then scanned the crowd for Elizabeth. He spotted her sitting alone on the grass under one of the many trees that bordered the front of the house. He knew Elizabeth had been here previously visiting Anne but had never toured the farm or vineyards in their entirety. Walking over to her, Thomas asked, "Would you like the grand tour now, Elizabeth?"

Standing up and smoothing her dress, she dimpled and took his arm. "Yes, you know I would," and they casually strolled away from the crowd. The vineyards lay behind the house on the far side of the fields unfolding up the gentle hillside. The groundskeepers had paid special attention to the area knowing this was a special day with many friends and important clients to be in attendance. The view could not have been better. The sun was setting with just a hint of pastel clouds on the horizon. Meadowlarks were singing, and farm animals were grazing or standing patiently. Thomas and Elizabeth strolled quietly amongst the rows of grapes as he explained the various methods of harvesting and other related duties associated with the business that Elizabeth's father was to take over. They were now at the very back of the vineyards completely out of sight of the house and guests.

Slowly Elizabeth stopped, removing her hand from his, and delicately placed her arms on his shoulders. She gazed at his rugged face then into his expectant eyes. They had walked some distance, and her feet were hurting in her new shoes. This was private enough, she alleged.

Then she broke the mesmerizing silence. "Are you planning to kiss me, Thomas?" She stroked the long tendrils of hair back from her face with one hand. "Because if you are, this is a good time for it. There is no one about to see us."

He moved his face toward hers, then stopped with only an inch between their lips, overcome by a heartfelt sense of respect and indecision. "I don't want to do anything that will make you think less of me," he whispered.

"Don't be a shy boy now, Thomas Clay." Despite the affront, her voice was husky and her eyes closed slowly, her thick eyelashes interlacing. She ran the pink tip of her tongue over her lips, then pressed them expectantly.

Thomas felt a most tempting urge to seize her and crush her body against his own. Instead, he touched his lips to hers as lightly as a butterfly settling on a petal. After a moment, he drew back. Her eyes flew open. They were as startlingly green as his.

"Damn you, Thomas Clay," she said. "I have waited so long, and that was the best you could do?"

"You are so soft and beautiful," he faltered. "I don't want to hurt you or make you scorn me."

"If you don't want me to scorn you, then you must do better than that." She closed her eyes again and leaned toward him. He hesitated only a heartbeat longer, then seized her, wrapping her in his powerful arms, and pressed his lips to hers. Soon noticing she had aroused more than just his attention, she leaned back, loosening her embrace but with her delicate arms still resting on his shoulders, and she huskily whispered, "You can't do much better than that."

"Oh, but I think I can. And you are right—there are no other eyes here," he said gently, pulling her close again.

"I fear I have been most gullible." She smiled, her cheeks blushing pink as rose petals. "But you would never take total advantage of my innocence here and now, would you, Thomas?" He had now lost all of his shyness.

"I am afraid you may have overestimated my chivalry, Miss Klein. It is my intention to do exactly that."

"I suppose that it would be of no avail if I should shriek, would it?"

"I am very much afraid that it would not," he said.

She swayed against him. "Then I shall save my breath," she whispered, "for perhaps I will find better use for it later."

They strolled back through the vineyards and mingled back into the crowd. *No one even missed us*, she thought with some relief, not seeing Thomas's mother watching as they had left the gathering and on their return. Frida treasured Elizabeth's company as much as Thomas did and was happy for them. Truly, Elizabeth Klein and Thomas Clay seemed blessed by all the gods. They were rich with affection and most pleasing to the eye. The most handsome couple. It would have taken the steeliest heart to begrudge them their good fortune.

The social lasted until nearly dawn the next morning. Upon the departure of the last guest, Thomas brought the buggy around and the exhausted Kleins stepped in, forever grateful for the wonderful evening. Fredrick had brought two horses out to escort Thomas and guests back to Darmstadt. Thomas would require one for the return trip after he'd returned the rented carriage to Mr. Dryden at the livery. Fredrick, too, was still concerned about the intentions of Horst. "I thought I would tag along and bring you back," he suggested to Thomas.

The return trip to Darmstadt was uneventful. It was now breaking dawn when Thomas escorted Elizabeth and her sisters to the door of their apartment, where they were met by their father.

"I'm glad my daughter was chaperoned by her two sisters." He smiled. "It's daylight." Jokingly, he added, "I hope your intentions are honorable, young Thomas."

"Well I do have intentions," he said. "How is Mrs. Klein?"

"Resting comfortably but in a weakened condition, I'm afraid. Thank you for your consideration, Thomas."

Stepping outside into the rising sun, Thomas returned the buggy to the stable and mounted the extra horse Fredrick had brought along as they turned toward home.

"Fredrick, there is so much to do before I am to venture to the Americas."

"Don't worry yourself. We have it under control. With your mother, Anne, Mr. Klein, and I'm sure Elizabeth, how could anything go wrong? Have you and her discussed your pending departure, my friend Thomas?"

"Yes, yes, of course. She understands the necessity of the trip, the need for diversification during this social and political upheaval we are experiencing. We have discussed it thoroughly, and she would join me as my wife if it were practical at this time. She is most excited that there may be a chance for moving to America in the future. As a matter fact, her older sister, Mary, and her husband will be making the journey soon, migrating to the city they call San Francisco. They are only waiting for Mrs. Klein's health to improve. Who knows when or if they will ever return to Germany, even for a visit or to see the family again. I'm afraid the recent rumors of the rich gold strikes in what they call California and the Oregon and Idaho Territories have caught their attention, and they want to be a part of that as well as get out of this deeply troubled country."

Thomas and Fredrick stopped the horses on the side of the road where the attempted attack on their lives had taken place only a few weeks ago. "Fredrick, my friend," said Thomas, "one of the most concerning reasons for my delay in getting on with this trip is my concern for our families with the pending threat of Horst."

Fredrick turned his horse to stand closer to Thomas. "Don't worry about Horst, Thomas. My friends staying here and waiting for things to cool off a bit in Hamburg will keep a careful eye on things. They will not allow any harm to come to the Clay family or the Kleins."

Fredrick then listened intently, engrossed in every word Thomas spoke of his plans and future ideas for the plantation on his return. He talked of accumulating wealth, as much wealth as possible that could be discreetly taken out of Germany when the timing was right. He spoke to Fredrick about purchasing a tobacco plantation or acreage to start one in America and of his interest in the coffee plantations in Panama. Finally the horses tired of standing and became restless, causing them to continue on.

"You know I would never leave Mrs. Clay in need, but if you do find suitable conditions in America, I would be extremely pleased to accompany you and your family there."

Thomas glanced over at him very touched by Fredrick's sincerity and dedication. "You know we would never consider a permanent move without you, my old friend."

They continued on in silence the rest of the way home.

Chapter 26

Clay Family Vineyard, Hesse, Germany

1862

It was a beehive of activity on the farm and vineyards as the time for Thomas's departure rapidly approached. Mr. Hollenbeck, the gunsmith, being Thomas's friend of many years, had presented Thomas with a scimitar, easy to travel with and excellent protection. He also provided Frida with the small pistol she had requested. It was one of the original Philadelphia Deringer single-shot, muzzle-loading percussion cap pistols—a single-barrel pistol with the back-action percussion lock system. The barrel was two inches long with rifled bores and a walnut grip. The hardware was a copper-nickel alloy known as German silver. She had stashed it away in a secure place in the house. Thomas had not had time to teach her to shoot or care for it yet, and Elizabeth also wanted to learn to use one her father had hesitantly agreed to allow her to use.

I will invite Elizabeth to the farm soon, Thomas reasoned, *and we will practice with these weapons. They will do no one any good if no one knows how to use them.* Putting words to action, he would make the trip to town the next day under the pretense of picking up some items for the farm.

The next morning as Thomas stepped out the door, his mother followed him and said slyly with a knowing grin, "Would you pick up a small bottle of lilac water for me from Elizabeth's store?" She always called it "Elizabeth's store" knowing she only worked there. That was for Thomas's benefit—she knew exactly what was happening and was pleased for it.

"You know I will!" Then mounting his horse, he made for town.

Leaving the horse at the livery, he walked rapidly across the street and down the two blocks to the Perfumeries Douglas where Elizabeth worked. As she was helping a customer near the huge front window, she saw him walking across the street. Having only a few moments until his arrival, she quickly tended the person, ushered her out the door, then looked into the full-length dressing mirror as she gave each cheek a solid pinch to make them rosy. "You have become a shameless and lascivious woman, Elizabeth Klein," she whispered primly, but her smug smile gave the lie to her self-deprecatory tone. She turned to greet Thomas.

"Can you come to the farm with me for a couple of days soon? I would like to teach you and Mother how to shoot and tend to the pistols you have both recently obtained."

"I thought you would never ask." She smiled. Then, with no hesitation, Elizabeth turned to the side door that led into the office where the store owner sat.

"I heard." Mrs. Hoogendyk sighed. "I will make do again without your presence as usual when Thomas is in town."

Hastily taking Thomas by the arm, Elizabeth said, "We will go and discuss this with my father."

"Well, I-I—" stuttered Thomas.

"There is no time like the present. You know all you have to do is ask, and you will receive," she replied, leading him across the street to her family apartment.

It was a day of no work for Manfred. He wanted to spend time with his wife, and she now required nearly full-time attention. His daughters, Mary, Elizabeth, and Anne, had taken turns staying with her while he worked at the Clay vineyards, but he wanted this to be his day. Thomas and Elizabeth burst through the door, and he rose to greet them, seemingly happy for their jubilant attitudes, neither of them yet fully comprehending the severity of her mother's condition.

Standing primly in front of her father, Elizabeth calmly asked, "Father, can I go to the vineyards for a few days and stay with Thomas? He wants to teach me to shoot."

Manfred just stood staring in silence, not too surprised at the request. From her earliest childhood, he had taught her to accept responsibility and to make her own decisions and abide by them. *Every young person wants to be grown-up*, he thought. *But the difference between a child and an adult is not years—rather, it's a willingness to accept responsibility, to be responsible for one's own actions.* She was no longer a child. She had learned well, and in the time since her father's war injuries, she had matured into a beautiful young woman.

Thomas was looking over her shoulder right into Manfred's eyes. *I think even I could have made a more discreet attempt at that request*, he thought, shuddering slightly at the look on Elizabeth's father's face. *I wonder if he has a pistol.*

Manfred diverted his attention from Thomas to his daughter then back to Thomas. "She will be properly chaperoned, will she not?"

"Yes, of course. Mother and Anne will be present at all times, and you will be there tomorrow at work, will you not?"

Despite the severity of the situation with his wife and Elizabeth's spontaneous request, Manfred could not help himself from laughing. After all, he had been working at the vineyards with Thomas for some time and thought he knew him quite well. As for Elizabeth, he was well aware of her impulsive nature and did not want to suffer the consequences of a denial. "You have my blessings." Then, adding to the humorous situation, he said, "Just don't get her home late."

Thomas and Manfred talked about the business, Thomas's pending trip, and the never-ending flow of emigrants leaving Germany while Elizabeth packed a few things for her trip to the vineyard. Not expecting such a hasty reaction from Elizabeth, Thomas had not brought the carriage.

"Don't worry," she confided. "I can ride one of your horses that Father has brought home."

With that, Thomas took her bag under his arm, and they strolled to the stable where Dryden saddled two horses for them. Noticing neither horse had a ladies' sidesaddle, Thomas commented as such.

"She won't ride the ladylike sidesaddle," Dryden said.

Elizabeth took the reins of one, led him outside, placed a foot in the stirrup, and swung into the saddle astride like a man. Her dress revealed a bit of her leg to a few inches above the ankle and was sure to raise eyebrows leaving town, but it did cover everything of importance. "Who would really care?" She laughed.

Turning the horses, they walked down the street that led to the outskirts of town. Horst was sitting in his shabby little room looking out at the street when they passed.

"I will kill him and have her yet," he said to no one.

Anne and Frida were relaxing as Thomas and Elizabeth arrived at the farm, and they helped her from the horse busy in chatter and gossip as Thomas tended the animals. When he returned, the women were still talking—he knew they would continue for hours. He told Elizabeth, "We shall start familiarizing you with the pistols first thing in the morning, as soon as I have checked the workers and stock," and bid the women goodnight.

At the end of the vineyard behind the house, Thomas had arranged a target practice area. Frida and Elizabeth joined him after breakfast. Thomas took out one of the pistols, both being the same. He explained the basics then instructed them on the loading technique. "You first, Elizabeth." Thomas had loaded it with half measures of powder to reduce the recoil. Then he showed her how to place her feet, position her body, and address the target. She was turned half away, presenting her right shoulder. Then with her left fist on her hip, he told her to bring up the weapon with a straight line to pick up the foresight bead in the notch of the back sight and fire as she swung through the target, rather than trying to hold her aim until her arm ached and shook.

He had sat up a row of blocks on top of one of the low benches at the edge of the vineyard twenty paces away. "Have at it," he said. "Knock them over."

With the first shot, he assessed, "Low." Then, with the second, "Still low and to the right." He reloaded swiftly as she changed pistols. With the third shot, she sent the block spinning and shattering into several pieces.

Elizabeth squealed gleefully and soon was hitting more often than she missed. "I should be given a prize for each hit," she demanded.

"What sort of prize do you have in mind?"

"A kiss might be appropriate."

"I love you, Elizabeth Klein," he said.

She felt glee to hear him say it then forfeited her position to Thomas's mother, who went through the same routine, except for the kiss with each successful hit. *An occasional hug from my son would be nice, though*, she thought.

"Hitting the target is much more difficult than I expected," Frida commented. "Elizabeth made it look so simple. What is the secret to becoming a good shot with a pistol, Thomas?"

"Simple enough," he replied with a slight grin. "Just point the pistol like you point your finger. You have become excellent at that over the years."

Turning without a smile, she replied, "Careful, young Thomas. I will not point this at you, but I may bounce it off your pate, young man."

They patiently practiced all afternoon, one shooting until she was tired, then the other. Elizabeth had, in the short period of time, become very accurate and swift in loading. She had a natural talent with this pistol and was soon a lethal shot. She didn't know it now but this gift would one day save her life. Thomas's mother, on the other hand, had practiced to the point of being efficient in both loading and shooting but still did not like the weapon, though she could and would use it, should necessity dictate.

Chapter 27

Clay Family Vineyard,
Hesse, Germany

1862

Time was quickly passing, and it was rapidly approaching the time for Thomas's departure. Fredrick and Manfred worked tirelessly with Thomas making last-minute considerations to every detail in managing the farm and vineyard, and Thomas had spent as much time with Elizabeth as possible.

Finally the day arrived. The wagon and team of horses were parked in front of the house. The horses were shaking their heads rattling their bridles and would occasionally stomp a restless foot. It was a warm beautiful day without a cloud in the sky. The rest of the family had noticed Thomas and Elizabeth standing together and was trying to give them one last moment of privacy before Thomas's departure. Standing alone with Elizabeth next to the wagon that would take him with his entourage to the docks at Nierstein on the Rhine River, only a few kilometers away, he somewhat shyly handed her a small package, both grateful for these last few moments alone.

"Oh, and what might this be?" Elizabeth smiled.

"Only a small gift I wish you to remember me by for the short time I will be gone. Please open it now before the others arrive and we all leave for the docks."

Carefully opening the small package with its fragile contents, she gasped. "Oh, Thomas, it is so beautiful."

"Knowing of your affection for the tiny, delicate, and very colorful little hummingbirds, I had the glass blower in Darmstadt make it for you months ago, anticipating this moment."

Caught without words by the tenderness he had displayed in giving her this delicate gift, she carefully rewrapped the very fragile little glass hummingbird back into its small nest in the box. "This will be with me wherever I go forever," she told him.

The others, being only but a few feet away, had all seen the gift and heard the exchange of words. Even Fredrick C. Burgdorf had a mist in his eyes.

Then Thomas said, "My absence from here will be but short."

Elizabeth looked up with a tear running down one cheek. "It will not be short, Thomas," she said. "Four or five months is a long time. Without you here, it will seem like forever."

"More likely only four months," he quickly replied.

"Thomas," she said in a throaty manner of voice he had not heard from her before. She stared at him with those deep-green eyes with such a serious expression as he had never seen before. "If you have not returned before five months' time, I shall come to the Americas looking for you. I cannot exist without your presence. We will be married and have a family. Of that I am quite certain, and the sooner, the better. Now let's get on with this departure. I do not want to be seen riding with you to the docks with tears running down my cheeks like some silly child." Her cheeks were wet, but she gave a slight smile.

Fredrick, Little Josh, and Thomas's mother all climbed into the front seat of the wagon. Thomas's sister, Anne, elected to remain at the house while the rest were to accompany Thomas the very short journey to where the small ship was docked that would start his journey. Anne was horrible with goodbyes and did not want to go through another when they reached the departing ship waiting on the Rhine River. Thomas and Elizabeth were seated alone in the rear of the wagon.

"I will send word on my arrival in the Virginias while making arrangements for a shipment of tobacco," he promised. "Then I will make the short journey to Panama in Central America at Colón and across the Isthmus of Panama, part by wagon then train from Gamboa to one of the oldest cities in Central America, Panama City, and the Tribaldos Coffee Company plantations. Then homeward bound I will be. Simple as that."

They had discussed the details many times during the past several weeks, as Elizabeth had made him voice it again and again. As the wagon bumped its way toward the waiting ship, Elizabeth said, "I want to miss not one detail. I want to live the next few months seeing your journey in my mind." But now Elizabeth was again struck with the reality of the pending trip. The sudden jolt that his words had caused, like a physical blow to the stomach, a feeling of profound sadness. She realized the reality of life without Thomas for the first time. It was to be only for a few months, but she was frightened and suddenly very lonely.

"I will miss you," she said again, seeing no reason to pretend otherwise.

They had both known that this day was coming. They were bound to be separated by the treacherous North Atlantic between Germany and the Americas. But Elizabeth never allowed that knowledge to lessen her absolute loyalty to their affection. Whatever might happen, however far apart they might be blown by the storms of the sea, they would, she swore, be together in the end. *Love can often be very ruthless but will not be denied us*, she thought. *We will endure this hardship.*

Too soon they had arrived at the small harbor and the waiting ship. Thomas's two trunks were hoisted by a huge sling with the other passengers' belongings onto the ship. Then turning and waving to all, he made his way up to the top of the platform connecting to the small ship deck.

Thomas stood on the platform leading from the dock to the ship in the bright morning sunlight staring down at his family. He was still only a lad. He was very handsome, and Elizabeth so enjoyed just looking at him up there on the docks and about to board the small vessel that would take him down the Rhine to its confluence with the North Atlantic, where he would board a large sailing ship bound for America. He was tall and muscular in stature, with long waving hair, ravens-wing black, falling nearly to his shoulders.

"Thomas—" The wind whipped her voice away, but his sharp eyes could read her lips. "I love you."

PART II

Chapter 28

Darmstadt,
Hesse, Germany

1863

Almost a year had passed since Thomas's departure for America, and Elizabeth had received no word. She had patiently waited for him five months, then six. By eleven months, she was totally distraught. She had been spending much time at the farm with Thomas's family since her mother's passing a few months after Thomas's departure for America. Her father and her younger sister, Anne, still maintained the small flat in Darmstadt, with her father making the short trip to the vineyards daily to work, but she preferred the farm and vineyards with Thomas's family. She was slowly recovering from the sorrow of her mother's death with the help of Thomas's mother and younger sister and preferred to stay there with them. She made it a point on her trips from the vineyard to her father's home in the city to stop at Mr. Hollenbeck's shop, knowing he would have news, if news of Thomas's voyage were to be had. She stopped to visit him often during the last year and was always greeted with his usual jovial smile and banter.

Walking into the shop this day, she had a terrible foreboding feeling. Mr. Hollenbeck was not smiling, just sitting behind his desk with a blank stare. For him, Thomas was not only a very dear old family friend but also somewhat of a son. He had not seen his own children for several years. They had sailed successfully to a new life in California, and it was now only him and his wife still living in Germany.

"Come and sit, my lovely child," he said when he saw Elizabeth. "I fear I have no good news."

Seeing Elizabeth enter the shop, Mrs. Hollenbeck entered the room and took Elizabeth's hands into her own, then gave her a gentle hug.

"I have heard that what could have possibly been the ship Thomas was sailing on was lost to a terrible storm, a storm as severe as any encountered in recent history," Mr. Hollenbeck explained. "Apparently the route chosen for this voyage was south down the west side of Africa then east across the Atlantic to the Virginias. I have been told that the ship could have been blown hundreds of miles off course to the south and west, and no one knows for sure where it went down or if there were any survivors."

Elizabeth sat down between the Hollenbecks, her head resting on Mrs. Hollenbeck's shoulder in total silence for several minutes. Her hair hung over her face, hiding her tear-streaked cheeks. Then slowly she stood. "I know he is not dead. If the ship that went down was indeed the one that carried Thomas, he has survived. I gave Thomas no more than five months to make his voyage and return here to me in Darmstadt. It has now been almost a year. I am going to America and will find him. I forwarded a letter to him in care of the Tribaldos Coffee Company months ago, advising him of my intent to leave in search of him, and now I am going." She made this statement with such conviction that it startled both the Hollenbecks.

If Thomas is still alive, she will find him, Mr. Hollenbeck thought, not even trying to talk her out of such an endeavor. "When you are ready to start this journey, consult with me, and I will make the arrangements for you as I did for your Thomas. But remember, you will not only be faced with the dangers of the Atlantic crossing, but also there is a terrible civil war in America between the states going on over there."

Digesting this new information for only a moment, Elizabeth got to her feet, thanking the Hollenbecks for their years of help and support.

"Do you need assistance home?" Mr. Hollenbeck asked.

"Thank you, but Fredrick is close by. He came to town with me and is now picking up supplies. I shall have a ride home with him."

Finding Fredrick, Elizabeth quickly told him of the news from Raymond at the gun shop. "Please take me home immediately," she pleaded. "I am going to America. I am going to search for Thomas, and I need to make ready directly."

That evening her father and her younger sister stayed on at the vineyards for supper. Thomas's mother always enjoyed the company.

Elizabeth soon made everyone aware of her pending journey, and no one tried to talk her out of it. The discussion was mainly of assistance to help her get ready for the trip. Everyone knew of her strong resolve and of the futility of trying to convince her otherwise.

Unexpectedly her younger sister, who had been sitting not saying a word for the entire evening, stood. "I am going with Elizabeth." Before anyone could interrupt her, she hastily continued, "With two of us, it will be much safer. If we are to go all the way to San Francisco in our search of Thomas, we can stay with Sister Mary and Edward." Anne had always been the most shy, timid, and nonadventurous of the three sisters, so this announcement took everyone by surprise. "I will not take no for an answer. I am going with you, Elizabeth. I do miss Sister Mary, and I know she will be so happy to see us if we have to go that far before finding Thomas."

"You do know the journey will take nearly a year and will be fierce and not so safe," Elizabeth warned. "A trip across the North Atlantic to Boston then south around the southern tip of South America then north to San Francisco."

"I do," she replied but not really having any idea of what Elizabeth was trying to tell her. Try as they might to persuade her otherwise, Anne proved to be as stubborn as Elizabeth, so the plans were made.

Mr. Hollenbeck had already advised Elizabeth of the route. It was the only one available now on short notice, as regular passenger service across the Atlantic was quite sporadic. If they were to make the necessary connections, they must leave in just a few days. They would be allowed a very small amount of space on the ship. All of their possessions to last them both for the year journey, if it were to take that long, would have to fit in one small suitcase, so it did.

Seeing the girls plan to leave Germany on such short notice and the dangers that they could face was very difficult for Manfred; Thomas's little sister, Anne; and Frida. If they survived the trip, all three of Manfred's daughters would be in America, and he knew he may never see any of them again.

Prior to their departure, Fredrick was unusually silent with little to say. He had taken the news of Thomas's disappearance very hard. Since Fredrick's arrival at the vineyards several years ago, Thomas had been like a brother to him.

Chapter 29

Darmstadt,
Hesse, Germany

1863

Thousands of passengers and emigrants left Europe for the United States in the 1800s. They sought economic opportunity, religious and political freedom, and the chance to join family members who had gone ahead. The passengers had sailed to America in ships that carried mail, cargo, and people. Conditions varied from ship to ship, but they were normally crowded, dark, and damp. Limited sanitation and stormy seas often combined to make them dirty and foul-smelling. Rats, insects, and disease were common and constant problems. There were serious outbreaks of cholera and typhus. These diseases were particularly bad when the passengers had been weakened by a poor diet and the never-ending issue of contaminated water. Passengers suffered many physical dangers on these crossings—fires, shipwrecks as a result of the unpredictable weather, and still the never-ending threat of privateers. One ship carrying passengers and some cargo caught fire, and 176 lives were lost. A few years before Thomas's voyage, an estimated 500 emigrants had died after a fire on the steamship *Austria*.

Anne and Elizabeth were seen safely aboard the small passenger ship that would carry them down the Rhine to the major port of Amsterdam, where the Rhine flows into the North Atlantic—the port that Thomas had left one year ago. The first few days of the voyage were not bad. Elizabeth and Anne whiled away the slowly passing of the hours and days with no real concerns toward the deplorable, overcrowded conditions on the ship. It was early spring, and they were allowed out of their small cramped quarters to spend as much time on deck enjoying the weather as they wanted. The weather was not bad, and the air was in fact rather enjoyable. They were rationed a very small amount of food that they had to prepare themselves, which presented no problems, as they both had spent much of their lives preparing family meals.

The first three weeks were rather mundane with hardly any change in the day-to-day routine. They looked forward to spending each day on deck in the fresh air. If it rained, they would find a small sheltered area on deck and stay until well after dark. This was always preferred over staying in the cramped and stench-ridden quarters below deck—a space that was shared with many people and only allowed flimsy curtains for separating the quarters of each family.

At three weeks into the trip, they were nearly three quarters across the Atlantic on their way to Boston. They were informed by Captain Sawyer that they were making excellent time and should reach their destination ahead of schedule. During the night they awoke to the sickening rolling and pitching of the ship. By morning they were being tossed about their small quarters dangerously. Their sparce furnishings often toppling onto them in the dark confines.

A severe storm had overtaken them unexpectedly. They were tossed in every direction, often rolling through the sheet curtains that separated their tiny quarters from their neighbors or finding one of the neighbors lying with them. The conditions rapidly declined even more, to a point of total pandemonium. Everyone was terrified and in varying degrees of panic. The food supply over the next many days would become nearly nonexistent, and under these conditions the water had become so contaminated, it resembled the overflow of the latrine area, which at this point seemed to cover the majority of the ship, with sewage flowing in every direction and most of the passengers below deck seasick and vomiting nonstop in these tight and enclosed quarters. The storm went on for days. With the heaving of the ship in every direction, not a single person could get to the top-level deck area where the conditions might have at least been more sanitary. Passengers were already starting to die from the prolonged fear of being tossed unmercifully about the ship, from hunger, from the contaminated food and water, and from disease.

Elizabeth and Anne huddled day after day in a corner of their tiny space, pasted against one wall so as not to have a neighbor be thrown on them or be thrown onto a neighbor. Some days due to the violence of the storm, no food or water was made available. They both were covered with stench and feared for their existence, concerned they would never reach their first stop in Boston let alone make it all the way around the tip of South America to California if necessary. They survived three weeks of these conditions before the storm let up enough to stand and walk freely without danger of being tossed into a neighbor or overboard.

It was the morning of the sixth week at sea when they awoke to these somewhat calmer conditions with only a light drizzle of rain. They had been huddled against a wall during the time of the storm and now could hardly stand. They had been wearing the same clothes and had nothing to change into. Their one suitcase was full of reeking, disgusting water. With the slowly subsiding storm and much calmer conditions, they staggered their way to the top deck.

Elizabeth and Anne stood inhaling the fresh air then moved to a corner of the ship with some degree of privacy, removing their clothes and standing under a steady stream of water flowing from a piece of torn canvas. They had placed their clothes under another stream of water within easy reach and were soon rinsed somewhat clean but felt they would never rid themselves or their clothes of the reek that had permeated their noses. They were some of the first up on deck, but soon many other passengers were starting to appear for the same reason.

Redressing in their wet clothes, Elizabeth suggested, "Anne, why don't you stay here and claim this spot while I try to retrieve our suitcase so we can wash our other belongings in this fresh rainwater?"

Anne did not reply. She was shivering with cold and shock as to the conditions they had survived the last three weeks.

Leaving Anne, Elizabeth carefully made her way down through the carnage and disgusting odor to their quarters and soon found their belongings, bringing them back topside to where she had left Anne. Removing their stinky belongings from the suitcase, she hung them under the stream of fresh rainwater to wash. Elizabeth had packed her most precious gift from Thomas—the tiny blown-glass hummingbird—very securely, and it had not been damaged. She stared at it longingly, missing Thomas terribly. They also found that with some modifications to the torn canvas, they could divert the rainwater into one steady stream and create a somewhat dry and comfortable area free of wind and prying eyes.

Later that afternoon, the sun suddenly appeared from behind the clouds and thoroughly dried them and their extra sets of clothes. Even though the area on deck they had fashioned into a simple living space was cold at night, it was far better than the horrible environments below, and the ship's captain did not make them return below deck for the remainder of the voyage.

The passenger list at the beginning of the voyage included 296 people. Nearly one hundred had perished in the last three weeks, and they still had another week before reaching the port in Boston. Elizabeth and Anne were very grateful that Captain Sawyer and his crew allowed them to remain in their slightly secure corner top deck until the ship was docked in Boston. Once arriving in Boston they still had about eight more months of seafaring travel before expecting to reach their final destination in California, if they did not get any news of Thomas before.

"Oh look, Anne," Elizabeth cried and pointed. "I can see what must be our first sighting of America and the Port of Boston there on the far horizon."

Standing with little interest, Anne said, "I can't wait." She had lost all enthusiasm for this trip to America, let alone continuing on another possible eight months rounding the tip of South America before heading in a northerly direction on to California. "I want to go home. I hated the entire voyage here. I hate this ship. I will go ashore and stay ashore until I can catch the next ship home. I will endure another two months at sea to go home, but I will go no farther away. Not now. Not ever," she cried, stamping her foot on the hardwood deck.

Elizabeth took her sister gently by the arm. "Come, let's prepare to go ashore now and have a wonderful meal and get a decent bed for the first time in weeks. We will go to the finest restaurant in Boston, see some of the sights, and enjoy ourselves on solid ground.

Looking and smelling like a goat in a pigpen, Anne shrugged. "You are out of your mind." She had never talked to Elizabeth in this manner before, and it was somewhat disconcerting. It was another five hours before they docked and passengers started to disembark.

Chapter 30

Chagres Rainforest, Panama

1863

Well, Thomas thought, *every new journey begins with the first step and this had better be a fast one.*

He jumped over a fallen palm and floundered into shin-deep water covered by a scum of puke-green moss. His only thoughts now were to get away from the beach that was soon to be inhabited by the native Caribs that sought him. He splashed inland through the spongy, wet, leach-infested vegetation for an hour, then stepped onto the slightly higher ground behind one of the giant fig trees that were abundant on this stretch of the coastline. Resting there and catching his breath, he once again glanced behind him, but there was no sign of pursuit into this repulsive environment. *Smart group*, he thought. *Who in their right mind would think to follow me into something like this stinking swill even if they were hungry and looking for a body to throw into their oversized soup pot?* His ship from Europe had been blown severely off course and wrecked on the distant reefs. He had no doubt he was the only survivor who'd made it to shore.

Thomas had run across a faint trail and attempted to follow it, and now he noticed it hooked sporadically to avoid fingers of swampy water leading landward from the coastal shallows he had recently left. The vegetation was changing too. The water-loving tropic willows and cypress that grew among a chest-high understory of ferns, reeds, and vines were fading into a more solid footing of slimy and slick leaves that fell liberally from the increasingly denser forest canopy. He had to watch his step. The leaves rotted away soon on this soil, but freshly fallen ones were slippery as banana peels, and there were other things a guy could step on in the dark too, like bushmasters or other poisonous snakes, poisonous tree frogs, and fatal black scorpions, all amidst the constant threat of alligators.

Thomas continued on as fast as the dreadful conditions would allow, pushing forever inland in what he hoped was a westerly route. As the light began to dwindle, he decided to make camp, but the mosquitoes didn't. He slapped his neck and got a handful. He thought he'd now traveled two miles into this denser jungle atmosphere, and with any luck he would've lost his pursuers, if any still pursued. It was unlikely any of that sorry lot would get far from the beach into this stinking underworld.

Thomas was totally exhausted and hopelessly lost, at least temporarily, so he located a slight hollow in one of the huge buttressed tree trunks and crawled into it. He was drained of strength, both physical and mental. Covering his bare skin from the mosquitoes as best he could, with only his thoughts for company, he curled into a tight ball and tried to rest. *Mosquitoes aren't really much worse in the jungles*, he reasoned, *than they are in the fields and vineyards in Germany on a summer's eve, but I don't enjoy them anywhere.*

He remembered the old Spanish doctor practicing in the hospital in Darmstadt who kept saying mosquitoes carried yellow jack in the jungles of the world. Most medical professionals were unconvinced of his theories on that subject, but—not being a medical professional—Thomas had an open mind when it came to the old doctor's opinions on yellow jack, jungle fever, *vomito negro*, or whatever else one chose to call it, all being the same. He had witnessed it more than once in his journeys in the tropics so far, and he didn't want to go through the kind of agonizing death the disease seemed to cause. They said a guy was immune to jungle fevers once he'd lived through a bout, but few lived through it the first time, and he did not want to find out firsthand if it was true.

Curled up in a fetal position in the bowl of the giant buttress-rooted tree with these thoughts in mind and the never-ending loneliness for his family and Elizabeth, Thomas finally fell into a fitful, restless sleep.

Chapter 31

Port of Boston,
Massachusetts, United States of America

1863

Once again gently holding Anne in her arms, Elizabeth continued, "Let's go ashore now, Anne. We will find a clothing store then a nice inn with a hot bath. When we are bathed and in new clothes, we will then go to the best restaurant in Boston. It will be refreshing—just you wait and see." She smiled. "Then we can talk more about continuing on or returning home to Germany. Our ship will be here for about a week taking on new supplies and repairing damages sustained from that storm. Let's make the best of our time here in America."

Anne was now crying. The trip had been so overwhelming with the miserable conditions, the death of so many of the passengers they had befriended, the lack of food and water, and the deplorable quarters. Now held in Elizabeth's arms, Anne sobbed uncontrollably until she had regained her self-possession. Finally able to speak again, she said, "I'm sorry, Elizabeth. It all was so terrible. I had no idea as to the poverties we would encounter." She halfheartedly let Elizabeth lead her down the boarding ramp, and they slowly strolled away from the docks into town.

Looking like two disheveled vagabonds departing the ship, they stopped at the first clothing store in sight and somewhat reluctantly entered. They certainly were not the only ones looking of this nature. Many of the passengers disembarking had not had the opportunity to clean up in any manner. As Elizabeth and Anne entered the store, a young sales clerk noticed them immediately.

"Oh, you poor dears, you must have just come in on one of the ships crossing the North Atlantic. Here, please let me help you." She guided them to the ladies' apparel and helped them pick out all the necessities along with several spare changes of each and a trunk for each of the two sisters. Before departing the ship, the captain had advised them that the remaining portion of the trip would be much less crowded and they would be offered a private room at a slight extra charge should they choose—and they would choose. The majority of the passengers would be remaining here in Boston for some time before continuing west or wherever they may be going. In spite of the civil war that recently started here in America, they soon found that it had little effect yet on the Boston area.

Next, upon the clerk's recommendation, Elizabeth and Anne found a small but very neat inn. They booked a room for a week and planned to take total advantage of the facilities offered. On entering the room, Elizabeth noticed a full-length mirror and stared at herself in horror. Her shoes were warped and misshapen from water damage and sun. Her dress was a jumble of torn, stained, and faded cloth. And her hair looked like she had been through a hurricane, which she had. Looking at herself, she was amazed the innkeeper would even consider renting a room to anyone who looked such a mess as her and Anne.

Turning to Anne, she asked, "Why did you not tell me I looked so horrid?"

"Well, I didn't mention it because I knew I looked the same or worse, if that is possible, and I did not want you to remind me of that sad fact."

They both chuckled for the first time in months, it seemed, then proceeded to bathe and dress in their new wardrobes.

Anne was the first into the tub of hot soapy water with just a touch of perfume. "Ooooooh," she sighed as she sank into the water until it covered her head. She soaked for an hour, washing her hair, then climbed out to make ready for Elizabeth's turn. When they were cleaned and dressed in the new clothes, each presenting the final touches for inspection to the other and in much better moods, they strolled on some of the nearby streets looking for a fine restaurant for their evening meal—their first real meal sitting at a table with linen and silverware in over six weeks.

Anne was feeling much better now with a bath, new clothes, a new hairdo, and a full stomach but refused to discuss the possibility of continuing the voyage any further. Meeting up with and chatting with many of the other passengers they had become well-acquainted with, they passed the rest of the evening in better spirits until they returned to their room totally exhausted and retired for the evening. Climbing in the cozy, warm, and comfortable beds—the first ones they had slept in since leaving Germany—they were both instantly asleep and stayed that way until late morning.

They awoke to the sound of a street vendor yelling of the quality of his goods to the passersby. This was a bustling port city with ships arriving and departing several times a day.

What am I to do? Elizabeth wondered. *I can't let Anne go home alone knowing the return voyage would probably be no better and even possibly worse than the one just encountered.* She did not want to stress Anne more with conversation of going on to California, but the ultimate decision had to be made: return home or continue? And she had to look for Thomas.

After another day of lounging, eating, and sightseeing, Elizabeth picked up the conversation once again with Anne. "I have hesitated to talk about going farther, but I have to continue on in search of Thomas."

Not replying for several moments, Anne finally sighed with the slightest hint of a smile. "Okay, I'll go on with you. I loved him too, you know."

Elizabeth sat there hardly believing her ears but overjoyed. "Well, we will continue on then. Our next departure is to be in just a few days, nothing too demanding. Our next port of call will be at Jamestown in Virginia. It will only be less than a two-week journey, and Captain Sawyer has assured me the weather appears to be holding nicely and should be very pleasant. Our ship will be loading tobacco there to go to South America, then on to California, I have been told. I will quickly inquire as to Thomas's possible visit in Jamestown and look forward to some positive news."

Chapter 32

Chagres Rainforest, Panama

1863

Thomas carefully rose and surveyed his situation and surroundings. No one had found him, and he had not been completely devoured by mosquitoes. He was desperately hungry. He'd read somewhere that you could eat the fruit of some kinds of mangrove and other fruit-bearing vegetation, but since he'd left the coastal area behind the day before, he hadn't seen any. If the frightening noises he'd listened to all night and now kept hearing were really monkeys, he wondered what a monkey tasted like. The never-ending and very hostile bellows of the howler monkeys made him think twice about tackling one of them for a meal. They were nearly as big as he was—and probably too tough to eat any way.

He had moved only a few steps beyond the spot he'd spent the night in, across a small inlet of slimy water to a slightly higher and dryer spot, and he sat down to regroup his thoughts before continuing. He was completely lost and realized he was accidentally turning back toward the coast and the group that may be looking for him.

A slight movement in the stagnant water drew his attention. Something was moving toward him just below the surface. He knew he was probably too far from the sea for it to be a shark, and he'd been told gators and crocs swam only in fresh water, so what could this be? A turtle? He grinned as he remembered the enjoyable turtle soup he'd had on the ship from Germany. Maybe he would have a decent meal again.

He was now on a small patch of semi-dry land, the only one around for a quarter mile in any direction. If he didn't give himself away by moving, the turtle might be coming out to sun itself. How would he kill and clean a turtle? *Probably cut its head off first*, he thought. He'd catch the brute first and work the details out while he built a cooking fire. He didn't move a muscle, and the thing kept coming. It was going to crawl out right between his feet. Thomas, being a very hungry man, tensed to grab it, his scimitar from Raymond Hollenbeck poised across his thighs. *Thank goodness I had this on me when the ship went down.*

Then the morning exploded in a hissing shower of salt and spray as a ten-foot crocodile was suddenly lunging for his face, tooth-filled jaws agape and still coming. "Shit," Thomas gasped as he jerked his head back and the jaws snapped shut where his face had been. The crocodile was halfway out of the water by now and, having seen its mistake, was opening its jaws for a second snap at Thomas's left foot. Startled and badly shaken, Thomas was now backstroking through the soggy muck and snatched his leg away in the nick of time.

The crocodile kept coming, a natural enough mistake on the part of the vicious and hungry reptile. As it opened its jaws again, Thomas shoved his scimitar into the hissing throat as the big jaws clamped down on the steel blade, forcing it to slice up through its tiny brain.

Jumping to his feet, Thomas stumbled back away from the thrashing crocodile. Then the crocodile's pierced brain stopped functioning, and the bloody body of the monster rolled and writhed in the wet grass. Thomas danced back farther to see what would happen next. Considering he'd only punctured its brain, it took its sweet time dying. It thrashed around with its tail and seemed to be trying to get back to the water while its giant jaws kept opening and closing. The body slid halfway into the saltwater—which crocodiles could swim in after all, Thomas noted—and then it stopped and lay quivering as a bright stain spread in the water like red ink.

Thomas bent to grab the rough, armored tail and hauled the crocodile partway up on the hammock, thinking, *No, you don't. You were aiming to eat me. Turnabout is fair play.* He took the tin of waterproof matches from his pocket and broke dry twigs and fronds, stuffed some dry grass stems in for tinder, and started a small fire while he pondered how one cooked a crocodile. He was sure he had heard somewhere that gators only swam in fresh water. But maybe crocs were different. *Or maybe they didn't read the same natural history books*, he thought, amused.

Using his scimitar he had just wrestled from the croc's mouth, he partially skinned the muscular tail as the first sticks burned to coals. The white flesh was tough and stringy, but he'd heard it was the best part. He hacked big chunks of tail flesh free and skewered them on a green stick to roast over the coals. It smelled better than it looked as it sizzled on the stick, and he couldn't remember when he'd last had a real meal. He had been shipwrecked and stranded in the mangrove swamps with little food and water for days before reaching the mainland he was now on.

After the first taste of the roasted meat, he decided this was not going down on his list of fine meals, but it did have a filling effect. When he'd eaten as much of the roasted meat as his stomach would hold, he cut off another large chunk for later and started moving further inland in what he hoped was a westerly direction. He still wanted to place more distance between him and his pursuers. Thinking he would soon find some kind of road or trail that would lead to his destination on the Pacific side of the isthmus, he staggered on through the dense jungle underbrush.

He was sorry for not paying more attention to his father's books on world geography, but who would have thought he would ever be trying to cross the Isthmus of Panama, walking with hardly more than the clothes on his back? The further he progressed, the more difficult it became. Never finding a road or even a trail, as he stumbled, his thoughts were forever wandering back to his home in Germany, his family, and Elizabeth. Slogging on, he thought, *Just to say "jungle" without seeing Central America doesn't mean much. A name like "green hell" would be closer but would still be hard to believe until seeing it firsthand.*

And he seemed as though he was attempting to bore through a big rotten apple. At times trees leaned at crazy angles, being strangled by elephant-trunk vines that were in turn being attacked by what looked like spinach-green barbed wire. There were palms that crawled on their bellies like reptiles and supported big red barbs. In such a wet, warm climate, the only limitation an inspired vegetable had to worry about was light. There were plants—half of them unknown to science—that could grow in water, on soggy soil, on dry soil, and even on bare rock but not in the deep shade. So, once the first-come, first-served trees got big enough to shade the forest floor in cathedral gloom even at high noon, nothing much else could sprout.

The never-ending bellows of the howler monkeys was starting to make the hair stand up on the back of Thomas's neck. Trying to scour up images from the depth of his memory about venomous reptiles, he wondered if he would recall what a bushmaster or fer-de-lance looked like. *Oh yeah*, he remembered. You seldom saw a fer-de-lance before it hit. It was also called a two-step snake. Two steps after it struck, you were dead. The bushmaster was bigger and a bit more sluggish than a rattlesnake and had no rattlers. The thought of the snakes made him most anxious, and he continued on, hoping he wouldn't encounter either and simultaneously relieved that he had recalled some of the details from the books in his father's library.

In the gloomy depths of the swampy jungle, Thomas came across a vine he remembered reading about. He snapped off several handfuls of its pungent leaves and stuffed them into his pockets. Although he couldn't remember what the natives had called the stuff, he knew it was used for a mosquito repellant. You were to lay the leaves on hot coals and stand in the smoke, smoking every inch of your body and hair. Stopping long enough to start a small fire, he placed a few leaves into the coals and smoked himself thoroughly. He hoped it would work, as another night with the continuous attack from the harassing little insects would drive him senseless. His first impression of the presence of the mosquitoes was wrong. They were much more severe here than anywhere in the world he had ever been.

Thomas was still in the low swampy lands and could see the ground was dropping even lower. He was traveling through a maze of old game trails among froggy-smelling mud and bigger ponds where ghostly gray tree trunks rose from water the color of ink, the smell of alligator hanging in the air and mixing with the dripping rain. As he kept going, it got worse. He staggered over islands that quivered underfoot and smelled like a stinking sewer-soaked mattress, and he knew he would be helplessly lost if he continued on in the dark. The bugs started working on any exposed flesh that had rubbed clean of the insecticide smoke, and he remembered reading about the poisonous tree frogs and bitter butterflies that were prevalent in the jungles of this area. Plus, he knew firsthand about the threat of crocodiles now. He was not too concerned with other animals in the jungle, as he knew that deep-jungle wildlife naturally sheltered themselves while it rained. Almost nothing big enough to matter lived on the soggy wilderness floor. Nothing even a deer would eat could grow in such dense shade.

Some of the mushrooms he had stepped on were bigger than his hand, very slick and treacherous to walk on. *One thing I don't need now is to slip on something in the dark and fall into or onto God only knows what.* It was time to stop and make a camp in this miserable little corner of the world. Thomas hacked a hanging mossy vine out of his way—at least, he hoped it was a vine—then slashed some leaves the size of elephant ears from a nearby tree and folded them over the small tepee frame he had leaned against a buttress root. *That ought to deflect the constant dripping water from the forest canopy high above*, he thought.

Knowing the mosquitoes would suck him dry unless he had a lot of blood, he started another small smudge fire. As it burned down to coals, he added more of the leaves he'd saved and once again smoked himself thoroughly. That night, most of his hide stayed reasonably covered with the smoke, and the frustrated mosquitoes hovered in a cloud around him, humming a high-pitched famine song but never quite landing on his smoked hands and face. *They just hover close enough to drive you crazy and make it tough to breathe*, he thought. If he puffed too hard, he sucked in bugs and had to spit them out. The taste was repulsive.

The moon was now down, but it didn't matter, as it would have been as dark as the inside of one of the black panthers that roamed the distant landscape anyway. As he sat in the nearly total darkness beside his small fire as his lean-to deflected most of the rain, his feelings finally registered on the possibilities of violent natives. *What will*

I do if I meet any more? he thought. *Well, I don't intend to meet any, so the fear is unwarranted.* That wasn't too comforting, though, as he knew it was very likely he would. The natives in Central America, he had read, were distant relatives of the ancient Inca, and as he had heard, they had a frightful habit of sacrificing strangers to the gods by dismembering their victims and scattering their body parts across the jungle floor.

Thomas had no food but the little bit of gator meat he could carry on him and try to eat before it spoiled. He knew that if necessary he could go several days without food, and water had not been a problem, as the jungle canopy never stopped drizzling rainwater. Gathering some dry limbs he found under one of the huge trees that had fallen some time in recent history, he returned to his small but somewhat dry shelter and placed them inside to stay dry. He then wiggled under the makeshift lean-to with some degree of comfort and leaned against the tree. As he gazed out at the fire, his thoughts once again returned to Elizabeth, then his mother and the rest of his family.

Thomas was sure that during his temporary absence that had turned out to be not so temporary, Manfred had taken over marketing and the other daily functions that Thomas had previously attended to and was functioning quite well. The grapes would now be very large, and the notorious vineyard would be doing well, he was sure. Thomas's family's vineyard had once again gained notoriety as one of the finest in Europe. His sister would be busy helping his mother with the bookkeeping and the other related duties necessary in running a business of this magnitude, and Fredrick of course would have the entire group of workers well organized and the transportation of the grapes to the markets well under control.

It had been over a year since Thomas had started this journey. His ship had been blown off course, whiling away months in the Atlantic. Then just as it seemed like the captain might be able to dock them, replenish supplies, and turn back to the course, the biggest storm yet hit. Thomas had never seen waves so huge, and he knew he was lucky to have survived, floating on a meager piece of deck, trying to avoid the sharp reefs and the attention of privateers who came in the days after to loot the wreckage.

Lucky or not, I have never felt loneliness like this before, he thought. He missed Elizabeth enormously, not to mention his old lifestyle in Germany. *If I ever make it home*, he thought, *I will never leave again.* Eventually he slept for what seemed a very short time and awoke, shivering, to a sliver of sunshine that had somehow worked its way through the forest canopy.

A bird that he'd never seen in any nature book sang a song that he had never heard. A fat lizard that could easily be mistaken for a small alligator covered with emerald scales came wandering along the fallen tree trunk, darting its ugly licorice-whip tongue to taste the bark ahead. It seemed to sense Thomas's presence without being able to tell his exact location, so it turned and darted the other direction.

This distraction helped Thomas to again focus on his existence here in this foreign environment and return to the reality of what lay ahead before he would reach the Pacific Ocean, near Panama City, he hoped.

He slowly crawled from his lean-to with nothing to eat and once again continued his trek into what looked like a solid wall of thorny spinach, then crossed a game trail that appeared to have a slight incline. The trail wandered somewhat upslope in taller timber, where the going was easier in any direction between the mossy, buttress-rooted pillars supporting the gloomy overhead canopy. It was along the edges of trails and rivers, where the sun could get at the warm, moist soil, that the classic green hell jungle grew too thick to push through without a machete. In the tall timber, one could walk for miles without tripping over a dandelion. The trick was not to get more lost than he already was. One buttress-rooted forest giant looked like the one right next to it, even though they were different species. So he had to navigate much like if he were at sea—by compass or by dead reckoning and the sun. *This will be tough*, he thought. He had no compass, the sun was very seldom visible through the forest canopy, and most of the trees looked alike.

The rain had started again but was broken by the leaves and branches above into steady streams that looked and smelled like monkeys relieving overactive bladders—and felt about as warm—he thought when he couldn't avoid it. Studying the view forward, he could see mostly only shifting veils of rain. The dim game trail he was following in the mist and steam seemed to dead-end several times, against a house-sized bolder or a tangled windfall of down trees, but he was able to pick it up again each time on the far side.

It wasn't getting any easier as he climbed higher. The path not even a narrow ribbon of bare dirt anymore. Someone or something still used the route often enough to keep it more or less open, but the grass and vines conspired to weave it into what looked more like a green runner winding on between even thicker vegetation. Much to his relief, though, it was getting much quieter. The howler monkeys had ceased their constant aggressive howling, and Thomas could only hear an occasional parrot. The dim trail was now leading him slowly up and out of the steaming rainforest. The savanna ahead was opening somewhat and required less machete work. He was starting to make better time. Thomas trudged the rest of the day in what he thought to be a northwesterly direction—hopefully toward the Pacific Ocean, Panama City, and the Tribaldos Coffee Company.

The days went by like this. The prevailing trade winds dropped most of their moisture on the Atlantic side of what he thought to be the Culebra mountain range, so once he was over the crest, the night air was clammy.

He knew one of the unexpected dangers of the jungle was the common cold. People expected jungles to be hot, and they were, a lot of the time. It was impossible to ramble through the jungle in an overcoat, but the rain would dampen people's clothes, and even sixty degrees would be cold enough to cause them to shiver uncontrollably. That was why pneumonia claimed so many lives among jungle travelers and dwellers, he had read.

Chapter 33

Atlantic Ocean,
Off the Coast of America

1863

Elizabeth and Anne soon found themselves enjoying the next leg of their voyage to the Virginias in much larger, more pleasant rooms and able to lounge on the deck under sunny skies with land in sight on occasion. In all, it was a tremendous improvement over the horrible voyage across the North Atlantic from Germany. Anne was in a jovial mood with the calm seas and warm weather.

"Where do you intend to inquire about the possibility of Thomas's presence here last year?" questioned Anne.

"I have been thinking of that for some time. Perhaps when we arrive at Jamestown, we could split up going separate directions and that way question twice as many merchants. I am sure if my handsome Thomas was here last year, someone will remember him."

Anne sat in silence considering the safety of wandering alone in an unknown seaport on the Virginia coast but decided not to voice her concerns at this time. She could see Elizabeth's mood was improving daily with the good weather and sailing conditions and the possibility of finding some positive news of Thomas.

The next nine days passed quickly with much anticipation as to what they may learn in the thriving community of Jamestown. Elizabeth had spent much time in conversation with the ship's captain, pestering him relentlessly as to where and to whom to talk to about the possibility of a visit here over a year ago by her Thomas.

Of course Captain Sawyer was only too happy to chat with her. She was beautiful, intelligent, and so persistent, he had no other choice. Usually he had only male passengers and some families bound for California, no one as pleasant as her to pass the time of day when not attending to the ship's needs. He was well-dressed in comparison to the other hands on deck, and she noted he was the kind of man who would look well-dressed in his long johns—he had a certain style. His manners were those of a gentleman, but fine manners did not necessarily make a fine man, and she was very alert for any clue as to any intentions of inappropriate behavior on his behalf.

"You must be cautious when we get to Jamestown," Captain Sawyer informed Elizabeth the day before their arrival. "It is a well-settled port with mostly respectable businesses, but a seaport is a seaport and can be quite dangerous, and we are still engaged in the bloody civil war between the states here. We were not affected in Boston much by this miserable war, but it's different here in the Virginias. Young women like you and your sister, with your most obvious attributes, will draw much attention, not all of it respectable. Your plan of sending Anne going one direction to make inquiries and you another is not a good one, in my opinion. I shall try to keep an eye out for you both, and I will advise the crew who go ashore to do the same, but nevertheless be very careful. The ship will have to sail on time regardless of your presence back here or not. Please remember we have no more than four hours here."

Thanking the captain, Elizabeth went to find Anne and make final arrangements to go ashore and begin a hasty search for any information that may concern Thomas. When the loading ramp was secured to the dock, the two sisters were allowed to go ashore first. They only had a few hours before the next promising tide and the loading of the cargo that was to go on to South America and then to California.

"Hurry, Anne, you go that direction down the docks to the south, and I will go the other direction. We will meet back here in no more than four hours, and please be very careful. I couldn't live if anything were to happen to you."

Elizabeth's departure was not unnoticed. She drew attention in any crowd, but in this accumulation of seamen, dock workers, and merchants, some paid particular attention. She meandered along the docks and streets talking to the merchants, seamen, and other vendors who would listen to her inquiries and descriptions of her missing Thomas.

Anne was strolling in the opposite direction, also talking to everyone who would listen, with no success. No one fitting the description of Thomas had been seen or at least remembered in the past few months. Discouraged and tired, she finally turned and started back to their ship, which would be departing within approximately one half of an hour. It was getting late, and Anne would not chance missing that voyage.

Elizabeth had wandered farther than she realized, desperately looking for clues as to a possible visit here by Thomas. Finally realizing the time and distance from the ship, she hesitantly turned around, deciding on a shorter route back through some alleys she had spotted earlier in the afternoon. She made the first corner just a block from the main wharf area and slightly out of sight of the main traffic of dock workers and vendors. So lost in her thoughts was she that when she turned, she caught just a fleeting glimpse of the man who grabbed her suddenly from behind.

Chapter 34

Chagres Rainforest, Panama

1863

The approaching savanna was not entirely void of trees, but the ones here were more sparse and a welcome relief from the nasty atmosphere Thomas had spent the last several days in. He was tired and hungry. *If I don't eat soon*, he thought, *my navel will be rubbing my backbone*. His thirst was not unbearable yet, as he drank from one of the steady streams pouring from the jungle canopy, as unpleasant as it was life-sustaining. *I should have tried to kill and eat that oversized lizard this morning.* However, the thing had not looked like an easy kill and was gone before he could reach his scimitar, the only weapon he now had, probably a good thing, as it may have been questionable as to who might have been eaten whom.

The land grew higher but not much drier as he marched day after day into the teeth of the trade winds. The long rains about to end for the year had greened the grass of the parklike highland mesas. But here and there, a half-drowned cactus held out, biding its time. The highlands, drained by countless seasonal streams, would bake dry sooner than the lowland jungles he had left behind. In a month or so, the hip-deep grass would be dry tinder and ready to go up in smoke at the first careless spark from a human or bolt of dry lightning from an even less-caring source. The highlands were erosion gone mad, and the trail ran in a twisted web of red clay to avoid the ravines and sheer cliffs all around. Thomas had to travel a mile north or south for every one leading west toward his final destination.

Progressing higher into the savanna, he knew it was getting close to the time the tropical sun would go down, and when that occurred it would be dark. There was no evening twilight—it would simply be dark. In the tropics, there were approximately twelve hours of dark and twelve hours of daylight, and it was about to get very dark. Thankful to be out of the threatening jungle with the continually screeching monkeys, Thomas started to look for a place to make a camp. His requirements were simple, a dry place to lie down and hopefully get some rest. He stumbled across an ancient tree half rotting on the ground, the trunk still intact. Gathering other pieces that had not completely decayed, he stacked the remnants against the trunk to form a shelter.

While breaking the pieces, he found some were infested with grubs. Most things in the jungle grew to many times what would be their normal size if they were anywhere else, and so was the case with these curly little soon-to-be gourmet grubs. They were a light color and resembled a three-inch marshmallow with a dozen legs. As hungry as Thomas was, he hesitated to eat one of the repulsive things alive. Gathering several handfuls of the wiggling little creatures, he laid them next to his shelter and started a small cooking fire. Not knowing how to kill one, he simply impaled several at a time with a small stick and roasted them over the fire.

Thomas's living habits had changed considerably in the time since his journey from Germany. He once would never have considered harming any garden pest, and now he was eating them. They had a flavor different than anything he had ever tasted, hence the taste was undiscernible but very edible. Thomas was ending his third day with nothing to eat, so he rapidly devoured the several handfuls he had gathered and, in spite of the now-dark surroundings, hunted for more with the light from a flaming stick.

His stomach full for the first time in days, he placed another piece of decaying wood in the fire and leaned back to enjoy. It was not cold, but this small, soothing fire in the total darkness on the savanna was comforting to his worried soul. Lying there with only his thoughts to keep him company, he gazed up at the stars wondering if perhaps Elizabeth may possibly be doing the same. On the higher-elevation savanna, the stars seemed within his reach. The tropical skies were crystal clear without the hint of a cloud or mist from the jungles below, and the celestial bodies lit up the landscape nearly as bright as day. Thomas was totally exhausted and soon drifted into a deep sleep.

When the no-nonsense tropical sun popped out at about six in the morning, he sat up and once again surveyed his surroundings. He had eaten heartily the night before, but not knowing when or where his next meal would come from, he repeated the grub feast before packing his simple belongings and continuing on.

Several hours later, Thomas stepped off the trail and leaned against one of the twisted windswept trees of the savanna. Looking forward, he saw miles of the same kind of country. *Where will this end?* he thought. *Will I reach the Pacific alive? Will I ever see my family again and my Elizabeth?* It was late afternoon and if the next hour or two were to pass in relative safety, he would have survived another day and was looking forward to the rest that darkness and a small fire and food would bring. *What food?* he thought. *Grubs again?* Always looking for some food source along the way, Thomas determinedly continued on until a small stream crossed the trail. Stopping and lying on the bank, he drank his fill.

With his thirst quenched, he sat up to once again survey his surroundings. The stream apparently originated in the higher mountainous region off to the north. It was crystal clear and very cold. *Fish*, he thought and studied the water systematically for any sign of movement. Out of the corner of his eye, he caught the slightest of movements, then saw the fish. Slowly moving back, he found a forked stick from a nearby branch. Cutting it to the proper length, then sharpening it to near needle sharpness, he fashioned a very functional spear. He located the fish once more and slowly moved the spear into place, hovering just a moment to make sure of his aim, then plunged it into the water directly over the midsection of the fish. He felt a hefty wiggle on the end of the spear and was quite certain of his success.

Thomas slowly slid the fish up the bank at an angle that would not allow it to slide off the spear. With it safely on shore, he picked it up and wondered about its species. Then he thought, *What difference does it make? I'm hungry, and it is a fish—a very large one indeed—and will make a good meal. Tonight I will eat.* Cleaning it then laying the fish in the grass, he once again studied the water up and down, looking for another. After spending considerable time and finding none, he lowered himself once again to the bank of the stream, drank deeply, then stood picking up his evening meal, and continued on.

Four hours later, the tropic moon shone down full from directly overhead, painting the waist-high grass of the savanna a soft shade of tarnished silver. He found a suitable spot beneath a small-canopy tree and made his camp. Being particularly tired this night, he didn't bother with a lean-to. It was cooler here at this elevation, so he started a small fire and roasted the fish. As the fire slowly turned from flame to a bed of coals, he placed the fish on its side then methodically turned it slowly to cook all sides evenly. This was the first real food he'd had in days, and he was not about to ruin it for a lack of attention. As hungry as he was, he could eat only half in one sitting, so he saved some for breakfast. Placing the leftovers on a small tray he'd fashioned from sticks and leaves, he then hung it from some low-hanging branches of the tree forming the canopy over his sleeping area. He enjoyed the fire then lost himself in dreams of more pleasant days gone by.

Thomas woke at the first hint of light and started a small fire to warm the leftovers from the night before. When he had only coals, he reached into the tree to retrieve the tray he had fashioned, and it was gone. Sometime during the night, some small animal or perhaps a bird had robbed him of his meager supplies—he would start the day trek with nothing to eat and enormously thirsty.

It was much easier to tell directions now that there was not the contentious cloud cover and he could see the sun. Being fair skinned and now in the open sun, he soon became fairly baked and was sure he resembled one of the lobsters that he had eaten coming across on the ship to the Americas. The trail he was following was wandering precariously around a hillside and into a washed-out canyon before returning to the more moderate terrain of the flatter savanna, being sparsely populated with various types of vegetation far different than the rainforests below.

On a tree above the trail and off to the right, Thomas spotted what looked to be green oranges—huge green oranges. He'd read someplace that oranges stayed green after full ripening in the tropics, so he hungrily grabbed and peeled one. Not knowing exactly when the season was for being ripe, he thought, *There's only one way to find out.* He stuck it into his mouth, chewed once, and spit it out in disgust. Obviously this was not the time of year for ripe oranges.

Gradually descending from the higher-elevation savanna, Thomas was once again approaching the rainforests far below. Through the mists, he could see a hint of the forest canopy poking through the clouds here and there like thousands of tiny islands. *I would rather take another thrashing than continue to descend into that darkening green underworld of giant trees and jungle,* he thought. Being weak as a result of the ever-nagging hunger, he sat down under a small tree that resembled a short palm tree, with its fronds nearly reaching the ground to rest, making a tidy and sheltered place, hopefully free of bugs. He had used the last of the pungent leaves he had stuffed into his pockets to smoke himself free of mosquitoes so he would have to suffer with them until he could find more when he reached the gloom far below. Dispirited he decided it would be fruitless to continue further this day. The lengthening shadows of the few trees on the savanna warned him of the soon-to-come darkness, but anxious, he pressed on a short distance further.

The trail he was following turned into a small canyon, and he came upon a larger tree that had tumbled from the bank above and lay at a steep angle, its top buried in the canyon below with the roots still clinging to the earth above, creating a small hollow. The hollow beneath was sheltered with surrounding vegetation, appearing as good a place as he would likely find before dark.

Just sitting there, leaning against the tree, he fell into a deep sleep long before dark. Sometime during the night, he woke to one of the most frightening screams he had ever heard. It sounded like the tortured cries of a child. He was sweating even though there was a slight breeze that should have had him shivering at this still higher elevation. He *was* shivering, he finally noted, but from fear. Another scream broke the silence.

Now wide awake, he thought he recognized the noise as that of an oversized cat. Probably one of the panthers that roamed the area between the rainforests and the savannas. It sounded farther away this time, so he relaxed, trying to regain some of the composure that had escaped him with the first scream of the cat. Hard as he tried, sleep was a long time coming and then very fitful.

Thomas awoke in the cold dark and lay very quiet, still, and confused. The fog moved around him in strange curls, moving across his body with transparent fingers with the slightest hint of moisture.

Chapter 35

Chagres Rainforest, Panama

1863

Thomas had fallen asleep with his mind filled with thoughts of his boyhood, his family, and Elizabeth, though he had no idea that Elizabeth and Anne had now departed Germany to search for him. Now he was a castaway, lying on leaves in a Panamanian jungle with a sinking feeling of crushing disappointment. He sat there in the total darkness waiting for the first hint of daylight, then stood quietly to survey his surroundings, looking for any possible excuse to delay his inevitable descent into the foreboding forests below. He knew he could have walked across the Isthmus of Panama in three or four days on a smooth road, but the Panamanian jungle proved to be a lot larger when one tried to walk a straight line through it.

I have to find something to eat, he thought. It had been two days again since he had eaten, and his weakness was starting to nag at him. His mind was not as crystal clear as usual, and as he stood there, he noticed a slight tremor to his legs. *This degree of fatigue and hunger can put a man back to the brink of savagery*, he thought, *both in the means he uses to get food and the lengths he will go to get it.* Cannibalism did not sound quite so gruesome at the moment—if there were anything or anybody to cannibalize. Wild country and wilder circumstances can thus render all theoretical ethics a little less than a topic for conversation.

As he foraged on the flat area he had spent the night, he noticed a plant that resembled a yuca, which he had read about in the distant past. If it were indeed a yuca, it would have an edible root similar to a potato. Digging up one of the plants and exposing the root, then cutting the root loose and peeling it, he placed it into the coals of the fire he had started earlier to warm his chilled body. It baked similarly to a potato and in no time, Thomas was eating his first meal in two days. The fibrous root was tasty though not exactly easy to eat. His limited methods of cooking rendered it stringy and tough. After eating several roots, he could feel his strength slowly returning and his thoughts also seemed to clear. He gathered as many of the roots as he could comfortably carry, not knowing when or where his next meal may present itself, and then he turned to gather his few belongings.

Out of the corner of his eye, Thomas caught a faint glimpse of movement in the undergrowth not but a few feet away. Hesitating only a moment, he cautiously moved toward the brush area where he'd spotted the movement. Lying tucked under a decaying log and partially covered with leaves lay a small unconscious native girl. She was shivering uncontrollably and appeared to be no more than four feet tall.

He was now very alarmed. *She can't be here alone*, he thought. Carefully surveying the area, he could see no other signs of life. As a matter of fact, this young girl was the first person he'd seen in the many weeks of travel since he was shipwrecked on the Caribbean coast and forced to flee into the jungle. Standing there very still, searching with his eyes for any signs of movement, and finding none—no further sign of other members of her tribe, clan, family, or whatever groups of natives were referred to here—he stooped, gently picked up the small child, and carried her back to the scant camp he had spent the night in.

She couldn't have weighed more than sixty pounds but did not appear to be malnourished. There was just something about the jungle dwellers that seemed to stunt their growth. He remembered in his reading of the many books in his father's extensive library about the indigenous inhabitants of the remote areas of Central America that these natives had something in common missing from their diet. Or maybe evolution favored short people, who had to duck fewer branches as they hunted in the forest gloom. She seemed as though she had been healthy before, with no noticeable deformities, and her hair was cut as if she had worn a soup bowl during the cut. Thomas had read that the Caribs and Arawaks in this region wore their hair this way. The Caribs were cannibals.

I have to get her warmed up and get some food and water into her, he thought, ignoring the idea that she may have a quick recovery and see him as her next meal. Placing some small sticks on the still-glowing embers of his previous night's fire, he soon had the flame sufficient to slightly warm her and some of the leftover yuca roots. He used a small branch and smashed some of the root into a paste. Then he gently raised her head and rubbed the paste on her lips, which she began to lick. He held one of the nearby leaves, still soggy with water from the previous night's drizzling rain to her lips, and she drank. Still unconscious and trembling, she was warm to the touch. *Maybe malaria*, Thomas thought. *Do natives in these parts even get malaria?* he wondered.

Throughout the day Thomas fed the girl small amounts of the paste and as much water as she would take. She appeared to be recovering, as her relentless shaking had stopped and she seemed to be more relaxed. Suddenly she opened her eyes and stared at him intently for just a few seconds, then jumped like a bolt of lightning, disappearing into the woods without a word. He just sat there staring at the space where only a minute ago a small unconscious child had lain.

Glancing around, he could see no sign of her. *Well*, he thought, *that's gratitude. I have shared my prized food with this helpless little urchin, and she is gone without even a smile.* It was now rapidly approaching nightfall again, so he decided rather than go on, he would spend another night at this readymade camp and continue on the next morning. He paused, though, giving much thought to the risk of staying here with the young native girl knowing of his location, but he considered it safer here than to continue into the unknown forests below, where anyone may be lurking and watching his movements.

That night was starlit with only a few wisps of very high clouds, and all was still. For a few minutes, Thomas's ears sorted the sounds of the night, which were few here in the highlands. After a restless night thinking of the day's events with the young native appearance here on this mountainside, he rose before day broke to continue the exhausting hike toward what he hoped was the Pacific Coast.

Still in the interior highlands, he could see far off in the distance the faint outline of a river winding its way through the jungle below. From this distance and height on the savanna, he could not tell how big it was or what direction it was flowing, but he hoped it was toward the Pacific Ocean. *If I can build a raft and possibly float the rest of the way, I may survive this ordeal yet.* Walking determinedly and not slowing or stopping, he plodded toward the river in the far distance. Knowing he would soon descend into the jungle, he kept a constant eye on the trail at his back, hoping he could identify some landmark once he was into the depths of the forests and not get totally lost again.

Once Thomas was through the wicked thorny growth along the sunny side of the tree line, the jungle opened up into a cathedral-like gloom. The massive trees on the buttressed roots shaded the soggy soil too much for serious undergrowth. He could see far despite the greenish gloom, and it was easy to walk between the big trees spaced four or five yards apart. The ground under his badly worn boots felt like wet paper pulp and smelled like rotting garbage. He couldn't see the sun, save occasional shafts of light lancing down high above through breaks in the canopy of green. There was no slope to the ground to indicate direction either. One tree looked pretty much like any other, so it would be easy to get turned around and lost.

Frowning, he thought, *I have been lost for weeks.* Once he hacked his way through the tangled jungle wall into the depths of the rainforest, he could no longer see any of the landmarks he had so carefully identified on his way down. Once he arrived at the area where the trade winds suddenly bounced and dumped a constant sprinkle, he was once more in true rainforest, where the tree canopy high above caught the short, almost daily showers of the so-called dry season. More accurately, the continuous wet season. The black leaf mold between the wide-spaced buttress-rooted jungle giants would be a slippery slime when it wasn't under running water. But at this time of year, the forest floor was firm enough for easy walking in most places.

He swung what he thought was a bit north again before reaching the really flat lowlands closer to the sluggish muddy river. Living in the more open lands of Germany, he had looked much at the sky and could tell time by the sun, but here in the depth of the rainforest, he could see no sun through the forest canopy. There, he had been able to tell directions by the shadows, but here there were no shadows—just the never-ending gloom of the forest. Even other telltale signs—like the side of trees that moss grew on correlating with certain direction—were useless, as moss grew in huge clusters on all sides of these giant trees, totally ignoring any law of natural arrangement. *Here we go again*, he thought. *How long will it take to find that river and make a raft? Anything will be easier than traipsing through this mushy mess.*

In the outer edge of the jungle area, he found the low-lying shrub for keeping the mosquitoes at bay and stuffed his pockets with the leaves, not wanting to chance running out again further into the forest. The river he had seen from high above on the savanna did not appear to be too far into the gloom he was now traipsing into.

Not too far, huh? he thought a few hours later with no sign of the river in sight. He stopped walking and started a fire, letting it burn down to coals then placing a yuca root to bake and some of the powerful-smelling leaves on to smoke the mosquitoes away. After eating his fill again and thoroughly smoking himself, he continued on, wanting to find the river before nightfall. Ahead, he saw the underbrush and snarled vegetation similar to what he had struggled through weeks before when he'd left the Caribbean side of the isthmus. Knowing that this impenetrable green barrier usually occurred only where there were openings in the overhead canopy of the rain forests, he enthusiastically hacked his way through the growth. The sluggish river lay before him and was running in a northerly route, possibly the right direction. Stepping out of the heavy brush onto a small sandy area, he smiled for the first time in days and asserted, *The gods are with me. It may be nearly black in color and thick with mud, but it's moving in the right direction, and I think a raft will float on it if I don't get eaten by a Cayman or some other hungry creature.*

Chapter 36

Jamestown,
Virginia, United States

1863

Someone very strong with rough, hairy arms and the smell of an ape—and probably the look of one too, if she could see him—grasped Elizabeth tightly around the neck, choking her. Then another had a fistful of hair, and they were dragging her further into another side alley. The two men grabbing Elizabeth worked efficiently, and the whole kidnapping had happened too fast for panic to set in.

Ugh, she thought, *two stinking brutes to handle one small person like me. They must be extremely desperate.* Over their struggling noise, a hoarse voice rasped, "She will bring a pretty amount at the slave market on the Barbary Coast, along with the others we have kidnapped." This she heard as blackness closed in on her vision. She had been struggling frantically to loosen her captor's grip around her neck, but she lost the battle and slumped like a ragdoll into his stinky, hairy arms.

The captor who had been strangling her released his grip and opened a door that was facing the small alley. The one who had a firm grip on her hair yanked her through the open door, slamming it behind them as he threw her to the floor. The room was filled with several other girls of varying ages in total horror.

"Not a peep from you," he warned as Elizabeth struggled to her feet, gasping for air. "I would be happy to cut your tongue off," he warned.

"Where you are all going, none of you will be required to speak anyway—you only need to be strong enough to endure hard labor and other menial tasks that do not require you to speak." He laughed.

Now fully aware and very angry, Elizabeth swept the hair away from her face, quickly moving between her captor and the other girls huddled behind her. She reached into the slight opening in the side of her skirt and hauled out the small pistol that Thomas had taught her to shoot on the farm and vineyards in Germany.

Taken totally by surprise of her rapid recovery and the sudden appearance of the gun now pointed at him, the man just stood staring. Steadily aiming the pistol at a point below the ugly brute's belt buckle, Elizabeth snapped, "You will not be cutting anyone's tongue, and furthermore, I will hastily blast away a portion of your anatomy located somewhat below the zipper on those filthy trousers you are wearing—a portion of your anatomy I'm quite sure you are very fond of. And if you even blink or utter the slightest peep, I shall start firing immediately."

He stood quietly with eyes bulging, not so much as blinking. Who would have ever guessed that this beautiful young lady dressed to kill would indeed be capable of killing on such short notice and in such a painful manner? As Elizabeth stood there with this ugly beast of a man in front of her and the kidnapped girls behind her, many things raced through her mind. She knew she had only a few minutes until her ship was to leave, and the captain had told her he would leave on time regardless of her presence on it or not.

"Lie on the floor," she snapped, "with your hands behind your head. Now."

He did so, dropping like a cannonball.

Elizabeth snapped again at one of the girls huddled behind her, "Rip a piece from your skirt and tie his hands behind him and gag him." One of the girls did so as Elizabeth opened the barred door, carefully casting a glance into the alley to look for any sign of lingering danger. Seeing none, she shouted at the girls still standing in a huddle in the back of the room, "Get out and run for your lives!"

Once outside, they scattered like quail in every direction, hopefully all to make it safely back to their homes where they belonged. She felt guilty not having more time to help the girls, but she had a ship to catch and must continue the search for Thomas.

Elizabeth gathered her skirt up and ran in a panic through the back alley and streets and was now only a few blocks from the ship she had passage on and could see it clearly. Running frantically and yelling, "Wait, wait!" she reached it just as they were raising the boarding platform. There was no sign of pursuit, and she now felt guiltier for not offering more help to the other fleeing kidnapped girls. As she caught her breath, she wondered, *Where did they come from? Where did they escape to?* Yet, to try to return now and miss the ship's departure would make all of her and Anne's recent sacrifices for nothing and most likely make the girls' situation no better and hers worse. The boarding plank was slowly lowered back to dock level, and she ran up it to the ship's deck.

Elizabeth did not have to look for Anne to see if she had made it back on time. As soon as she was aboard, her little sister hung on her like a limpet and fired questions that took a considerable length of time to answer.

Chapter 37

Chagres Rainforest, Panama

1863

Thomas still had enough yuca roots to eat for a few days, and water would not be a problem, as it would still rain frequently on the river, so his moods raised considerably. Here in a tight turn of the river, debris had swept ashore in a heap—probably by the wind, as there didn't seem to be enough current to create waves. Surely amidst this pile, there must be a corner away from the ceaseless rain and mist that he had once again descended into at the lower elevations.

Wearily, he circled the huge pile of drift knowing that not only he, but any number of beasts may well be looking for the same dry habitat. Finally confident that he was the only living thing—except perhaps snakes, bugs, and spiders that were at times as big as his hand—he ducked under an overhanging root thrust up like a tentacle from the root mass of a great uprooted tree. Stepping over a smaller trunk, he found himself in a shadowed and somewhat secure place, a small room half-covered and rather dry. He hung his wet shirt—or at least what tatters were left of it—on a limb sticking out. Then he gathered large slabs of bark from the drying trunks and placed them overhead to further shelter him from the dripping rain. Wiggling his toes through his boot soles, he had an idea—the bark would work much better than the worn leather at this point. He used some vines to tie bark pieces to his feet before examining his shelter further. Then Thomas gathered more large bark pieces to form better sides under the roof, and in a matter of minutes, he had an orderly and dry little room lacking only a small fire and some food.

What more could I ask for? he thought and immediately thought of home in Germany with family and Elizabeth. A fire he could soon have, as he still had a comfortable supply of matches in his waterproof tin, but he didn't want to waste his meager food supply. His stomach growled, protesting his modest discomfort. *Be still*, he thought. *You will have nothing to gain by complaining. You will be likely without food soon, and who knows when you'll find some again.* Exhausted, he lay down on the dry sand.

Sleeping in his clothes for weeks had rendered them badly wrinkled and permeated with odor that he was sure any company would have objected. However, he was alone, and it just didn't matter. Even so, at this camp here by the river would be a good time to wash them as well as his itching body. Always aware of the alligators or crocodiles—whatever one chose to call them, as the difference was not so obvious to him—he placed what was left of his clothing in the river to soak then gingerly stepped in himself. The water was warm but very dark in color due, he guessed, to the surrounding soil conditions, and he wondered if he could possibly come out clean or would his skin be the color of some of the natives he had read about indigenous to this area. He had seen pictures of them and read about them but had not met any yet except for the small child in the highlands two days before.

The thin veneer of his previous civilized existence was wearing as thin as his clothes, which were no more than rags that covered very little of his sunburned and gaunt body. Having had no haircut for months and not shaved for the same length of time, he knew he must look pitiful. But the water was too muddy to make a reflection, and again he reminded himself that it just didn't matter. Carefully but thoroughly washing every inch of skin on his body, using coarse sand for soap, he began to feel better. Surveying the murky water and finding nothing obviously hostile, he once again submerged his whole body and scrubbed his hair hastily, also with sand, then used a stick as a comb to remove some of the tangles. It worked to some degree, or at least he thought it did, but he still had no means to see the true condition of himself.

Feeling much better and slightly refreshed, he found a renewed determination to survive this misadventure and endure. Even though it had been over a year since leaving Germany for America to establish a trade for tobacco in the Carolinas and coffee in Central America, he felt a renewed faith in his original goal. The vineyards and processing plants in Darmstadt were surely well taken care of by the crew that had been in place when he left.

Returning to his small but comfortable shelter in the huge driftwood pile, he started a small fire, letting it burn down to coals, and placed some of the powerful-smelling leaves to smolder and smoke. Now totally void of all clothing, he stood over the smoke, turning slowly in every direction to take full advantage of its powerful mosquito-repelling odor. Once this was done, he stepped aside and bent over the coals to let his hair hang freely in the smoke. He soon realized this was not a good idea, though, when he smelled burning hair and stood up, hair ablaze. Grabbing his scimitar and taking a handful of hair, he started sawing at it until it came free, then repeated the process until he was nearly bald. It was not a painless process, and his eyes were watering severely when he had completed the task. He wondered what Heinrich, the barber friend in Darmstadt, would think of this haircut.

Within the smoldering coals he placed another yuca root and sat down to wait patiently until the root was cooked to perfection. The small fire in his temporary shelter was enough to keep him contented, and the faint glow from the fire was encouraging. He'd had hardly more than just a tree to lie under or next to for weeks. He would spend this night in relative comfort and then explore his surroundings at first light tomorrow. Perhaps he could even get started on a raft that would carry him ultimately to civilization.

Civilization. That sounded somewhat foreign, as it had been over a year—and felt like longer—since he had been in any kind of a civilized environment. With nothing but his arm for a pillow, he curled into a nearly fetal position close to the small fire and slept soundly. A deep, dreamless sleep for the first time in months. There seemed to be some degree of safety in this shelter, whether real or only imagined did not matter now. He was emotionally fatigued and beyond physical exhaustion.

When Thomas awoke, he could tell the sun was at its zenith, and it was sweltering hot in his temporary shelter. Sitting up, he brushed the sand from his torso then stood and stepped outside. He was greeted by the screeching sound of the local birds and again the aggressive hooting of the howler monkeys. *Annoying but not all bad*, he thought. He remembered reading something about how all the animal noises assured there was no immediate danger nearby and one only had to be cautious when it was deathly quiet. *Quiet in the jungle probably never exists*, he thought.

Eating more of the roasted yuca root, he sat on a nearby log and carefully surveyed his surroundings. The sun had moved a bit farther to the south, and he was now sitting more comfortably in some partial shade. His eyes traveled slowly along the shoreline of the river. He watched every shadow as it slowly changed positions, watched the general movement of the dense vegetation that grew along the river's edge, trying to make out any suspicious movement or anything that may present a threat. Nothing. For the first time in months, he started to feel at ease and just sat and enjoyed the sluggish river slowly moving by him toward the sea. Which sea, he was not quite certain, but wherever it went was better than there.

Slowly, he stood up and walked a short distance down the sandbar. This was on the outside edge of a large curve in the river, so the undergrowth in this area was very sparse and made the walking easy. After a few hundred yards, and finding nothing of particular interest and nothing to use for building his raft, he turned back in the direction he had just come and once again stopped at his hut. The insects were nearly unbearable, so he added some sticks to the smoldering coals, smoking his body thoroughly again with the powerful odor of the mosquito-repelling leaves he had carefully hoarded. This being done and offering at least temporary relief, he continued walking up the river looking for some debris for his raft.

As he came to an end of the vegetation-free area along this curve in the river, he spotted a very substantial grove of bamboo. Large stalks, with many that had been blown over and were lying in a disfigured tangle that would require some effort to separate and get to the river to start the raft. At least, he hoped they would float for a raft, as he had seen many large swirls in the river that he took to be very large fish, large enough to eat him in his entirety. Plus, the alligators. Neither were things he wanted to encounter on a firsthand basis.

After surveying the pile of bamboo, he picked a likely spot to remove the first log, approximately six inches in diameter and twelve feet long. Laboriously pulling the small log from the pile, he drug it back to his hut not more than two hundred yards downriver, then returned for another. The heat was now unbearable, so upon returning with the second log, he sat down in the shade on the back side of his hut. That offered some relief from the heat, and leaning back against the hut, he was soon asleep. The year of travel with limited food had taken its toll on his physical well-being. He was just a husk of the person who had left Germany. He dozed but roused with a start when the monkeys would howl unusually loudly or the other birds were more boisterous.

Stirring now that the sun was setting behind the tree line and the air was somewhat cooler. He knew at this time of evening the insects would soon be vicious again, so before attempting another hike up the riverbank, he once again smoked his body with the insect-repelling leaves. He was running low on these precious leaves so would have to make a short journey into the jungle for more. He knew it would be several days of hard work here to finish the raft, and if it floated and was stable enough to carry him downriver, he would need a substantial supply of the leaves for the trip. In the cooling temperature of the early evening, he once again walked upriver the short distance to the bamboo pile.

Noticing a faint trail at this point, he decided to make a quick venture into the jungle for more leaves. He knew there were some not far, as he had seen them while coming from the highlands down to his hut on the river. *This will have to be fast*, he thought. In the tropics there was no twilight or dawn, and he knew it would soon be pitch black until the moon came up, if it did. There was often a heavy fog setting in when the sun went down, with temperatures cooling and making the darkness feel like it came even sooner.

As he took a few steps farther into the undergrowth, the sight straight ahead made his skin crawl. Within moments, panic nearly took over. Straight ahead of him in a wrinkle of grass hanging from the dense snarl of growth in the riverbank, he spotted a snare. A snare would have been placed by natives. Friendly? Who was to know? The sand around the snare was plainly disturbed, and there were flecks of blood, mostly mixed in with the sand. He put his finger on the thicker spot of blood and noticed it was still moist and obviously very fresh. Thomas realized that just his presence there at that time represented a danger. He stood completely still and quiet, carefully looking in every direction for any sign of movement.

Chapter 38

Atlantic Ocean,
Off the Coast of America

1863

Captain Sawyer was waiting his turn for Elizabeth's report. The ship was underway again, on time, and he invited Elizabeth and Anne to dine with him that evening. He wished the sisters to retell the story once again so he could try to make sense of what had happened just prior to their departure from the harbor in Jamestown.

Elizabeth was again anxious and excited to be underway. They had encountered no evidence that Thomas had been seen in the Virginia area. Sitting with Captain Sawyer at dinner, she listened carefully to Anne's account of the afternoon's events but couldn't help simultaneously mulling over the journey ahead. The captain had said they should have fairly good weather for another month until their next port of call in Colón on the Caribbean side of the Isthmus of Panama. With the war between the states still in process, they would still have the danger of Union and Confederate ships crushing off shore until they rounded the southern tip of Florida heading more or less for the eastern shores of Cuba. Captain Sawyer chose this route to possibly avoid some of the more unfavorable weather in the southern reaches of the North Atlantic and the difficult route between the many island chains south of Cuba.

Elizabeth finished, and before the captain could question her, she shifted in her chair and slid her plate aside irritably. "Captain Sawyer?

Would you please enlighten me as to the route and timeframe we are taking on the next leg of our journey?"

"I know you're anxious, but couldn't we finish dinner and recount your harrowing event with the other kidnapped girls before we get into the formalities of the mundane trip ahead?" The trip ahead would be anything but mundane, they still had to sail around the Atlantic side of South America then around Cape Horn or through the Strait of Magellan with some of the most dangerous waters in the world, and he did not want to worry them needlessly yet.

"No. I would like to know now. I would like to know every detail of the rest of the journey to Panama then the route on to the Pacific. I would like to know as much as you about the islands we may pass, the other ships we may expect to encounter, the weather Thomas may have encountered, anything that may lend a clue as to what may have happened to him. He couldn't have just disappeared from the face of the earth. I feel strongly he is alive, and I must find him."

The captain shouted for the cabin boy to clear the table and brought out many charts and maps of the area they would pass through the next few weeks. They reviewed these into the wee hours of the morning. "Okay, lass, it's time to retire for the night. You and Anne can sleep until noon if you choose, but I have a ship to master. I am going to bed, and I would suggest you do the same."

The two girls retired to their room in quiet conversation about the information they had received from Captain Sawyer. In spite of the late hour, Elizabeth was restless, and sleep did not come until nearly morning. They both woke early to the chattering of seagulls. *We must still be close to land*, Elizabeth thought. After dressing, they moved to the ship's kitchen and hastily ate a brief breakfast before going to the main deck to find the captain. Far off to the starboard side of the ship, they could barely make out the faintest outline of land. *I wonder exactly where we are and how far we traveled last night.* If Thomas's ship had wrecked, as they had been led to believe, could he have somehow passed here? By this very spot?

They whiled away the hours of the morning and early afternoon before encountering the captain.

"There you are." He smiled. "Did you rest well?"

"No, I am anxious to talk more of what may have happened to the ship that Thomas was on."

"Ah, lass, it's been more'n a year since his disappearance. No one knows where that ship may have gone down. The only thing known for sure is that a ship bound to the colonies did possibly get blown off course over a year ago and has not been seen or heard of since. Some wreckage did wash ashore down the coast south of Colón on the Caribbean side of Panama during that time, but it would seem highly unlikely it would be your Thomas's ship. They would have been blown weeks off course in a terrible storm to be that far south."

"Where are we now? How far did we come last night?" Elizabeth snapped.

Captain Sawyer placed his hand on her shoulder. "Take it easy, lass. We will get to Panama when we get there. We can only go as fast as the wind will allow. I'm just the weathervane—I don't make the wind blow. Now is the time for you to call upon your true strength. You must be braver and stronger than ever before, both for you and for Anne. Soon we will be facing the worst of this journey. We will be facing seas far worse than any encountered yet. And you must face the possibility that we will never hear evidence of your Thomas."

For the first time in months, tears streaked down Elizabeth's cheeks. "I'm so sorry. It's just been so long, and I do miss him terribly." She leaned on Captain Sawyer's shoulder and sobbed. It was a long time in coming. The shock of hearing Thomas may never be found, the harrowing trip across the North Atlantic, and the kidnapping in Virginia had finally hit, and Elizabeth once again was totally exhausted.

A few minutes later, she looked up at the captain, drying her eyes on the handkerchief he offered. "No one ever told me life was easy, and for me it never was, until I met Thomas. I am now a stronger person than ever because of this last year of hardships and indecision. We will succeed in this journey, and we will succeed in finding news of Thomas. Good news or bad, we will find evidence of his whereabouts."

"Good. Now let's review these maps for the route you are so concerned about, and I will enlighten you until you know all I know about the area— or until you become totally jaded with the subject. You do know that there are no pictures to look at here," he suggested slightly sarcastically.

She slugged him on the shoulder, smiling at the joke—at least she hoped it was a joke—but the last many weeks sailing with Captain Sawyer had taught her he was a difficult man to read. Not only was he the captain of the ship but also the ship's doctor, and he had administered treatment to all aboard the last couple months, everything from scurvy treatment to complicated surgical procedures to care for other delicate matters. He was a very serious man with the slightest room for some humor and a tremendous amount of compassion for those injured or ill.

"Pay attention here," he suggested. "In three days we will be passing south of the Florida Keys then moving back into the gulf as soon as we pass Cuba. After that we will be headed just south of the Cayman Islands then more westerly toward the shores of South America. Then south to the Port of Colón in Panama, where the Rio Chagres flows into the Caribbean Sea."

"Why that route? It looks like you could have picked a more direct route than that!"

Lifting an eyebrow then crossing his arms across his chest and adjusting his reading glasses a tad, he said, "Because that's the way I want to go. It is my ship, you know."

"Ooooh, well, then how much longer before we get to Colón in Panama? I have things to do also, you know."

"We will get there when we get there—not a day sooner." Then smiling, Captain Sawyer added, "Young lady, you are most persistent and often a little annoying." He was joking and had tremendous empathy for Elizabeth and Anne. At this point, humor was needed and was accepted gratefully. "We will get there in approximately six days from where we are now, weather permitting."

"Weather permitting, weather permitting, weather permitting. When we get to California, I hope I never hear 'weather permitting' again," Elizabeth said, ambling off to talk to Anne. On her way, she leaned over the starboard rail looking for land or anything but the never-ending waterscape. This was still a dangerous area in the Caribbean Sea, with the perpetual threats of pirates and hurricanes.

Chapter 39

Chagres Rainforest, Panama

1863

How did I miss this before? Thomas wondered. The snare was only a few feet from the bamboo pile he had been cutting logs from. And he was quite sure that whomever had set the snare and then removed its contents knew of his presence. Very quietly making as little disturbance as possible, Thomas turned and took a few steps back toward the river.

Something was amiss. There were no wildlife sounds, no noise from the monkeys, birds, or whatever else made noise in this living hell. He stood there with sweat dripping from his ashen cheeks and chin. It was hot, but this perspiration was from nerves not the heat. The hair at the back of his neck was standing, and he could feel the eyes of whoever was watching him—maybe peaceful but probably not. Not knowing what to do and armed with only a scimitar, Thomas slowly turned in the most nonthreatening manner he could and walked back toward his small driftwood hut.

His mind was racing with possible actions he could take. It was nearly totally dark, so he crawled into his hut and sat in silence, not moving, just listening for any sound that would warn him of a foreign presence. He could not consider sleep—he was alarmed and trembling from indecision. *Why isn't Fredrick C. Burgdorf with me now?* Thomas felt he would need all the help he could get before the next sunrise, if he were to see another.

All night he sat, not daring to sleep but occasionally nodding off, only to wake with a start. After about a million years, the sun finally peeked over the canopy on the far side of the river. Hesitantly, Thomas crawled out of the hut and stood looking around. As he turned downriver, he stopped in total surprise. Sitting on the sand in a half circle no more than twenty feet from him were six small natives. They wore nothing but a string of small shells around each person's waist. They made no motion, just sat and stared, not intimidating. They each carried a small reed tube of about four feet long with a dart sticking out of its end. Thomas had once read of these blow guns and knew they were extremely accurate and dangerous. Not knowing what the protocol for this situation required to guarantee that he was not to be their next meal, he held up his hand, palm out, in what he hoped to be a universal peace sign. He was tired from little sleep the previous night and quivering from fatigue and hunger.

One of the little natives stood up smiling—if one could smile with a bone in his nose—and spoke in perfect Spanish, which Thomas also spoke fluently. "Don't be frightened and shake so miserably. We are not going to eat you. You have done us a great service." The man bowed slightly. "You saved one of us, and we are grateful."

Thomas just stood there not understanding what he was talking of and not knowing what to say anyway. Finally he blurted, "You speak Spanish."

"Yes," the man replied. "The missionaries on the far side of the mountains taught us. Hail Mary." Continuing, he said, "On the mountainside, you found one of our children suffering from what you people with funny white skin call malaria. You nursed her to health, allowing her to return to us."

I didn't "allow" anything, Thomas thought. *Upon regaining her consciousness, she just jumped up and ran away.* But he made no issue of the little natives thinking what they wanted, considering his situation. They all stood then, and he noticed one of them was the little girl he had taken care of on the mountain the day before entering the rainforest in the great river basin.

Timidly, she stepped forward. "Thank you for saving my life and allowing me to return to my people," she said in Spanish. "Many would have done neither. When I woke I was frightened and ran, not knowing your intentions." Having said this, she extended her hand. "This is a small gift for you. I know it means much to your kind." Snugly wrapped in a small palm leaf was a beautiful and very large blue pearl. "Our people dive for these and use them in trading with the missionaries and with others of your kind in the community of Colón, many days' travel from here. We will go there again soon to trade."

"*Gracias. Es hermosa*," he stammered, telling her it was beautiful.

She stepped back into the small cluster of her people, and they all stood looking at Thomas as he stared back at them. No one spoke. After a few minutes of this awkward silence, he finally said, "I am quite hungry," while thinking, *And I hope you are not.*

The native who had spoken first replied with what could have been a grin, with his pierced nose wrinkling. "How could you catch food making so much noise?"

To this, Thomas said nothing. Somewhat rankled, he thought, *Catching food in the middle of the Central American rainforest is nothing I've ever given much thought to before. I wonder how you would do in a sword fight on a rolling ship in a heavy storm.*

Again a few more minutes of silence and then with another slight twitch of his nose, the man said, "Come."

Thomas hesitantly followed them on the faint game trail he had seen the snare on the day before. Not wanting to go too far from the river and get lost if they abandoned him, he voiced his concern to the leader of this small band.

"Why would we leave you? We will go a short ways to our camp and eat and drink. It is back away from the river a ways where there are no insects. Only you funny white people camp close to water where all the mosquitoes live. We only go there to gather food and fish." Again with the twitch of his bone-pierced nose, it looked like he grinned.

Running to keep up with the little natives, Thomas soon reached their camp of considerable size. The others knew they were coming and had prepared their version of a feast. Thomas was apprehensive as to what this may be. However, after reviewing the food as it was unwrapped, he hastily agreed it was a feast. For the last month and more, he had eaten scarcely more than crocodile meat, bugs, roots, one green orange, and a fish.

Unwrapping something from huge palm fronds that had been lying in the coals cooking, they spread out the meal on the small dry grassy area between two huge old trees—roasted monkey, some kind of bird, fish, a fruit that Thomas was totally unfamiliar with, and something else that resembled huge grubs. He did not try those. The drink was from a mild, slightly fermented fruit that he found was not so mild when he tried to stand and toppled embarrassingly onto the seat of his britches. He drank no more but did have his fill of the other items on the menu except the things that looked like grubs.

The natives, after having their fill, seated themselves around a small fire and soon were asleep, totally ignoring Thomas's presence. Knowing he could never find his way back to his hut by the river in the dark, nor was he in any condition to do so, he remained sitting where he had just landed, rolled over, and went to sleep. The brew they had consumed had taken its toll.

When the morning sun arose amongst a flurry of activity from the children playing and the start of the natives' daily activities, Thomas found the old man that he had talked with the day before. Maybe he could guide him to some close civilization or at least give him directions. They had another meal of the same as the night before, and then the man agreed to talk.

Thomas's situation there at that location at that time was of no concern to the native leader or any of the others. When Thomas questioned him as to how to get to a town or inhabited area, the man only silently stared. He did speak Spanish as well or better than Thomas, but Thomas's questions did not make sense to him. After many tries of Thomas explaining that he wanted to reach a tribe with the funny white-skinned people like himself, the man understood but asked why he would want to go there. Finally the man said, "There is a village with only your people a short distance down the river. Maybe three or four days' travel."

Noting that natives would travel three or four times faster on foot than the river could flow, Thomas assumed it would be at least a week on a slow-moving raft. The old man had no interest in guiding Thomas further but did have one of the younger men take him back to his hut on the river.

Before Thomas left their camp, the leader did instruct him on how to find some nearby fruits and more yuca roots, and he gave Thomas a small fish trap. Then he said that if Thomas's skills were like other white men's, he would starve before reaching the village downriver. With this comment, there was no semblance of the smile.

Chapter 40

Port of Colón,
Panama

1863

In spite of a few storms that Elizabeth and Anne worried would turn into hurricanes but passed them by, Captain Sawyer sailed the ship into the Port of Colón on schedule early in the morning. It was a beautiful area surrounded with palms and all manner of tropical vegetation native to the area.

The two sisters had spent countless hours in discussion with Captain Sawyer on the best approach to finding any lead on Thomas. This was also a very dangerous port for anyone, male or female. It would most undoubtedly present more than the average amount of challenges for two beautiful young ladies like Elizabeth and Anne to be wandering alone. They both were fluent in Spanish and French, as their native homeland of Germany bordered France and Spain. With some effort, they had mastered these two languages, which were not uncommon languages in Germany. They felt comfortable with these verbal skills in questioning the locals of their search of Thomas. But still, it was a port of mainly sailors, merchants, and diseases—and of course the miners going to the California goldfields who had landed there by the thousands to cross the Isthmus of Panama, saving months of dangerous travel around the cape at the south end of South America by ship. Captain Sawyer did not want the girls to go ashore alone.

"Tell you what I can do," he suggested. "I can't go ashore with you—I have this shipload of tobacco and other cargo to unload here and then a sizable amount of other local goods to replace it with before continuing our trip around the horn then on to California, but I will send one of our crew with each of you. Perhaps that will make this fool's errand a bit safer for you."

Elizabeth was somewhat annoyed with that comment, but she gratefully accepted the offer. "I do not want to experience another ordeal like the kidnapping in the Virginias and would welcome the chaperone. Can we depart first, before you start unloading?" she questioned.

"No, you can't! We need to establish a presence here before you step foot on that dock. We want all of those around to know you are a part of this ship's inhabitants. You two have no idea as to the amount of danger you're getting into even with my men escorting you. Stand near the rail for a day or so, and enjoy the scenery and port activities. Make yourselves visible so everyone will know you are a part of us here."

Elizabeth and Anne agreed to this plan and did as asked, wandering the deck all day and into the evening. They did enjoy the activities of their surroundings. As usual the sisters dined with Captain Sawyer that evening, and after what seemed would be endless haggling, they received his permission to go ashore with their respective chaperones the next afternoon.

Elizabeth stared across the table at the captain. "Why afternoon and not morning?"

"Because the mornings usually have heavy steam or fog rising from the ground around the bay, and the visibility would be somewhat limited. I want the two of you to be very visible at all times."

Chapter 41

Chagres Rainforest, Panama

1863

Upon Thomas's safe arrival back to his hut, his guide waved and faded back into the jungle. Thomas never saw any of them again.

It was late, and he knew it would soon be dark. Knowing he was close to ending this ordeal with only perhaps one more week without civilization, Thomas reluctantly climbed into his hut, smoked himself to ward off the insects, ate some of the smoked fish the little tribe had sent with him, and lay down for sleep. Sleep did not come easily this night, for he was very eager to finish the raft and get on his way downriver.

The old man had told him he was at the beginning of a river that would flow into the mighty Chagres River. Thomas could hardly comprehend his location. He had studied maps and history of Panama in his father's library growing up, but that seemed in another world and a time long ago. From what he remembered from those old maps, he had been forced ashore someplace between Colón and the ancient harbor of Portobello. He had then made his way up out of that steamy hell and over a mountain range in the central area of the isthmus and crossed the lower San Blas Range and was now somewhere on a major river that would lead him to the Chagres River where he may find civilization.

Still lying there unable to sleep, he allowed his thoughts to wonder of his mother, Elizabeth, Fredrick, and all his friends in Darmstadt. His thoughts of them had been dormant for much of the last few months' travel in this miserable jungle. It had caused much agony to think of his loved ones at home, so he refrained from that thought process as much as possible, concentrating only on survival. It had been so long since he'd started what was to be a six-month journey. What could he expect when he returned home? Did he still have a family, a fiancé, and friends? Or had some or all disappeared after this length of time not knowing if he was even still alive?

At first light the next morning, Thomas was up and walking rapidly to the bamboo thicket up the river. He had cut eleven more logs of the right size with his machete and dragged them out to the river, skipping any noon meal and ignoring the brutal heat. It was now dark, and he could hardly see his humble hut. Walking back to the camp, he dragged one of the logs and would get the rest to his camp the next day. He wanted to build the raft near his makeshift hut so he would be close to his meager belongings and food supply, not knowing if there may be any more visitors or what kinds of traffic, if any, the river may afford.

Starting a small fire, he smoked himself, ate a hasty meal, and lay down for another pitiful night of sleep. Thomas spent two more days cutting bamboo logs and strangler vines. The following morning, he started lashing the logs together with the vines and was nearly half completed by dark. He could finish tomorrow, then gather what food he may find from the forest and begin the next leg of his journey down the river.

Leveraging the raft into the river with a long pole was easier than Thomas had imagined. He had loaded his belongings onto the raft and was slowly floating away from his home in the driftwood pile on the river bank. He had been there for nearly two weeks, the longest time he had spent in one place since leaving his home in Germany. Not once looking back, he slowly drifted downriver with a current flowing no more than what he estimated to be two knots. At this rate, he thought it would take another year to get anyplace with any degree of importance.

Before departing, he had constructed a canopy made of palm fronds over the raft in anticipation of the severe heat he would encounter on the river. He had constructed what were called sweeps—long oars on each end of the raft that he could handle by standing in the middle to manipulate the direction the raft would float. He wanted to stay in the middle of the river, as that seemed the most rapidly moving water.

Day after day, he floated with no real change in scenery. He would stop at night on small islands, of which there were many, and smoke himself thoroughly to keep the insects away. At times during the day when he could find an area along the river with more sparse vegetation, he would stop and forage for more food. He was getting very tired of the roots and various types of fruits the natives had assured him were safe to eat. He had tried without success to use the fish trap they had given him. The river was too murky and dark to see even an inch into its depth, so Thomas resigned himself to having only roots and fruit.

Nine days later, he could see the river was now flattening more and would soon merge with another, larger river, which he assumed to be the Chagres. At the confluence, Thomas stopped, pulling the raft up on the shore for some critically needed repairs. The vines he had used for lashing the logs together were unraveling, and the palm-frond canopy was in shambles. He spent two days there making the necessary repairs and gathering food. He was quite sure he would soon be reaching a village or town. With the repairs successfully completed, he once again maneuvered the raft to the center of the river and continued down the Chagres.

Two days later he spotted a village in the distance on the east shore of the river. Somewhat apprehensive, he piloted his raft toward the shore of the village. His first encounter with natives had been fruitful with no undesirable issues, but would this encounter be the same? Cautiously, he maneuvered the raft close to a group of people who seemed to be observing him from the edge of the water, curious but not alarmed. Clearly they had seen other white-skinned people before, and he seemed to present no threat.

Chapter 42

Port of Colón,
Panama

1863

The next morning Elizabeth paced the deck until she nearly had a path worn into it. The steam and fog did lift by noon, as the captain had predicted, and she ran across the deck and grabbed Anne. "Let's go," she said.

As promised, Captain Sawyer had two escorts waiting on the gangplank leading to the dock. They were the captain's most fierce and dangerous deckhands and would indeed discourage any unwanted advances toward these two charming young women.

According to plan, Anne went one direction and Elizabeth another. Elizabeth would stop and question each street vendor, and she stopped at every storefront quizzing owners and helpers relentlessly with a complete description of Thomas. No one remembered seeing such a handsome black-haired, green-eyed young man.

The sisters and their escorts repeated this process for days, and it was on the third and final day before their scheduled departure from Colón that Anne got their first bit of news. She was visiting with a merchant trading in the colorful handwoven baskets, sandals, and other handmade items made by a native tribe deep in the interior at the headwaters of the Chagres River.

Anne frantically raced through the town looking for Elizabeth, soon spotting her across the street chatting with a group of pearl divers who had just arrived in Colón. The pearl divers had recently come from the San Blas Islands and were a wealth of information with a wealth of pearls but had no news of Thomas. Very disappointed, Elizabeth slowly turned to seek another group to chat with when Anne caught up with her, yelling uncontrollably. Anne grabbed Elizabeth by the arm and started dragging her toward the other side of the small town, babbling about a wild story that the interior tribe had told her.

In their haste Elizabeth and Anne had both lost the bodyguards, and it wasn't until they had reached the area of the natives' display that the men caught up, swearing and puffing. One of them said, "I have fought in many battles at sea and on land and have never been as tired as I am following either of you two for a day."

Smiling sweetly, Anne chirped, "That's okay. It's good practice and keeps you in shape for your next battle. And from what I hear of our pending trip for the next couple of months, you may be called on sooner than you think."

Anne filled Elizabeth in on her conversation with the natives about encountering a very tall, black-haired young man with a scraggly black beard and piercing green eyes on a beach near the headwaters of the Chagres. Apparently he wore but very little shredded clothing and no shoes but for the bark pieces tied to his feet. This made no sense—how and why could Thomas have been there? It was some fifty kilometers into the interior of the isthmus toward Panama City. Elizabeth was somewhat in shock. When the shock gave way to excitement, her words made no sense at first.

As Anne and the two chaperones sat and listened, Elizabeth began to speak more coherently. This was the first concrete evidence she had heard of Thomas surviving his fated voyage from Germany to the Americas over a year ago. She expected to possibly hear of information concerning his shipwreck from a passing seaman or from a merchant, but not to hear of Thomas in the interior with a band of natives. It was almost too much to comprehend and, she thought, highly unlikely.

After regaining some of her composure, she began her interrogation of the spokesman of the tribe for three hours, until nearly dark. This proved not an easy task. The tribe spokesman did speak Spanish, but it was more of a local dialect and was very difficult for Elizabeth to understand. She questioned every detail of their finding of this man who resembled Thomas, then requestioned, then formulated the questions yet again in another manner so as not to miss one tiny detail or bit of information these people could have.

The story was hard to believe, but Elizabeth had no doubt it was Thomas who had passed through the native village. Thomas had survived a shipwreck somewhere in the Caribbean Sea, then made it to the shore someplace south of Colón, then traversed through the lowland swamps and over the mountain range to the head of the Chagres River, where he was last seen on a handcrafted raft floating down the river and ultimately toward the town of Gamboa, not far from Panama City. By dark, Elizabeth had exhausted herself and the native tribe and could get no further information, so she reluctantly followed her group back to the ship.

The ship was scheduled to depart the next morning to continue with its valuable cargo around the southern tip of South America, and Elizabeth was quite sure it would do so with or without her. She knew of the overland trail from the Port of Colón to the Port of Balboa near Panama City, following the Chagres River at least part of the way. After some of the torturous sea travel they'd experienced, she had given this route serious consideration. It would have saved her months of sea travel south around Cape Horn, but at this time it was nearly impossible. It would have been nearly sixty miles of pure hell on foot dragging her baggage. The area was infested with insects carrying malaria, which did not always kill but made one very sick with recurring visits for life. Then there was black vomit—or yellow jack or yellow fever, all one and the same—which usually did kill, but if one survived, one rarely ever experienced that horrible sickness again. The route across the isthmus was also infested with a variety of small venomous snakes that could kill in seconds as well as massive snakes up to twenty feet long that could coil around one's body, inflicting hours of torture to crush and kill a victim before eating it. Elizabeth determined these reasons to be good incentive to continue on with Captain Sawyer, which she hoped would be safer.

The entourage climbed the boarding platform and was directly confronted by the ship's captain.

"News travels fast," he said grinning from ear to ear. Some of the deckhands had heard parts of the conversation she'd had with the natives from the interior and had passed it on to the captain upon their boarding earlier. "Please rest a bit then freshen up and join me for a late supper. We must make final preparations so we can embark shortly after the midnight tide."

With that, he swiftly turned, barking last-minute orders to the crew. There were many preparations still to be done before setting sail, and he wanted to hear a full account of the afternoon's events over the evening meal with Elizabeth and Anne.

Chapter 43

Port of Colón,
Panama

1863

Elizabeth and Anne wearily walked to their room but were too excited to rest. The afternoon events were completely overwhelming. They had hoped and prayed for good news of Thomas but were still in a state of apprehension and now disbelief. Soon strolling to the captain's quarters for supper, they knocked on his door and were quickly dragged to a well-set table.

Captain Sawyer was even more excited than the girls. Over the past few months, the girls had shared the stories of most of their lives with the captain, and he had developed an unembellished kinship with Thomas even though he had never met him. He now wanted a full and most accurate account of the discussion Elizabeth and Anne had had with the interior natives, and he wanted more than ever to assist in discovering Thomas's current whereabouts. He gave each woman a partially filled glass of the finest wine aboard ship, being well aware of their young ages and fearing to give them too much. They all touched glasses to his simple but powerful toast: "To a speedy reunion with our Thomas." They all sipped, and then the usually more quiet and shy Anne burst into talk.

She would recount some of the natives' stories, and then Elizabeth would interrupt reliving the same tale but adding more that she remembered. This went on for hours, with Captain Sawyer only interrupting and cross-examining when both women spoke at the same time, until the captain had pieced together the full story of Thomas's misadventures that had contributed to his disappearance. It was approaching daylight when he suggested they all go to bed and pick up the story in the morning. Elizabeth still had many unanswered questions as to their next steps but reluctantly agreed to call it a night. They all were fatigued, and the ship did need an alert captain to continue on the voyage.

The sun was shining at full height when Elizabeth awoke, but Anne was still sleeping soundly. Elizabeth quietly dressed and was soon on the deck. Making the rounds, she found the captain standing alone near the bow staring at nothing in particular but deep in thought.

Catching a glimpse of movement from the corner of his eye, he turned to face her. "As I understand this tale," he started, "you did send a letter to Thomas approximately six months after his departure from Germany. And to your knowledge he has never responded."

"Yes, I sent the letter to the Tribaldos Coffee plantations in Panama City to the attention of Thomas Clay. It seems his father had a relationship with the company before his death in Germany." Folding her arms and looking out across the vastness of water, she asked, "What am I to do now? He may have made it across the isthmus and may have reached Panama City and the Tribaldos Coffee Company, but this ship will pass through the Strait of Magellan and again head in a more northerly direction for San Francisco, passing right by Panama City, days out at sea. This route, you have shared with me many a time. Then I will be forced to catch another ship back to Panama City, losing many weeks in my search for Thomas." Her eyes were misty. She felt she was so close, but time was not on her side. Every day that passed was one more without his presence, and she now believed stronger than ever that he was alive and well, but where, she did not know.

Captain Sawyer now faced her. The slight breeze ruffled her hair and blew her dress gently to one side. *What a lovely couple they would make,* he thought, *if we could just find the lad. This search seemed so hopeless in the beginning months when I first learned of the women's plans, but now—who knows?* he thought. *Maybe Thomas did in fact survive the ordeal and is indeed in Panama City, or maybe someone at the Tribaldos Coffee warehouses has information concerning him. I have put up with these two for months—he smiled to himself—pestering me to go here, stop there, and I've had to try to keep them somewhat safe all that time in their search. What will another couple of weeks' sailing time matter now? I have no perishables, only a hold full of timber for the shipbuilders in San Francisco and a small fortune in bales of tobacco from the Virginias, and two more weeks will not sway their value any more or less. As soon as we round the tip of South America through the strait and turn north again, we could make a slight detour in to Panama, this time on the Pacific side, and spend a day or two with these Tribaldos people.*

"Well," Captain Sawyer finally said, gazing past Elizabeth at the bright-blue sky and the equally bright-blue ocean on the horizon, "here is what you can do. You can look for Thomas in Panama City. We should be there in a few weeks."

Looking at him in a puzzled manner, Elizabeth asked, "What do you mean? We are bound for San Francisco."

"*Were* bound," he replied. "We are changing course and will visit Panama again. Perhaps there is some hope, and I think I would like to see this thing through. We are now going around the horn and once again to Panama, and I pray for good news there." *But first a safe trip around the horn*, he thought. "I can't waste any more time than that on you two vagabonds," he said, smiling.

Anne was now on deck and scurried over to where Elizabeth and the captain were standing. Elizabeth was again stunned by the gruff older man's generosity and willingness to help continue in the search. Anne, being the perceptive young lady she was, took one look at the situation and said, "What's happening now?"

Elizabeth was speechless, so the captain told Anne the same as he had told Elizabeth. "I can't afford to waste any more time on the pair of you vagabonds, but we will reroute to the city of Panama to see what we may see," he said grinning.

The two stood staring at the captain with a totally newfound respect for him. Then Elizabeth, true to form, snapped, "When will we be there?"

And once again repeating himself, Captain Sawyer replied, "We will get there when we get there. I'm just the weather vane—I don't make the wind blow," and they all laughed.

Chapter 44

Chagres Rainforest, Panama

1863

Thomas greeted the people in English and received no response. He then tried Spanish, and they were more than willing to respond. They had traded with other Spanish-speaking white men before, he soon learned, and most of them seemed to be quite happy with the results.

Thomas spent two days in this native village. He had nothing to trade but did still have a few pieces of gold coin left in the now-battered pouch he had carried across the mountains, along with his remaining few wax-dipped matches, which he was using more sparingly as there were only maybe a dozen left. The natives dressed in cotton trousers, and a type of serape hung from their shoulders. He was able to purchase both that fit comfortably and discarded the rags he had worn for the last year. They offered him food and drink, talking freely of their existence here being a tribe that relied on trading. They frequently traveled down the river to the small community of Las Cruces near the Panama Railway to trade their wares for the few items their simple existence required.

Upon further inquiry, they informed Thomas it was only another two or three days' journey to Las Cruces and the community was inhabited by mostly natives and a few white men from far corners of the outside world. The railroad was only a few years old and apparently had no scheduled stop at Las Cruces. Being totally unfamiliar with the functions of a railroad system, having never seen one before, Thomas had no idea how this was to be dealt with when reaching that destination but decided he would deal with that upon arrival.

After a couple of days resting and talking to the natives, he decided to continue on the last leg of the journey to what he hoped would be civilization. Sliding his raft back into the river and waving his farewell early in the morning of his third day there, he lazily continued the float downriver overwhelmed with excitement and trepidation, desperate to get word back to his family of his well-being, such as it was, and eager to negotiate a way back home.

The trip seemed to go slower. Traveling until well after dark then stopping to rest until the moon rose, casting its odd shadows on the river, Thomas started again with no sleep. He desperately hoped to make it to Las Cruces in two days. At first light the next morning, his eyes were desperately searching the river bank on each side for some sign of civilization. Disappointed at seeing nothing, he hung his head as his raft slowly drifted along. He had neglected to ask which side of the river the community of Las Cruces was on but was quite sure he could not miss it.

About noon, rounding a huge bend, he spotted the community and the tracks of the railroad nearby. Not wanting to waste any time now, he turned the raft sideways and used the large sweeps like oars to assist its speed. Finally arriving at the small dock system and hastily jumping ashore, he tied the craft off and surveyed his surroundings. Walking up the bank to the village of thatch-roofed dwellings, he made

inquiries as to the procedure for getting on the train. He was informed that the train had just passed going toward the town of Aspinwall on the Caribbean side of the isthmus, but would be returning tomorrow morning toward Balboa and Panama City.

Having no choice in boarding the train in either direction this day, Thomas walked the narrow streets of the community, stopping to chat with anyone who would listen. He had few takers in this respect. No one seemed at all interested in his misadventures or his arrival from the jungle by way of the river. Being very hungry, he purchased a type of bread-and-cheese sandwich and an earthen mug of tepid beer of some type from a street vendor, then sat in the shade of one of the jungle giants lining the river.

The raft was in bad need of repair again, but having no further use of it, Thomas gave it to a small native boy fishing close by. It was late afternoon, but time seemed to stand still waiting for the pending darkness and the arrival of the train the next morning. One of the natives he had talked with earlier indicated that one only need stand in the center of the railroad track, and the train would stop to pick up anyone going its direction. Not knowing how fast this train would be traveling, Thomas decided it would not be wise to stand in the center of the track but off to one side and wave it down. A wise decision, he later found out. The train was not moving fast, but it took some distance to stop, and he would have surely been run over.

Thomas ran to the front of the train where the operator of the steam engine hung out of the window, impatiently waiting for him, and climbed aboard. The operator motioned him back to the passenger car directly behind the engine. It was crowded with people of all walks of life traveling this route across the Isthmus of Panama, saving thousands of miles to sail around the southern tip of South America. From the Pacific side, they could head north to the port in San Francisco then inland to the California goldfields.

Chapter 45

Caribbean Sea,
Off the Coast of Panama

1863

Captain Sawyer set sail south, and at the end of that first day, Elizabeth found herself well out to sea but still in sight of land.

"Where are we?" Elizabeth inquired of the captain when they crossed paths on the deck.

"We are now just passing the northern border of Colombia. We will go further out to sea and much further away from its shores. It's a very dangerous area, and I do not want to encounter any of its pirates or military, both being about the same."

"Are there any important sea ports on this Atlantic side of Colombia?" she inquired. "Any we may be stopping at?"

"I have visited only one, Cartagena, and wish never to go there again. Or any other place on Colombian soil. A most unpleasant experience, which nearly cost me my ship and crew." Captain Sawyer shook his head disgustedly. "The next few days we will be sailing well out to sea to avoid any vessels coming and going in or out of not only Colombia but also Venezuela and Guyana. In a few weeks, we will be close enough to see parts of Brazil but will have no reason to make any stop in that area either. I will point out, however, when we pass the northern border of Brazil and cross the equator. Those crossing for the first time have to undergo an initiation and pay allegiance to Neptune, god of the seas. It will be, however, a very short initiation, as I am most anxious to get around the infernal tip of South America, the sooner the better, and be into the calmer Pacific Ocean."

"Anne and I are most anxious to observe the crossing of the equator and tend to our initiation and pay our dues, but you do seem somewhat concerned about this pending trip around the Cape Horn area." Elizabeth peered south.

"I am. It's very dangerous, with some of the wildest waters in the world. Since the 49ers started around this route, there have been over one hundred ships lost with nearly one thousand five hundred lives. I have made the trip seven times, once all the way around Cape Horn and six through the straits. And each I swore would be the last, but alas here we are again."

"What are the 49ers?" Elizabeth asked.

"That's what we call the gold miners going to California. There's been a rush to get there since 1849, and it doesn't seem like it will slow. Everybody wants a chance at striking it rich."

The further south they went, the cooler it got, and it was soon too cold to spend much time on deck. The weeks of sailing into the southern hemisphere sluggishly passed with very little excitement for the two sisters but with much preparation and anticipation for Captain Sawyer. The straits were a most important passage through Chile to connect the Atlantic and Pacific Oceans, eliminating the necessity to go all the way around Cape Horn on the southern tip of South America, where the two oceans meeting caused some of the wildest and most difficult waters in the world. Some waves rose as tall as a ten-story building, not to mention the howling gale-force winds and sneaky icebergs. Captain Sawyer had made the trip around the horn once, surviving that trip with ship intact and no lives lost and vowing to never do it again.

In the telling of this harrowing journey later to Elizabeth and Anne, he said, "Traditionally, when a sailor rounded the horn, they were then allowed to wear a gold hoop in their ear, the ear closest to the horn."

Looking at him with a slanted smile and cocking one eyebrow, Elizabeth asked, "If you made the trip around the horn, why are you not wearing a ring in your ear?"

"Don't you remember?" he said, smiling. "I do have a wife in Boston—therefore I wear it in my nose."

She punched him playfully and remarked, "My Thomas will not be led by a ring in his nose."

They saw but a few ships on their route through the Strait of Magellan and none presented any reason for a second glance. Successfully navigating this route, and now on the next leg traveling north once more but on the west side of the continent, Elizabeth inquired once more of the captain—but in a much more pleasant manner—"When do we expect to arrive in Panama?"

"It will be hardly more than three weeks now," he replied. "The weather will be warming, and we will be into somewhat heavier shipping traffic. Here we will have to be more aware of our surroundings. Pirates and other ships that may wish to do us harm and relieve us of our cargo, which includes you two charming young women, are always a concern, so help me and the rest of the crew keep an eye out for such unsavory characters."

Captain Sawyer paced the decks relentlessly, watching carefully for anything on the horizon that moved. He stayed far out to sea, avoiding any land mass that may hide another ship. Even though he was concerned, he knew it was highly unlikely that another ship could overtake him if he could spot them first before they got close. His own vessel, he knew, was heavily laden with goods but still was very sleek and fast. *One of the fastest on the sea*, he thought, and he was comfortable and proud of that.

Chapter 46

Panama Canal Railway, Panama

1863

Upon boarding the train, Thomas had no problem striking up a conversation. It seemed as though everyone in this coach had questions as to who he was and how he had arrived here in the middle of Panama. The questions never stopped. The others were miners, farmers, merchants who hoped to start businesses in California or farther north in the Idaho Territory. There were entire families who had left different parts of the American East Coast to travel this route to the West Coast, not wanting to brave the trip across the Great Plains. There were people from various countries in Europe too, all hoping for a more prosperous life in the American West.

Sitting on the bench seat that ran the length of the coach on each side, with only a narrow aisle between, Thomas was engrossed in conversation. He was hungry for news—news of any kind. The couple sitting directly across the aisle from him happened to be from Germany and shared about the political and economic situation there. It was now extremally unstable, and Thomas feared for his family. To date more than one million Germans had been forced to flee Germany, most settling in the great America. The questions from the other passengers around him were never ending, so Thomas told and retold his story many times during this last leg of his journey in Panama. The train was soon to arrive at the end of the railroad in the community of Summit, some ten miles short of the port cities of Balboa and Panama City.

From Summit, some passengers hired mules and rode, some rode in dilapidated mule-drawn carts, and many walked the remaining distance to the port on the Pacific Ocean at Balboa or Panama City, hoping to catch a ship for the remaining journey to San Francisco. Before long, Thomas realized that for many, this part of the journey was extremally disappointing, as regular scheduled sea travel from Panama to San Francisco had not yet been established. Many waited for weeks or months to board a ship, and hundreds died of neglect on the shores of Panama, never having a chance at their dreams in the American West.

Thomas, however, had decided to make a hasty trip to the Tribaldos family coffee warehouse in Panama City, part of his original mission to explore the possibilities of establishing a trade agreement for coffee to be sent to Darmstadt in Germany, politics and economy permitting.

Upon arriving in Balboa, Thomas made his way with much effort to the heart of this thriving and bustling city. Speaking Spanish fluently, he had no problems in communicating with the local populace and was soon directed to a community bath house for a much-needed shower. He cared not to think how long it had been since his last one. There was a barber shop handily located next door. He had not had a haircut or shave since he had cut his own flaming hair in the river hut prior to making the raft. Again he wondered what their barber in Darmstadt, Heinrich, would think.

After the bath house and then the barber shop, Thomas walked across the street to a clothing store and fit his frame—once heavy and muscular but now very thin—with new clothes and shoes as well as a spare set of each for his return trip to Germany.

Finally, with directions from the store owner, Thomas made his way to the Tribaldos Coffee warehouse and asked to speak to Eladio Tribaldos, one of the owners. Immediately, a man came running down a set of stairs, his office being on the second story with a view of the harbor and busy streets surrounding the warehouse.

"You are Thomas Clay!" he cried.

"I am," Thomas replied.

Chapter 47

Tribaldos Coffee Company, Port of Balboa, Panama

1863

"I have news for you from your home in Darmstadt in Germany," Eladio Tribaldos said as he approached Thomas. "I received a packet from your family a few months ago. They sent me a packet of inquiries, expecting your arrival here some time ago. I have a letter for you also. From the dates on these packets, it seems you have been missing for over a year." Throwing a big arm out to each side and raising his chin, he added, "Good God, son, where have you been? I was hopeful of your arrival here, but after so long, I certainly had my doubts you were still alive. Come with me to my office, and let's open that and see what we shall see. I have more to share with you, Thomas, much more." Shouting to one of the servants, Eladio ordered sandwiches and sangria to be sent up immediately.

They walked up stairs to his extravagant office.

"Sit," Mr. Tribaldos commanded, pointing at a comfortable chair. "Our refreshments will be here momentarily."

Completely overwhelmed with the barrage of news and the lavish surroundings, Thomas collapsed into the chair. He'd had so little real food for so long, had survived the shipwreck that had eventually landed him on the Caribbean shores of Panama in the first place, had survived the alligator attack early on his journey into the bloody jungle, traveled unguided across the country of Panama with no more than the ragged clothes on his back, been sleeping on the ground for so long, and ultimately ended here with Mr. Tribaldos. He was mentally fatigued and totally exhausted.

"You are a lucky young man," Mr. Tribaldos interrupted his thoughts. Those Indians in the interior usually stick poison darts into people and make some kind of an offering to their gods with their heads. How did you manage?"

"Well," replied Thomas, "I didn't try to change their religion or make them wear pants."

Eladio raised his hands with a chuckle. "Fair enough," he said.

With a combination of much apprehension and excitement, though, Thomas turned to the items from his family and debated which to open first. The packet contained two letters from home, one from his mother and one from Elizabeth. He hastily chose the one from Elizabeth first. The servant arrived with the sandwiches and the cool drink. With a sandwich in one hand and a glass of sangria sitting in front of him on a small end table, he picked up the first letter and began reading its lengthy content out loud. Mr. Tribaldos was as excited as Thomas for the news within, and Thomas was afraid if he did not read it to him, Mr. Tribaldos would rip it from his hands and read it himself. Thomas was surprised Mr. Tribaldos had not already opened and read it.

My dearest Thomas,

It has been nearly a year since you left, and we have heard no word from you. Our cherished friend Mr. Hollenbeck had news that one of the packet ships crossing the Atlantic for the Americas was lost in a severe storm, very possibly with no survivors. He thought it possible the one you were on.

I feel in my heart you have survived and are alive so am forwarding this letter along with one from your mother to the Tribaldos Coffee Company in Panama City, knowing in my heart you will eventually manage to make your way there. Your dear friend Fredrick,

Sister Anne, and Little Josh are all in good health but completely distraught not knowing your fate.

Their fears combined do not equal mine—I miss you so, and there is not an hour of any day or night I do not think of you.

Mother took a turn for the worse shortly after your departure for the Americas and sadly passed. My father, considering all, is doing well and has totally recovered from his wounds in the revolution. He and Fredrick have taken excellent care of the farm and the Clay vineyards. With Mother's passing, my older sister, Mary, and her husband left for San Francisco to try their luck in the California goldfields. I also will be leaving Germany soon accompanied by my younger sister, Anne, attempting to trace your route to America to see if there is any news of you, my dear Thomas.

Ultimately, Anne and I will join Mary and Edward in San Francisco. We think Mary is staying in the Hayes Valley area of San Francisco not far from the docks, while Edward is working away in what is called Sutter's Mill mining area.

I can never forget you and will always love you, my Thomas. I will suffer severely and have a very difficult time in life without you if that is my destiny.

To you my heart and all my love,
Elizabeth

Thomas sat in stunned silence for but a few seconds. In his entire life he could not remember shedding a tear, but they now ran freely in a constant stream from each eye. Mr. Tribaldos slowly stood from his chair, also with moist eyes, having heard every word of Elizabeth's letter. Crossing the small room, he placed his arm around Thomas's shoulder. Thomas wept pitifully for—he didn't know how long—then dried his eyes on a handkerchief Mr. Tribaldos had offered.

He was both relieved for the news from Elizabeth but deeply saddened by the loss of Elizabeth's mother and the grief he had caused her and the family. *Will I ever see her or any of them again?* He hesitated on the unopened letter from his mother with Mr. Tribaldos's arm still on his shoulder.

"Open it, son. I am right here with you and am quite sure things will work out fine."

Thomas's mother's letter was much a reiteration of Elizabeth's. She was doing well with the help of Elizabeth's father—Manfred—and Fredrick and little Josh. Thomas was emotionally drained and very concerned for his future. He had little money left—certainly not enough to return home—and no place to stay here in this South American city.

Mr. Tribaldos squeezed his shoulder tenderly, then smiling radiantly down at Thomas, said, "Now for some good news." He took a sip of his sangria. "I received much the same news from your family as you months ago. Along with the letters, they sent a substantial amount of funds for your needs, should you reach here. Fearing you may have suffered some disastrous condition, they wanted to make sure that if you made it this far, you would have some money."

It had been over a year since Thomas had left Germany on his trip that was to have taken no more than six months. He would likely have been out of money in that time anyway, even if he hadn't lost most of it to the bottom of the ocean. Thomas and Mr. Tribaldos talked away most of the afternoon, mainly of Thomas's life in Germany, of his father's demise, then of his meeting of Elizabeth, of the family farm, and of his ultimate trip to the Americas. Thomas told him of his ship being blown weeks off course and of the emergency landing on an island for much-needed repairs, then on to South America, only to smash into some unknown reef and lose the few remaining poor souls. He explained he was the only survivor, to his knowledge, to make shore on the beach of Panama. Mr. Tribaldos was a thoughtful and caring man with children of his own and knew Thomas needed this time to relax and talk.

Finally Mr. Tribaldos asked, "What will you do now, Thomas?"

Chapter 48

Tribaldos Coffee Company,
Port of Balboa, Panama

1863

Standing up and smiling, looking out the window at the distant harbor, Thomas replied, "I am now going on to San Francisco in search of Elizabeth. Depending on the route of her ship, she may already be there or soon will be. I will send a packet home to my mother, advising her of my misfortune, my good health, my meeting with you, and my decision to continue on to California." He once again had cash in his pocket, food in his stomach, and another real purpose other than that of just surviving from one day to another.

"Good decision, lad," Mr. Tribaldos spoke loudly, gently slapping Thomas on the back. "You shall stay here with us until I can arrange passage for you to California. You will not have to wait long—I get special consideration from the shipping lines because of the vast quantities of coffee I ship to San Francisco and other California ports of call. Come, let us go home for the evening. I will instruct my people to get you passage on the next ship out with my merchandise. It will be no time at all until we have you in California searching for that Elizabeth you seem so fond of."

Guiding Thomas down the stairs from the office, Mr. Tribaldos yelled at his workers and shouted orders to get the young man board on the next ship bound for San Francisco. They walked to the rear of the warehouse and climbed into the carriage that the man's stable boy had made ready, apparently knowing it would be needed soon by hearing Mr. Tribaldos's boisterous yelling in the warehouse.

They arrived soon at his home in the cliffs overlooking the harbor, and Thomas was made comfortable in a large and very lavish guest room, the likes of which he had never encountered. He thought his family had a very pleasant but modest home in Darmstadt, Germany, but this guest room looking over the Port of Balboa on the Pacific Ocean was far from modest. It had a four-poster bed with a canopy and mosquito netting, huge windows looking over the ocean, and a water closet with bath tub, sink, and wash basin, all with running hot and cold water. Fresh towels were hanging near the tub with perfumed soap in a dish.

The maid escorting Thomas to the room reminded him that the evening meal would be hours away and he had plenty of time for a bath and a rest if desired. She indicated if he were now hungry or thirsty, she could bring some refreshments. He was in fact both hungry and thirsty, so she returned shortly with a platter of sliced roast beef, thick slices of cheese, and a chilled pitcher of sangria. Thomas wondered if these people drank water—so far he had only seen sangria but certainly was not complaining.

Later Thomas was summoned down to the main sitting room for a formal introduction to the Tribaldos family members. Conversation was plentiful, and all were curious to hear of his adventures in crossing the country of Panama on foot using the godforsaken route he had followed. There was the old Balboa trail from the Caribbean Sea to Panama City, a well-established though dangerous trail, but Thomas's route had been far south of that established path and in totally uncharted territory. With the barrage of continuous questions from each family member and their insistence of reliving every detail of the trip, Thomas was soon wishing for the sullen, silent natives he had encountered weeks prior. The evening meal was served well after dark, which was the custom of the area, and it went on and on, course after course, until well after midnight. *Why did I eat the earlier snack?* he wondered. Finally, stuffed as a goose or turkey at Christmastime, and having drunk too much of the sangria, Thomas was able to excuse himself and retire to his room.

The gas lights were lit and turned low. Not knowing for sure how they worked, he did not bother to turn them off. He had slept in no real bed since leaving home so long ago. The ocean voyage from Darmstadt partway across the Atlantic until the horrifying storm had offered only a small pallet and mattress. Then later the jungle floor had presented no degree of comfort. Thomas tumbled into bed with thoughts of getting a letter off to his mother first thing the next morning, then continuing on to San Francisco in search of Elizabeth as soon as possible. He slept with much comfort and more soundly than he had in months.

Waking in the early morning and enjoying another hot bath, he heard a gentle knock on the door followed by the maid's voice announcing breakfast would be served in the main dining room in fifteen minutes. After leisurely drying his skin with a fluffy white towel, Thomas dressed in a change of new clothes and went down the stairs to the dining room, marveling along the way at the furnishings of this beautiful household. Perhaps, after all, the coffee business could be a rewarding venture.

As they all gathered around the table, Thomas was again bombarded with questions concerning his adventures crossing the Atlantic and arriving here on their doorstep. He was again overcome with the food and drink—not sangria this early morning, but mugs of steaming black coffee, the likes of which he had not had in a long time.

After Thomas had gorged himself with food, ready to burst from the many cups of coffee, he saw Mr. Tribaldos boost his sizable frame from the chair at the head of the table. "Feel free to rest and do as you please, Thomas, but I must go to work. I want to check on your passage to California. We know not if Elizabeth has reached there or is still en route, but we will have you prepared for either event. And then we must discuss your future in the coffee industry when you return to Germany."

Thinking for only a moment, Thomas replied, "I think I would like to go with you, sir. If I would not be a bother, I would like a tour of the warehouses, and if given enough time before my departure, I would like to visit one of the plantations." Thomas, of course, hoped *not* to have enough time for this, as he desperately wanted to continue his way as soon as possible to California in search of Elizabeth, but if time permitted, it would be a wise business choice. Before affording the luxury of his bathing that morning, he had written a letter to his mother in Germany, giving her a full account of his adventure to date and his intent to continue on to California. Mr. Tribaldos then sent it with a servant to the dock area to ensure it would receive proper attention and routing to arrive at its destination in Germany in a timely manner.

"Please, do accompany me to my office, and I will make sure you receive the grand tour of our operation here in the city. It will require some time to reach and tour our plantations in the interior of Panama at Boquete. Rest assured, you will have one of my assistants at your complete disposal for your remaining time here. But let's first check on your boarding schedule. If we do not have the time to do all you wish before your departure, we can continue with this endeavor upon your return from California once you have found the girl." He smiled.

"Thank you for all your help." Thomas returned the smile. "I would have assuredly perished by now without it. Upon finally reaching Panama City, I was utterly exhausted and knew not where to turn next."

When they arrived at the warehouse, they turned the team and buggy over to the stable boy, and Mr. Tribaldos's casual demeanor instantly changed, yelling orders at everyone there. He soon had workers scattering in every direction.

Before Mr. Tribaldos could ask about Thomas's boarding schedule, one of his aides raced to him with a note in hand. "This just came from one of the ships in the harbor, *La Bestia Real*." Thomas knew this translated to "The Royal Beast." "It will be leaving on the evening tide for San Francisco. Per your instructions, they will have a suitable room ready for master Thomas."

Chapter 49

Tribaldos Coffee Company, Port of Balboa, Panama

1863

Clasping Thomas's arm and smiling, Mr. Tribaldos yelled, "Let's hurry, lad. I did not imagine such quick results. I will send the stable boy quickly home to snatch your possessions. You will accompany me here until his return. Is there anything I can help you with before we put you on that ship bound for California this very evening?"

Having anticipated a long wait in Panama before expecting a space on any ship to California, Thomas thought, *Is there no end to this man's connections in this part of the world?* He knew of the long waits for passage and the fate of some who never received passage, often leading to their untimely demise. He felt somewhat guilty but not enough to deny his quickly reserved slot on this ship, even if it had at times been a livestock hauler. Wading in animal dung, he could handle; a lengthy stay in Panama delaying his search for Elizabeth, he could not. Thomas's needs now were simple, and he did not know what he would require once reaching there.

Looking at Mr. Tribaldos, he simply replied, "I know nothing of my accommodations on this ship. Perhaps some food and water and my personal belongings?"

"No worry about that, lad. The skipper of that ship is a dear friend and usually only transports cargo one way and who is to know what on the return trip. You will be well taken care of to your destination."

The stable boy soon returned with Thomas's meager personal belongings. Thomas had come to trust Mr. Tribaldos and considered him a dear family friend. As Thomas took stock of his items, he had a sizable amount of money in the belt around his waist. Not knowing of the dangers that may lie ahead, he was somewhat uncomfortable carrying that amount of cash.

As it became time to leave for the dock that was near, he hurriedly took Mr. Tribaldos aside out of hearing distance of the others. "Sir, as you know, I am carrying a considerable amount of money, of which I am not comfortable in doing. I know not what I will be encountering and would not wish to lose it all, should something happen."

Mr. Tribaldos looked at Thomas with some concern but without saying a word.

"Could I leave half of this here in your safe hands until my return? Perhaps you can put it in your safe or possibly invest it for me? Should I not return in a reasonable time, please return it to my family in Germany. I think you have the directions for that."

Mr. Tribaldos considered Thomas with a serious expression. "That's a wise decision. I wanted to suggest that to you but thought not to question your wisdom nor make you suspicious."

To that, Thomas only smiled. They walked up the stairs to the office, where Thomas removed his money belt and left half of its contents and the blue pearl in Mr. Tribaldos's safe hands.

Grabbing a leaf of paper from his desk, Mr. Tribaldos said, "Let me give you a receipt, for whatever purpose it may serve. One never knows what the future holds for either of us. I may not be here upon your return, and you may have to deal with some other."

With that, they moved down the stairs and to the waiting carriage. Mr. Tribaldos said, "I will escort you to the ship and make sure of your safe boarding and introduce you to the captain. Worry not—you will be in respectable hands until you get to California. I would suggest, however, that you not leave the ship at any port you may pass before reaching your destination. There are a many horror stories of things that happen to lonely sailors who go ashore at some of these banana republic docks you may pass in Nicaragua, Honduras, Guatemala, and Mexico, should your route pass there."

Upon arriving at the dock, Mr. Tribaldos authoritatively escorted Thomas up the loading ramp of the *La Bestia Real* to the captain's quarters, where he formally introduced Thomas to Captain Justin.

Chapter 50

Port of Balboa,
Panama

1863

Captain Justin was slightly taller than Thomas's six-foot height but outweighed him by at least one hundred pounds. He had not an ounce of fat—pure muscle—and Thomas was still very thin from his trek across Panama.

With the formal introductions made, Mr. Tribaldos turned, clasping Thomas's hand, and wished him, "Godspeed, son. I shall anxiously be awaiting your news." That being said, he returned down the boarding ramp to the carriage, removed his hat, and waved again. Thomas stood on the deck waving back, and they were soon hauling anchor with the sails set and moving toward open water.

Once in open water and sailing at a good speed, Captain Justin hailed Thomas. "Come, let us find you a proper place to rest your head on this journey to California. I have promised our friend Eladio Tribaldos that you would have nothing but the best on this ship."

"That will not be necessary." Thomas smiled. "I will be forever indebted for this hasty boarding and departure to continue on to San Francisco."

"Bahhhh," Captain Justin loudly replied. "Eladio is a trusted ally, and you shall in fact be treated royally on this voyage. He has told me some of your tale about leaving Germany. I will be looking forward to hearing your story in its entirety soon." With that, he led Thomas to a spacious cabin with a table, a chair, a bunk, and a chest under the bunk for his belongings. "This will be your home until we get there. Make yourself comfortable. I will send for you when our evening meal is ready. You will be dining with me in my quarters until we reach our destination. We have much to talk of."

Still exhausted, Thomas put his things away, then lay on the bunk. He was soon sound asleep but awakened sometime later for the evening meal in the captain's quarters.

Briefly enjoying the meal and wine, the captain soon excused Thomas, knowing he was in no condition for serious discussion that evening. "We will talk again soon," he said. "Our first port of call, pending good weather, will be in approximately a week at Puntarenas in Costa Rica."

For the next few days, Thomas did nothing but sleep and eat. He was too weak to be of any useful assistance on deck but was steadily gaining weight and strength. Captain Justin and Thomas talked frequently over the next few weeks. Thomas had related his life history as much as he could remember from his family's first days in Denmark and their experiences with the corsairs.

"A brutal and bloody group," Captain Justin commented. "I have had more than one bout with that ruthless bunch."

Captain Justin also divulged most of his life history with Thomas. He shared that he seldom had the opportunity of conversation with anyone with Thomas's background, education, and worldly experiences. Captain Justin had been born and raised in Sweden. His family had a fleet of ships scattered around the world, so he had worked as a cabin boy on his father's ships starting at the age of six but was always accompanied by his private tutor. Then he attended the Catholic University of Ireland in Dublin. After that, serving as second in command on one of his father's merchant ships for a year, then his own command, he had spent several years in the Mediterranean Sea, where he fought many battles against the Barbary pirates, sometimes called the Ottoman corsairs. Eventually tiring of the family business, he severed that tie and came to South America to start his own merchant company serving

South America to California. He went on to conclude he was considering broadening his horizons in the future to include an occasional trip into the Indian Ocean then on to South Africa and Madagascar.

With much conversation, the two men had become good friends. Captain Justin never tired of Thomas's stories of his childhood in Germany or his newfound search for Elizabeth. Thomas also found Captain Justin's adventures much more entertaining, and they chatted the hours, weeks, and months away as they had time, steadily making their way north and west to the fabled city of San Francisco. They made stops not only in Costa Rica but also at two ports in Nicaragua, then on to Honduras and Guatemala. Given the advice of his dear friend Eladio Tribaldos in Panama City, Thomas did not venture ashore at any of these ports. He had rested well, eaten well, and regained most of his weight and strength. He was once again healthy and worked as much as possible, helping where he could on the voyage.

They were now on the long but undisturbed final leg of the voyage and would reach its terminus within approximately two weeks. Thomas was filled with trepidation and much excitement, not knowing what to expect when reaching the city. Captain Justin had shared his extensive knowledge of San Francisco with him, advising as to how to reach the area that Elizabeth would hopefully be staying with her two sisters. He also warned of the dangers of San Francisco's Barbary Coast area and gave Thomas the names and locations of some of his friends he could count on for guidance and help.

Thomas was grateful for all this advice, but his mind still fretted. *Will she be there? Will I find her? It's been so long now. Will she have changed? Of course she will have changed—we've both changed.* The questions went on and on in his mind.

Chapter 51

Pacific Ocean,
Off the Coast of South America

1863

Elizabeth and Anne were very busy during these next few weeks prior to reaching the City of Panama. They were busily making plans to continue their search for Thomas in an orderly manner, with their first stop to be at the Tribaldos Coffee warehouses close by the dock area in Port of Balboa near Panama City, the captain had informed them. Captain Sawyer was very familiar with the area, having docked there many times over the past few years either taking on trade goods or offloading such goods before going on to California.

One day while on deck with the girls and listening to their relentless conversation of what they would do first when landing in Balboa, he said, "Sometime later tonight you should see some lights off our starboard side. We will be rounding the northwest side of Colombia and will be no more than a few days on to Port of Balboa. We are nearly there."

Both girls noticed how haggard and unkempt Captain Sawyer had become. He and the other crew members had taken turns keeping up a guard for other ships. The constant watch had taken its toll on them all.

Three days later in late afternoon, they sailed into Port of Balboa. "We were very lucky," he told them. "We managed to circumvent contact with any other ships over the last few weeks and avoid dangers they may have presented. It will be late when we are finally secured at the dock, but before you start pestering me, I promise *you will be the first ashore with me,*" he hastily added. "I know Eladio of the Tribaldos Coffee Company very well, and we will visit him first."

Elizabeth was shaken with their arrival here. *If we hear of no more news of Thomas here,* she thought, *we may never get more news. It would be highly unlikely I could ever mount or afford an expedition into the jungle near the headwaters of the Chagres River.*

That evening the two sisters had their meal with the captain. He had thoroughly cleaned up with a fresh haircut and shave and his finest suit for this occasion. The mood was somber with hints of joviality as they discussed the possibilities of the next day. Tomorrow as early as possible, they would once again be setting foot on solid ground to resume their questioning of the possible whereabouts of Thomas. This was a much safer port than the one they had last visited in Colón, but the captain still insisted he go with them for at least a short time. He would leave only a skeleton crew aboard ship and give the rest of the crew a three-day pass to enjoy what they may before resuming the last leg on to San Francisco.

Once on shore with the girls, Captain Sawyer started in a specific direction. "Let our first stop be at the coffee company," he announced. "I would like to introduce you to Eladio. I do know him quite well, as I have occasionally stopped here for some of his goods to take on to California."

The three started to walk the few blocks toward the coffee warehouses but were completely overwhelmed with the hustle and bustle of the area. The docks as well as the area surrounding them were jammed with hundreds of people staying in makeshift tents and shelters of all kinds. There were families, miners with equipment, and all types of tradesmen who had traversed the foot trail across the isthmus from Colón to Balboa. They were now stuck here with no ships available for passenger boarding to California in the near future. Many of these people would be forced to wait for months and be charged exorbitant prices for just a seat on the next ship if and when it were to arrive. The conditions were deplorable with few sanitary facilities, little food except what they had managed to drag with them across the isthmus, and very little shelter. Many had perished here waiting for a ship, and the two sisters gave thanks once again to Captain Sawyer for his faith and assistance in helping them this far.

Now offering an elbow to each, he said, "Come, let us depart this unfortunate mass and try for an appointment with Eladio at the Tribaldos Coffee warehouses."

They made their way through the multitudes of people and eventually arrived at the warehouse district without incident. It was so good to have set foot on solid soil, the girls and Captain Sawyer found it rather difficult to walk without swaying side to side. It would take a few days to rid themselves of their sea legs. Elizabeth and Anne were both totally stunned with excitement. They had been months on the ship from Colón on the Atlantic side of Panama to Balboa on the Pacific side.

One or the other would point out a quaint shop here, another there, and nearly forget their purpose, when Elizabeth shrieked, "There is the Tribaldos Coffee Company office. There, on the other side of the street." She broke from Captain Sawyer and Anne, running in the direction of the office, and would have just burst in unannounced if her friends had not caught up with her and insisted she regain her composure to proceed in a more gainly manner.

"Get ahold of yourself, child," the captain stuttered, having never seen Elizabeth behave in quite this manner. "Calm yourself so we may enter and ask of Eladio. Just quiet down so you can speak coherently. Trust me, if there is any word of Thomas here, we will get through this, for better or worse."

With this being said, he opened the warehouse door, and they proceeded to the far side of the building weaving between huge bags filled with coffee beans. Some of the pallets piled high with bags were marked for delivery to coffee merchants in California, and he noticed a smaller pile marked for delivery to a Two Rivers Coffee company in Idaho Territory. *Hmmm*, he thought, *I wonder where that is*. Spotting an employee near a door with a sign overhead stating in bold red letters *OFFICE*, he inquired, "Is Mr. Tribaldos available to have a word with us? Please tell him Captain Sawyer would like to speak with him if he could spare a moment."

Elizabeth could hardly breathe, and she was clutching Anne's hand so tight, it had turned blue at the fingertips. They waited only a few minutes, and Elizabeth was turning very pale.

Chapter 52

Tribaldos Coffee Company,
Port of Balboa, Panama

1863

"**B**reathe, child," the captain warned urgently. "Don't faint on me now."

Elizabeth took a breath and soon regained her glimmering beautiful complexion with somewhat of a smile.

Then Eladio stepped through the door. He immediately saw Captain Sawyer standing there and roared a greeting before putting him into a bear hug that nearly lifted the captain off the floor. "It's been a long time, my old friend. Where have you been? Still chasing rainbows from continent to continent?" Releasing the captain and glancing behind him at his two companions, Eladio saw Elizabeth standing in front of Anne and did a double-take gasping with his mouth open. "Would you be Elizabeth?" he said softly.

They all just stood staring at each other in total bewilderment. How could he know or recognize her? Then they all started to talk at once. It was total pandemonium. Not a word spoken by any made it through the racket or made any sense. Finally Eladio shouted, "Please come up the stairs to my office, and let's sort this out. You are Elizabeth, and we have much to talk about."

Upon the group's arrival at the top floor where the office looked over the harbor, Eladio instructed them to all sit down, and then he started.

"Your family in Germany sent a packet here in care of Thomas Clay. That packet arrived months ago, and I put it away for safekeeping, assuming that Thomas was to arrive shortly after. I had done business with the Clay family years ago and naturally assumed Thomas wanted to pick up that old relationship and perhaps do more business at this time. It was but barely a month ago he arrived here with the wildest story I have ever heard, and he opened the packet that you had sent. In that packet, along with a letter from his mother, a letter from you, and some much-needed funds was a small hand-drawn portrait of you, Elizabeth. One drawn, apparently, from what I could gain, by Thomas's younger sister, Anne, who shares the same name as your sister here, Anne. The portrait bears such striking resemblance and such remarkable detail of yourself, there could be no mistaking it was you, Elizabeth, just standing here in my door."

Hastily continuing before anyone could interrupt, he relayed the tale Thomas had shared with him about leaving Germany for America to seek a suitable place to relocate and also gain information as to exporting tobacco from the colonies back to Germany. "Then he was to have come here to Panama to make my acquaintance and reestablish a coffee-exporting business through me, also back to Germany. It seems as though his ship was blown way off course, floundering for months in the Atlantic, then ultimately wrecked someplace in the Caribbean. Somehow he then managed to make shore south of the Port of Colón. Then over the mountains he went with Caribs in hot pursuit, then into the headwaters of the Chagres River, where he befriended a group of natives that nursed him somewhat back to health. He then floated down the Chagres to Gamboa, where he caught a ride into Panama City and ultimately met up with me!"

He paused, then went on, "But now, how did it come to be that the three of you are here at my door a month after Thomas passed through, and I would assume you are looking for Thomas?"

They all sat in silence for a moment glancing from one to another until Elizabeth began. She was so overwhelmed at first, she could hardly speak. Slowly her story unfolded, and she told Eladio of the preparation for Thomas coming to the Americas. She spared no detail, and Anne or

Captain Sawyer only interrupted when Elizabeth momentarily faltered in relating an emotional highlight in the trip to this point. It had taken nearly eight months to get here to Balboa, Panama.

It was getting late in the afternoon when there was a lull in the conversation. Eladio had already sent a messenger boy to speak with his wife, Alicia, of the arrival of these guests, and she would be expecting them. It was now in one of these lulls that he suggested that they make leave of the office and go to his home for the remainder of the evening to continue on with the discussions and plans for the next leg in the trip in search of Thomas. Captain Sawyer politely declined, as he had responsibilities aboard ship, but he did say he would have the girls' meager belongings brought to the Tribaldos home for their stay that night.

"Rest assured, you will be very comfortable there." Captain Sawyer smiled. "I have in fact stayed there on occasion in my travels, and I'm quite sure you will find it most refreshing after spending the last many months confined to the ship."

Anne and Elizabeth both stood to give the captain a hug and thank him for all of his considerations. Then Elizabeth said, "Please be very careful with my trunk while getting it to Mr. Tribaldos's house. Not that any of my things harbor any value, but I do so cherish the gift Thomas left me with before leaving Germany, the little glass hummingbird. I fear if it were to be broken now, I would also perish." The captain assured her that his men would be instructed to be most careful, and so they parted, the girls going home with Eladio and the captain back to his ship docked not far away.

Working his way back through the crowds in temporary shelters on the docks and surrounding area, he thought, *My God what a pathetic existence this is for the poor people waiting for passage to the American West.* He knew that while many were headed for the goldfields in California, some were hoping for a homestead further inland or another business venture. *If we reach San Francisco in a timely manner with our cargo intact,* he thought, *I will have made a fortune. Enough is enough. I will return here once and give free passage to as many of these poor souls as I can carry back to California—a small token of thanks to my longevity in this dangerous business of crossing the oceans. I'm tired of it. I will gather my most beautiful and patient wife from Boston, and perhaps we will settle someplace in the great American West. Perhaps that Idaho Territory—I bet it's beautiful there.*

Eladio escorted the two exhausted sisters to his home, and they were immediately taken under the protective wing of his wife, Alicia. Their trunks also arrived from the ship at about the same time, undamaged with its contents in order and suffering no damage. The captain had threatened the delivery crew with their lives if anything were to happen to Elizabeth's little glass hummingbird that Thomas had given her so long ago. Alicia ushered the girls into the parlor, all the while delivering orders to the serving staff for preparations of a feast in honor of the two guests.

Chapter 53

Tribaldos Residence, Panama City, Panama

1863

The evening meal would be in several hours, as was the custom of most Latin American families. It was just too hot during the afternoons to eat or do anything requiring much manual effort, so most people whiled away the afternoon in the shade someplace and then got busy again when the sun went down. It was customary to indulge in the evening meal quite late, eating one course after another until all were too stuffed to eat more and too tired to talk anymore.

Alicia sat and chatted with the two girls, listening to the retelling of their experiences over the last year.

"I knew in my heart he was alive—and still is," Elizabeth said.

When the two were too tired to continue further with the tales of their journey, Alicia escorted them to their rooms to freshen up before the evening meal. Anne was shown to one lavishly appointed bedroom with, much to her surprise and delight, a bath with a water closet, a beautiful oval white marble tub with matching washbasin.

"Make yourself comfortable and take advantage of that tub." Alicia laughed. "As you see, I have laid out an outfit of new clean clothes for you. I'm quite sure they will fit. I have a son and two daughters, the daughters being twins. They will be joining us later for dinner. You appear about the size of my daughters, and I'm sure they will not mind loaning you these garments. They have way more than they will ever wear. Their father spoils them shamelessly," Alicia said with a radiant smile.

Putting her arm around Elizabeth, she led her to the next guest room, also as lavish as the one Anne was in. "This is the room your Thomas stayed in a month or so ago," she said. "As you see, I have had the maid lay out a change of clothes for you also. Please, make yourself comfortable and also take advantage of that tub." She smiled again.

Anne started water into the tub and climbed in as soon as she could peel out of her threadbare clothes. She sat down in the tub and let the water fill to nearly overflowing, with just her nose and eyes above the water. *Holy mother of God*, she thought. *I have never enjoyed anything so much as here and now. I have hated every minute of this trip, but this truly makes it worthwhile, and I am starving and ready for a real meal other than the ship's same old salted pork and biscuits.*

Elizabeth collapsed on the bed in total exhaustion, not daring to move for a few minutes. She did not trust herself to even walk the few short steps to the tub. Could it really be true that only a month ago Thomas had bathed in that tub and rested for at least one night on this very bed? Again she was overwhelmed with emotion. *I have to get myself together*, she thought. *Now is not the time to collapse into a melancholy state of lethargy and slow the search for Thomas. We are so close. We still have much to do and a month or more to travel, but I know we are close to Thomas. We will find him. Hopefully he has reached San Francisco and has made contact with Sister Mary there.*

Slowly she got up and started water in the tub, then literally peeled out of her clothes. As she turned to step into the tub of hot water, Elizabeth caught sight of herself in the full-length mirror mounted in an oval oak frame attached to the wall. She hardly recognized the person staring back, even being tall, she hardly weighed a hundred pounds. Taking a long luxurious bath with lavender soap, she thoroughly cleansed herself and slowly sank beneath the water to scrub her mop of tangled hair. She had not had a real private bath for months and was totally enjoying this badly needed one. She soaked in the tub for an hour before climbing out to dress and get ready for the meal she was so looking forward to.

A real meal with real plates and real silverware and fresh clothes and other women to talk with. Not that the captain hadn't been good company, but at times he hadn't, and she laughed to herself about that. She was sitting at the dressing table applying makeup Alicia had left out and putting the final touches to her hair with a comb and French barrettes also left in case of need. And indeed they were needed. It had been a long time since she was really clean, dressed up, and anything resembling her former self before leaving Germany.

A maid knocked at her door to announce dinner was about to be served. Elizabeth stepped out into the hall where she joined Anne to be escorted to the beautiful formal dining room where the other family members were assembling and milling around discussing daily events. The two girls were busy complimenting how wonderful each other looked and talking of the delightful bath and real soap and shampoo and new clean clothes and on and on as they followed the maid into the dining room.

Upon entering the lavishly decorated dining room, Elizabeth stopped dead still, with Anne running into her. Anne stepped around her and gasped in total wonderment and surprise. Neither had ever seen such a lavish setting as they were now standing in. Eladio and Alicia noticing the amazed look on the two sisters' faces and immediately came to their rescue.

"Come," Alicia said softly, taking each girl by the hand and leading them further into the room. "Please allow me to introduce our three children."

They are absolutely beautiful, Elizabeth thought, but she was somewhat taken back by their appearance. They were standing at ease and conversing in perfect English. All three had the typical light-skinned, blue-eyed, blond-haired features of the other Americans that she and Anne had met months ago when first arriving in Boston—they had absolutely no resemblance to their parents. She soon learned the three children's birth parents had been robbed then killed while staying in one of the camps waiting for passage on to California four years ago, and the Tribaldoses took them in and subsequently adopted them.

Alicia now caught the attention of her son. "Please, Richard, step over here. I would like to introduce our guests." Richard, being very accustomed to dinner guests and not the least bit uncomfortable or shy, accompanied his mother and the two girls. "Richard," she continued, "this is Anne Klein. Anne, this is our son, Richard."

Anne was totally enamored with this handsome young man only slightly older than her and was barely able to stammer a hello.

"And this is Anne's sister, Elizabeth."

Seeing her sister's hesitant attitude toward Richard, Elizabeth took a step closer, not being in the least bit intimidated by the charming young man, then curtsied slightly and took both of his hands in hers saying, "We are delighted to make your acquaintance. Your father and mother have told us much of you."

With this introduction completed, Eladio caught the attention of his two daughters, who immediately joined them. "Marie, I would like you and your sister, Linda, to meet Anne and Elizabeth Klein. They have just arrived here from Germany by way of rounding the south tip of South America."

"Oh my," Marie commented, "I think that was indeed a long voyage. We are so happy to meet you both," she continued with a radiant smile, absolutely delighted to have new friends.

Eladio soon had everyone seated, and the food and sangria were plentiful. The conversation was of a variety but mostly a reiteration of what had preceded Anne and Elizabeth's arrival here in Panama City. Elizabeth once again told nearly all of her and Anne's life story and Thomas's attempted trip to the Americas and what was known of his cross-country journey over the mountains from the Caribbean Sea to the Chagres River and then on to Balboa and Panama City. The mood was light, the conversation stimulating, the food and wine impeccable, and the hours late when Elizabeth and Anne excused themselves, as they were both very tired and in severe need of rest. The Tribaldos children guided the two sisters to their respective rooms, wishing them well and agreeing to continue the conversation at breakfast the next morning.

Chapter 54

Pacific Ocean,
Off the Coast of America

1863

A shout interrupted Thomas's thoughts. The lookout in the crow's nest above the sails shouted, "Land sighted on the starboard side of the ship!" It was early morning, and they hoped to dock late afternoon.

Thomas was suddenly filled with a calmness he had not felt for quite some time. He had his confidence back and knew he would find Elizabeth if it was meant to be. He was prepared for whatever lay ahead. Standing at the rail alone, he watched the shoreline approaching rapidly. Captain Justin was strolling from one area on deck to another, yelling orders for a quick and orderly docking.

It was the fall of 1863. There was a chill to the air, but the atmosphere in the dock area was one of excitement. People were swarming the dock in preparation of offloading the goods from the ships. Wagons filled the busy streets, transporting the goods from another ship to the warehouses. Various types of seagoing vessels were either docked and unloading or anchored in the harbor awaiting a berth. There was much activity, shouting, an occasional fight breaking out as a result of, Thomas imagined, short tempers with so much work to do. Thomas stood watching the excitement and turmoil.

The captain had advised him many times on the voyage what to expect on arrival, and it was exactly what he had predicted. Thomas wanted to go ashore immediately. He wanted to locate Captain Justin's friends for assistance in locating the area Elizabeth may be staying if she had arrived here yet.

Soon the captain noticed him pacing the deck and made his way to Thomas's side. "Do you go ashore now, my friend? Or wait for a fresh start in the morning?"

"I cannot wait. You have given me many weeks of instructions and directions. Now I must go ashore. I will locate the contacts you have given me and see some of the city this evening."

"Be very careful," the captain advised his friend. "I should go with you but have much to do here to make ready for the return trip to Panama. Go with God, my friend, and watch for me here again in a few months. Good luck, Thomas."

Thomas had already brought his bag of belongings to the deck. The captain guided him to the loading ramp then waited as Thomas descended to the crowded wharf below.

Thomas walked to the hotel that Captain Justin had recommended, booked a room, then went out to see the sights of the city. Having just arrived from Central America with a pocketful of money, he was in good financial standing. Far better than most he noticed hanging around the wharf, looking for a quick dime. This was indeed a rough area, a rougher crowd.

Happy to be away from the dripping jungle, fever ridden, and stifling with heat and humidity, where he'd battled with the elements on a daily basis just for survival for months, he was now wandering the streets soaking up the lively atmosphere.

Somewhere along the route that night, Thomas happened upon Jason Klaus—a young man he knew from the old country. He too was originally from Denmark and shared the same last name as Thomas before his family had changed it to Clay. Thomas thought perhaps they may be related in some way but only knowing him for such a short time, years ago, he was somewhat hesitant to discuss the matter with him now.

Jason Klaus and Thomas stopped at a few dives for some mugs of beer and a bit to eat. Thomas especially liked Hongkong Bohle's dive, where they had a sandwich and ale. Then they made their way back up the street. Jason took a room at a hotel not far from Thomas before they parted company, agreeing to meet again the following morning.

Chapter 55

Tribaldos Residence, Panama City, Panama

1863

The next morning, breakfast was as lavish as the dinner the previous evening. Captain Sawyer was in attendance, as Eladio had sent his carriage early to the ship to pick him up. Plans were now being made to continue on to California to locate Elizabeth and Anne's older sister, Mary, and her husband, and hopefully Thomas would have made contact with them.

"You know," Eladio said, addressing the two sisters, "when Thomas was here, he left a sizable amount of funds with me from what your family had forwarded here to his attention. Per his instructions, I have invested it in the growing coffee industry and in only one month, that investment has increased considerably. What are your suggestions concerning this investment? Do you need funds to continue on to California? I could easily liquidate that investment should you require me to do so."

Thinking deeply for a few minutes, Elizabeth replied, "No, let's leave it for the future. When we find Thomas, we may need it. Anne and I are okay financially for the immediate future, and we will hopefully find our sister in San Francisco. We can stay with her for a while as necessity may dictate."

It was agreed that they would stay for another two days, giving the girls a bit of a rest and company with the Tribaldoses. Captain Sawyer could also use the time to acquire more goods, primarily coffee, to take on to California. He thought again while going back through the throngs of people clustering around the dock area in the most miserable and unsanitary of conditions, *If we safely complete this trip on to California, I will be a very rich man and do everything possible to improve these horrid conditions. I will have my wife in Boston join me here to help. Then perhaps later we will go on to that fabled Idaho Territory in the great American West to live out our lives.*

On the evening of the second day, he met the girls and the entire Tribaldos family at their warehouse for final goodbyes. They all knew they may never see each other again but still promised to do so as time and circumstances would permit.

Blazes, thought Anne, *I do not want to set foot on that swaying ship ever again. I could stay here and work for Eladio and marry Richard and live happily ever after, if not for Elizabeth and Thomas.*

They then worked their way aboard the ship and made ready to leave on the evening tide.

The next morning, well out to sea and heading in a northwesterly direction, the girls came topside to chat with Captain Sawyer.

"Well"—he laughed—"just like old times, huh?"

Anne threw a not-so-friendly punch at him and missed, laughing. "When this voyage is complete and we set foot in California, I hope never to be forced to get on another ship. At least," she quickly added, "never to be out of sight of land again. Never ever. I hate this mode of travel." Then she paused and tilted her head. "I'm hungry, sir. When do we eat?"

The captain chuckled and led them to his quarters for a perfect breakfast of salted pork and biscuits accompanied by a cup of very good coffee from the Tribaldos plantations.

"Ugh," Anne said, "I will not be able to survive on coffee alone for the next several weeks."

Chapter 56

Pacific Ocean,
Off the Coast of America

1863

When Thomas awakened, he felt the slow, long roll of the sea. He opened his eyes to realize he was chained to a ship's mast with several others, and a brutal booming voice making it known to all that he was First Mate Bully Borger of the *Mary S.* Thomas rolled over, surveying his heavily chained confinement, then cursed himself for a tenderfoot and a dupe to have been shanghaied like any drunken farmer visiting the city. *How did this happen to me?* Thomas thought. *Perhaps no reason in particular. I was just at the wrong place at the wrong time.* He had taken a mug of ale he shouldn't have taken, and it must have been drugged. The sun was at its full height, shining relentlessly in his eyes, and he could feel that he had been severely beaten, not to mention chained.

Knowing the uselessness of resistance at this time, Thomas just leaned against the mast and rested. His newfound friend was lying on the deck beside him, yet to regain consciousness. A few spattering drops of sea sprayed, and he attempted to stand up on the deck, liking the feel of the water on his battered skin. He was able to stand slightly crouched over at the end of the chain. The ship was still at anchor, and beyond its deck the gentle waves slapped against its side, a pleasant sound, despite the circumstances, a sea sound. The salty air, the water lapping, and the ship lazily swaying on the waters of the bay were somewhat of a comfort—if comfort could be had at a time like this.

Thomas thought of yelling to gain someone's attention for his perilous situation, of his kidnapping and of being held prisoner, but he saw the first mate standing with his cat o' nine tails poised and ready to lay the whip to any who made a noise. Thomas could see one poor victim already beaten nearly to death, presumably for trying to sound an alarm, so he kept quiet.

It was late that afternoon when the ship weighed anchor to begin its voyage to the South China Sea, they were all told. Only a few hands were seasoned seamen, and it was total bedlam using the new recruits in getting sails raised, tensioned, and properly tended with First Mate Bully Borger yelling and using the whip on anyone who floundered. All were trying their hardest to do well at a job that was in most cases totally foreign to them. Many of the kidnapped men were human derelicts thrown together from far and near by decoy advertisements circulated by the wily crimps who would collect a one-hundred dollar bonus for every man secured through their sinister methods, regardless of whether he was a sailor, soldier, peddler, doctor, or farmer.

Thomas's newly made friend Jason Klaus was slowly regaining consciousness. Thomas figured Jason must have been unconscious for nearly eighteen hours, so it was good he was slowly coming around, but Thomas feared he would panic when he found himself chained to the mast and make a serious commotion just to get beaten to oblivion again. Thomas sat next to Jason and tried to get his attention when he had finally regained full consciousness. Thomas sat motionless and kept a serious look in his eye to signal to Jason to remain quiet. Jason had enough wits about him to do just that, feeling the chains also binding him.

With darkness approaching, First Mate Bully Borger stomped over to where Thomas and Jason sat leaning against the mast, still in chains. "Well, I see you are both awake and well enough for work. You!" he shouted, pointing at Thomas. Thomas gazed steadily at him. "Yes, you, you black-haired, green-eyed devil. What is your name?"

"It is Thomas Clay," he said, still staring at the first mate.

"Well, Thomas it is, and I want you up that shroud to the crow's nest," he yelled, pointing up to the enclosed basket some seventy feet above the deck. "I want you to replace that derelict heathen up there and shout down everything you observe from that crow's nest, understand?"

Thomas nodded.

"We want to stay as far from all other ships as possible, and we sure don't want to hit any floating debris." Undoing the chain that bound Thomas's hands to the mast, Bully jerked Thomas to his feet and kicked him on the thigh, sending him stumbling toward the shrouds leading up to the crow's nest.

Rage had built up in Thomas from the kidnapping and beating and now the kick that nearly sent him to the deck. He spun to face Bully Borger only to see him with whip raised, ready to fillet him.

"Don't try it unless you want to be fish bait," Borger said. "I can fillet you in seconds, and I assure you it won't be pleasant."

Thomas slowly turned around, taking his rage out in climbing up the shroud. He had done this many times on the *La Bestia Real* crossing from Panama to California, so this was nothing new. *I will have my turn at that monster one day*, he thought.

Laughing, Borger turned to Jason still sitting and chained to the mast. "Your name!" he yelled.

"Jason Klaus."

Borger looked at him, smiling. "Any relation to that black-haired devil up there?" he asked, pointing up at Thomas.

"How would I know? I just met him last night," Jason replied tartly. Borger smiled, raised the whip, and brought it down across Jason's back, ripping the shirt from his body and leaving several horrible slashes across his skin.

Wincing, Jason smiled up at him. "Is that the best you can do?" he said and received another smashing blow from the first mate's whip.

Borger glared down at him then laughed. "Anything more you want to say?" he asked in a conversational tone.

Jason glared at him with teeth clenched. Thomas had witnessed the beating from far above and started down.

Looking over his shoulder, Borger noticed Thomas's hasty descent and yelled, "Back up with ya or you will get the same thing when you get down."

Thomas paused but a moment, seeing the futility of his actions, then turned to climb back up, hoping Jason was not severely injured.

Turning once again toward Jason, smiling with broken and black teeth, Borger asked, "Anything else you want to say?"

Jason just glowered, knowing another word would probably get him killed, and he wanted to survive and feed this barbaric brutal man to the sharks. Borger continued to glare down at him for a minute then carefully bent and unfastened the chain that was securing Jason to the mast. Noting Jason's scowling contempt, he replied, "Try something, sonny. I would love to lay this whip to you again."

They both stood, Jason sick from the foul substance added to his mug of ale the night before, rendering him unconscious, and now the beating with the whip and Bully Borger just smiling, ready to strike again.

Thomas, seeing the events unfold from high above, shouted down, "Not now, Jason. We will have our time another day."

"If I were you," Borger said to Jason, "I would listen to your overly optimistic friend up there. Nothing would suit me more right now than to beat you and throw ya overboard—and him too," he said, pointing up at Thomas. "Probably save me a lot of trouble with you two in the future if I were to do just that," he muttered. "Now, boy," he yelled at Jason, who was standing and trying not to collapse from abuse. "I want you over there with that bucket. Start scrubbing this filthy deck. You two and the rest of the crew brought aboard with you last night have made a frightful stinking mess on this deck, and the captain wants it cleaned up. Now!" he screamed, and Jason stumbled over to the bucket, lowering it over the rail with a rope to let it splash in the water below then hauling it up again onto the deck to start scrubbing. "Get used to it!" Borger yelled at him. "That is what you are gonna do from now on. Or at least until we get to the South China Sea."

Jason stared in disbelief. *The South China Sea?* he thought. *That's halfway around the world.*

Chapter 57

Pacific Ocean,
Off the Coast of Central America

1863

So on the ship and the captain and the Klein sisters went, day after day, week after week, with the monotonous regularity of the never-changing view of only the deep, cobalt-blue ocean and its occasional curling white caps warning of an approaching storm. Captain Sawyer knew they were having extraordinary luck with weather—no severe storms, good and steady wind, and only an occasional sighting of another distant ship. It was only about a three-thousand-mile route plus or minus a few hundred miles, depending on currents and fickle directional winds, so it shouldn't have taken more than about one month.

That month had passed, but the presence of birds gave warning of the proximity of land. They were species that neither Elizabeth nor Anne had ever seen before, but the captain assured them they were of a type that did not range far from land. They would soon be in California's fabled city of San Francisco.

The sea was changing in color, taking on a slight yellowish hue from period to period. When the girls asked about this, Captain Sawyer explained, "The rains of the great storms that have preceded us have discharged their muddy flood waters into the sea. We are very close to land now."

It was early morning on a fall Sunday when the watch called out, "Land in sight!"

The girls heard this announcement and immediately dressed to join the captain on deck. On the horizon on the starboard side of the ship, they could now see the faintest outline of the California coast. They had been traveling most of 1863 in their quest to find Thomas. Elizabeth and Anne stood in awe staring at the slowly approaching land mass that would ultimately determine their final route into San Francisco harbor. They had pestered the captain for so long with so many questions and now were totally speechless, each in her own private world wondering what would come next. What would become of them if they could not locate their sister in San Francisco? They had planned for months for this day in the event their journey eventually led them to California. All of the plans now seemed vague and pointless.

The definition of the approaching land mass was becoming un-fathomable in size and was extremally thought-provoking to Elizabeth. *Exactly what are we going to do first?* she thought. *Can we even locate Mary's home let alone Thomas, who may be God only knows where by now? Maybe he found Mary's home and left some word. Maybe someone at the port remembers him. Maybe, maybe, maybe,* she thought. She was trembling now, partially because of the slight cool breeze blowing across the ship's deck but mostly in apprehension. This was a rare time she considered any doubt of ever locating Thomas.

Captain Sawyer noticed the girls standing by the rail and approached them, smiling radiantly. Then noticing the panic on Elizabeth's face and her visible shaking, he gently squeezed her arm. "This is not the time for doubt or major work, lass. You have been through hell—so to speak—over the last year, and now it is your time to shine."

"I know we have discussed our disembarkment with you many times in the last month," she managed in a very shaky voice, "but I am scared, scared to death."

"Everything will be fine—wait and see. We do have a plan, you know. We have discussed it many times before. I will not be able to escort you ashore on our arrival in a few hours. My presence will be required here aboard ship with the pesky custom officials and the other responsibilities required in offloading our considerable amount of goods. I do, however, as I have promised you many times before, have our charming young man Timothy, who is very familiar with not only the dock area of San Francisco but the city and its surrounding area as well. As you well know by now from the stories the crew of this ship has shared with you over the last several months, Timothy is also quite handy with a pistol and a blade, which of course will be at his side at all times. Once reaching the docks and unloading our goods, I will remain there for the required time it takes to find your sister's home. You will return here to your cabins on the ship each night as necessity dictates until you have accomplished what you must here," he said again smiling. "You will see—this will work out. Now let me prepare for our arrival with no more distractions."

"That's not going to happen," Anne chirped. She did not share Elizabeth's concerns and would readily jump ship and swim to shore to once again get her feet on solid ground. It was now becoming another new adventure, and she felt ready for it. "What is that gap in those mountains we seem to be headed for?" she inquired.

"It's the Golden Gate." Captain Sawyer good-naturedly frowned. "Now no more questions for at least the length of time it takes to get there. I have much to do."

"What is the Golden Gate?" Anne again hastily inquired before he could get away.

With his hands on his hips and staring at her not pleasantly, he said, "The Golden Gate is a strait on the west coast of North America that connects San Francisco Bay to the Pacific Ocean."

"Will it be as dangerous as the Strait of Magellan?"

"*No.* Now may I get to work?"

"Of course, Captain. It's your ship. Do as you must."

As good natured as he usually was, Anne still had a way of rankling his wits. Turning and stalking away before she could get another word out, he immediately started snapping orders to the crew to assure safe passage through the strait into San Francisco harbor.

Chapter 58

San Francisco Bay,
California, United States

1863

The closer they got to the harbor area and the distant city, the more hesitant Elizabeth became. *Lord have mercy*, she thought. *How are we to find anything in that mass?*

The harbor was overflowing with shipping traffic, and Captain Sawyer had to navigate slowly and carefully, often dropping anchor for short periods of time to avoid a collision with another ship. At one of these short intervals, he told the girls, "It's too crowded to make dock this day. We will have to spend one more night here on board in the bay then try for a mooring on one of the docks tomorrow."

Elizabeth heaved a sigh of relief—she was not ready yet to go ashore—and Anne pouted. The captain laughed at the both of them.

This last night on board the ship was one that would be remembered forever by the sisters and Captain Sawyer. Earlier in the day when it was apparent they would not be able to reach one of the docks, he had sent Timothy and another crew member ahead in one of the small lifeboats to purchase some fresh food for what may be Elizabeth and Anne's last night aboard ship. They had been instructed to bring back the finest and freshest produce, crab, lobster, abalone, oranges, and whatever else may be available for that evening's meal. Not only did they get the goods the captain had ordered, but Timothy had also hastily visited several of his old haunts inquiring of the possible whereabouts of the girls' older sister, Mary, and her husband, Edward, promising to return sometime the next day to check on the results of his inquiries. Timothy and company returned with so many fresh goods, they nearly capsized their small boat, and the ship's cook soon went to work preparing for this meal.

They were positioned in the harbor to take full advantage of the splendid view offered by the sun setting over the city and the twinkling lights that soon started to show. The captain had tables set on the deck, and all hands on board were invited to join him and the Klein sisters, as they had come to be known, for this evening meal. Timothy had done a superb job in collecting nothing but the freshest of items available in the market area on the docks. The meal would have been impressive even to a king and queen. The event was not an unusual one for the crew, as the captain had done this very thing on various occasions before when reaching a distant port after a long voyage. He treated the crew fairly, and they in turn returned more than a fair day's work.

The crew members enjoying this meal all took turns in last-minute questions to Elizabeth and Anne about their plans now that they had potentially reached their destination. The conversation was casual, and the sisters truly enjoyed their company. Timothy was relating his shopping experiences for that afternoon with some embellishment. He jokingly told of his traumatic time in warding off the aggressive vendors and the painful search for nothing but the finest and freshest produce, including the huge avocados, pomegranates, and other fine fresh citrus fruits.

"Oh brother," Elizabeth finally voiced after this long but enjoyable tale. "We are in California, you know. And I have read these things all grow wild here just ripening and ready for the taking."

Timothy had succeeded in entertaining the group, if for no more than just a few minutes. The entire group was laughing and enjoying the occasion.

The captain now stood holding his wine goblet high. "A toast to the two most lovely young ladies in the realm and to their successful efforts in locating this Thomas that Elizabeth seems so fond of."

She had grown accustomed to his occasional chiding of Thomas and laughed with the rest.

"On a more serious note," Timothy said, "I have put out some feelers while ashore for the whereabouts of Elizabeth's sister and her husband. They seem to be well-known here in San Francisco. It seems they have accomplished a tremendous degree of success in the goldfields to the northwest of the city during the last few months. I am hoping for current news of them when we reach port tomorrow morning."

The sisters were undeniably delighted with this news and all the other news that Timothy related. This social lingered on until quite late in the evening. Elizabeth once again regaining her composure and now ready for whatever the morrow would bring. Finally tired and nearly bursting from the effects of all the food eaten and wine consumed, they excused themselves and made way to their cabins below deck, wishing all the best in case they were never to be seen again. Not knowing what the next day would bring, they packed nothing, anticipating at least a few more nights on board the ship after spending the days ashore searching for Mary and Edward and of course Thomas.

Elizabeth was now over the melancholy mood and once again ready to face the next day with hope. Sitting alone in her lonely little cabin, she opened her sea trunk and tentatively took out the small, well-packed glass hummingbird Thomas had given her so long ago. Holding it now gently in her hands, she said a prayer asking for strength to face the days ahead, then rewrapped it, placing it back in a secure spot in the trunk.

Chapter 59

San Francisco,
California, United States

1863

It was a very foggy and misty morning. The dock area—hardly more than a hundred feet away from the ship, with the shoreline perhaps a bit farther—was hardly visible from the deck. There were people milling around below, but none had a defining characteristic. The two girls had dressed more like guys than girls, hoping to attract less attention and knowing it would be far more comfortable roving around the city with Timothy dressed in this manor than in their usual feminine attire. They did somewhat resemble swishy guys at first glance, but under close examination with their shapely lines, there would be no mistaking they definitely could be nothing other than beautifully disguised women.

Timothy and the Klein sisters walked down the steep gangplank leading from the ship to the dock. "Take special care," he told them. "This fog is like pea soup, and we could easily become separated." Tim stepped foot on to the dock, first noticing a few people very close to where the gangplank touched the dock. Stopping, he turned his back to the small group standing close by and waited, holding his hand up to help the sisters with the last step onto the dock, Elizabeth first, then Anne. Elizabeth turned toward the less congested side of the dock, taking only a step, leaving slightly more than two paces between her and her sister.

A figure suddenly appeared in front of Anne, and she screamed "Elizabeth!" For a moment, it was frantic pandemonium. Elizabeth turned rapidly, and Timothy grabbed the two figures close by that seemed to be embracing Anne. Then Elizabeth screamed again—this time with joy. Tim was at a total loss.

The two embracing Anne were her sister Mary and brother-in-law Edward. They had received a message late the night before due to Timothy's inquiries as to the possible location of their living quarters and had come immediately to the dock area locating the ship. They had been waiting for hours in the dark on the dock, anticipating the gangplank to be lowered and hoping to make immediate contact with this ship's captain to learn the whereabouts of Elizabeth and Anne, if in fact they were here.

It had been nearly two years since Mary and Edward had left Germany for the great American frontier and the goldfields of California. They had left shortly after the girls' mother had sadly passed, nearly a year before Elizabeth and Anne's departure in search of Thomas. The reunion here was totally incomprehensible. Edward had just returned home after a lengthy time at their mine and was planning to leave again that very morning, had they not received word last night that the two sisters were possibly there and looking for them.

The fog had started to lift, and the sun was almost able to peek its way through the damp haze. They were all still standing there at the bottom of the gangplank while everyone was firing away questions and answers when Captain Sawyer, looking over the ship's rail noticed them there on the dock speaking loudly, waving their arms wildly, and still embracing one another. He came running down to add more to the confusion. It took only minutes to unravel this scene, and Captain Sawyer then invited them all back on board to a more comfortable location to continue their conversation. Soon leaving them in his quarters, he returned to the ship chores of offloading the cargo, which would take nearly two days.

The sisters had so much to discuss. Mary told them of their humble little cottage in Hayes Valley only about two hours away and couldn't wait for them to come and stay. Elizabeth informed them of the disappearance of Thomas and of what they had learned of his journey here to California. This immediately brought on a more serious mood. Mary and Edward listened carefully now to every word of this incredible tale. They had only known Thomas briefly before leaving Germany but were quite fond of him. Finally Edward interrupted and insisted they all gather their things and return to their home in Hayes Valley. The packing of the two sisters' belongings took but a short time, and Edward had returned to the stables not far away to bring the team and carriage to the gangplank.

With all the turmoil, the group had forgotten about Timothy and now found him assisting in the removal of the enormous amounts of cargo being slung over the side of the ship by the dockside cranes. Taking only a short reprieve from his duties, he assured them he would join them for a supper before leaving port again. They thanked him copiously, for without his assistance, they may have never found Mary and Edward.

They next found the captain in the midst of the proceedings shouting orders, waving his arms, pointing his finger and using the language only a sailor knows best. Elizabeth and Anne had become somewhat accustomed to this behavior over the last year and found it quite amusing but not at all flattering. Now noticing the group, Captain Sawyer dropped from his perch on the rail of the ship, and he also agreed to join them along with Timothy for supper one last time before leaving harbor, knowing full well they would never cross paths again. He had become quite attached to the two Klein sisters and would miss them terribly. After this trip with them for the last several months, he knew his life would never be the same. Fate had a very fickle way of twisting one's future from what one felt was a given factor to something totally the opposite.

Edward had returned with the carriage and, with Timothy's assistance once again, they carried Elizabeth's and Anne's trunks down to the waiting carriage. Edward assisted the three women into the wagon, Mary dressed in the latest San Francisco fashion and the other two still in their masculine attire but quite happy with this for the moment. Edward clucked at the horses, lightly slapping the reins against their rumps, and started the short journey home. They wound their way through the busy, dirty, and congested streets in the dock area, and in a short time they were in the less inhabited and far more rural countryside.

Anne dominated the conversation, and the others laughed and humored her. Over the next hour, though, the conversation returned to Thomas and what they must do next. He had never made his presence in San Francisco known to Mary and Edward, but Elizabeth was quite certain he had made his way here. Eladio had told them he'd personally put Thomas on the *Bestia Real* with Captain Justin Klaus in Panama, and no one had any reason to believe the ship had failed to reach this destination here in San Francisco.

It was late in the afternoon when they reached Hayes Valley and Mary and Edward's quaint little cottage, as they referred to it. Quaint it was, but a little cottage it was not. Sitting in front of the residence, Elizabeth gasped in astonishment. It was in fact a beautiful three-bedroom home on two levels. It was of the Victorian style separated from the stable by a white picket fence. The lawn was manicured and smooth as a billiard table with beautiful flowering shrubs and a small garden on the opposite side of the stable. The creek running by the edge of the property had been partially diverted to water the horse pasture. Anne stared in amazement at the beautiful surroundings with the horses grazing peacefully in the pasture.

"I see horses," she said with a questioning look, "but where are the cows, chickens, and pigs?"

Mary chuckled. "We grew up with chickens, pigs, and cows, and I hope to never touch another udder, gather another nasty egg, or slop another pig. We have vendors close by supplying us with milk already in a bottle, eggs already in a bag, and a variety of choice cuts of pork."

Ugh, Anne thought, *and I hope to never see another piece of pork.*

"Edward has done very well at our little mine, and we can afford these small luxuries. Come now, let's all go inside and make ourselves comfortable." Mary guided her two sisters into the house, all three babbling on of this and that. They had so much to talk about. Then, showing them up to their rooms to freshen up, she went back downstairs to help Edward with their luggage.

Elizabeth watched out the upstairs window and waved down to catch Edward's attention. "Please handle that blue trunk with extra care—it has my hummingbird in it."

Hmm, he thought, *makes sense to me. A hummingbird in your suitcase.* Then he gently carried it up the stairs to her room.

Elizabeth made no attempt to explain the bird in the suitcase now. She had been nearly a year onboard a heaving, rolling ship with very little privacy except for a few days in Boston, then months later a few days in Panama. She adored Captain Sawyer and his crew and would be forever grateful for his kindness, but she did miss other female companionship. Anne had been a great sport, but it had been only her, and there had been only so much they could talk about.

Mary and Edward brought in fresh vegetables from the garden and some lingering fruit from the small orchard and prepared a hearty but light meal. Even though it was late fall, it was still sunny California, and many crops were still flourishing. With all sitting around the table, the talk soon returned to Thomas.

Elizabeth commented that Timothy, still in harbor on the ship, could spend the next two days helping them look for Thomas before he would be required with the rest of the crew to return to Panama. The captain had sworn to make at least one more trip and pick up as many passengers as possible from the deplorable conditions they faced on the crowded docks in Balboa. He was now a very wealthy man and would charge not one person he could pack onto his ship for the return trip to California.

It was Edward who finally interrupted the conversation. "I think I have a plan," he interjected. "Mary and I are very familiar with the city and the surrounding area. Let us all go to the dock early tomorrow morning. There we will meet up with Timothy. He can escort you two in one direction, keeping you out of trouble I hope, and Mary and I shall go the other. Before dark we will meet up back at the ship to compare notes."

The plan was agreeable, and Elizabeth and Anne went to their rooms.

Still sitting at the table, Edward looked deeply into Mary's eyes with a concerned stare. "We have to find him," he said. "It very well could be Elizabeth's ruin should we fail."

Chapter 60

San Francisco, California, United States

1863

The next morning was only slightly overcast when they returned to the dock and hailed Timothy, who must have been expecting them. He was leaning on the rail above and immediately waved before climbing down the rope ladder. The gangplank had been removed for the night and had not yet been placed back into position for the continuing process of offloading cargo from the ship's hold.

Edward soon explained their search plan for the Bay Area and the city.

"A good plan," Tim agreed, and he started off with Elizabeth and Anne in a direction that led to dockside pubs, inns, and hotels.

"Perhaps Thomas stopped at one of these soon after leaving Captain Justin on the *Bestia Real*," he advised the sisters. "I know the first thing I would do would be to look for a pub with some cold ale."

They searched diligently for hours, weaving their way through the masses of people doing business in the area. Timothy was not but a few feet from the two sisters but did not appear to be with them. He was casually observing their progress but diligently watching out for them. He thought they'd have better success in questioning the mostly male populace without his immediate influence. Everyone wanted to help a beautiful young lady in distress, and they continued on leaving no stone unturned. The girls questioned every street vendor, giving a detailed description of Thomas. They questioned the pub owners, employees, and patrons of every business in the area but had no luck.

Anne wanted to find some news of Thomas as badly as Elizabeth, but she was tired. "I have an idea," she said, smiling sweetly at Elizabeth. "Why don't we question the brothel owners?"

"There is no humor in that remark! My Thomas would never visit one of those houses," Elizabeth snapped. "If you were not my darling little sister, I would throw you in the bay." Then realizing Anne was only trying to relieve the tension, they both chuckled.

Both tired but not discouraged—this was only their first day— they stopped at Hongkong Bohle's dive. It was no better nor worse in appearance and atmosphere than most of the other places they had already visited, but they were soon to learn it was a very danger-ous establishment. They sat at a street-side table, with Tim joining them, when a gangly waitress with a tattered apron ambled out to take their order.

Timothy ordered a beef sandwich and a mug of ale. The two girls surveyed the skinny waitress with a not-so-neat, mop-appearing hairdo, badly stained apron, and bare feet and hastily reconsidered their decision for a meal. Anne was tired and sat next to Tim as he ate the sandwich and drank the contents of the mug, neither being very appealing. Elizabeth wandered a short distance from the two and was talking to a street vendor selling shrimp—something she was not at all familiar with but found very interesting. She was warily giving a complete description of her handsome Thomas to the sleepy-eyed vendor, who was paying little attention, only nodding occasionally and waiting on other customers while pretending to listen to Elizabeth.

"He is well over six feet tall with long wavy coal-black hair, broad in the shoulders, well-educated, and the greenest eyes," she was saying.

The waitress who had just waited on Timothy and Anne overheard and perked up an ear at the description. She raised her voice to get Elizabeth's attention. "Did he pass through here about a month ago?"

"Yes, yes, yes, he did," cried Elizabeth.

The gawky waitress went on, "He was a big handsome beast, he was. Tall, broad-shouldered, and the most beautiful smile I have ever seen. He was a nice lad and tipped well."

Anne and Timothy had both heard the exchange of words and were soon surrounding her.

"Whoo, hold on," she stammered with all three of them firing questions at the same time. "Please if you must, but only one at a time. I have only one mouth and can only answer one question at a time."

Raising her hand to silence Anne and Timothy, Elizabeth said, "The big handsome beast was my husband-to-be."

"You lucky thing," the waitress sighed and then smiled. "What can I tell ya?"

"Did you really see him?" Elizabeth begged.

"Of course I saw him—how could a girl miss someone like that? He was very tall, broad-shouldered, and had, as you have described, the greenest eyes and blackest wavy hair a girl could wish for. I think he had just got off a ship fresh in from Panama. Had a German accent, he did, and was quite a polite gentleman. I knew that Captain Justin he sailed with too, although he would never pay me the time of day. Your young man…I think I heard him telling another gentleman he was with that he had been shipwrecked in the Caribbean and somehow wound up here sometime later in this lovely city of San Francisco."

Elizabeth could not believe her eyes or ears. This wayward, gangly waitress had suddenly become the most beautiful woman in the world. The questions went on, and she finally said, "I have to get back to work. The boss is staring at us and may fire me and throw you all to the dogs."

"Wait," Elizabeth cried. "When do you get off work?"

"About midnight," she replied with a tired sigh.

"Will you meet us then? I will make it well worth your time. What is your name?"

"My name is Lolivey," she said hastily. "Now begone with you, and I promise to meet you later, out front but not in sight of this place. The boss is a hateful person and would not hesitate to have us all thrown to the curs roaming the streets just for the fun of it." Hastily she turned and scurried back into the alehouse, looking back over her shoulder at them only once.

"Who were those people you were just talking to?" the proprietor snapped.

"Only a couple of tourists," she said, "off one of the ships in the harbor."

"They looked very well off to me," he grunted and looked out again to see if they were still around.

Lolivey thought, *I hope they are gone and do not come back tonight. It is dangerous here during the day, and the night is much worse. But if they do return, I will meet them and again tell them what little I know.* She started wiping the bar down. *They do seem to be nice people for a change, and that Thomas was quite a delightful young man,* she again thought wistfully.

After their brief but informative conversation with the waitress, Elizabeth and Anne quickly returned to the ship, with Timothy struggling to keep up. *A lot of help I would have been in an emergency,* he thought, *I can't even keep up with these two, let alone keep them out of trouble.*

Reaching the gangplank leading up to the ship's deck, they climbed up and found Captain Sawyer in his quarters poring over receipts and other paperwork.

"And what brings you two aboard again so soon?" he said smiling. "I thought I was rid of you for at least a couple of days.

"We have found someone who knew of Thomas. She is a waitress at what they call Hongkong Bohle's dive about an hour down the street from here."

"What in God's name were you doing there?" Captain Sawyer replied. "Half the people that frequent that place are never seen or heard of again. Where is that Timothy? He should never have allowed you into that neighborhood. I will have his hide."

"Oh but he did escort us there," Elizabeth replied haughtily. "And we did gain news of Thomas, and we were never in any danger. He was there hardly more than a month ago."

Before Captain Sawyer could say more, Elizabeth went on, "Mary and Edward are to meet us here before it gets dark. They went one way this morning, and we went the opposite, agreeing to meet up here. We have made arrangements to meet that waitress, Lolivey, when she gets off work about midnight."

The captain just sat there staring at the two, knowing further reprimand or argument would be futile. "All right," he said, "when the others get here and we all have had a bite to eat, I will send a heavily armed escort of my best men back with you to meet with that waitress again if you think it will do any good."

"Thank you. Thank you so much," Elizabeth said.

The two girls returned to the deck and were hanging over the edge anxiously awaiting Edward and Mary's return. It was now getting dark, and they were becoming alarmed. *Where are they?* Elizabeth thought. *Please don't let anything have happened to them. We are so close to Thomas now.* She was pacing the deck when her sister and brother-in-law came wearily aboard looking totally disappointed.

"Sorry, Elizabeth," Edward said. "We have turned over every leaf and talked to so many vendors, dock workers, and all types of other people in the area and have no positive news to report."

Elizabeth then informed them of the chance meeting with the waitress at Hongkong Bohle's and the subsequent conversation about Thomas, and their plan to return again later that night to talk with the waitress Lolivey.

Edward stared at her with a weary expression. "That's a bad place," he said. "You two charming young ladies were lucky to get away from there alive and unharmed. Here on the West Coast of this relative new world of America, there are never enough willing and able-bodied volunteers available to man the requirements of the endless fleets of ships coming to the area. A great number of the African and even some European ships are resorting to a more straightforward method of recruitment that does not depend on volunteers—namely kidnapping men to serve as sailors by coercive techniques such as trickery, intimidation, and violence. Those engaged in this form of kidnapping are known as crimps, and the practice is most commonly referred to as shanghaiing. It is a booming business here. One of the favorite hangouts is commonly reported to be Hongkong Bohle's of San Francisco. Apparently," he continued, "the crimps look for vagrants, plucking them out of taverns and boarding houses or off the streets. They are usually rendered helpless by the tavern keeper drugging their drinks or just whacking them on the head in the shadows. The term *shanghaiing* came about probably because Shanghai was a popular destination of the ships with abducted crews. It's not only that place that supplies the crimps with men for unwilling crews on ships but also the brothels with young women."

Elizabeth had heard of the shanghai business, a practice as old as the age of sail, and suddenly she felt as though ice water were running through her veins. She refused to consider that this may have happened to her Thomas.

"It will be extremely dangerous to return there in the dark," Edward continued.

"Captain Sawyer is sending a heavily armed escort with us," she said. "I must get further news—if there is any more—and this woman, the waitress, knew him, Edward. We have to return."

"And we shall," he replied with a look of apprehension. "If we have some of the captain's men, we should be reasonably safe."

Captain Sawyer had just come topside and overheard the conversation. "And I shall be accompanying them also," he commented. "We will be leaving soon after we have had our evening meal. Come, let us eat so we can get on with this. We do not want to miss this waitress."

Captain Sawyer had instructed six of his most trusted men to arm themselves with a rifle and pistol each from the arms locker below deck while the rest of the party was eating. They had done so and were now waiting at the head of the gangplank for the captain and the tiny group to finish. The captain stood and walked to his waiting group.

"I would like two of you in front of us," he said, "one on each side, and two behind. I will also be armed, and I know Edward is also carrying a pistol in a shoulder holster. Likewise Timothy is well-armed and will be wandering about detached from this group but within easy hailing distance should he notice anything alarming or we are in need of his services. We are now ready to head back to that ugly part of town the tavern is located in. Now let's make way."

The captain's group was a forbidding pack to cast an eye on as they made their way with no difficulties and hopefully another meeting with Lolivey. They all stopped a block away so as not to alert the patrons of the tavern, not knowing who were patrons and who were employees ready to grab any unsuspecting soul.

Timothy, true to character, strolled up to the tavern casually looking around, then went inside and sat himself at the bar to order a mug of ale. He soon caught Lolivey's eye, and she nearly dropped her tray of dirty mugs.

Slowing her pace as she walked past, she said, "Watch the drink. May have knockout drops. I will meet you as soon as possible around the far corner."

Nodding, he gripped the mug as if to take a drink then casually placed it between his knees and dumped the contents on the sawdust floor. *This is the oldest trick in the book*, he thought, *knockout drops in your drink then staggering out nearly unconscious to be whacked on the head and thrown onto an outbound ship that was short of help.* Timothy shivered. *I nearly drank that. It may have been okay but probably not, and I already have a job, don't need to be on another ship working for free with an enormous headache.* In a few minutes he got up and pretended to stumble and slightly stagger his way out of the foul-smelling and smoke-filled dive but keeping as safe a distance as possible from a rowdy group of men. Reaching the door, he then turned immediately left, running hard, and made his way out and across the lamplit street then into the shadows of an alley. Watching for any sign of pursuit, he waited but saw not a shadow of immediate danger.

Noticing the captain's group somewhat scattered and also watching from about a block away, Timothy casually removed his seaman's cap as if to wipe sweat from his forehead, then placed it back on his head. The captain did the same to acknowledge the signal. Now it was just a waiting game.

Chapter 61

Hongkong Bohle's,
San Francisco, California, United States

1863

Hongkong Bohle had in fact noticed Timothy's presence in the pub. *A very strong looking and healthy young man*, he thought. *He will bring a pretty penny to one of the more unsavory ship captains waiting shorthanded in the bay*, he supposed and had ordered for Timothy's mug of ale to be drugged.

Outside the door, in the shadows of the adjoining brothel, three huge unwashed thugs had been waiting for Timothy's exit. His speedy turn just out the door and dash across the street into the shadows saved him—the thugs barely missed snatching him so remained in their place of concealment to wait for the next victim.

Lolivey nervously finished her shift in the pub an hour later than usual. She had no way of knowing what may have happened to Tim or if Elizabeth could even get here to this loathsome place unmolested and alive. Walking out the door, she noticed the three thugs still standing in the shadows but was not particularly alarmed by their presence. They had been a permanent fixture concealed there just waiting for victims to kidnap. They had been there for as long as she had been working here in this terrible place. As long as she was staff, she reasoned she was safe from the kidnappers, as her presence was needed in this dive and Hongkong Bohle would presumably leave her alone as long as she worked there. She hated it, though. *I am sick of this place, this life, and this festering city*, she thought, *but were else could I go?*

Turning her head to cautiously survey the surrounding area, she noticed movement in the shadows of an alley behind the streetlight to her left. Hesitantly, she walked in that direction, knowing full well the thugs by the pub door would be watching her. She would do nothing out of the ordinary—she did not want Hongkong Bohle to be alerted as to any suspicious behavior on her part. Although he may have some use for her at the pub, he would not hesitate to have her thrown into the bay if she crossed him. Walking slowly down the street and trying to avoid other foot traffic, she continued toward the tiny one-room flat she was living in, passing the shadowed concealment of Captain Sawyer and his group as she did so. She whispered, "I will wait for you behind that old rundown building there to my right," and slowly passed on to the rendezvous point.

Moments after she passed, they all slipped through the shadows to join her. Captain Sawyer instantly had his crew around her, and Elizabeth held out her hand in greeting. They did not want to frighten the poor girl but neither did they want any harm to come to her as a result of their presence. This was a precarious meeting place for all, and the captain soon made the suggestion that they return to the safe confines of the ship to continue the conversation with the waitress Lolivey. The group in its entirety was soon aboard the safety of the ship.

Mercy, Lolivey thought after being ushered through the heavily populated streets surrounded by the ship's crew and Elizabeth then onto this ship, *what have I got myself into now?* She knew with Hongkong Bohle, if she came to work, toiled extra hours for nothing, and kept quiet, she would mostly be left alone. With this group, she knew nothing. They could all be crooks, thieves, or also part of the slave traders that inhabited the area along the wharf. She had immediately been at ease with Elizabeth earlier on the street in front of the pub. *But what do I know?* she thought. *If I always made it a practice to make good decisions, I wouldn't be in this quandary now.*

Chapter 62

San Francisco Bay,
California, United States

1863

The captain dismissed the crew who had accompanied them to retrieve Lolivey, leaving only Elizabeth and Anne still here in the captain's quarters. Mary and Edward were returning home, as it was now quite late and soon would be breaking dawn, and the captain had insisted the girls spend the night on board once again in their old rooms after they had a chance to talk more with Lolivey.

Lolivey had been standing off to one side of the room like a mouse in the corner trying not to draw any attention to herself. Elizabeth had stayed close to her during the walk back to the ship, trying relieve some of her obvious apprehension, but she could see the waitress was now getting very nervous here thinking she had been a fool. Lolivey thought, *This ship may just leave port with me aboard to a fate unknown, but could it be any worse than my miserable existence back at the pub? Probably not.*

Elizabeth now devoted all of her attention to Lolivey with a smile that seemed to help melt away her uneasiness. "Please sit." Elizabeth gestured toward one of the chairs at the small table. "Can we get you anything to eat or drink? This has been a most stressful evening, and you must be exhausted and hungry." Elizabeth was still smiling with a radiance that was slowly dissolving Lolivey's fears.

The girl replied, "I am hungry and would like just a bit to eat, and the whole bottle of wine, should you have one. At the pub I get very little to eat or drink, and I am still quite nervous as to your intentions for me. I simply agreed to speak with you in the alley on the wharf, and here I am aboard a ship in the harbor bound for where, I know not. Not only am I hungry and thirsty, I'm also quite frightened."

Realizing the situation she had put this girl in, Elizabeth sat down beside her and took her hands in her own. "I am so sorry. We only want all the information you may have concerning the whereabouts of Thomas Clay, whom you have claimed to have noticed in front of your pub about a month ago. And we will pay you for your time here." Elizabeth then started with a barrage of questions until the girl held up one of her hands.

"Please, I am most hungry and thirsty, and it is almost daylight."

In her haste, Elizabeth had forgotten to have Anne get them all something to snack on and a bottle of the captain's wine. While Anne was preparing a sandwich, Elizabeth searched the wine cabinet and took out one of the finest bottles it sheltered. As *long as I am just borrowing this*, she thought, *it may as well be the best bottle in the cabinet*. Lolivey inhaled the sandwich and was looking at Anne for a replacement, and she almost immediately got one. While Lolivey was eating the second, Elizabeth started again talking, this time starting at the very beginning of her relationship with Thomas, the apparent difficulties he had faced in getting here to San Francisco, then her and Anne's wearisome voyage in getting here also.

Lolivey listened attentively, slowly eating her third sandwich and drinking the wine from the bottle, ignoring the goblet they had sat out for her. By now she was at complete ease with this situation and most willing to cooperate.

"What can you tell us of my Thomas?" Elizabeth pleaded.

Her hunger completely satisfied, and feeling the effects of the wine, Lolivey started, "This much I know for a fact. It had to have been your Thomas that was here. I saw him but for no more than an hour but such a handsome a hunk as that a girl would not forget. He was so well-spoken and sure of himself. He was telling another nearly as delightful and charming young man as himself of his tale of crossing the Atlantic in a ship bound for the Virginias to buy tobacco for shipping back to Germany. Seemingly somewhere along their route on the coast of Africa before making the turn across the Atlantic, they encountered a hurricane, its force greater than anything seen in recent history. They were blown and tossed about for days, suffering extensive damage to the ship with many poor souls lost overboard. The ship then floated aimlessly for over three months before coming to rest on an island somewhere in the Caribbean Sea. According to what I overheard from the exchange between Thomas and his friend, the ship had not only been badly damaged and barely afloat, but they had lost all navigational equipment, and not even the captain of that disabled vessel knew for certain where they were. Ultimately, the few crew members and passengers remaining alive, including Thomas, were able to repair the ship to an extent of getting it once again under sail.

"Nearly out of food and water, they managed to fill the ship's casks with fresh water from the frequent tropical storms and the ship's stores with coconuts. On this inadequate food and water supply, they eventually made it to the shore of South America, someplace in Panama, but were still badly in need of further repair and food. According to Thomas, it was in an area they thought may have fresh water coming down from the distant cloud-shrouded mountains. The captain sent a small boarding crew of three ashore to investigate a possible campsite for the remaining passengers, and no sooner had they set foot ashore when they were set upon by a group of Caribs, native Caribbean cannibal head hunters, and all were slaughtered but for Thomas barely escaping with his life into the jungle. He made his way deep into the jungle in an attempt to avoid that 'bloody native group,' as he referred to them."

Elizabeth and Anne sat completely spellbound by the story that was unfolding, the story as told by Thomas to his newfound friend Jason Klaus over a mug of ale and overheard by the waitress Lolivey.

She then continued, "Your Thomas, as you fondly refer to him, did manage to struggle through the jungles and mountainous regions crossing the Isthmus of Panama and eventually made his way to the

Balboa docks in Panama on the Pacific Ocean, where with the aid of some coffee plantation owner he caught further passage on to San Francisco on the *Bestia Real* with that Captain Justin, another very handsome and gorgeous specimen of man who frequents the wharf area when in port.

"I saw your Thomas just that once and only for maybe an hour. I nearly got beat from my boss for loitering around listening to his tale. But I'm afraid I was not the only one listening. I am quite sure later that same evening he was shanghaied into the services of a shorthanded ship bound for the Orient. As I have overheard it mentioned, him and his friend Jason Klaus were both shanghaied and not a word have I heard of either of them since. And I certainly would remember them if I were to have seen them again."

It was now nearly ten o'clock in the morning, and none of the three ladies realized how much time had passed—they had been up all night. The captain had busied himself with his duties, not wanting to interrupt, but had on occasion stepped into his quarters to check on them.

Realizing the time and the fact that it was totally daylight, Lolivey jumped as if her seat were on fire. "Oh, good lord," she wailed, startling Elizabeth and Anne, who were totally mesmerized with her story. "I am already hours late for work. They will flay me alive for being this late. I have to go now."

"Wait!" Elizabeth pleaded. "We have much more to talk of." Thinking quickly she said, "Will you let the captain's men safely escort you back to your apartment to pick up your belongings then go to Hayes Valley with us? I know our sister, Mary, will not mind, and she will probably have work for you. Please, please give this consideration."

Lolivey stared unbelieving at Elizabeth's offer for only a moment. "Using the word *apartment* for my bed between two buildings covered by a sheet of old boiler plate to shed some of the rain is flattering. If you are really serious and I can work to pay my way, I will certainly give this more than consideration—I will go with you. The captain's men needn't accompany me anyplace. I have nothing but these filthy rags on my back, and I have no family anymore, so no reason to return to that horrible place. We can go when you wish."

Elizabeth and Anne sat in total astonishment as to the developments of the last twenty-four hours. The captain, hearing the last of the exchange, offered to have one of his men accompany them home when ready.

Taking Anne aside, he continued, "You have a safe haven here now with Edward and Mary. If you are careful, this will be a reasonably safe place to continue your search for Thomas. This is the last place he was seen, and perhaps your newfound friend Lolivey or some of her acquaintances will eventually shed more light on his disappearance. Please, this is no time to give up hope. You will see, my child. You will see.

"I will keep in touch with you through Timothy, and now, God willing, I will be leaving with favorable winds tomorrow morning. My man will see you home now. I plan to return here with a load of passengers from those horrible overcrowded conditions on the docks of Panama, as I have promised, and should be safely back here in about two months, maybe a little more. And if you are about, I'll see you and Anne again then. Now get on with you so I can finally get some work done."

Elizabeth placed her arms around Captain Sawyer's neck, burying her head on his shoulder, and wept. They had been through so much. She and Anne loved this man with all their hearts. His wisdom, compassion, endurance, and insight into their very souls had kept them alive and well for such a long time, it seemed. He was truly a gentleman and one of the most successful sea captains in recent history. The captain was a bit misty too.

Once they had regained their composure, he continued, "Timothy has asked to be relieved of further duties aboard this vessel and will remain here in San Francisco. Should you have troubles or need anything—anything at all—leave word for him on the docks and he will soon be at your beckoning."

With the farewells finally in order, the three girls made way to the ship's departure platform, meeting the escort who patiently waited to see them safely home to their sister's in Hayes Valley. Elizabeth and Anne took one final survey of the ship knowing they may never see it or any of the crew members again. They could not locate Tim, so they left the ship sadly.

With Elizabeth, Anne, and their newfound friend Lolivey comfortably seated in the bouncing carriage with his most trusted escort driving, Captain Sawyer turned back to his duties of making the ship ready for its next morning departure. "I pray," he said aloud, "she finds that young man Thomas alive and well."

Chapter 63

Pacific Ocean

1863

For the first few months, Thomas and Jason and some of the others on the crowded ship were forced to spend twenty-four hours a day on deck. There was not enough room in the cabins below to accommodate all of the new hands and the cargo. This was changing on a regular basis, however, as many were dying from beatings, malnutrition, and disease.

One night while lying on the deck, Thomas gazed up at the blanket of stars. On the ocean, at this latitude, the stars appeared close enough to touch. Enormously lonely, he thought, *Sometimes the most significant things in a man's life are the ones he talks about least.* It had been that way with Elizabeth and him. No day passed that he did not think of her much of the time. In Germany, she had been continually with him, and when they were together in those delightful days, they did not find it necessary to talk a lot because so much of the time there was no need for words. Those moments were something special that occurred between them that they both understood. The happiest hours of his life were those when he was riding with Elizabeth around the vineyard or sitting across a table from her at their humble household in Darmstadt. Whenever he thought of her now, he remembered her face by candlelight. It seemed he was always seeing it that way. The soft sounds of the rustle of her dress, the tinkle of her spoon in a glass, and her voice, never raised and always exciting.

The days were filled with the various tasks assigned to Thomas and Jason. They worked harder than all the others, and they were amongst the fortunate few to avoid more abuse from the cat o' nine tails ever present in the first mate's hand. They kept quiet and did their jobs, waiting for the day they could escape. Never speaking during the day, they would have the evenings—after eating the stinking refuse fed them—to share feelings, thoughts, and escape plans.

Jason would talk for hours of helping his father rebuild their home and outbuildings on their small estate that had been burned and demolished after the corsair raids on the coast of Denmark. The corsairs, he would say, were such a brutal, bloody, ruthless group that would take each and every person, young and old, into captivity. Jason's mother and older brother had been taken captive on one of the raids, never to be seen again. He and his father had only avoided capture because they were away purchasing trade goods for the family business, only to return and witness the total carnage and destruction of the family estate.

"You are a very bitter man, my friend," Thomas would say when Jason would constantly perseverate on the atrocities committed by the Barbary pirates.

"Bitter, I am not," Jason spat. "But lonely, yes. I have missed my mother and brother immensely even though it has been so many years. I feel we will never hear from them again." Silence passed between them, and Jason added, "And you, Thomas? You have not spoken much of your early childhood. Did you assist in the building of your family estate in Denmark before being forced to flee to Germany?"

It was now dark, and Thomas was staring at the blackening sea. "I did not," he replied. "At least not in Denmark. By the time I was born, all the buildings were done. I was very young and do not remember, but I was told we had fine horses and carriages—"

"And slaves?" Jason smirked into the darkening sky.

Ignoring the sardonic comment, Thomas continued, "Many of my ancestors who built the first houses were also kidnapped by the corsairs or Algerian pirates and became slaves."

"We were all white slaves," Jason commented. "We were literally thousands of whites enslaved to Algiers, Tunis, and elsewhere. As for that, there have been white slaves for hundreds of years. Every time the corsairs raided a North Atlantic country, they would kidnap its inhabitants, taking them to the Barbary Coast slave markets for ransom or selling them outright into slavery. It was the way of life, and most of the populace of the North Atlantic coastal communities lived in constant fear of those barbarians."

"Let's get on to a lighter subject," Thomas finally said. "Slavery has been in existence since the beginning of mankind and is not likely to stop."

Thomas and Jason had made friends amongst the other captives on deck. Though an escape plan was seldom discussed with any of the others, the captives quietly thought of Thomas and Jason as the men who would lead such a daring undertaking—if and when the chance arose. But to openly talk of such a thing even though they had been shanghaied into service on this unpardonable ship would be mutiny, an offense punishable by death.

PART III

Chapter 64

Hayes Valley,
California, United States

1863

As the girls bounced along toward Hayes Valley, the mood was somber. None of them had had any rest for well over twenty-four hours. Elizabeth was deep in mystified thought. She pondered as to the health of her father, of Thomas's mother and little sister, and of course Fredrick C. Burgdorf and little Josh. Thomas also was always on her mind, but the search once again seemed hopeless, and her dreams of finding him here in San Francisco had been thoroughly dampened. Maybe some other person in the dock area would have more positive information. Half asleep, they arrived at the house with Mary and Edward walking out to greet them.

Mary noticed Lolivey tucked in between her sisters and inquired, "And what do we have here?"

Elizabeth, hardly awake, reiterated the basics of the tale Lolivey had shared with them about her chance meeting with Thomas, explained that she now had no job to return to or place to stay, and asked if she might continue on here helping out with the chores around the small acreage in return for a room and board.

Casting an eye on this girl's pitiful appearance, Mary said, "I think we can do better than that. Come with me, child. Let's get you cleaned up and a place to rest. Are you hungry or thirsty?"

"No, ma'am," she replied half-asleep. "Just tired."

"Come, then. Please follow me." Thanking the driver, Mary helped the three girls from the carriage, instructing Anne and Elizabeth to get some rest, then led Lolivey into the house to a room with a bath. Handing her a robe and fluffy towel then turning her back to the girl, she instructed, "Throw those rags over there on the chair, and get into the tub. There are soap and shampoo on the end table next to the tub. Feel free to use as much as necessary." Mary had never been known for mincing words. "When you are done, give a shout, and I will have you some clean clothes."

Embarrassed at her unkempt personal appearance, Lolivey mumbled to herself, "I haven't always been in this condition. I hope soon to have the opportunity to enlighten this generous family as to the excuse for my miserable condition."

Opening the bathroom door and stepping out, Mary sighed. *God, I wonder how long it has been since that poor girl has had a bath and clean clothes.* She went to her wardrobe and picked out a wonderful new dress with all the other necessities—new shoes and a stylish jacket. *No hurry,* she thought. *It will take that young lady some time and perhaps another tub of water to become presentable.*

After an hour and hearing nothing from the girl in the tub. Mary quietly knocked on the bathroom door then opened it a crack to tell her she was bringing her fresh new clothes. Lolivey was lying on the bed in her robe curled up into a small ball and sound asleep. *Well,* Mary thought, *these will keep until she is rested and wakes.* Folding the clothes across a chair, she quietly left the room and went downstairs to join Edward.

"The girls have had a rough time of it," she commented. "They all need rest and time to recuperate. That poor little rascal Elizabeth and Anne brought home appears to need some care indeed."

All three girls slept through the afternoon and all that night. When getting out of bed the next morning, Anne had overheard Lolivey in the next room fumbling with her new clothes and lightly knocked on her door then opened it a crack. "Can I help you with anything before we go down to breakfast?" she asked.

Lolivey faintly replied, "Please, if you will. It has been so long and I have nearly forgot how all the items fit."

Anne then entered the room and helped her new friend dress for the day. "Wow." She gasped when completed. "You look absolutely beautiful."

The girl smiled timidly. "I am so embarrassed, I haven't always been in the deplorable condition you found me."

Anne only smiled. "Come, let's get some breakfast. I'm starved."

Together they went down the stairs to the kitchen, where the aroma of frying bacon permeated the room. Elizabeth and the others gasped when they saw Lolivey nervously walk into the room. To say she was gorgeous would have been an understatement. Anne had helped her with her hair, and the new clothes fit perfectly, flattering her figure.

She stood still for a moment while they all stared, and then she slowly turned in a circle. "Well, how do you like the new me?" she asked with a radiant smile.

In the matter of a few hours, having bathed, a good night's sleep, and the new clothes, she had undergone a complete transformation. With her appearance so drastically improved, she was losing her shyness. They all stood at a loss for words.

Then she broke the silence. "Let's eat. I'm starved."

With all sitting at the table but Mary, who was busy serving up the bacon, eggs, and pancakes, the group was once again all talking at the same time, Lolivey now being the center of attention.

Finally Edward brought some manner of order to the conversation. "We all know of ourselves and our adversities in getting here to San Francisco," he said, "but how on earth did you get here in your apparent condition—" He corrected himself. "I mean, in your condition when joining us yesterday at the ship, quite different than now." He smiled.

"Not so long a story or different than many others here," she said. "I came west with my parents from Illinois. There in Chicago, my father owned a very successful hardware and lumber store. My parents made the decision to move west to California 'to experience the endless opportunities of the great west,' he would say. We made this journey west in a covered wagon over the Oregon Trail. Not a bad trip at all. In fact it was quite an amazing adventure and very beautiful." Her vocabulary was changing from the rough wharf and bawdy pub-like expressions to a quite sophisticated manner. "My mother and father were very happy during the trip here, with our only real hardship being the infernal heat and dust. We were very well provisioned and lacked for hardly anything. With not a specific destination in mind, only 'onward to California,' as they would say, we finally arrived in San Francisco.

"We took a nice home back a ways from the city in the hills over-looking the bay. One day shortly after arriving, my mother became very ill with a high fever and severe stomach issues. Father brought in the most reputable doctor in the area, and she was soon diagnosed with something referred to as stomach cancer. She only lived another four months and was very ill and incoherent before passing. My father had loved her with a passion like no other and never really recuper-ated from that loss. Even with me around he was in a constant state of depression—he had lost interest in everything around him and often just wandered our home confused.

"A few months after her death, he went to town for supplies, and I never saw him again. Later, after I was forced into the slave labor situa-tion at Hongkong Bohle's, I heard of my father's probable kidnapping to a shorthanded ship with its destination being that of the South China Sea. If that is true, I fear I will never see or hear from him again. I am now fifteen years old—my last birthday was a week ago."

Even Mary had stopped her scurrying around the kitchen to listen to this child's story.

Chapter 65

Hayes Valley Homestead, California, United States

1863–1864

The next few days passed swiftly with everyone finding their way into a new and very different way of life. The two Klein sisters helped their older sister with the household chores but rested when the opportunity presented itself and made no attempt to return to the city for another three weeks. Lolivey had become a trusted friend and addition to the family. She made herself useful in every way possible and was more secure now that she was settled in with this family than she had been for some time. She helped clean, cook, launder, and tend to the few head of livestock in the pasture, and she never wanted to return to that dreadful city even though it was only a couple of hours away.

Every spare moment the girls had was spent in conversation about the dreaded group referred to as the shanghaiers. They talked much of Thomas's experiences as related by Lolivey and also by what Eladio in Panama had informed them. This and the speculation of what may have happened to Lolivey's father consumed most of the girls' free time. Edward had returned to his mine in the goldfields near Sutter's Mill and would probably not return until early spring. Mary had told them he was often away for months at a time and she constantly worried for his well-being.

As winter wore on into the early spring of 1864, Elizabeth was getting unusually fidgety just sitting around the little farm. She had accepted what had most likely happened to Thomas but would never give up hope. She felt it was again time to return to the city to see if Timothy had any new information on Thomas's disappearance. She made plans to meet him the morning of the day after tomorrow. She was now familiar with the surrounding area and would use the horse car line from Hayes Valley into the city. This was a wooden rail system with horses pulling the cars down the track—a system very similar to the one Thomas's father had used in Germany to move grapes and produce from the family farm to the markets in Darmstadt.

On the morning of Elizabeth's departure, Anne and Lolivey accompanied her to the terminal wishing her Godspeed and good luck. It was a beautiful ride of only about two hours. She was now relaxed and less anxious than she had been since leaving Germany now over a year ago. She had at least a hint as to what had probably happened to Thomas and had resigned herself to accept whatever fate would bring from this point forward. Upon arriving at the dock area, she found Tim waiting for her. He was just standing by the pier with a seaman's cap covering his long curly hair. He was leaning against a huge anchoring post with one foot up resting on his other knee and his thumbs hooked in his pockets.

"I was starting to worry," he said loudly over the noise of the congested area. "Come, let's get some lunch and a mug of ale."

"It will have to be somewhere here close by," she replied with a grin. "I do not want to get out of sight of this horse-drawn train and certainly do not want any dockside greasy, dirty, and dangerous pub like the last one you took me," she teased. "However," she admitted, "if it were not for that experience, we would not have found Lolivey or obtained the news of Thomas, as disturbing as it was."

Tim stepped closer, offering his elbow for her arm. "Over there is a pleasant shop with food and drink that is to the liking of my empty pocketbook, and I hear it has scrumptious food. Probably shrimp or some kind of fish but good ale I'm told."

"The treat is on me this time." Elizabeth laughed then added, "Have you ever in your life had a meal that did not include alcohol?"

"Not that I can remember."

She chuckled. They sat and talked the hours away. Tim had gained no new news of the disappearance of Thomas, but after Elizabeth told him Lolivey's own story, he added, "I will also make some inquiries as to her father. As you know, I do have a good pulse on things that happen here in the city."

They had been talking nonstop to this point. Then Elizabeth looked him in the eyes and said, "Timothy, just what do you do for a living while you are here in port and not on a ship?"

He wrinkled his face with a slight frown. "You really do not want to know."

They had become acquainted over many months of travel, but she knew little of him. "Well, that's good enough for me, my friend."

Noticing it was about time for the horse train to return to the valley, Tim politely stood and escorted Elizabeth down the block to the loading platform. Helping her aboard, he said, "As usual, Elizabeth, leave word if I can be of assistance, and I will continue my inquiries of Thomas and Lolivey's father."

On the trip back to the valley, Elizabeth thought long and hard, *What am I ever to do? What will Anne do? We can't live in this constant state of indecision mooching off my sister and Edward forever.*

Returning to the valley she found Anne, Lolivey, and Mary all three waiting at the station. Elizabeth jumped off the train and energetically gave them a complete rundown of the day's events, including a recap of her discussion with Tim. "He will not only continue looking for news of Thomas but will also try to find some evidence on Lolivey's father's disappearance." Walking back to Mary and Edward's home a short distance away, the ladies talked continuously, with the subject finally turning to the future of Elizabeth and Anne's stay here in San Francisco.

"Right now we have the funds to return to Germany," Elizabeth commented, "but if we stay on here sharing in the household expenses and depleting our meager resources, who knows what will happen?"

Anne finally spoke up, "I want to stay here. I miss our friends and family, but I do not want to get on another ship going anywhere and certainly not for another year-long trip back to Germany. I want to go into the city and find a job. Who knows, I may find a very wealthy man to marry and live happily ever after." She sighed. "But in the meantime, we will help Mary here with expenses and continue to live here in San Francisco searching for news of Thomas. If we leave now to return home to Germany, it will take nearly a year for news of Thomas to reach us and then another year to return should necessity dictate, and I am not up for that," she said with emphasis on *that*.

Mary quietly interrupted the conversation. "Please, Edward and I are very well off now—actually, we are quite rich. The mine has proven to be a mother lode, as they say. Edward has discreetly managed to get all the gold to date from the mine here to the Wells Fargo office in the city. He plans to spend only another few months working then sell the claim. I have tried to convince him to quit and sell out now. I fear for his life sneaking all that gold back to the city every few months. It is only a matter of time until the news gets out of his success and he will be robbed and killed like so many others. We have plenty enough now to last more than a lifetime, but he wants to continue in this risky business for a little while or until the mine plays out. He has promised me no more than a few more months here, and if the mine still continues to be productive, he will sell and we will return to Germany. You needn't worry about expenses here. We welcome your company and wish you to stay as long as you like, and that's final."

Elizabeth had not said a word for several minutes, listening to the exchange of words between Anne and Mary.

Mary then continued, "We are happy to employ Lolivey here at our home too, and when Edward and I return to Germany, she can return with us or stay on here as she wishes. I have by the way sent word home of your safe arrival here and of the news of Thomas."

By the time they walked through the front gate into the yard, everyone had ceased to talk, and the rusty gate hinges made a louder than usual screeching sound, snapping Elizabeth out of her deep thoughts. Feeling guilty for not taking the time to write home before now and leaving it up to Mary, she promised herself to do so the following morning.

Dinner was prepared, and Elizabeth expressed her thoughts now on the subject of staying. "With your permission, Mary, and Anne's insistence on staying, we will remain here at least for a while. I would, however, like to get a job in the city. I'm afraid I will become very bored just sitting around waiting for information, and there is little we can safely do to help with Tim's discreet inquiries on our behalf."

Anne, being most aggressive in her pursuit of employment, was first to get a job. With Timothy's assistance, she had made inquiries in a dozen different places and finally had a positive interview at Maguire's Opera House on Washington Street, between Kearny and Montgomery.

She announced one evening at dinner, "It is not far from the end of the horse car line on the pier and will be a quite safe journey to and from work."

Elizabeth looked at her disbelievingly. "You're going to work in an opera house? When you sing, you sound like those rusty hinges on that old gate outside!" she said with a chuckle, "but we all love you and will come to hear you."

Mary just stared in disbelief.

"The opera house? Well, it's not just an opera house, as you should know," Anne explained. "It's also a theater where plays are given, and I shall have but a minor role in the next production. The pay is not good, but as I progress into one of the finest actresses around, I will get a raise, they have promised," she countered, smiling. "And I do not have to sing."

They all laughed.

Chapter 66

San Francisco, California, United States

1864

As summer came, the job at the theater was taking much of Anne's time, and Timothy or one of his cronies did keep a constant eye on her coming and going. With her frequent trips into the city, they figured, Tim could easily pass on any news he may gain on Thomas or Lolivey's father, though to date that amounted to very little. Occasionally a ship would reach port from the Orient, and he would discreetly question the crew members about a tall, well-built young man with raven-black hair and green eyes they may have seen in their travels. With the bribe of a mug of ale for information, most all reported to have seen such a person of this description and would consider revealing a location for another mug. It seemed as though every ship in the Pacific Ocean had seen Thomas after a mug of ale. Knowing the evidence was mostly erroneous did not discourage Tim's determined and discreet inquiries. Sooner or later, legitimate word would come to him, and he by nature was a patient man.

Elizabeth had many job opportunities but nothing safe or suitable to her taste. Lolivey had warned her of the many hazards faced by a beautiful young lady working in this city. Elizabeth had always wanted to practice medicine to eventually become a doctor, but the opportunity had never presented itself. She took advantage of this time to volunteer her services at St. Mary's Hospital in the city—an experience that would become most valuable to her for the rest of her life.

Edward had made another extremely profitable and successful trip to his mining claim near Sutter's Mill and had made arrangements now to sell the still very active claim for a handsome price. He and Mary were already way beyond rich and would just add the proceeds from the sale of the claim to their very fat Wells Fargo account, to be used as needed upon returning to Germany, which would be soon, they hoped. Even with the hundreds of ships in the harbor, it was extremely difficult to obtain passage on one in a timely manner. They may have to wait for up to six months, and then who was to know what accommodations they may find? Many of the ships had terrible reputations for abusing passengers with crowded living quarters, bad water, and tainted and short rations. Many of the ships required the passengers to bring their own food, only for it to mysteriously disappear once aboard. Still, they did not wish to stay here in this rough-and-tumble western frontier and longed to return to the more sophisticated culture in Europe. They had made much preparation for their return and were now finishing the formalities of turning the house over to Elizabeth and Anne. Lolivey had decided to stay on here with the sisters in San Francisco, having no idea what the future would hold for her but still harboring some small hope of locating her father. It was a very busy time, when Captain Sawyer conveniently returned from his last Panama trip.

He had made one trip to Panama and back with a load of passengers from the horrible congested areas of the docks where they had been badly mistreated. He was hailed a hero for that benevolent act. Upon arriving in port, he sent word to Mary and Edward to expect him for a visit and dinner, he hoped, as he wanted to once again see them and the girls.

It was a delightful reunion. Elizabeth and Anne loved this gracious man and had prayed for his safe return for months. They all talked the night away, reliving his adventures as well as the trip with the girls through the Strait of Magellan and the meeting with the Tribaldos Coffee growers in Panama, then their ultimate landing here in San Francisco, until the sun was just barely peeking its way through the foggy mist.

Finally with a short lull in the conversation, Captain Sawyer said with a tired sigh, "I am now ready to retire. I will return to Boston with one final load of freight. I will then gather up my most patient and beautiful wife, gather all of my worldly belongings into the ship's hold, and return here in a couple of years. I have a buyer for the ship upon my return here, and my wife and I will most likely settle up in that new Idaho Territory."

Edward was very tired and couldn't believe what he thought the captain had just said. "Did I hear you right?" He said, "Did you say you were preparing to return to Boston soon?"

"Yes," Captain Sawyer replied. I will leave in just a few days.

"Could you possibly make room for two more people and the few belongings we will be taking with us? We are turning the house over to Elizabeth and Anne and returning to Germany."

It was now the captain's turn to be surprised. "You and Mary are leaving this great American West to return to Germany? What about the girls? Thomas?"

"We are tired of the life here," Mary said. "I have lived in constant fear for Edward's life since we arrived here. Edward was fortunate locating that gold claim and has nearly killed himself working that mine alone all this time. We are now quite well off, thanks to his efforts, but we do wish to return home. The girls will be fine here. We have given the house to them and will leave them enough income to survive for a few years."

Looking at the girls then back at Mary and Edward, Captain Sawyer slowly replied, "I would be honored to have your company on my return trip to Boston."

"We are quite settled here now." Elizabeth smiled weakly. "We will continue to wait for any news of Thomas. With Anne working in the theater making countless friends and Timothy doing whatever he does on the docks and me at the hospital, we have managed to accomplish a very good network for news from all kinds of people. We will get news of Thomas, of that I'm quite sure."

The next few days were busy. The girls helped Mary and Edward with packing the last-minute things needed for their long journey home. They were taking only very few personal things, leaving nearly everything here for Elizabeth and Anne, but it was still a painstaking ordeal and very emotional. The girls knew they may never see their sister or Edward again. Lolivey had known them for less than a year but loved them all dearly—they were now the only family she had.

The final day arrived and the captain had sent several crew members from the ship with a large freight wagon to pick up Mary and Edward with their belongings. Tim was also in attendance for the occasion. With all the help, it took no time to load their few trunks into the wagon then make way to the ship.

It was late afternoon, and the sun was setting into the pastel clouds, a perfect evening with only a slight breeze gently rocking the ship among the faint odor of the harbor. The captain had the ship's cooks prepare a meal, not lavish but suitable and simple. No one was in the mood for more than just something casual this evening. They had been saying their last farewells for days, and there was little more to discuss. Elizabeth, Anne, and Lolivey were of course very sad about this departure, but it seemed to be the destiny accepted by all. The captain had promised to see them again when he returned to San Francisco in a couple of years. Perhaps this would come to pass—they hoped so.

Walking down the gangplank with Tim, who would accompany them to their home in the valley, they stopped and waved one last time. Mary and Edward were leaning on the ship's rail in an embrace with visible tears streaming down Mary's face. Elizabeth thought, *Damn those corsairs, damn those pirates, damn those shanghaiers. If it were not for them, we would not be experiencing this sorrowful parting.*

With this, Tim helped her, Anne, and Lolivey into the wagon, clucked to the team and gently slapped the reins on their rumps, and they started their way home. Neither Elizabeth nor Anne could bear to turn one more time for a final wave, so they stared straight ahead. Lolivey did turn and wave. She was sobbing uncontrollably as Elizabeth gently put her arm around her shoulder, leaning her close to hold her tightly for a few moments.

Tim spent that first night with them after leaving the ship but returned to the wharf late the next day, "to continue on with my duties." The days and weeks that followed were melancholy, as once again the Klein sisters settled into the new routine without the stable environment of their older sister and brother-in-law. Lolivey had soon bounced back to her lovely self—working hard at all everyday tasks around the small farm and helping the sisters immensely. Tim would visit occasionally, and life went on.

Chapter 67

Hayes Valley Homestead, California, United States

1864

It had been several weeks since they had last seen Timothy when one evening he walked into the yard. He had taken the horse car line out to Hayes Valley so had no animal to tend on his arrival. Elizabeth saw him first, then Anne. Lolivey was moving the few cows they had recently acquired around behind the barn in the pasture so did not know yet of his presence. They could see by the look on his face, he was disturbed with some news. Usually even with no news, he greeted them smiling and waving from a distance. Today he just stood at the gate watching them.

Elizabeth stopped breathing with a terrible feeling of foreboding—she had hoped to never have negative news of Thomas, hoping and praying only for the best, but she could tell from the look on Tim's face, he was deeply troubled.

"What is it?" she finally approached him and asked.

"I'm sorry Elizabeth," he said softly. "I do not have any news of Thomas."

She sucked in a huge breath of air, having nearly fainted. "Then what is it?" She gulped. "You nearly scared me to death."

"I think I may have located Lolivey's father. Is she here?"

"She is," Elizabeth replied somewhat relieved but still apprehensive. "Wait a moment and I will get her."

"No, please, let us talk of this first," Tim replied. "It may be good news but certainly in not the best of circumstances."

They walked into the house and sat at the dining table while Anne poured them all a cup of coffee then sat down herself and placed her elbows on the table with her chin resting on folded hands and her eyebrows slightly raised. "Okay, bub, let's have it. Whatcha got?" Anne's vocabulary had been changing while working at Maguire's Opera House, picking up on the slang from the stage hands and at times talking like a sailor, which worried Elizabeth to the limits of her patience.

"If it's truly him," Tim started, "he is confined to a chain gang working around the city where necessity dictates a labor crew. The supervisor of this work group is none other than one of the hoodlums from Hongkong Bohle's nasty organization. They seem to kidnap vagrants and put them to work on this crew, then hire the crew out at a handsome price to do repair work around town. As I understand—if it is her father—he is in pitiful condition and looks as he may drop dead at any minute. I will need Lolivey to accompany me to the area, not a safe one, to make a positive identification."

With this being said, Elizabeth excused herself and slowly walked to the pasture behind the barn and motioned to her friend. Lolivey hastily crossed the pasture toward Elizabeth, and as she approached and noticed Elizabeth's anxious look, she asked, "What is it?"

"Timothy is here in the house." Elizabeth paused a moment, not knowing exactly how to continue, then added, "He thinks he may have found your father alive—not well but alive—here in San Francisco."

"Oh my God." Lolivey gasped, nearly collapsing if not for Elizabeth's hold on her. She was momentarily struck with silence.

Chapter 68

Hayes Valley Homestead, California, United States

1864

"Elizabeth, it's been so long—over three years—how could this be? And where?" Lolivey faltered, and Elizabeth gently led her into the house. Anne saw them coming and had poured another cup of coffee. Lolivey collapsed into the chair with the cup in her hand and stared wide-eyed at Tim. He glanced back and forth from one sister to the other, unsure of how to start.

Regaining some of her self-possession, Lolivey shakingly asked, "Have you seen him, Tim?"

"Lolivey, I do not want to get your hopes too high. I have not personally seen him—one of my associates has reported to have witnessed a man of your father's description confined to a chain gang working in various parts of the city. He was able to get close enough for a short but incoherent conversation with this man. What brought this man to attention was his constant rambling of his departed wife, his beautiful daughter with her whereabouts unknown, and his own miserable condition. It was reported to me that he is in very shaky health and probably soon to perish. My contact did inquire as to how he happened to be in that situation, and it seems he was originally removed from the streets by one of the crimps but in too poor of condition to be placed captive on one of the outbound ships. He was instead placed in a cell someplace to regain some degree of his strength then later placed on a work detail. I think, if it is him, we can—probably for an exorbitant fee—have him removed to your custody. Most likely he does not produce enough work to warrant his pathetic meals, and his captors would like to be well rid of him."

Lolivey sat with both hands tightly clenched around the cup in thunderstruck silence. No one was moving, nor had a word been spoken for several minutes when she finally raised her head and looked once again at Timothy. "When can we go to see him?" Lolivey had hardly returned to the city since she had escaped from the clutches of Hongkong Bohle's to the small farm with Anne and Elizabeth.

"It is too late this day," Tim said and smiled softly. "If it's okay, I will spend the night here and we will go tomorrow morning at first light. The workers your father is attached to—if it is truly him—start work at daybreak and work until dark."

"I am afraid of being discovered," Lolivey said. "If anyone from that dreadful place I was forced to work at on the wharf sees me, we will all be in serious trouble."

The three girls and Tim talked for hours of a plan to accomplish the task of visiting the area her father would most likely be working in at first light the next morning. They finally decided they would first only observe then return home to make further plans of rescue. To totally conceal her identity, Lolivey would accompany them dressed as a boy. She was now sixteen years old and even though a beautiful young lady, she was skinny with more of a boyish figure, yet to completely develop the well-rounded and most noticeable characteristics of the other two girls. She could easily pass for a boy if she dressed like one and put her long hair under a cap.

At first light they were in the city and casually walking down the street in a direction of the last sighting of the work gang. This early in the morning showed little foot traffic, and the usual crowds had yet to materialize. Elizabeth, Anne, and the boyish-looking Lolivey strolled along engaged in light conversation, trying not to seem too obvious, and Tim and company were scattered about watching their every movement so they could hastily intervene should anything suspicious or threatening occur.

After an hour or so of travel, they saw the work gang slowly repairing one of the boardwalks in a rather seedy section of the city next to the bay. The usual early-morning fog was still dense, and they could hardly see further than the work gang. With this condition, boldly now the girls walked up to the workers. There were not many—it would not require much time to identify the person thought to be Lolivey's father.

Lolivey's mouth fell open, and she covered her face with her hands and gasped. "It is him."

Standing there at the front end of the group with a chain fastened to a manacle around his ankle, he was painstakingly removing a decayed old board from the walk while another shackled man replaced it with a new one and another secured it into place with sledge and nails. The rest were loaded with boards cut to a length, handing them forward one by one as needed. Even observers could see it was a conscientious effort on the behalf of all to maintain any degree of order, saving each the painful snap of a whip.

How could anything like this take place now in this day and age? Elizabeth thought.

The guard of this pitiful and nonthreatening group was standing at their rear facing the bay enjoying the stub of a foul-smelling cigar. He paid little attention to the group, and Elizabeth could see a single large key hanging from a fob in his hip pocket. Where would one go if they were to escape? Probably wouldn't make it a block before collapsing with weakness anyhow.

Tim was watching very closely from a short distance away, with other members of his group strategically concealed on all sides, should anything threaten the girls.

Elizabeth whispered, "Are you sure that is him? The one you are staring at and he staring at you?"

"Yes, that tall one in front. I'm sure it's him. He's skinnier now than I and looks in terrible shape, but it's him. I know it's him."

Anne stood to one side to listen to the exchange then lifted her head, looking straight at Timothy, not far away, and catching his eye. *Well, there is no time like the present*, she thought. *This is as good a time to save this poor soul as any, if it is going to happen.* Raising her arm, she made a gesture of turning a key then pointed at the guard. Then with her thumb and forefinger, she pinched, still pointing at the guard staring over the bay through cigar smoke.

Good God, Timothy thought, *is she suggesting we rescue him* now? *We made no plans for any more than just a quick look.* Then, looking around to make sure there was no one close by or watching, he hastily took two quick steps to where the guard stood and delicately removed the huge old key hanging from his hip pocket and throwing it in an arc over his shoulder—a high arc that landed neatly in Anne's outstretched hand. Timothy quickly engaged the guard in conversation about the women of the brothels and fine ale, so they stood locked in conversation, laughing and looking out over the bay and the rising fog.

With the key now in hand, Anne held her finger up to her lips as she faced the captives and quickly but silently jumped forward, placing the huge old key into the keyhole in the lock on Lolivey's father's ankle chain. *This better work*, she thought, *or we all may be in this same predicament very soon.* As Anne turned the key, the manacle popped opened and the man slowly stumbled out and away from the rest of the group. This whole chain of events had only taken about five seconds—the rest of the group stood in shocked silence. Anne, still facing them with her finger to her lips in a gesture for silence, handed the key to the next in line, and the three girls walked off with the bent and crippled old man in tow.

They made it to the first alley and turned out of sight, then continued on as fast as the old man could travel. They were desperately trying to put as much distance as possible between them and the work crew. The guard had his foot on the first rail of the pier railing with his elbows resting on the top rail still looking out into the bay, completely unaware of what was going on behind him. Timothy was standing with his back to the rail keeping an eye on the guard and looking past him at what was happening to the work gang. Most of them were old hands and silently unlocked their own ankle bracelets then passed the key to the next in line. The noise of the seagulls and the awakening of other activities out on the water helped to conceal the noise of unlocking each ankle bracelet in turn.

Unbelievable, Timothy thought, all the while prepared to throw the guard into the bay at any second, should he notice what was going on. Timothy watched as the last man in line unfastened his bracelet and casually strolled in another direction. The guard was still engrossed in telling tales of the many brothels and fine ale houses.

A minute later the lack of any work-related sound from the crew behind him alerted the guard to something wrong. Still facing the bay with a vile smirk, he said to Timothy, "Watch this. I'm going to take this whip to each and every one of those lazy beggars. Have to do it at least once a day just keep their attention on work." Then he turned slowly, obviously enjoying every second of the thought of inflicting pain on the work crew.

"What the hell?" Not a soul was in front of him, just a pile of empty manacles. He hadn't noticed Timothy slowly squatting next to him, so he was surprised by the powerful grab around his ankles. Timothy quickly lifted and dumped the cruel guard over the rail head first into the bay.

He landed on his belly making a gigantic splash with the wind knocked from his lungs. Gasping for air but inhaling water. In this weakened condition, he barely struggled to a dock support. He clung there for minutes before he could even gasp air let alone yell for help. Timothy and crew vanished without a trace, and the girls with Lolivey's weak and ailing father were safely back to the stable where they had left the team and buggy.

All loaded hastily into the wagon, then slowly made their way back toward Hayes Valley. The whole chain of events had taken hardly more than two hours. Elizabeth, Anne, and Tim were sitting in the front seat, with Lolivey and her father in the rear. Lolivey's father was in no shape to carry on a conversation and probably did not even fully comprehend all that had just happened, though he did introduce himself as Hank. Lolivey was making no real attempt to prompt him into any discussion. She just sat beside him holding his hands in her own and watching him stare at the passing countryside. She realized it would take time for him to regain any mental awareness, if he ever did.

In the front seat, Elizabeth stared wild-eyed at Anne. "What in God's name were you thinking of, Anne? I was scared to death, and we made no plans to rescue him today, only to make sure it was him."

Anne smiled. "I don't know what I was thinking." She turned to look over her shoulder at Lolivey and her father. "But it did work." Then she snickered. "Poor Tim, however, had to throw that wicked man into the bay, and what a splash he made. I truly hope the sharks got him. A few have been sighted this close to shore, you know."

The conversation the rest of the way home was light, with all of them grateful for the successful rescue of Hank but still somewhat shaken over the day's events. Tim reasoned there would be little fallout over the event because the thug he had thrown into the bay, if still alive, would be too embarrassed to let word of this event spread. All of those other captives would of course embellish this tale, and each would claim to be the hero saving all the others. He chuckled at the thought. This would certainly help to keep the girls out of the limelight, but the thug he had thrown into the bay would be looking for *his* hide, Timothy realized.

Let him try for it, he thought. He would just throw him into the bay again.

Chapter 69

Hayes Valley Homestead, California, United States

1864

When they arrived home, the girls hastily made up a comfortable room for Lolivey's father, Hank. Tim helped in getting him cleaned up and into new clothes. Hank was cooperative but just stared at the events going on around him.

Day after day, Lolivey worked tirelessly with her father as time permitted. She would remind him of small bits and pieces of their former life together, but he never responded with more than a blank stare, seemingly not comprehending a word she had said. Slowly he was gaining weight, consequently regaining some of his strength. On occasion, she would walk with him around the pasture behind the barn then up and down the road out front, the one that ultimately led to the city.

They all lived with some concern of a possible visit from the waterfront thugs that had once haunted Lolivey's life and probably had shanghaied Thomas into service aboard a ship. Anne was still working at Maguire's Opera House and reported a possible sighting of the thug that Tim had thrown into the bay. She felt thoroughly disappointed that the sharks hadn't gotten to him.

Other than that, life was relatively simple. One day Anne and Elizabeth received a packet that their father and Thomas's mother had mailed months ago. The vineyard was prospering. Their father had moved the short distance from Darmstadt to the vineyard for convenience purposes, Little Josh was maturing into the most delightful young man, and of course Fredrick C. Burgdorf was becoming impatient with life there without Thomas and Elizabeth and wanted to also follow to America. He'd heard of the fabulous goldfields in the new Idaho Territory. Having been previously notified of Mary and Edward's return to Germany, their father, Manfred, now residing at the Clay vineyard, was anxiously awaiting their return for a full report of their time in America.

Setting the letters aside, Elizabeth turned to Anne, both smiling and puzzled. "Are we doing the right thing, Anne?" she asked. "Do you think we will ever get news of Thomas? Staying here and not returning to Germany. Are we truly making the right decision?"

Anne stared back and, for a change, was dead serious. "Oh yes, Elizabeth," she said slowly for emphasis. "We are doing the right thing. I know it. You will hear of Thomas again. I don't know if I will, but I feel it deep inside that you will one day be reunited with your Thomas. I don't know when, but you will."

"What do you mean?" Elizabeth hastily replied, "You don't know if you will?"

"Just a feeling," Anne said.

Elizabeth immediately stopped the conversation with a deep-rooted feeling of foreboding. Anne was at times a challenge, but Elizabeth loved her dearly and did not wish to face the possibility of a future without her.

Later that evening after supper, when Lolivey had taken her father to his room and made him comfortable, Elizabeth once again struck up the conversation with Anne. She had taken a few well-deserved days off from her position at the hospital, and Anne was resting here at home between performances at the theater.

"Anne," she said, "I am tired of it here. It is comfortable and somewhat safe. We could probably spend the rest of our lives here with relative security, but I want to move on. I'm quite sure news of Thomas will follow wherever we go."

Anne, having achieved a reasonable degree of success in the theater as a promising new, young, and beautiful actress, sat bolt upright. "What are you talking about?" she nearly shouted.

Elizabeth was startled—she had seldom heard Anne raise her voice—but continued on, "I don't like it here anymore. I want to move on. This place is just closing in around me. It is time to go."

"Well, just go then," Anne retorted, "because I, for one, am going nowhere. I like it fine here." Then she added with some hesitation, "And I think I like the theater."

"Please, Anne," Elizabeth pleaded, her eyes starting to tear. "Won't you at least give some consideration to going on with me? I just couldn't think of going on alone without you. You are my little sister, and I do not wish to even think of a life without you."

"Just where do we intend to go?" Anne huffed. "I do so love the theater, and it is certainly a challenge. There is no end to how good I can get—"

"But," Elizabeth interrupted, "no actress is really ever good enough. I have seen you, and you are amazing, but the crowd is such a fickle beast. Some actresses think the people love them, and that's certainly not the case, and it's nonsense to think that. They love the roles you play or the way you play them, but not you. Tomorrow it could easily be another, and you will not always be young and beautiful."

Anne sat in silence for a moment thinking. "I have been doing well enough." *Well,* she thought, *to tell the truth, no, I haven't.* Not as well as she wished, nor as well as she must. As much as she loved the theater, it was a means to an end rather than a way of life. She wanted to find a place for herself, a place where she belonged, a place that was hers. She was lonely, and she wanted to marry a wonderful man like Elizabeth's Thomas and have children. The people of San Francisco loved their theater, although just thinking of this amused Anne, for the everyday life she and Elizabeth had lived was much more exciting and dramatic than any play she had been in.

Elizabeth had detected an uncertainty, perhaps a doubt, in Anne's resolve. "To be an actress," Elizabeth continued, "is to be a vagabond, admired on the stage, and at times despised off it, always at the risk of the crowd's pleasure or displeasure of one's performance. Forever vulnerable."

Anne's resolve was visibly weakening. "Where are we going?" she asked her sister.

"To the fabled new Idaho Territory," Elizabeth replied. "I have thought this out carefully. We will go from here in San Francisco to Portland, Oregon, by one of those new steamships. Then we will just have to figure it out for the rest of the journey."

"What do you mean 'just figure it out'?" Anne replied incredulously. "I too have seen maps. I also have read the stories of the fabulous wealth in the goldfields there in the Idaho Territory, but Elizabeth, do you know how far that is? And, oh by the way, I am not the least bit interested in spending another day on that Pacific Ocean in any kind of ship—steam, sail, or anything else, if there is anything else."

"You said, 'Where are we going?' Does that mean you are going with me?" Elizabeth said, now smiling.

Anne flipped her hair. "Yes, it does, and just when are we to leave? I am now between performances at the opera house and will give my notice tomorrow. That miserable group can find someone else to fill my shoes, if that is possible." Anne was now infected with Elizabeth's enthusiasm of this next adventure. "We will go to that Idaho gold country, and I will find a rich man and marry him and have children and live happily ever after!" she announced, beaming.

Elizabeth squinted her eyebrows into a frown and commented, "How many charming young men or old rich ones have you proposed to by now, Anne?"

"A bunch," she replied. "And you wait—one will take me up on it one of these days, and you will be an old maid, and I will be married with a family. You can come visit as a favorite aunt." She chuckled. Not only had Anne picked up slang terms and a questionable vocabulary from the theater group she had worked with, but she had also started to speak with considerable sarcasm.

Returning to the room after having made her father comfortable, Lolivey heard the last part of the sisters' conversation. She was visibly upset as Elizabeth turned from the dining table toward her. "What is to become of us, my father and I?" she remarked with tears starting down her cheeks.

Walking to her side and placing her arm around her shoulder, Elizabeth said, "Please let me explain our thinking, Lolivey."

Anne, still seated at the table in silent observation, thought, *This should be interesting. What's to explain—we are leaving?*

Elizabeth gave her sister a quick unapproving glance, hoping she would remain silent for a few minutes without butting in. She said to Lolivey, "You will still have this house to live in," reiterating that Edward and Mary had left each of the girls a small trust fund that, with some care, would last several years. "Not knowing where we will ultimately settle again, we will need someone here to receive mail from Germany and keep an ear out for news of Thomas. Timothy will still keep a watchful eye over you and your father, and we will keep in touch the best we can. There is one of those new telegraphs here in San Francisco, and I have heard it will soon be in Portland, Oregon, if it's not there already, and then who knows? I'm quite sure it will also be further north into the Idaho Territory soon. Please, for us, continue on here with your father, keep an eye on this place, and support him to a complete recovery, and keep Anne and me informed as to current events here, as you can."

Lolivey looked slightly relieved but was still crying. "We will stay here and be forever grateful for it." She sobbed. "But I will miss you both terribly." Glancing over at Anne, she repeated, "Both of you."

It was settled.

Chapter 70

Pacific Ocean

1864

Months after escape talks had first hatched on the ship, Jason had graduated from the official deck scrubber and had taken over Thomas's position of manning the crow's nest high above the deck to watch for other ships passing too closely or dangerous flotsam in their path. He had just thrown his leg over the basket of the crow's nest to begin his careful descent down when a sudden roll of the ship tore loose his grip on the rim and he tumbled headfirst toward the deck nearly a hundred feet below. He was windmilling head over heels with the sky coming into his vision, then the deck, then the sky, then the deck. There was no fear in him—he just accepted this as an inevitable end to his short life and actually welcomed this end over the terrible conditions he and Thomas had faced day after day on the stinking ship deck that was rushing up to meet his head-on fall.

A cotton rope suddenly wrapped around his windmilling leg, slowing his descent. His mind flashed on his task earlier in the day—he had taken one end of the rope up the mast to the crow's nest and secured it to replace a worn rope, and now that very rope had him entangled. Jason felt the rope come to its end just a moment before his head would have smashed into the deck. He felt his hair sweep the deck then rapidly recoiled as the rope jerked him back up nearly twenty feet then dropped him again almost to the deck. Before it could jerk him up again, it loosened itself from his leg, dropping him only a few inches to the deck. Badly shaken but with complete poise, he got up, rearranged his tattered clothing, bent with a graceful bow to all hands on deck that had witnessed the occurrence and stammered, "A planned maneuver."

Thomas—standing near where Jason had come to rest and having witnessed the complete chain of events—gasped hoarsely, "I have never seen anything like that before in all my time at sea. I have never heard of anything like that before. That was not a planned maneuver. That was shit house luck, Jason. You should be dead with your head smashed like a melon." Thomas was standing in total disbelief along with the rest of the crew.

Jason smiled. "What an exciting descent. I may try that again sometime."

Chapter 71

San Francisco,
California, United States

1864

The Klein sisters had asked Timothy to assist in booking passage on a steamship, *The Swallow*, which would be leaving in a few weeks in the summer of 1864, running from San Francisco up the coast to Portland, Oregon, with many stops in between, and he had done so. Elizabeth and Anne, with the assistance of Lolivey, had carefully packed each of their two trunks, with special attention to the one with the glass hummingbird, the beautiful and fragile gift Thomas had given to Elizabeth years ago upon his departure from Germany.

Tim arrived at their home in Hayes Valley early one morning with a carriage to take them to the departure dock of *The Sparrow*. He brought the trunks out to the porch, leaving them in a neat stack, then moved the carriage around for the final loading of the trunks. As Timothy placed the trunks one by one into the carriage, Elizabeth barked at him, "Be careful with that one. It has my hummingbird in it."

Tim looked at her quizzically. *Huh, a bird in her suitcase*, he thought, the same as Edward had with the same warning nearly a year ago while unloading the trunks at the house. But Timothy had learned long ago that it was of no use to question either girl of their motives or reasoning. He just smiled and continued on with the efforts a little more carefully. Once finished, he assisted Anne and Elizabeth into the wagon. Lolivey would not accompany them to the dock. She dared not leave her father alone yet and had said her goodbyes previously, only waving now as they departed with Tim for the docks once more.

Anne was seventeen years old and Elizabeth nineteen but both worldly way beyond their years. It had been more than two years since Elizabeth had last seen Thomas. His memory, though, would be with her until her dying day. She thought, *Whatever is to happen, I shall not forget him, ever*.

The Klein sisters now safely loaded on the ship with luggage intact and made their way to their respective rooms. Opening the door into her room, Elizabeth gasped in astonishment, "This is the most lavishly decorated room I have ever seen."

Standing next to her, Anne chirped, "Why not? I hate ocean travel, and you forced me into this once again. I personally instructed Tim to reserve the nicest rooms available. It is only for a few days, and we may never have the luxury of a roof over our heads again, let alone something as nice as this." With this, she turned and flounced into her room adjacent to Elizabeth's. "I will knock when I'm ready for dinner," she concluded, shutting her door.

The evening meal on the top deck was equally as pleasant as the rooms. Once seated, Anne commented, "I could get used to this life-style very quick."

"Well, enjoy it now. I fear some of the remaining trip may be quite different and not so comfortable."

A few days later, *The Sparrow* and all passengers left the Pacific Ocean, passing Astoria, Oregon, and entering the Columbia River. They continued through the passage to the confluence of the Willamette River, then up the Willamette to dock in Portland. The girls required the assistance of a carriage to take them to a modest hotel away from the docks. It seemed the further from the docks one could get, the safer it would be.

Anne immediately fell in love with this booming little town of about three thousand people. Even though it was small, it was much more refined and sophisticated than the larger rough-and-tumble city of San Francisco of about seventy-five thousand. *I think I could be very content here, but that will never happen—Elizabeth has her mind set on that Idaho Territory for some reason, and I know she will pester me to accompany her there no matter what. And I probably will go.* She sighed.

After a week in the hotel, they found a less expensive but quaint little boarding house called the Shaw House, closer to the outskirts of town. Elizabeth and Anne had been here only a week when one afternoon while having lunch at a small pub, a friendly voice hailed them from across the street. It was Albert, a stagehand who had once worked with Anne at Maguire's Opera House in San Francisco. He had noticed them through the open window and immediately walked across the street to join them.

"Anne!" he exclaimed. "What on earth are you doing here?"

"Well, I might ask you the same."

He sat down with the sisters, and they were soon engaged in conversation of old times in San Francisco and their respective trips to Portland. They chatted the afternoon away. Albert had just returned from the Idaho Territory's capital city of Lewiston, which was several days of travel up the Columbia, Snake, and Clearwater Rivers. The girls were very lonely but now cheerful in mood, and they pestered him relentlessly for hours with questions of the area, travel on the Columbia River, rumors about the Snake River, and what other modes of transportation could be expected on their journey northeast. Albert was part of a touring group of actors and actresses, none of which were very good, but they were still thoroughly popular in the Oregon mining camps and the new boomtowns in Idaho. The group he was with was now playing here in one of the tent theaters that had been erected around town to accommodate such events.

The girls were thrilled of the stories of his group's trip to Lewiston, the capital city of the new Idaho Territory. They planned to continue their journey on north through Lewiston then on to one of the booming mining towns, perhaps Pierce, Florence, or maybe even the Warren's Diggins. Elizabeth had not decided yet which would be their ensuing terminus. She did know she had not liked living in San Francisco—in fact, she had liked no part of that ugly and menacing town that Thomas had disappeared from—and was very happy to be away from that unhealthy environment. She was still very concerned for the safety of Lolivey and her father in Hayes Valley but knew Timothy and company would be watching over them.

Albert bid them farewell for the day but promised to meet again the next morning for breakfast at the Gem Saloon. This establishment was not only a popular tavern but also known to be a very good establishment for day-to-day meals. Albert was prompt the next morning but was forced to wait nearly two hours for the Klein sisters to arrive. Anne as usual had lost track of all time and apologized abundantly for their tardiness. She had drug Elizabeth all over that section of town looking in the window of this store then another and another, none of which were open early but were still quite appealing to look at. Even though San Francisco had been several times larger than Portland, they had never spent time shopping there. It had just been too dangerous, and they had never felt safe enough to meander any of its streets.

Upon their arrival, Albert politely rose and seated Elizabeth then Anne. After ordering their breakfast, Elizabeth inquired, "Please, Albert, tell us of what to expect between here and Lewiston. We will probably not be here long, and I would like to know all I can before we leave. We will need to prepare well from here on, as I have heard there are few towns, even small ones, between here and Lewiston."

"Correct, you are," advised Albert. "There has also been a few Indian uprisings on the overland route, but you should be relatively safe from that issue going by boat up the Columbia."

Anne threw both hands into the air, interrupting, "Oh my God, not another boat."

"It will be another boat ride for you," he continued. "That's the safest way on to Lewiston in the Idaho Territory. The first part being from here in Portland down the Willamette River to the Columbia."

Their food arrived, and Albert paused to shovel two forkfuls into his mouth before proceeding. He was famished after waiting for so long.

"Then up the Columbia to Bonneville will be by paddle wheeler, probably the *James P. Flint*, at least that is the one our group took for the first section of the trip upriver," he continued, barely pausing to chew his food. "We had to spend two nights at the Cascade Rapids waiting on the mule-drawn rail cars to the middle section of the Columbia around some bad water at Hood River, then the next section of the Columbia on another steamship called the *Idaho* up to the next portage by rail, around the Celilo Falls, then back to another steamship, that one being the *Colonel Wright*, as I remember, then on to Lewiston at the confluence of the Clearwater and Snake Rivers. Don't remember all of those stops for sure, though—we had been indulging in too much ale most of the way. The small city of Lewiston will be on the east side of the Snake River and is a wonderful and quaint little town. I think you will love it there."

"Will the trip be safe?" Elizabeth inquired.

"Of course not." Albert frowned. "There are gamblers on the paddle-boats. Gamblers and robbers and seedy saloons in the portage towns. The risk of Indian attack on the portages themselves. However, they would be more likely to indulge in petty theft rather than attack on well-armed travelers. Everything is dependent upon the captain's ability to keep the paddle wheeler on course so as not to hit a rock or floating debris resulting in the sinking of your craft."

Both girls sat in anxious silence. This was not what they expected to hear.

"These riverboats do have fairly nice accommodations but hardly what one could refer to as luxurious, and two beautiful young ladies traveling alone in an area mostly inhabited by lonely miners? Not one inch of that trip will be remotely safe."

They continued to talk again for hours after breakfast before Elizabeth excused herself to return to the Shaw House. Anne stayed on with Albert, and he gave her a guided tour of the small town of Portland, which would take all of about three hours on foot.

"See that huge tent over there?" He pointed. "That is where we are now playing. Anne, you were quite good—as a matter of fact, you were better than good. Would you consider joining this small performing group at least while we are here in Portland? You will of course go on, I know, but at least think of doing a few performances here."

"I will talk of this with Elizabeth. She did not approve of me continuing on in the theater in San Francisco, and I'm afraid she will not be at all happy with this and may want to move on soon, but who knows? We will talk of it, Albert. It may be fun for only a few performances."

Chapter 72

Portland,
Oregon, United States

1864

Two days later Elizabeth and Albert sat in the front row of the tent theater watching Anne's performance as she sang. The games around them in the tent had slowed, and here and there men had even ceased to drink. One and all, they all watched her. There was about her none of the brassy boldness of the usual tent-theater and gold-country performers. She looked fresh, young, and lovely. She was like a girl from home, yet with that extra something that stirred the blood of every man in the huge tent. As she went on from song to song, moving gracefully about the stage, her eyes moved from man to man throughout the crowd, making each one feel that she sang to him alone. She had a quick, easy smile that pleased a man. Along with it, she had an honest and straightforward no-nonsense demeanor.

Elizabeth sat watching in total admiration. *She is so good. So much better than when she first started. Perhaps I should have never convinced her to leave San Francisco to follow me into God only knows what. Perhaps we will stay here for a while,* she thought. *I really like this quaint little town, such a refreshing change from Frisco. And Anne is happy doing an occasional performance here.*

With Anne once again consumed with the theater, such as it was at the time in Portland, Elizabeth spent all of her free time in the area's

Chinatown. She volunteered her time in treating the injured and sick as well as learning more of the ways of the Chinese medical practices with herbs and other homeopathic remedies and procedures. She had become a legend in the small community as the beautiful white lady who helped all.

The Klein sisters remained in Portland for three months before mutually agreeing to continue on up the Columbia. They had just received news from home in Germany. The packet had arrived at their home in Hayes Valley, where their dear friend Lolivey and her father were still residing. Lolivey had forwarded the packet on to the attention of Elizabeth at the Shaw House in Portland, where Elizabeth and Anne were still residing. Edward and Mary had made safe return from San Francisco to Darmstadt in Germany. Elizabeth and Anne's father, Manfred, had been staying on at the Clay vineyards owned and run by Thomas's mother, and they were planning to be married. They read that that occasion was to be concluded by the time Elizabeth would receive the packet.

Fredrick C. Burgdorf had survived another confrontation with Horst and had seemingly sealed the villain's unconscious body in a packing crate marked *Farm Implements* being shipped to South Africa. This confrontation had taken place all in Horst's own warehouse in Darmstadt. The warehouse had also mysteriously caught on fire and no longer existed. With Manfred now assisting in the business of the vineyards, Fredrick was feeling antsy, having heard of the tremendous success and wealth of Edward and Mary in the mining fields of California. He had decided to also move on to that great American frontier to try his luck.

Little Josh, whom Thomas had rescued from the slums in Darmstadt when only a small child, was now a burly and handsome teenager and would also be accompanying Fredrick to the American West. As near as Elizabeth could comprehend of the dates, knowing the length of travel time depended on one's methods of travel and routes, Little Josh and Fredrick were possibly en route now. They of course had the Hayes Valley location and had promised to eventually pay a visit there.

The letter was quite long and went on with news of other friends and neighbors in Germany. The gunsmith, Mr. Hollenbeck, and his wife were also coming to the American West. Their children had migrated several years earlier, and they were excited to reunite with them and the new grandchildren all living in what was now referred to as the Idaho Territory. Elizabeth remembered Raymond Hollenbeck had been a friend of Thomas's father, and then a mentor to Thomas after his father passed. He was a dear friend to the family who had helped with all the travel arrangements for Thomas then later for Elizabeth and Anne. *That dear man and his wife probably also helped with the travel arrangements of Fredrick C. Burgdorf and Little Josh*, Elizabeth thought in reading the letter for the third time. But it was unclear as to who had left first, the Hollenbecks or Fredrick and little Josh.

Lolivey had also forwarded a short note of conditions in Hayes Valley. Their small farm was in excellent condition due to Hank's complete recovery—he was now the best of handymen. However, they had dared not make a visit into the city of San Francisco, fearing exposure to Hongkong Bohle's ruthless group, and still depended on Timothy for goods and services not readily available there. They were quite comfortable to just limit their existence to the Hayes Valley area. There had been no news of Thomas—he seemed to have vanished from the face of the earth.

Elizabeth and Anne took turns reading the letters out loud to each other, over and over. Elizabeth had not lost hope of Thomas's healthy return but was facing the reality of possible life without him. After reading the letter from home many times, Anne thought, *With our father marrying Thomas's mother, will that make Thomas and Elizabeth brother and sister?* It was a subject she knew Elizabeth would have already thought of, and Anne certainly was not going to bring it up.

"Well, now what?" Anne asked.

"We will leave here as soon as we can make arrangements," Elizabeth answered her sister. "I want to move on."

"You make the arrangements," Anne said. "I'm going to start packing. I am tired of the theater again, at least here in this one-horse town."

"One-horse town?" Elizabeth repeated. "I thought you loved it here."

"It's just the same old faces with only a few new ones now and again. The new has worn off, and I'm not the extravagant star I was a few months ago. A new face will replace me soon. Of that, I'm quite sure."

Chapter 73

Portland,
Oregon, United States

1864

Elizabeth had made the arrangements. They had planned carefully with two more trunks of provisions in case there were no available hotels or boarding houses available along the way.

They were settled comfortably in their cabins on the *James P. Flint* when it pulled away from the dock in Portland in early morning. The fog was heavy, rendering poor visibility.

"I hope this captain knows what he is doing." Anne groaned. "If we are to crash into something and sink, I would rather it be here close to Portland so we could at least have some civilized place to swim to."

Elizabeth just shook her head. "Anne, you can at times be the most exasperating person I have ever known. Think of something positive for once."

"Okay," she replied with a grin on her face. "I hope you marry your brother."

With that, they both broke into laughter. They were sitting in their cabin on the starboard side of the paddle wheeler gazing out the window at nothing but the heavy fog and making small talk. While in Portland, they had talked to many travelers who had made the trip either from Lewiston down to Portland or were going upriver from Portland to Lewiston, but nothing had prepared them for the breathtaking beauty they would soon experience. The trip down the Willamette to its confluence with the Columbia was completed before the thick fog rose, and they were well on their way up the Columbia before they could see anything more than a few hundred feet away.

Suddenly the sun peeked its way through the clouds. The canyon walls rose up on either side of the river, and they were staring at splendid timber-covered mountains with snow still on the upper levels. The birds flocked from the trees along the shoreline, and majestic eagles were visibly in abundance. The numerous valleys along the shore were filled with a variety of huge animals called elk. And the occasional stream running into the river was often blocked by a beaver dam. It was lush everywhere they looked. Thick moss hung from the trees near the water's edge. Tremendous flocks of geese and ducks were continually rising from the waters in front of them. It was a sight of such beauty as they had never witnessed before in their entire lives.

This was the new world, the new American frontier. *This is what Thomas dreamed of, what he always talked of, and now here I am,* Elizabeth thought. Sitting spellbound in observation of all this grandeur, the girls had missed lunch then hardly noticed the slowing pace of the small steamship. *It should be hours yet before dark and our first scheduled stop for the night,* Elizabeth thought. When she inquired about it, she learned apparently there was some issue with one of the boilers on the steamboat, dictating the necessity for an early stop along the shore.

The steamboat slowly made its way to a secluded cove that would be partially protected from the wind. At times earlier in the day, the wind had whipped down the river with such force, it could take one off their feet. Repairs would be required prior to the continuation of the trip, so they would spend the night tied here in the cove then continue on tomorrow, they were told.

The sisters were standing by the railing in front of their cabin, completely fascinated at the raw beauty they were witnessing, when the huge bell mounted to the front of the ship boomed away, breaking the silent splendor.

"It must be suppertime," Anne announced. "Come, let's see what the menu has in store for us this first night."

Walking down the stairs to the huge dining room on the main level, they met and greeted many other travelers heading in the same direction, some well-dressed in suits and evening dresses but most in plain frontier clothes more suitable for unpredictable events on the journey upriver. These steamboats were reported to have a reasonable safety record, but on occasion, one would sink for some reason or another and the only survivors, word had it, were the ones that were prepared for such an event. Elizabeth and Anne chose a table for two next to the window to take advantage of the mesmerizing view that was still on display just before the coming dark.

Chatting and enjoying her meal, Anne noticed a solidly built man with a thick chest, wide shoulders, and a block head perched on his neck slowly ambling his way through the crowded dining room toward them.

When he reached the girls' table, he asked brusquely, "You two traveling alone? Either of you married? I'm ah rich mine holder and in need of ah wife."

"You need a bath too," Anne quickly replied, swiveling in her chair to face him more directly. Albert had warned them that they may be approached by any number of men of this type, but both Anne and Elizabeth were still taken by surprise.

"We are not traveling alone," Elizabeth hastily added, "and our husbands will be joining us soon."

"Humph." He breathed deeply. "I watched you board alone this morning in Portland. Where were these husbands you talk of when they were needed? In one of those many trunks you drug on by your selves? I'll be keeping ah eye on ya both. Either one of ya will do." Repeating "I need a wife," he turned and ambled off.

"Well," Elizabeth said, "there is one you can marry and probably *not* live happily ever after with."

Anne sat gazing at Elizabeth for a moment with her fork halfway to her mouth. "I'm beginning to change my mind about marrying and having a family if the likes of that creature is all I have to choose from."

The rest of the evening went without incident, and they returned to their room. The repairs were completed before daylight the next morning, and the vessel was well underway again long before the sun came up. The trip, they had been informed when boarding the day before, would take about twelve days, give or take a day or two.

"What will we do upon our arrival in Lewiston?" Anne finally asked.

They had talked little since boarding, Their concentration focused wholly on their unbelievable surroundings. They had passed Multnomah Falls on the starboard side of the boat, a most beautiful and splendid sight. A short time later, another falls appeared to resemble a bridal veil when the constant wind dispersed the mist causing this visual phenomenon. "The spirit of puffing wind," Anne commented. "Is the rest of the way and our destination in Lewiston as beautiful as this?"

Elizabeth frowned, not wanting to divert her attention from these unbelievable surroundings. "We will get a room somewhere in a boarding house or hotel until we can join a group going on into the heart of the territory's mining district. Maybe we will go to Pierce or Florence or even to Warren's Diggins. It really doesn't matter to me—we will continue on to whichever one we can get to first with the most ease."

"Nothing here is with any ease," Anne commented, faintly smiling. She knew she was annoying Elizabeth with her continual sarcasm. After losing time yesterday because of the faulty boiler, they would have to spend another night on the river before reaching the first portage at Bonneville, a bad section of the river filled with severe rapids and nasty outcroppings of rocks, making it impossible to navigate. At Bonneville they may be forced to camp for at least one or maybe two nights, as their steamboat, the *James P. Flint*, would unload them and the other passengers then begin the trip back down the river with cargo and other passengers immediately. It was a never-ending cycle. Elizabeth and Anne had been informed that due to the amount of travel now on the river, it would be next to impossible to obtain lodging at any one of the few otherwise seedy hotels they may not wish to stay at anyway. They were prepared for this possibility and actually looking forward to it. Sleeping under the stars sounded nice.

Arriving at Bonneville, the beginning of a five-mile stretch of river that extended to the Cascade Rapids, about noon they disembarked and left most of their luggage at the Oregon Steam Navigation

Company office to be loaded onto one of the horse-drawn rail cars that would take them the five miles upriver and around the Cascades to catch the steamboat *Idaho* offering service on the next section of the Columbia as far as Celilo Falls. The Klein sisters did not bother to wander into the small community at Bonneville. There was a young man loitering at the docks who was more than happy to help with only two of their trunks to a campsite amongst a group of mixed cottonwood and pine trees next to the river, making for the perfect place to spend the night or maybe two, since the rail car schedule was sporadic at best. The horse-drawn train had not arrived at Bonneville yet, and they were informed it may be a day late—possible Indian trouble.

They had set up a very comfortable camp, though it took more time than expected and it was approaching dark. They got a small fire going and hung a line nearby between the trees to hold up a makeshift tent. Their bedrolls were stretched out on a mat under the tent. Their meal consisted of a can of beans warmed over the small fire, a slice of bread cut from a loaf that had been tucked away in a trunk, and a tin of peaches. Anne had strolled up the beach a distance, gazing over the moonlit river, and Elizabeth was carrying a bucket of water the few steps from the river to their camp when the undesirable smelly miner who had approached them the evening before on the boat suddenly appeared out of the darkness. He startled her, and she spilled most of the bucket down her dress.

"Miss Klein," he said. "I got your name from that steamer's captain. I've been thinking—"

"Oh, you have? A refreshing change," Elizabeth said in a strong manner, trying not to show her fear.

Frowning at this remark, he continued, "Wet or dry, you're the handsomest woman I ever did see. You've got spirit, and a fine, sturdy body, actually a very appealing body—a decent combination. Why to you, I bet child bearin' would come easily as rolling off a log."

Elizabeth looked at him with a steady gaze, not knowing where his actions or this conversation would lead next. "Sir, if it is left to me," she said despairingly, "I would rather roll off the log."

"Ma'am, I'm telling you. You got the build for it, and that's what I'm looking for. I want you for my wife. You just natural couldn't do any better than to marry me. Why, we could have ourselves a fine family in just no time at all." Then hearing Anne approaching, he turned and walked away into the darkness. Looking back over his shoulder, he added, "I don't intend to let this proposal stop here—you can count on that."

What a proposal, she thought. *He didn't even bring flowers, and he nearly scared me to death.*

"What did that unwashed but 'very wealthy miner,' as he says, want?" Anne inquired.

"Children."

"Children? Well, why didn't he come shopping to the right store?" Anne gasped.

Elizabeth laughed. "Must you always be so blunt? You're a lady."

"That I am," she replied. "That I am. And a lonely one."

In a time and place when women were scarce, the Klein sisters would average a proposal every other day, the proposals coming from old men and young men; from established miners, ranchers, or businessmen; from drifting cowhands, prospectors, and every variety of male creature about.

"And some of them really mean it," Anne said one night as she and Elizabeth were discussing it, "but most are only talking and would be frightened to their death if you said yes. To them this is a lonely time for their kind here, taking no pleasure in returning to an empty house or tent just to hear nothing but the echo of their own voice. With us it's different—we have each other, we are a family, we laugh together, we cry together, and you put up with me." She smiled.

Chapter 74

Columbia River Gorge, Oregon, United States

1864

The morning after the miner's surprise proposal, Elizabeth and Anne strolled up from their campsite on the river to the small community of Bonneville looking for a place to have breakfast. They did not want to get caught with dirty dishes stuffed into the trunk if the rail cars were to return for them and other passengers early.

The wind was howling down the canyon fiercely, and they could hardly stand and walk against it. Their camp was somewhat sheltered in the cove surrounded by trees, so they'd experienced hardly more than a mild and comforting breeze there. Now out of the trees, they felt this was brutal. The canyon was over a mile wide here, with the mountains on either side of the river still visible but only from a distance. The terrain was flattening and much more barren than what they'd seen in the gorge so far. The shores of the Columbia now had only scattered vegetation that appeared to be stunted in growth from the constant and severe winds. The few trees dotting the landscape all leaned the same direction. This was by far less appealing than the splendid section of river to this point from Portland.

Finding a small wood-framed shelter with a sign stenciled *Eatery*, Elizabeth pulled the door open, and the wind slammed her and the door into the side of the building, knocking her to the ground.

"Be careful of that wind," the proprietor announced from across the room. She had witnessed this occurrence several times a day for years. "I am going to put that door on the other side of the building one of these days," she said. "I have few enough customers as it is, and I surely don't want to discourage any away because of that door slamming them into the side of the building every time one opens it."

Fairly shaken, Elizabeth did not notice who was attached to the helping hand that was offered. She only took it to finally stand against the wind and make her way into the shabby little building. Anne was standing just inside the door waiting for her to enter. The light was very poor inside, and it took a moment for Elizabeth's eyes to adjust to the dimness. Noticing the helping hand was now attached to her elbow, she turned and gasped. It was the same man who had approached them on the boat and then at their camp last night.

"I'm still proposing matrimony." He grinned.

And seeing some humor in the situation, Elizabeth replied, "And I would still rather fall off that log."

"Can I buy you two breakfast?"

"Why not?" Anne chimed in. "Please, join us." It seemed safe enough inside the dim-lit building with the few other patrons sitting and now staring at the trio.

After they'd sat at a table, he on one side with Elizabeth and Anne side-by-side on the other, Anne without hesitation asked, "What is your name?"

"Frenchy."

"Frenchy? That's not a real name. I think it is a nickname." Asking again but phrasing it a bit differently, she said, "What is your God-given name, the one you were born with? The one your mother and father called you?"

"Well, it's James P. Warren."

"How on earth did you with a name of James P. Warren ever get a nickname of Frenchy?"

"Don't know," he replied, "but I do have a town named after me."

The proprietor interrupted them with cups of steaming coffee. "What do ya want to eat, bacon and eggs, or eggs and bacon?"

Looking at her perplexed, Frenchy said, "Bacon and eggs."

"Same for me." Elizabeth grinned.

Then the server looked at Anne. "And what will it be for you?"

"Eggs Benedict, light on the hollandaise sauce, fried shredded pota-toes, and fresh orange juice." Anne had grown fond of the juice, having lived in Hayes Valley, California, for two years. Then she added, "Real cream and granulated whole grain raw sugar for my coffee." She re-turned the stare with a sweet smile.

"Right, got it." The proprietor snorted, turning away to get them all bacon and fried eggs dripping in bacon grease but looking tasty enough.

The miner sat gawking at Anne then turned his attention to Elizabeth. "I think she will make a much better sister-in-law than a wife."

This man Frenchy, or James P. Warren, whichever one chose to call him, was turning out to be a delightful and quite wealthy man with a sense of humor. They learned that the town of Warren's Diggins, which they had already considered visiting someday, was named after him. He was the first one to have discovered gold in that wealthy basin. Even though Frenchy had been serious about his crude proposal, he dropped that subject and carried on with answering hours of questions from the Klein sisters. He was the first person who'd spent much time in the great country beyond Lewiston that they had an opportunity to talk to in person.

It was now late in the afternoon, and they were still talking about the mining industry, the river route ahead, the capital city of Lewiston, and possible Indian trouble when the station manager strolled in an-nouncing that the rail car had just returned but would not leave until noon the next day.

"Why noon?" Elizabeth inquired.

"Because that's when I want to leave. Make sure you're on it or you will be left behind," he snapped at the girls, not seeing Frenchy in the dim light.

Standing then facing the station master, Frenchy stared at the man with a gaze as cold as ice. "Would you care to rephrase that comment in a kindlier way to these two young ladies?"

Without hesitation the station master pleaded, "Beg your pardon, ladies. Please be ready to board the rail car by noon tomorrow. That is as soon as I can be ready to get you all around the falls to the next available boat going on further upstream. And if you are late, I'll wait for you." Then he turned and hurried out the door.

"Good for him," said Frenchy. "I will now humbly accompany you to your camp to guarantee you have no further problems of any kind." Frenchy's rough mannerisms and slang had suddenly disappeared. He had once been a refined, well-mannered gentleman, but the time in mining camps with other rough-and-tumble men had dimmed his sophisticated ways, and he had fallen to that lifestyle with its crude mannerisms. "Come, let us go now."

When they'd returned to their camp, the girls invited Frenchy to stay for another can of beans warmed over the fire with a slice of bread.

"Not to offend you, and if I may, please allow me to add something to this meal."

"No offense taken," Anne hastily replied. "How long will it take? I'm hungry."

"Only a moment," Frenchy replied. "I am barely out of sight on the other side of the trees. I was watching over you last night to make sure nothing were to happen. I'm not the only one a-wantin' to marry ya." He grinned as he reverted back to his slang. Then turned away to bring something more desirable to the table than canned beans.

The next morning the girls were up before dawn with a fire brightly blazing to take the chill from the morning air as they anxiously awaited Frenchy's company. He arrived midmorning and graciously accepted a steaming cup of coffee. They had broken their small camp down and were ready to go. Frenchy helped them with their two trunks, handling them both with care. Elizabeth smiled, seeing no need to warn him to be cautious of the glass hummingbird carefully packed inside. Another bird-in-the-trunk comment was not something she wanted to address this morning, so she was relieved she didn't need to. She did allow the wishful melancholy thought of Thomas's return to enter her mind, though.

With Frenchy's assistance, they were safely loaded onto the rail car before noon for the short journey on the tracks around the unnavigable section of the river. They would soon arrive at Hood River for the next leg of river travel. The rail cars used for the portage were a vital part of the Columbia River travel and were relatively new. Prior to their completion, travelers would have to walk carrying their belongings around the non-navigable sections of river. At times a pack string of horses would be available for this endeavor, but that option could not be counted on.

"This is absolutely wonderful," commented Anne, particularly about the padded seats on the horse-drawn rail car. The horses plodded along at a slow gait to pull the passenger car, which towed the baggage car attached behind. The tracks were now about a half mile above the river overlooking its more barren splendor.

"It's not as beautiful as the lower gorge we came through the last few days, but it is beautiful. It's just beautiful in a different way." Frenchy was seated behind the girls and would continue with them as far as Lewiston, only a few days further upstream.

This first portage around the horrifying Bonneville and the Cascade Rapids went pleasurably with no incidents, and by two o'clock they had reached the dock to board the next steamboat taking them up to the next portage around the Hood River Rapids. Once around the Hood River Rapids, the steamboat was waiting at the dock, so they could unload their baggage from the rail car directly onto the steamboat and not worry about making another camp by the river this night. By the time all passengers had removed their luggage from the rail car then loaded on the boat, it was nearly dark. They would spend the night on board here and start early the next morning for Celilo Falls, where they'd have to do the final portage.

Elizabeth and Anne had been informed upon boarding that this leg of the trip would only be one day, maybe two, weather permitting. *God.* Elizabeth inhaled heavily. *"Weather permitting" again. I had hoped to never hear that phrase again after getting off Captain Sawyer's ship.*

Approaching the Klein sisters, Frenchy beamed. "How would you two like to join me for dinner tonight? I'm buying!"

"You're buying?" Anne retorted. "The meal is included in our fare!"

Frenchy rolled his eyes. "It was only a figure of speech, Anne. And please disregard any reference to matrimony I may have unwisely made to you before, but do join me at a table for the evening meal. We still have much to talk of before reaching Lewiston."

"We will assuredly do that." Elizabeth chuckled. A few weeks earlier Frenchy had made the trip downriver accompanying a sizable shipment of gold from his mine in Warren's Diggins to be deposited into the Wells Fargo bank in Portland. The mine was several days east of Lewiston by stage and then further by horseback in the wilderness of the Salmon River drainage to Warren's. He did not intend to travel all the way back this season. The area was above six thousand feet in elevation and would soon be snowed in with nothing but a very treacherous way in or out, by snowshoes only. He had made a small fortune from the mine and would make another in selling it, which he intended to do soon. He now wanted to spend some leisurely time in Lewiston and maybe even take the three-hundred-mile trip south to the new Boise Basin mining area. He had heard much about the opportunities there and thought much about that. There he may also find a wife, he thought—he knew for sure, though, it was not going to be Anne, and Elizabeth had informed him of Thomas, so she was not an option either. He wished her well with that continuing search, and as he bid them goodnight, he assured both sisters he would always remain friends.

Chapter 75

Columbia River Gorge, Oregon, United States

1864

The next morning the trip upriver was enjoyable with a very different beauty. The canyon was flattening out, with the mountains farther in the background. The terrain had changed from fantastic, tree-covered mountains coming right down to the river's edge to now nearly desert. The girls were once again spellbound. Frenchy had given them a mile-by-mile dissertation of what to expect around each sweeping bend of the river. It was another incredible day for them, and any possible danger was the furthest thing from their mind while in Frenchy's company.

They did make it to the Celilo Falls portage that day.

At first light, Frenchy again assisted them in loading all of their belongings onto another rail car for that final portage and the remaining trip by steamboat to Lewiston. Not being so lucky this time, they would have to spend the night in another camp alongside the river at the end of the portage waiting for the boat to return from upriver at Lewiston to pick them up. The girls were becoming exhausted by this loading onto the boat then transferring baggage to rail car then reversing the feat again and again. This night here on the shores of the Columbia in another secluded cove would be their last before reaching Lewiston.

"I will help you with your camp," Frenchy advised the two, knowing they were both exhausted. "And I will place my own bedroll closer than usual. I did see two unsavory looking gents watching you unload earlier."

"Thank you so much, Frenchy." Elizabeth smiled. "If I were not still so in love with my Thomas and still having hope of news from him, I would certainly give serious consideration to your proposal. You would have to bring flowers, though." She grinned.

He chuckled. "Deal." Frenchy had placed his bedroll only a few feet from the girls, and took leave. He would return soon, he promised. "I have to run up to the Oregon Steam Navigation Company office and make final arrangements for some implements I purchased here on my way downriver to Portland a few weeks ago. I should be gone about an hour, two at most, and will not be far away."

The girls nodded. Having had such a relaxing evening the night before and an uneventful day aboard the ship today, they had no reason to suspect any danger at their camp tonight.

Frenchy had been gone no more than an hour and Anne was sound asleep when Elizabeth heard faint rustling in the undergrowth between their camp and the river. She had been staring at the fire, which now impeded her night vision, but squinting carefully she could see what she thought to be a figure sneaking toward their camp. The small derringer had never left her possession since leaving Germany. It was always, without fail, hidden in an inside pocket concealed by a fold of her dress. Thomas had taught her how to use it, and she was capable of using it well.

Reaching into the pocket, Elizabeth held the small pistol in her hand. The derringer was a .44 caliber, and it had two barrels. Elizabeth was calm and not frightened. *Probably someone who just has lost their way, and I've overreacted in thinking they're sneaking through the brush,* she thought. Taking no chances, though, she hissed at Anne to wake up. "We may have a worry."

A man suddenly popped threw the undergrowth no more than fifteen feet away. The firelight was glinting from his ugly, menacing eyes. "No use in yelling for help," he said. "I saw that chaperone guy of yours leave. He will not be back soon enough to do either of you any good. It's been a long time since I have seen any women as handsome as y'all. You'll do just fine." He smirked. He was holding a knife at arm's length in front of him, waving it slightly in an intimidating way. "Just cooperate and no one will get hurt, not much anyway." He leered. "One false move, though, and you will both wind up as fish bait."

A tranquil had surrounded Elizabeth. She had the pistol in her hand, and there was no way this ugly creature would get another step closer to her and Anne. "Sir, if we are expected to cooperate, may I inquire as to your name?"

"Luther," he said. "It's Luther, but what difference does a name make at a time like this?"

"Well, Mr. Luther, as you can plainly see, I have this handgun pointed directly at your middle. It may seem small, but it does make a very large hole."

He had not noticed her quickly draw it from her pocket. He thought she just had her hand in her pocket, but he now realized it held the deadly little weapon. Luther raised his foot to take a step closer when the slug staggered him accompanied by its bellowing roar echoing over and over in the confines of the canyon. He backed up two paces, shaking his hand in disbelief and extreme pain. His thumb was lying on the leaf-covered ground, and the place where it had been naturally attached to his hand just a moment before was streaming blood freely down his remaining fingers and puddling on the leaves next to the thumb.

Elizabeth took a step back from him then paused, the derringer still in hand at arm's length. "Mr. Luther, I would suggest you take your thumbless and wounded hand and get somewhere right away. You are going to require medical attention, I think." Her heart was pounding heavily, and she could not seem to swallow, but she held the pistol steady.

Luther took a step toward her with rage in his eyes.

"Mr. Luther, I have another barrel. If I must shoot you again, I will, and this time it will not be only your thumb missing."

He stared at her disbelieving, his eyes nasty and ugly.

"Go now," she said again. "Go where you can get help, Mr. Luther. You are going to need it."

Suddenly his expression changed. His eyes widened, he gasped, and his skin had turned an ugly gray. He backed away holding his bleeding hand then started through the brush in a stumbling run.

Through the trees Elizabeth caught a glimpse of his horse and watched him clumsily mount and ride away.

Anne was sitting up in her bedroll looking at Elizabeth disbelievingly, having just been woken from a sound sleep. "What just happened?" she hooted.

"I just removed that creature's thumb with this pistol." Elizabeth's legs had started to tremble, and she collapsed in a heap next to Anne.

Now noticing the thumb hardly more than a step away, Anne managed, "What are you going to do with the thumb?"

Hearing the shot, Frenchy had come running down the slight incline from the freight office. "What happened?" he shouted. "I heard a shot."

"Elizabeth just shot someone's thumb off," Anne called.

"What?"

Anne was sure that he had heard her and did not reply a second time. She was also visibly shaken and was holding Elizabeth. Within just a few minutes, the quiet little camp was crowded with people coming to investigate what had happened. The girls had made many friends on the trip upriver, and no one would see any harm come to them. Several had known Luther—he was a perpetual trouble maker. They would all be on the lookout for this man but doubted that he would be seen again. He had been known as a coward taking advantage of weaker people and primarily picking on defenseless women. This time it had not worked—the Klein sisters were not weak and certainly not defenseless.

The small group that had gathered around the Klein sisters slowly moved off in all directions to make sure the would-be molester, Luther, was not still in the area. At this time a cattle rustler, bank robber, or plain old thief may be forgiven but not any man who would harm a woman or child. This was a hanging offense.

When Frenchy was finally contented the disgraceful Luther was nowhere around, he made sure the girls were once again comfortable then walked back up the trail to the station in the dark to finish his business. "This is a rugged, harsh, and at times lawless land," he said to no one. "I hope we make it on to Lewiston with no further problems. These two may have a chance of survival there. They are tough little mutts. Who knows?"

Anne and Elizabeth were still sitting by the campfire reliving the events of the last hour.

"Elizabeth, I saw where you were pointing that pistol, and I think I remember you saying if you were forced to shoot again, he would be missing more than just his thumb. Would you really have shot off his manhood?"

"No, I wouldn't have taken the chance of shooting at and missing a most likely small target." She laughed. "I would have elevated my aim a couple of inches and put a hole through his more-than-ample-sized gut, very possibly eliminating his miserable existence and saving any other woman his unwanted aggressive behavior."

Chapter 76

Columbia River Gorge,
Oregon, United States

1864

In the morning, the next paddle wheeler returned from upriver early, and they all boarded to continue up to the confluence of the Snake and Columbia Rivers. This leg of the trip, Frenchy had advised the sisters, would take two to three days, weather permitting, Elizabeth cringed. *Weather permitting again*, she thought. This day they made nearly fifty miles. The wind was not howling down the canyon, which would have slowed their upriver progress. They overnighted at another secluded cove just before dark and did not have to leave their relaxed cabins aboard the paddle wheeler. They would continue on at first light, they were told.

"God," Anne said over dinner on the small paddle wheeler, "maybe we can sleep in in the morning. I'm exhausted."

The boat left at daylight the next morning continuing upriver. The weather was cooperative, and the river was now passing through more desert-like terrain but was still beautiful. The rapids on the river were more frequent than what they had encountered in the lower Columbia but less severe and required no portages. The sisters were enjoying this portion of the trip. Frenchy would pay them a visit at noon and then again for the evening meal. He informed them about everything he could think of—he talked of his many trips up and down the river, about the country beyond Lewiston. He talked of the mining camps at Pierce, Florence, and Warren's Diggins. He told them of other significant small communities along the Salmon River not far east of Lewiston—White Bird and Gouge Eye. He talked of the few settlers along the Salmon River who were also prospecting for gold. In general the girls wanted as much information as possible of the area.

That night again in the boat's dining hall, the girls pestered him for more information. "We only have a few more nights on the river," he informed them. "You better make every moment count. You will not be entering into the kindest of environments. Lewiston is still a new and rough little community."

"Does it have a theater?" Anne asked.

Thinking a moment, Frenchy replied, "Not a formal one that I re-member, but I'm sure some of the occasional traveling shows will have a tent theater up someplace."

"Good." Anne beamed. "I will sing again for those who will listen," she joked.

Looking across the table at her, Elizabeth held out both hands. "Why not sing now? We love your performances, and I'm sure the captain, crew, and other passengers wouldn't mind."

And she did just that. Walking over to the captain's table, Anne boldly inquired if he minded if she were to sing a few songs for him and the guests. "Not at all," he replied, "but wait a few minutes and I will have the deckhands prepare a small stage for you."

Fifteen minutes later, Anne was on that stage singing a cappella, a most difficult task, but with her practiced talent, she managed easily. She gracefully carried on from one song to another, stopping only for an occasional drink of water and her acknowledgment of the applause of the crowd that had gathered in the dining room.

On one pause a man yelled out, "That's Anne Klein—I saw her performing in Portland. Bravo, bravo."

Another miner yelled out, "And I saw her in San Francisco. We have a real celebrity here on the river."

Her performance lasted for over an hour there on that stage in the dining room of the paddleboat on the Columbia River. Elizabeth sat spellbound with moist eyes. *She is so unbelievable, I should have never persuaded her to leave San Francisco. She is a celebrity, and what will she do in Lewiston, Idaho?* Upon completion of her performance, Anne received a standing ovation with Elizabeth and Frenchy in the lead. She was once again all smiles when she returned to the table.

"God," she said, "that was delightful. It has been so long since I have performed. It is such a love-hate affair, though. When I'm performing regular, I hate it, and when I'm not performing, I love the thought of it. What do you think will ever become of me, Frenchy?" she asked, laughing.

"You are bound for glory," he said. "A rare talent. But not too good to be wasted here in this lonely western land. We will enjoy you for as long as you are here."

The next day their small paddle wheeler docked just before dark at the confluence of the Snake River and the Columbia. They would have to change boats again to yet a smaller steamship for the remaining portion of the trip up the Snake River. The captain announced they could all remain on the ship this night and unload onto the smaller Idaho-bound vessel tomorrow morning. It would take them five or six days to go from here at the confluence on to Lewiston. They would have to stop at a number of small ports to load and unload goods and supplies as well as an occasional passenger. The Snake River was much smaller than the enormous Columbia. It was just one of many tributaries to the Columbia before it found its leisurely way to the Pacific Ocean.

Sitting at the dining table that night with Frenchy, Elizabeth asked, "Where does this Snake River come from? It is so much different in appearance than the Columbia."

"I have been to the headwaters of this very river," Frenchy replied. "It is about thirteen hundred and fifty miles in length and lies at the bottom of the deepest gorge on the North American continent. Its headwaters start in that Wyoming area, and it ends here at its confluence with the Columbia River. It is not navigable in the section between Lewiston and the Boise Basin mining area, but that section of the river does have a fleet of steamships built there and servicing that area, I'm told. However, I have personally never seen one there. I do plan to visit the

Boise Basin sometime in the next few months, though. I hear it is a booming area and destined for great things."

Elizabeth shifted in her chair and looked pointedly at Frenchy. "Will we ever see you again?"

"Of course," he replied. "I'll be sitting right here next to one or the other of you for the next several days."

She punched him. "You know what I mean—after we dock in Lewiston in a few days, will we see you again after that?"

"Yes, of course," he said with a reflective smile. But deep in his soul, he felt quite sure he wouldn't see either of them again after reaching Lewiston.

Once aboard the last steamboat, they labored their way up the Snake River, bucking roaring rapids, dodging rocky outcroppings, and avoiding floating debris of all kinds. It was a beautiful experience, something they would never have dreamed to exist while still living back in Germany so many years ago. It was times like this that Elizabeth thought most about Thomas. She had such a longing for him, it was overwhelming.

Part IV

Chapter 77

Lewiston,
Idaho Territory, United States

1864

Finally the afternoon arrived when, rounding a bend in the river, Elizabeth and Anne sighted Lewiston no more than a mile ahead. It was both enormously exciting at first and, the closer they got, somewhat disappointing. They had finally reached their immediate destination but the capital city of Idaho on the banks of the Snake River was only a boat dock and a few buildings. Frenchy had tried to tell them it was a small but growing community, but this seemed just small.

"Oh my God!" Anne exclaimed. Then turning and staring at Elizabeth, she began a side-splitting laugh.

"Well, at least you're laughing." Elizabeth sighed.

With her laughter subsiding, Anne said, "What in heaven's name are we to do here, Elizabeth?"

"We will think of something," Elizabeth replied uncomfortably. "We always do."

The small steamboat was crowded with passengers, mostly miners but some families too. Some were continuing on further by stagecoach to distant mining boomtowns, and some were remaining here in Lewiston. As usual, Frenchy was by their side assisting them when it was their turn to disembark. Their trunks were placed in a neat pile on the small dock, and he had made arrangements to have a wagon carry them and the baggage to the Luna House, a hotel of sorts more or less in the middle of town, only a few blocks away. They would stay there for a few days until they could find a less expensive boarding house.

It was late evening when the Klein sisters were finally settled into the Luna House, and again Frenchy had asked to accompany them to dinner. Being totally new to the small town, they agreed it was a grand idea.

Even though most of the buildings in town were visible from the balcony of the Luna House where Elizabeth and Anne now sat in the chilly air, they had no idea which one housed a restaurant and which other may hold a less appealing business. After all, this was a frontier town inhabited in large by miners and other businessmen catering to the mining needs.

Before leaving Germany several years before, Elizabeth had known of this place she was now sitting as a vague idea called the great American West. It was a place where people by the thousands went to start a new life and rarely ever returned from. The east she knew, as she had spent time in Boston on the trip here from Germany, was a place of established families, businesses that had been in operation for many years, children whose great-grandparents had grown up together, and it had been a good world in so many ways, a safe world. That was not true here. Everything was new; everything was building. It was rough, hard, and unpolished. The law was around but never in the way. Men were expected to handle their own difficulties, and courage was the greatest respected virtue, with integrity a close second. Many a man whom one might call a bandit to his face would think nothing of that but would shoot you if you called him a liar or a coward.

Frenchy joined them on the balcony. "It's a good country," he said. "Please don't judge it too harshly. We're young yet. We're still growing up. Where society does not yet have the organization to handle trouble, we have to handle it for ourselves."

Elizabeth was once again in a very melancholy disposition. She sat in silence on the balcony staring out over this small town, her hands folded in her lap and a slight moistness in her eyes. She could see the Snake River on one side of town and the Clearwater River on the other. The trees were all bare under the gray sky, but she could imagine them full and lush in the summer sun in six months. The area did have a certain appeal, she supposed, but she was so lonely. The years had gone by and the chance that Thomas had survived and she would ever see him again grew slimmer. She had tried to tell herself to no longer think of a future with him. But she would still suffer from the occasional tremor of hope that even now sometimes took her unaware when she found herself dreaming that she might yet see him again.

Chapter 78

South China Sea

1864

Thomas and Jason labored relentlessly day by day. They each had mastered every job aboard ship, and either could manage the ship easily, should the opportunity ever present itself. Prior to entering a port, all hands not absolutely necessary in maintaining the ship functions would be taken below deck and put in chains then threatened with death should they utter a sound.

The bitter days edged slowly by, and weeks passed into months; then years were gone by, and still they remained prisoners of a sort. They were allowed to roam freely on the ship's deck with no restraints when at sea but were always chained in the hold days before reaching any land mass or port. They were moved from one ship to another as needs changed, usually to combine crews with another ship due to the high death rate in the cruel circumstances.

Thomas and Jason had been forced to serve on three different ships in the last several years, all of them in deplorable conditions. They were amongst the few that had survived the continuous abuse. They had gained a reputation as that monster with the raven-black hair and green eyes and his blond sidekick not to be trifled with.

Chapter 79

Lewiston,
Idaho Territory, United States

1864

Anne and Frenchy were carrying on about the beauty of the two rivers bordering two sides of the town and analyzing whether the surrounding barren, rock-covered mountains added any real appeal to the area when Frenchy noticed that faraway look in Elizabeth's eyes. Standing up, he interrupted her thoughts of Thomas with a hearty "Come now, let's wander the streets of this delightful town and find a bite to eat."

He led them only a few blocks in a westerly manner to a small but quaint little restaurant located next to the Hotel de France, which was still under construction but held promise of being a magnificent establishment. It was warm inside, the food was excellent, and they had a commanding view of both rivers. It had a rare ambiance and did wonders for the mood of the two girls, who were extremely exhausted after their steamboat rides from Portland.

Upon completion of the meal, Frenchy escorted them back to their hotel and lingered a short time for talk. "I will be leaving tomorrow morning for the Boise Basin mining area," he said. "It is about three hundred miles away. There's been talk of moving the capital there, but I won't hold my breath for that to happen. It has been most enjoyable being in your company for these last several weeks. But I must be leaving. The weather will soon turn bad, and I must negotiate several severe mountain passes before reaching Fort Boise."

There was silence for a few moments. Then Anne asked, "Where is this place you talk of?"

"See that Snake River right over yonder, the one we have been coming up for the last several days? If you could follow it up to the south for a few days, you would ultimately come to Fort Boise. At this time it is not navigable, so I will have to take another established route by stagecoach part of the way, then horse, and then continue on again by stage."

"Sounds exhausting," Anne replied. "Would you consider staying here with us if one of us agreed to marry you?"

"God no. Elizabeth is in love with someone else, and you would drive a sane man insane."

They both punched him, laughing. They had grown very fond of him, and he would be sorely missed. The conversation lasted another two hours, with both Elizabeth and Anne pestering Frenchy with question after question about the mining camps. The mining camp of Pierce had been a hot topic on the boat upriver, as were Florence and Warren's Diggins. He told them what he knew of each as well as the planning it would take to travel to each. None were easy to reach. He told them of the community of Mount Idaho not far to the south of the small settlement of White Bird on the fabled Salmon River, which would run into the Snake not far from Lewiston. There was also a promising mining area rumored to be on John Day Creek on the Salmon River upriver from White Bird, and then a short distance further upriver still was the new community of Gouge Eye, also located on the Salmon River. "Learn all you can of these places," he advised. "They are important areas, and if you remain here long, you will find a knowledge of their locations most interesting and beneficial."

Finally the conversation slowed, and Frenchy stood to bid them farewell. Both girls sadly gave him a lingering hug and made him promise to find them if and when he were to return to Lewiston. Once again Frenchy felt that foreboding of never seeing them again but said nothing of the thought. Out on the street, he turned and waved one more time up at the girls. "I am a lucky man to have made the acquaintances of those two," he said to no one in particular, "and I shall miss them."

The girls sat for another few minutes enjoying the scenery of the rivers then retired to their respective rooms. *Not bad*, Elizabeth thought. *Not quite as nice as the beautifully decorated rooms on the riverboat up the Columbia Gorge but not bad. We will remain here a few months, make plans to go on to a fabulous boomtown like Florence or Warren's Diggins, and who knows? Maybe we will become as wealthy as Sister Mary and Edward.*

Chapter 80

Lewiston,
Idaho Territory, United States

1864

Lewiston was very busy in the morning. Even being very small, it was an inland seaport. *It will grow to be something amazing,* Elizabeth reasoned.

Her first stop was the bank. She would need money, as they had nearly exhausted their available funds coming up the river from Portland. Mary and Edward had left her and Anne as well as Lolivey enough money to last a few more years if they were careful with their finances, but she and Anne had used little of those funds. They both had worked since Mary's departure back to Germany and were at the moment still quite financially secure.

Elizabeth's next stop was a return trip to the small port area where she had seen an office for the Oregon Steam Navigation Company. She left a packet to go to Lolivey back in Hayes Valley near San Francisco. She had left word in the packet of where they were staying in Lewiston and hoped any word from home in Germany would be forwarded to them here. She also ventured to ask for any possible word of Thomas, as Timothy was still looking for any information concerning his disappearance from the wharf area of San Francisco.

This being done, Elizabeth returned to the Luna House to meet Anne for an unhurried lunch—she had skipped breakfast and was famished. Upon entering the small hotel and going to Anne's room, she found her still asleep at nearly noon. "Good Lord, Anne. Are you going to sleep all day?"

"Why not?" she replied in a half-awake inertness. "What else is there to do in this place? I definitely don't think there is a theater I could trouble for employment." Then she rolled over and fell back into a very sound sleep.

Elizabeth left Anne and returned to her room, which had an entrance onto the balcony. *I think I'll just sit here and rest myself*, she thought. *We are not in a hurry to go further for a while. We have to stay here for at least as long as it will take word to return from San Francisco. And it is reasonably safe here.*

With that, she ordered room service for lunch and would sit awhile and make plans for the winter here. They did intend to eventually go on to one of the new mining camps to seek their fortunes. She laughed to herself. Who knows what lies ahead for anyone? What destiny was in store for her and Anne? *We have been wandering halfway around the world. We have survived the trip across the North Atlantic, a kidnapping on the East Coast, the dangerous voyage around the tip of South America, and an attempted kidnapping on the Columbia River only a few weeks ago, which resulted in the kidnapper losing his thumb. I hope our luck holds until we are done with this nomadic lifestyle,* she thought. *We will eventually settle, hopefully with a family. Damn you, Thomas, where are you?*

Elizabeth had finished lunch and half of her second cup of chicory and was rising to leave when Anne finally joined her. Seeing Elizabeth's half-finished cup of very dark brew still sitting on the table, Anne took a large swallow of it.

Wrinkling her face and gagging, she coughed. "What is this?"

"It's chicory. It grows here, I'm told. There is a place called Carney Orchards and Gardens over by the river that grows the root."

"That was the worst tasting stuff I have encountered in a while. Do they have coffee here?"

"Not today," Elizabeth responded. "They're out, and it won't be in until next week on one of the riverboats coming from San Francisco."

"I'm trapped here in this barren place with no obvious means of support, there are no more than twenty buildings in this entire town, most of which could use a severe facelift, no theater to perform in, and no coffee. Elizabeth, I'm going home. This is atrocious. I did not like California. I did not like the cold, wet, rainy Portland in that Oregon place, and this is the worst yet. There are no trees in sight anywhere, and I'm sick of this place."

"You've only been here one night, Anne. Give it a chance. Let's explore the town and see what it has to offer."

"Explore it? What's to explore? You can see it in its entirety standing right here on this flimsy balcony, which I must add, if you lean on the handrail, you will probably fall right through onto the street below."

"Come on, Anne," Elizabeth said more sternly with a frown. "Let's go for a walk and see what this community has to offer. It may just have one redeeming quality that even you may approve of."

"I doubt it, and I'm not going anywhere until I get a cup of coffee and something to eat."

"Well, eat you can do but no coffee, only chicory."

Scowling, Anne reacted. "It'll have to do. God, I do not like this place."

Elizabeth sat down with her while Anne had a plate full of ham, eggs, and fried potatoes with onions. A few bites into the meal, she looked up at Elizabeth smiling. "This is very good. The chicory is really not that bad. How do you put up with me? I'm impossible even to me."

"You do have your trying moments," Elizabeth said. "Anne, I do not want to return to Germany ever. I have resigned myself to a probable life without Thomas, but I haven't completely given up hope. Even without him, I do not want to go back. Everything there in Darmstadt would just remind me of him. Our father married his mother and is now running the farm and vineyards. Fredrick C. Burgdorf and Little Josh may be on their way to this western frontier, and I just couldn't face life back there. Maybe someday but not now. If you must, please go—I will not try to talk you into staying again, but I'm not leaving. I want to go on to the fabulous goldfields of Pierce or Florence or Warren's Diggins. It is just something I feel I must do. Thomas and I talked of these places often, and just think of the fortune Sister Mary and Edward made in California. We may do the same here. Should I ever return to Germany, I would like to return in the same style as them."

"Now that's my old Elizabeth," Anne said cheerfully. "Let's go for that walk and check this town out. If I do return home, I'm not planning on doing it soon. The gold towns have a certain allure for me too. If we can't get wealthy from our own claims, maybe we can marry rich miners."

"You probably let the best one get away when Frenchy left."

"Yes, well we would never have gotten along very well anyway. He just didn't seem like the type that would let me be boss and spend all his money."

Elizabeth laughed ostensibly, and they went down the stairs for a stroll through the town, even if it were only hardly more than twenty or thirty buildings with narrow dirt streets that turned to knee-deep mud even if it only clouded over and didn't rain. They walked south away from the river on Second Street toward a slight rise, passing the construction of a huge building that would be the Hotel de France.

"Wow," Anne exclaimed, "when this thing is completed, it looks as though it will be as nice as anything we saw in San Francisco. I would just love to stay here sometime."

Passing the building and walking another block in the same direction, Anne let out a yelp. "Will you look at that?" In front of them stood a storefront with a huge tent in back. The sign on the building read *Gorstein & Binnard Store and Theater*. Anne had performed in many places over the last few years and recognized the tent theater for what it was immediately. She guided Elizabeth, intent on finding out all the details of the theater.

Upon entering the huge tent, they found no one in attendance. The tent had a small stage with rows and rows of benches made from tree rounds for legs and wooden slabs for seats. In the far corner next to another flap door, there was a makeshift bar made of a slab of wood perched over two whiskey barrels.

"I can work here," Anne said. "I'm sure this is for traveling shows. I probably know the members of the next one to perform anyway. I can possibly perform here on occasion, and you can go out and find people to heal, fix, or whatever it is you do to them." Both girls laughed at the joke. Elizabeth had taken the remark as intended. She had worked as a doctor assistant in the hospital in San Francisco and then in herbal and natural healing procedures in Portland's Chinatown, where she was known there as the white lady who treated all.

Strolling out of the huge tent, Anne led Elizabeth around to the storefront and they went inside. The proprietor was a squat, chubby little guy with suspenders holding his pants up to an elevation just under his more than ample belly. He wore a derby cocked off to one side of his head while he rolled an unlit cigar from side to side of his mouth. Looking the two girls over with a quick glance, he said, "What can I do for you two? Whatever it is, I can tell you I haven't had any company as nice as y'all here in recent times."

Anne looked him over with an appeasing eye and decided he was totally harmless. "I am a performer from San Francisco and would like to know when the next performing group is expected to play here."

"Tomorrow night. They will be coming in on the overland stage from over west of here later this afternoon and will have their first show tomorrow evening. Want me to introduce you to them?"

"No, thank you," Anne replied politely. "I am quite capable of introducing myself."

"Suit yourself," he replied, turning away to wait on another customer. "Need somethin', jus' give me a holler."

They walked out excitedly chattering and giggling at the prospects of Anne being able to perform.

"I am so anxious to see you on stage again, Anne. Your performance on the riverboat was so astounding. I have never heard you sing like that before. As a matter of fact, I didn't even know you could sing like that." Rounding the corner, they walked down what was labeled on a lopsided wooden sign as *E Street*. They continued on only a few blocks, never losing site of the river or their hotel. The town was quite small, not much to see here in this area. "Let's go back to the Luna House and clean up for dinner."

They sat on the upper tier of the hotel watching the setting sun sink slowly to the west nearly into the river before disappearing behind a low mountain. The few clouds that had accumulated were of beautiful shades of pastel colors and held promises of another beautiful day tomorrow. They were both silently mesmerized by the breathtaking view when Anne broke the silence.

"What are your immediate plans here, Elizabeth? One moment you're talking of our staying on here for a year or more; the next we are to move on to one of the rich mining camps, then on to another and another? This indecisiveness is starting to wear on me, and I'm the one who just came on this trip for the ride, for the sake of a different life other than what we knew in Germany. It was just a lark as I looked at the journey in its infancy. This morning I looked into the mirror in the room and noticed some new wrinkles. I am nineteen years old. Before I know it, I'll be in my twenties, and I need to settle down and get married to a rich man and have kids."

Elizabeth chuckled and said, "You have been going to marry anyone, rich or poor, for the last four years. The status of his wealth has only become a consideration more recently. Frankly, I don't think you will ever get married." Then she added, "If you do, he had better be a strong man as well as rich—I'm afraid you would be a very challenging wife."

"What's wrong with that? I would make a good wife—I'm just not going to wash dishes or clothes, clean house, change diapers, or any of that stuff. The rest of it sounds fun."

Elizabeth just looked at her sister, speculating if she were really serious or just in one of her impish moods, and decided on the latter. "Well," Elizabeth finally replied, "even I'm not sure what the immediate future dictates for us, but I am working on it. I do know this, you will probably get a performing job of some kind at that Binnard tent theater. I have been informed by some of the staff here that there are two doctors in town, so perhaps I can get a job with one of them. I know that our allowance from Mary and Edward is not going to last forever." Then with that faraway look, she thought again, *Damn it, Thomas, where are you? I can't wait forever.*

It was a snowy, beautiful evening, so the sisters decided to eat in Elizabeth's room with the view off the balcony rather than go down to the hotel dining room. The food was good but consisted of mostly beef, either boiled or fried, and beans with roasted root vegetables. All were local products and readily available without having to have them imported by one of the many riverboats navigating the Snake and Columbia Rivers at considerable expense. The two girls talked abundantly about anything and everything during the course of the meal.

Anne finished eating first then excused herself to retire early. "I want to get to the theater early tomorrow morning to see who will be performing. It's highly unlikely they will give much consideration for a few days, but I will at least audition if they will consider it."

Elizabeth stood to give her a hug. "We both know you will do well. Meet you here for breakfast?"

"Sure thing," Anne replied and strolled the few feet over to her room.

Chapter 81

Lewiston,
Idaho Territory, United States

1864

Elizabeth awoke with a start, sitting straight up in bed and breathlessly panting, "What was that?" A new river paddle wheeler had arrived and blasted a horn that sounded like the collapse of a ten-story building. It had not only warned the dock of its arrival but also awakened the entire town.

Dressing then walking out on the balcony, she found Anne already seated having a steaming mug of chicory. *God*, she thought, *what I would give for a cup of real coffee. Maybe some will come in from that new boat that just arrived.* They had a quick breakfast, and Anne hurried off toward the theater. It was still early, so Elizabeth walked down the stairs to the street and turned toward the dock area.

All the streets as they existed at the time had a numerical or an alphabetical designation. The streets running north and south were numerical, and the streets running east and west were alphabetical. First Street ran parallel to the Snake River and ultimately ended at the edge of the Clearwater River on the north. A Street ran parallel to the Clearwater River and ended on the west, running into the Snake River. The town lay in the inside of an L shape with the Snake River bordering the town on the west and the Clearwater on the north. It had been an easily defendable community in its infancy, only having two sides to watch, the south side and the east end. There had been but few skirmishes with Indians over the years, and they had not been serious, with no lives lost on either side—just a lot of commotion with wild shots being fired by the community defenders and a lot of arrows falling harmlessly onto some of the buildings on the south side. Those skirmishes had come to an end in more recent times, and things were relatively peaceful now. The most recent skirmish was political activists from the Boise Basin area forcefully retrieving records to move the capital to Boise after the territorial legislature's vote. But for the moment, the streets seemed calm again, especially with the fresh layer of snow covering the dirt roads.

Elizabeth strolled on down Second Street toward the small harbor at the confluence of the Snake and Clearwater Rivers. The boat that had just arrived early that morning, making all of the noise and waking everyone in town, was a new and larger craft than the others that would run this section of the Snake River hitting the Columbia and on down to the last portage, having the capacity of picking up a greater load of passengers and cargo. It was an impressive steamship built near here in Lewiston just up the Clearwater less than a quarter of a mile in a vacant space next to Robie's Sawmill. It was advertised with a big canvas banner: *Built by the Oregon Steam Navigation Company* and was named the *Tenino*.

Elizabeth perched on an old oak barrel and watched as the boat was offloaded of passengers and cargo. This had been its maiden voyage and appeared to have been a very successful one. It was reported that one trip with a steamboat of this size could net the company over $50,000 in about a week's time.

She was watching the passengers unload when one passenger caught her attention. He was a big man with long greasy hair and several days' growth of whiskers on an otherwise ugly face. What had caught her attention was the dirty bandaged hand held in an even dirtier sling hanging around his neck. She gasped. *Is that Luther, that foul creature whom I removed his thumb with one shot from my pistol downriver in the fall?* She was sitting slightly off to one side of the boarding ramp in the shade of some shrubbery growing on the riverbank, and he did not see her. She sat in total stillness, not moving even an eye. He was a frightening creature. She and Anne had no allies in this town now that Frenchy had left for the Boise Basin area, and she was frightened.

As she watched him amble on up the path that would turn into Second Street, she thought, *What is he doing here?* but then reasoned, *Why wouldn't he be here?* There had been no investigation of his assault or her consequential shot that had removed his thumb. *Who would recognize him now except me?* Elizabeth stayed on the oak barrel for the next hour contemplating her next move with his presence in town. Finally she reasoned, *If I was successful in stopping him with one shot from my pistol, I think I could do better next time with two shots, possibly causing his untimely demise. I'm sure there is some law here,* though she had seen no evidence of it to date. *I have to find Anne,* she thought. *He may recognize her.* But then she thought probably not, as the encounter on the river had been very fleeting and Anne had been lying down. *Nevertheless, I have to warn her.*

Elizabeth hurried up the street that Luther had traveled only an hour earlier but saw no evidence of him again. His first stop would probably have been at the saloon two blocks over to the east. Elizabeth hurriedly covered the four blocks up to the Binnard tent theater and found Anne rehearsing for that evening's show.

Seeing Elizabeth enter the huge tent, Anne jumped off the makeshift stage and ran laughing to her. "Sure enough," she cried, "I know one of the managers for this traveling show. They played in San Francisco a while ago, and he has given me a small singing part. They will only be performing for two weeks, but it's better than nothing, and I'm sure another group will be coming in soon."

Noticing the panicked frown on Elizabeth's face, Anne asked, "Aren't you happy for me?"

"Luther is here," Elizabeth whispered. "I just saw him unload from that noisy steamboat that arrived early this morning."

"You mean the man that attacked us and you shot his thumb off?"

"Yes, him, and he is here."

"What will we do?" Anne asked with wide eyes. "Frenchy is not here anymore to assist us, and I don't even own a gun, let alone know how to use one."

They both collapsed onto the slab bench gazing at each other. The stage manager for the theater group, Mr. Trabuco, walked through the tent and saw them sitting there. "Why the long faces, ladies? You look like it's your last friend you've lost."

"The problem is we have but few friends and can't afford to lose any of them." Anne groaned. "And there is an appalling and treacherous man here possibly looking for Elizabeth and me."

"Well, what's to worry about? Me and the rest of this theater group are certainly no strangers to adversity of any kind and do know how to handle appalling and treacherous men." Smiling, he sat down on the next bench facing them. "Tell me about it," he said.

Elizabeth gave him a blow-by-blow detailed account of what had happened with Luther in the camp downriver, finally finishing the story with a tear slowly running down one cheek.

"Well," he said, "what did you do with the thumb? That's probably what he is after."

Both girls gasped at once. It had been a grisly incident, but they immediately recognized the humor and wisdom in his comment. He had put the incident to a lighter note, relieving the girls of some of their stress.

"Come, please, the both of you. Join the theater group with me for dinner. For as long as we are here, you have nothing to worry about. You will be well taken care of."

It was a perfect evening with the group. Anne had a few old friends in the assembly from San Francisco, and the Klein sisters were guaranteed that no harm would come to them while the performing group was in town.

New Year's Eve and the following few days were peaceful. Anne performed with the theater group on a nightly basis and was a smashing hit. Elizabeth was in the audience for every performance. During the days, Elizabeth familiarized herself with the streets of town, stopping at Vic Trivets store on one edge of town then the schoolhouse closer in. On the same street as the school was Dr. Newell's house and office. This was the third doctor's office she had seen today. Scattered throughout town, there were a business on one corner, a family residence on another, a school on another corner, a blacksmith shop the next, and so on. *No rhyme nor reason for this layout,* she thought. *Whoever is responsible for the layout of this town must have spent too much time in the saloon over by the river.* Then she thought more seriously, *There are a lot of doctors in such a small town, and I'm not sure that is a good sign,* she alleged. *But maybe one of them will need help and I can get a job.*

Farther up on another street to the south near the end of town, she passed the jail. It looked like it couldn't confine a dog, let alone a human. *I wonder if the dilapidated jail that probably would not hold a criminal contributes to the fact that the cemetery seems to be full. There are five churches, three doctors, and a new mortuary.* With this thought fresh in mind, she turned and hurried down the street that would take her back by the tent theater where Anne was preparing for her nightly performance.

Smelling the sweet aroma of fresh-baked pastries, Elizabeth stopped at a small bakery and picked up some fresh quiches to take along to the theater to share with Anne. After the performance at the theater, Anne and Elizabeth walked toward their hotel. One of the stagehands escorted them. The girls thanked him, and he turned and walked back toward the theater.

"What are we to do when this traveling group leaves? In another five days," Anne added, "we will have no support, and the terrible Luther may still be in town."

Elizabeth shrugged. "Not sure, but we will be just fine. We'll think of something. We always do." Subconsciously, she slid her hand through the fold of her dress into the hidden pocket that concealed her derringer. A comforting feeling. *God,* she thought. *I never believed I would see the day when I would have thought a gun in my hand would be comforting, but it seems to have become a way of life over the past few years since leaving home.* Closing her eyes, she sighed and thought, *Ohhh, Thomas, where are you? If only you would just show up here in this little town! I need you so. Anne and I both need you.*

Luther did not show his face in Lewiston. The girls were forever watching for him, and he was always on their minds, but there was no sign of him or what he was up to. Luther apparently had only been passing through and was sighted on a stage going toward the mining towns of Florence and Warren's Diggins, perhaps even farther to the new, fabulously rich Boise Basin area.

Chapter 82

Lewiston,
Idaho Territory, United States

1865

The following months were stunning. The weather was warm but not hot. The traffic on the river was, as always, interesting to watch. The springtime brought a continuous flow of goods and passengers coming up the river to Lewiston, then a like amount returning back down. People would disembark, stay a few days, months, or in some cases longer periods of time, and others that had been in town a while would go back down the river to Portland or other destinations unknown.

It was a very busy little community, and Elizabeth was beginning to love it. In January she had paid a visit to each of the three doctors in town over the last two weeks and had been offered a position with each. She had extensive training in the hospital in San Francisco and again had achieved a tremendous degree of success as a healer in Portland's Chinatown. Elizabeth was fluent in English, German, French, and Spanish and could speak some North Germanic languages too, including Danish, Swedish, and Norwegian. This ability had proved very helpful while working in the hospitals in San Francisco and Portland.

Elizabeth had ultimately agreed to work for Dr. Robert Newell. Her command of languages was extremely valuable here in the western frontier of America. This was such a new land, and everyone was from somewhere and often did not speak one word of English. Dr. Newell was a well-respected and liked doctor in town with a practice that kept him working eight days a week, often with patients who spoke no English. It was a perfect match. Elizabeth immediately took a sincere liking to Dr. Newell and his family. His practice was in a room on the lower level of his home, so she had every opportunity to become well-acquainted with his entire family and took advantage of every minute of it. It had been years since she'd enjoyed a real family environment with children, and she had longed for it on a daily basis.

Elizabeth and Anne had been in Lewiston for four months when the next news packet arrived from Lolivey in Hayes Valley. Elizabeth opened it to find a lengthy letter from her father. Things were not going well in Germany. The various revolutions had threatened the livelihood of the Clay farm and vineyards. Manfred and Frida were forced to sell the farm and were in the process of moving back to Denmark. Mary and Edward had fled back to Denmark as well, with their fortune intact, thank goodness. Her father wrote an address of a relative in Denmark where Elizabeth and Anne could get in touch with them. Thomas's little sister, Anne, with the same name as her own little sister, had been fortunate enough to graduate from the university in Darmstadt. Fredrick C. Burgdorf and little Josh should have arrived in San Francisco some time ago, but Lolivey had not seen hide nor hair of either of them. Timothy was still working the dock area in San Francisco and had sent his affections and well wishes, but not a word from Thomas.

Carefully folding the letters and tucking them away with her other most prized possession—the little handblown glass hummingbird that Thomas had given her as a gift—Elizabeth sat on the chair next to the trunk. She was void of emotion but still had that unquestionable drive to continue on to Warren's Diggins, which she had heard so much about for the last few years. She had the deep-seated feeling that Warren's Diggins held her ultimate fate. She would share this new information from home with Anne later this evening.

Another traveling theater group had arrived in town, and Anne was happy as a lark performing with them. She seemed to have no end to friends in the theater or passion for the work. Elizabeth was happy for Anne's continued success.

That night was Anne's first performance with this new group, and after the show, they walked home together in the semidarkness, the only light being of the ambient glow from the store windows. They walked arm and arm in a melancholy mood as Elizabeth shared the news from home with Anne. They were both at least satisfied with their existence here in Lewiston but not happy. Anne was still threatening to marry every new man she met, and Elizabeth was just discontent, not sure what she really wanted.

"I still want to go on to Warren's Diggins," she finally stated forcefully.

"Well, let's go. I can pack tonight, and we can possibly catch the stage out in the morning."

"No! Not this soon. I mean maybe in a few more months. I just wanted you to think about it, not just up and leave in the middle of the night. We now have friends here and responsibilities."

"Well, you may have friends and responsibilities here, but I have only friends, and they are at best fleeting. I certainly have no responsibilities, and you know me, you just yell, 'Frog!' and I jump and ask how high on the way up."

Laughing and now in a lighter mood, they reached the hotel, bidding each other a good night and retired to their rooms. Undressing, then bathing, Elizabeth donned her nightclothes and slipped between the fresh clean sheets of the bed with a sigh. But sleep would not come to her for hours. Once again, Thomas slipped his way into her mind. She thought of him less and less now, but when she did allow her thoughts to return to him, as if she had a choice, they were vivid and would stay with her for hours as she tried to sleep. He was alive, and she knew it. As to whether she would ever see him again, that was the questionable part.

Elizabeth walked down the street toward Dr. Newell's office the next morning. She was irritable from lack of sleep and not in her usual jovial mood. Dr. Newell's three children saw her come into the back room, and they immediately flocked around her, improving her disposition immensely. But even this was not a complete cure this morning. *I really want my own family*, she thought. *I'm tired of waiting. I'm going to be just like Anne—I will up and marry the next man who makes a decent proposal. If he brings flowers.* Then she laughed at herself. *Good God, how pathetic.* She sighed. *These kids will just have to do for the time being*, she thought, *and I do love them. Just because I'm nearly an old maid, I won't just settle. He will have to be a tall, handsome hunk with lots of money, lots of wavy black hair, green eyes, a kind and considerate disposition, a big home, and... God*, she thought again, *I've just described Thomas.*

Elizabeth had become acquainted with nearly everyone in town, as most at one time or another had paid a visit to the doctor's office for every conceivable issue from arthritis to gout, heart conditions to asthma, and of course wounds caused by knives and shootings. She was known as the queen of setting broken bones.

"How did I ever get along without you, Elizabeth?" Dr. Newell would say at least once every day.

"You didn't. You were a miserable, short-tempered, overworked man who yelled at everyone and—"

"Enough," he would say, laughing. "We all love your presence. Mrs. Newell is desperately looking for a husband for you so you will stay here in Lewiston permanently."

"Well, if she finds someone, it will be a miraculous achievement. I certainly have been unsuccessful in that field." She had told them her whole life history, and they were well aware of her sentiments for Thomas, but that was a long time ago in the past, and it was time to move on.

Elizabeth worked tirelessly with Dr. Newell and never complained about the long hours. He did compensate her well, and she was not forced to draw on her trust account left by Sister Mary. Anne also had amassed a small fortune from working with the traveling theater groups. They were both quite wealthy for the time. The days slowly turned into weeks, and the weeks turned to months, and sooner than they realized, they had been in Lewiston for over a year.

At dinner one evening in early 1866, Elizabeth once again hesitantly proposed the subject to Anne of going on to the mining town of Warren's Diggins, not sure of what her reaction would be now. Anne apparently liked Lewiston at this time—at least she had stopped complaining about it and was not threatening to marry every new miner who came to town. In fact, Elizabeth had been the one harboring those thoughts now but would never mention them to Anne.

Anne stood up from the table. "Let's go pack now before you change your mind again. I am tired of this town. It was a thriving, exciting town last year when we got here and we thought it would grow, but since they moved the state capital to Boise, this town has just settled, as you often say. Warren's Diggins is a booming town, and I have heard it has more than ten thousand people there. I have made a small fortune from the miners visiting the theater here in this little town of Lewiston. Just think what I can do with all of those men in Warren's!"

Elizabeth shuddered. "Please say no more. Let's just go. But not tomorrow. I will have to give notice to Dr. Newell and his family, Anne. I have become very attached to them and they to me, and not just on a professional level. They are a sweet family—I will miss them tremendously."

Chapter 83

Lewiston,
Idaho Territory, United States

1866

It was only two weeks later, early one Sunday morning, that Elizabeth and Anne were packed and ready to leave. Dr. Newell's family as well as many others in town whom the sisters had befriended were there to see Elizabeth and Anne off. There were two other families who were relocating to the new capital city of Boise about three hundred miles away. They had made room for Elizabeth and Anne with all their worldly belongings, which consisted of two sea trunks each, with Elizabeth closely guarding the trunk containing her priceless gift from Thomas, the glass hummingbird. She had marked this trunk with one corner painted a bright pink she had purchased at the local hardware store. However, when the owner of the store found out what the paint was for he promptly returned Elizabeth's money. It was to be a parting gift, he said. This bright pink trunk of Elizabeth's would never be mistaken for another. If nothing else, the people of this small western town were extremely friendly and generous. The Klein sisters would be dearly missed.

Richard Rhett was the driver of one of the wagons, the one Anne would be riding in, and she pestered him relentlessly at first about the route. Would it be dangerous? How far? Were there Indians? Would they meet other travelers? How long would it take?

"Well," Richard drawled in a slow mutter that drove her impatient waiting for his total response, "this first leg of the wagon road begins here in Lewiston and will end at Mount Idaho, some seventy-fives miles up the road. This here route will climb out of this here Snake River Canyon, and then we will cross through the edge of the Craig Mountains, and we'll end up at the eastern edge of Camas Prairie at Mount Idaho." Then slowly continuing on, he added, "It is used by a multitude of folks—some are miners, some trappers, some are gamblers, outlaws, some are girls of the night," he continued with a twinkle in his eye, "and some are immigrants like you two. There are farmers, merchants, and of course all those Chinese miners and the US Army. This road here is a major route into the interior of Idaho country, Mount Idaho."

God, Anne thought, *if he drives this team as slow as he talks, we will never get there.* She did not dare ask about the rest of the trip from Mount Idaho to Warren's, but he volunteered anyway.

He slowly went on to tell her, "The next portion of the journey to Warren's Diggins after leaving Mount Idaho and Camas Prairie would be on the newly completed Milner Trail going on through the mining town of Florence, then across the big Salmon River by ferry and up French Creek to Warren's," describing every turn in the trail, every leaning tree, and every rock outcropping and throwing in an occasional story about the dangers of Indians.

By the time he was finished, Anne was sound asleep leaning against one of her trunks. *I can't wait to get to Warren's and for this trip to be over and away from this windbag*, she thought just before drifting off to sleep in the warm midmorning sun. She knew that once in Warren's Diggins, she and Elizabeth would bid them farewell, and the two families would continue on south to the Payette lakes, the Meadows, and down the Weiser River ultimately reaching their destination of Boise months later. It would be a long, fierce trip for them, and she was glad she and Elizabeth were going no farther than Warren's.

The first day out of Lewiston they made fourteen miles. "Not bad," Richard commented. "Our teams of horses are getting used to each other and the terrain. This is a good camping spot. You girls know how to pitch a tent?"

"Of course," Anne replied sharply then stiffly walked away to find Elizabeth. *Pitch a tent, look at this, look at that, start a cooking fire, fetch water. It's only been one day out, and I'm ready to go back to Lewiston. Actually I liked it there,* she thought. *I didn't have to do anything but go to the theater and sleep and eat and look pretty.* Spotting her sister across the camp, she called out, "Elizabeth!"

Noticing her, Elizabeth walked in her direction. "Isn't this a grand adventure? So beautiful climbing out of that river canyon we have been living in for the last year, and this camping spot along the creek is just wonderful."

"Look at me," Anne cried. "Dust in my hair, dust on my face, dust on my dress, dust in my mouth—I'm a mess."

"You are a mess," Elizabeth replied chuckling. Then taking her in her arms, she said, "But you are a beautiful, talented mess, and you have proven many times before that you clean up nicely."

Anne smiled with a tear starting in each eye and leaving a small trail in the dust on each side of her face. "You are amazing, Elizabeth. A few minutes ago I was ready to return to Lewiston, to the Luna House, to a bath and a comfortable bed, and now you have discreetly talked me into staying and continuing on with you again on this horrid adventure. I'll probably never see the inside of another theater."

The two girls took out the tent and were struggling to put it up when Richard came to their rescue. "Let me help."

"We have done this before," Anne snapped.

"Maybe, but with no obvious amount of success." He laughed. "The way you are going, it will be daylight tomorrow morning before you're done setting it up and then I'll have to take it down for you before we can break camp and move on."

Anne gave him a slight but sarcastic bow. "Have at it." She sniffed.

The camp was in a sheltered bend in the creek bottom with a wide expanse of meadow out in front of their tents and a cooking fire. Elizabeth helped the other two women preparing their meal over the open fire. They were well-stocked with food, and it was a much better meal than her and Anne's warmed-up beans and bread back on the Columbia River over a year ago.

The next morning Richard helped them take down the tent and put everything back in the wagons. He was short but a powerfully built man, nearly bald at the ripe old age of twenty. An excellent hand with the livestock and very useful around the camp. *Maybe he's not such a windbag after all,* Anne thought smiling. *He is quite pleasant to have around, and his wife and two children are just beautiful.*

It took five days to get the seventy miles from Lewiston to Mount Idaho, and Richard as well as the man driving the other wagon had handled the trip without any major happenings. Anne was becoming quite impressed with their routine and even ventured a haphazard apology for her previous conduct and a compliment on the men's accomplishments.

On arrival at Mount Idaho, Elizabeth questioned Richard about their stay here. "Can we stay at that hotel, Mr. Rhett? I see the L. P. Brown."

"We can," he replied. "It is the only one for the next forty miles of travel between here and Florence. We will need to reprovision here and switch out our teams of horses for mules. The mules will be stronger, and our horses are worn out. The forty-mile stretch between here and Florence could take us at least five days—it's going to be brutal, and I'm not sure what the accommodations will be like when we get there. I have heard it is a very wild town. Sometimes there are rooms available, but usually not. The miners are flocking in and out of that camp, and it has little or no law, I've been told. We will be here for a few days before continuing on through the Florence Basin and down to the ferry crossing on the big Salmon River not far from the community of Gouge Eye."

The accommodations at the L. P. Brown Hotel were comfortable with a bath house that the girls as well as the two families they were traveling with took advantage of. Anne hated to go a day without a bath and made that discomfort clear to everyone. On the trail up from Lewiston, Richard had even dammed up a portion of the small creek at one of their camps to quiet her about not having a bath.

"Richard, is there a theater in Florence, even a tent theater I may perform in?"

"Don't know for sure. I heard of a traveling troubadour going through there a few months ago, and two of them were shot. Whether they were in a theater or otherwise, I'm not sure."

"I'll pass," Anne replied. "But maybe I can do a small show here in Mount Idaho for everyone before moving on in a few days."

"Maybe," Richard said, not paying any attention to her continuous prattle.

Anne and Elizabeth enjoyed their time here at the hotel. They enjoyed the families they were traveling with but thought the two families would like a break from them, especially Anne, before traveling on to Florence. At dinner the third night in the hotel dining room, which was just an extension of the owner's own living quarters, Anne announced, "I would like to do a short performance for you all if allowed."

"What kind of performance?" Richard asked with a slight smile and a raised eyebrow.

"I could stab you with my fork, Richard. As usual it will be a song routine only."

"Oh, please don't stab him." His wife laughed. "He is only kidding." And everyone around the table laughed. Richard continually hassled Anne, and she found it amusing. When the tables were cleared and moved to one side, Anne stood on one of the chairs in front of her small audience and once again gave a recital that brought tears at times and laughter at others.

She is so beautiful and talented, Elizabeth thought. *Her disposition could use some improvement, though.* She sighed.

Chapter 84

Mount Idaho,
Idaho Territory, United States

1866

By the fourth day in Mount Idaho, Richard had reprovisioned their supplies and made the necessary trade for mules to pull the wagons. The following morning they were on the trail again bound for the boomtown of Florence.

"You warned us of the condition of the trail," Elizabeth said to no one in particular as she stood knee deep in mud and mosquitoes, assisting in pushing a stuck wagon out of a muddy bog. Anne was right beside her covered in mud and laughing.

"You should see yourself, Elizabeth," she hooted. "The only places you do not have covered in mud are your elbows."

They had only been on the trail a few hours when they encountered this first swampy area. It did not look bad until they were halfway through it and the wagon wheels were buried nearly out of sight.

"We will unhitch one team and pull one wagon at a time with two teams," Richard shouted to the group.

They spent until dark on this first day stuck in the mud only seven miles from their starting point. The camp that night was miserable—the mosquitoes were unbearable, and there was no real way to clean up without being eaten to death by them. The sisters woke early the next morning to the sound of Richard yelling and getting the camp ready to move on. They were red and itching with mosquito bites welling up anywhere on their bodies that was not covered with mud.

Elizabeth sat facing backward in the lead wagon watching every move made by the one following in the rear. *At least we are not covered in dust*, she thought. *However, dust would be a vast improvement over these infernal itching insect bites.* The next few days went about the same—one hour they would be stuck in a swampy bog, and then they would climb out into the most breathtakingly beautiful views one could imagine. At times they were above the trees with the trail going up or down a long bare ridge, so they could see to the west the deep gorge with the Salmon River in the bottom. At other times they could see off to the southwest and grasp the amazing snow-covered peaks of what Richard called the Seven Devils in the Snake River drainage.

"I see absolutely not one devil over there, let alone seven," Anne retorted one afternoon after being informed of their name. "Where is this devil?"

"Look in the mirror." Richard chuckled.

She was being jostled around in the back of the wagon facing Richard and his wife riding on the seat, and she saw no humor in his remark.

"And you may see a devil here if your continued sarcasm does not improve soon," Richard said, smiling and taking off his hat to rub the mosquito bites on his bald pate. They at least tolerated each other now, Richard with his stoic mannerisms and Anne with her continual sarcasm. As they entered a large meadow with a beautiful stream flowing through it, Richard commented, "Barring any unforeseen difficulties, this will be our last night on the trail before reaching Florence."

"God, I hope so," Anne replied. "I'm nothing but one large itching, red, muddy mosquito bite."

"A slight improvement in appearance." Richard chuckled.

She rolled her eyes. *He is impossible. How does his wonderful family stand him?* she thought.

The evening of the eighth day, they came into view of Florence. They had been making less than ten miles a day with their large heavily laden wagons. The town was off to their right less than a mile away, but they could hear the rinky-tink sound of an out-of-tune piano in the distance. Then the sounds of several shots firing simultaneously. No one had to tell them what that was. Elizabeth sank down in the back of the wagon with only her eyes peeking over its short sides. *What are we going to experience next?* They made their way cautiously on to the very edge of town, sighting a hotel on the outskirts. It was nearly dark.

Richard and Derick, the driver of the other wagon, did not want to go farther after dark in this dimly lit booming town. Stopping in front of the hotel—if that was what one could call this structure with a shattered sign hanging by one corner—Richard jumped from the wagon and hurried in to see if there were any rooms available. He returned a long minute later. "We're in luck. They have three rooms left tonight."

Observing the hotel carefully, Anne thought, *Luck? This structure appears to only have a total of three rooms. I wonder what is wrong with this hotel, and I bet there is no bath.*

"Here, let me help you unload your trunks. We don't dare leave them in the wagons overnight." Richard spoke in a low voice, not wanting anyone else to hear. They would have to leave most of their gear in the wagon, which would be in the corral with the horses behind this pathetic edifice posing as a hotel, and he did not want to make everyone else in the immediate area aware of that fact. Derick managed the families into their rooms without incident then helped the girls with their trunks to their room, paying special attention to Elizabeth's pink trunk housing her precious treasure from Thomas.

The hotel was a single-story structure with three bedrooms. When all three rooms were rented, the proprietor slept on a floor mat in front of the fireplace. "An evening meal will be served," he said, "for an additional twenty five cents to each. The meal will be Moors and Christians," he said. Seeing the group's puzzled expressions, he continued with a chuckle, "Rice and beans." The rice was a soggy, sticky mess, and the beans were as solid as a plate full of little pebbles. "Can't get those beans any more done. We are above six thousand feet here in elevation, and if I were to cook them until they were soft, they would boil away for a week or more. Sure won't do that—I got more important things to do than sit here and watch beans boil for days on end. If you don't like 'em, don't eat 'em. You can have your two bits back."

Elizabeth glanced at Anne, who was just sweetly smiling across the table at the children.

When the proprietor got up from the table to get the coffee pot, Anne slowly moved her head from side to side mouthing, "If you don't like 'em, don't eat 'em." The kids broke up laughing.

"What's got into you?" Richard asked the kids, having not seen Anne's pantomime. "Hush and be polite."

Anne rolled her eyes and winked, and they all made an attempt to eat the Moors and Christians.

Richard moved his chair back from the table and stood up. "May I ask what's for breakfast?"

"Sure, it will be leftover Moors and Christians."

Looking around, Richard noticed the looks of disapproval on the rest of the group's faces. "Let's put this to a vote," he suggested, not wanting to start the next day with everyone hungry and also not wanting to unnecessarily offend the proprietor. He shrugged. "Who wants to stay for breakfast?" Not even a smile. "Who would rather get an early start and forgo breakfast to eat later on the trail?" Every hand shot up, with the children raising both hands. It was a unanimous agreement.

Later in the evening, Elizabeth and Anne had moved closer to the stone fireplace, sitting on short homemade three-legged stools, when Richard and Derick joined them. The other women were busy putting the children to bed.

"I suppose," Anne said, looking directly at Richard, "a bath is out of the question."

"Not at all. I noticed a horse trough behind the hotel in the corral. It is above freezing, so there is no ice on it," he said chuckling.

Anne stared at him for a full minute before heaving a sigh. "Come on, Elizabeth. Please stand watch for me to make sure no one else is watching."

"You are kidding," her sister said incredulously. "You're not really going to bathe in this cold, dark night in a horse trough?"

"Come out and watch." With that, she got up and grabbed the towel hanging by the hand-washing basin beside the door on her way out.

The men just stood in astonishment. Who in their right mind would take a bath in the near-freezing horse trough in the middle of the night in a mining boomtown with drunken miners shooting out lights, yelling, and fighting? Anne Klein did, and when she was finished, Elizabeth gasped as she too climbed into the near-freezing water. After the quick bath, they both returned inside to stand shivering but clean in front of the fireplace. Not a one of the three men said a word. Even the boisterous Richard was silent, only smiling, undoubtedly thinking of what a sight that would have been with those two bathing in the horse trough in the middle of the night.

After warming themselves, they all went to their rooms. Anne and Elizabeth chatted for another hour before drifting off to sleep. They were exhausted after spending the last several days being thrown around in the back of a wagon like sacks of flour. Morning came too soon. They dressed and carefully loaded their trunks into the wagon, which was already out in front of the dimly lit porch. It was an hour before daylight. Richard wanted to get through the small town while most were asleep, leaving less of a chance for trouble. Just outside of town, the road forked, one fork going in a southwesterly direction and the other going in a southeasterly direction. Richard chose the route going southeast. They were now less than twenty miles from the main Salmon River crossing that lay over three thousand feet below them in the canyon bottom.

Leaving the large flat meadows surrounding Florence, the old wagon road traversed along a heavily timbered ridge that would often be blocked by a windblown tree lying across the road. They would have to stop, climb out, and move the tree—or, if it was too large to move, they would have to saw it and roll a piece out of the way for the wagons to pass through. After the third forced stop, Richard once again climbed down cursing.

"The wind howls across these high ridges, blowing down trees and drifting up snow. I don't know why Milner built this trail here."

"Well, where else would he have put it?" Anne shrugged, smiling sweetly. "It all looks the same to me. One place looks just as good as another."

Richard just looked at her then busied himself with the long-handled double-bit ax to chop another tree out of the road. An hour later, they made camp in a meadow just below the tree line. Richard and Derick had decided that even though it was only fifteen miles down the mountain to the river, they would camp here in this meadow with plenty of grass and water for the horses.

Neither had made this trip before, but Richard had talked with many who had. He had been told that there was no water beyond this point before reaching the river, other than some mineral water coming from a small hot-water pool in a cave nearly three quarters of the way down. If they were to have any trouble on the narrow, steep wagon road, delaying their arrival to the river, they could possibly spend another night on the hillside with no feed or water for the livestock. The weather was beautiful here and, unlike the Florence Basin they had just passed through, there were no mosquitoes. No one even bothered with a tent. They were now at a much lower elevation on the mountainside and could see the Salmon River, just a thread of blue in the bottom of the gorge, where the ferry boat crossing would take them across the river to another road that would continue up the other side of the mountain to the boomtown Warren's Diggins. From where their camp was, they could see much of the road across the canyon snaking its way up the mountain, switchback after switchback.

The next morning was a lazy one. Richard said there was no hurry. "If we have no trouble, we will be at the boat landing early afternoon and can cross then, depending on the ferry availability." So far since leaving Florence, they had met not one other traveler coming up the mountain from the river. This was the main north-south route between Lewiston, nearly a month's travel behind them, and Warren's, still several days' travel left from that point.

They were only two hours down the trail when they rounded a bend on the steep hillside. The wagon road narrowed, hardly wide enough for travel with a sheer drop-off to their left, hundreds of feet to the river. The horses were passing the narrow section onto the wider area, and the wagon was only a length away when the inside rear wheel hooked on a rock ſticking out of the sheer rock wall the road had been cut through.

The wagon lurched wickedly, smashing into the rock wall, ſtopping and jerking one horse back on its haunches and causing total pandemonium. One horse was down, and the other turned sideways, teetering as if to fall to his death over the canyon wall at any minute. The sudden ſtop had thrown Derick over the cliff, where he was left hanging with a death grip on the bridle reins ſtill faſtened to the team.

"Hang on!" Richard screamed from the second wagon. The road was too narrow to get around the team pulling his wagon so he crawled down the wagon tongue between the horses, jumped to the ground, and ran to the ſtalled wagon where Derick was hanging over the cliff. The reins suspending Derick were only flimsy leather ſtraps, barely one half inch in width, and Richard knew they would break with the slighteſt bit more pressure.

Derick was swinging lazily back and forth in the breeze, looking up then seeing Richard. "Whatever you're a-gonna do to get me out of this fix," he shouted, "you better hurry. I am afraid these reins I'm a-hanging from are going to break any second, and that river down there a-thousand feet or so looks mighty cold."

Richard climbed into the wagon with Elizabeth, Derick's wife, and two children paralyzed looking over the edge at the river a thousand feet below and Derick ſtill swinging back and forth. Grabbing a long coil of heavy-duty rope lying across the loaded wagon—the same rope they had used frequently to pull out one ſtuck wagon or the other— he haſtily tied a loop in the end then threw it over the cliff to where Derick hung.

Juſt as the rope hit Derick, the downed horse ſtruggled to his feet, lunging forward and snapping the wheel off the ſtuck wagon. They went but two ſteps before ſtopping again. Derick had managed to get his arms through the dangling rope juſt as the reins he was hanging on to snapped. Richard had no time to tie the rope off to anything solid and was left grasping it where he ſtood in the back of the wagon.

"Help me," he snapped at Anne, shaking her back to the reality of the situation. "Tie the end of this rope to something solid fast before I'm drug over the cliff with Derick."

Anne sprang into action, tying the rope to the wagon wheel against the cliff, then was back with Richard to help him ease Derick to the end of the slack. She quickly glanced over the edge of the cliff to where Derick was swinging back and forth but with the loop around his arms and shoulder.

"Hold on just a minute," Richard shouted down to the dangling man. "I have to rest my arms a moment. I'm going to try to pull you up."

The horses were shaking, and Richard knew he had to secure them immediately before they ran off down the narrow road, dragging Derick along the cliff. They were both brutally frightened but did allow him to work his way between them to tie them to a hackberry bush growing out of the canyon wall. When this was done, he worked his way back between the shaking horses and climbed into the front of the wagon. Anne and Derick's wife were attempting to pull Derick up the cliff face. Richard grabbed the rope behind the two women and gave it a heave with all his strength. Inch by inch, they slowly pulled him up and over the cliff edge into the wagon.

Derick lay there in the wagon only a moment and then shakily got to his feet and removed the loop from around his chest and arms. "Thanks for the lift."

They all sat there in silence for another moment before hearing what appeared to be another team and wagon coming up the canyon from the opposite direction. The other wagon stopped about a hundred yards away at the next switchback. The road there was wide enough for the wagons to pass. Two miners from the other wagon jumped down and ran up the trail to where the small group sat recovering where the team was still tied to the bank.

"Looks like you could use some help."

Richard related the chain of events leading up to their present condition, and the two miners helped move the team then unload all the damaged wagon's contents and carry them down to where the road was wide enough for the wagons to pass. After the team was calmed down and secured, they all aided in carrying the load from the wagon down then returned to the damaged wagon perched precariously on the narrow road.

"The road is too narrow to get between the cliff and the wagon to hold it up while we move it down to the horses," Richard said. "We'll have to try to hold this rear end up from the back. Let's have the ladies handle the tongue to steer this thing down, if we can lift the rear wheel enough to matter."

Elizabeth and Anne as well as the two other women positioned themselves along the wagon tongue, lifting it to steer. The four men had climbed over the wagon to the rear and heaved up, trying to lift it enough to move. If it started moving too rapidly for the women to handle, they could always drop it, they reasoned. It was too heavy to hold for more than a few seconds at a time. They would lift and let it roll ten feet, then drop it, rest, then repeat the action.

An hour later they had the wagon to the wide spot where the horses were tied. Then Richard brought the second wagon very carefully down the remaining hundred yards to the wide spot. The group stood for a few moments talking more with the two miners.

"We can stay for a while and help you fix that wheel," one of them said, "but we do need to get on along as soon as possible. Would like to get out of this infernal canyon up into the tree line and water before dark. Probably won't make Florence before tomorrow but do need to be on our way soon."

"Thank you," Richard said, "but I think we can manage. We do have a couple of spare wheels, and we can use that old log laying over there to lever the back up. Should be able to handle it okay."

The miners moved their wagon by, and then one of them yelled back, "There is a hot springs in a cave back down about another hundred feet if anyone has a hankering for a bath." Then they moved on up the road.

"That must be the mineral water hot springs we heard about," Derick breathed.

Everyone's mood was still very solemn. The four children were still shaking, but not a one of them had muttered a sound of distress or had shed a tear. Richard's wife raised her head with a slight smile—she was usually quite shy but was now the first to speak.

"I, for one, could use a bath. This has been a most demanding and exciting day." With that, she started down the road that was hardly more than a trail.

The other women and the four children followed closely behind. The hot spring was not deep, but there was a natural pool a little larger than a wagon positioned under an overhang in the cliff. They all took turns bathing in the delightful hot mineral water and were ready to go when the two men had finished the repair on the wagon wheel and had moved down the road to where they were, still somewhat shaken by the day's catastrophic events.

Bringing the wagons to a halt then securing the team to a nearby bush, Richard announced, "I am due for a bath also. It's only another hour before we reach the ferry crossing on the Salmon River. How 'bout you, Derick?"

Derick nodded then shook his head. "I think I could use a bottle of whiskey about now more than a bath." But he indulged in the relaxing warm spring. "Hanging over that cliff took ten years off my life. Thanks for the rescue," he said to no one but meant it for all.

Chapter 85

Salmon River Country,
Idaho Territory, United States

1866

The group arrived on the Salmon River just before dark. The ferry tender walked over to greet them. "I can take you all across tonight or wait till morning, your choice."

"Do they have lodging on the other side?" Elizabeth asked. She and Anne as well as the other two women and children were still severely shaken by Derick's fall.

"They do have some accommodations, but they're all filled up. I heard them tell those two miners who just went up the trail, you probably passed them. They only have a few rooms over there, and they are generally taken."

"With your permission," Richard spoke up, "we will camp here tonight and cross the river tomorrow."

"Permission granted." The ferry tender grunted. "Make yourselves at home anyplace you can find a flat space to lay down."

Richard and Derick unhitched the horses and staked them out just down the river a couple of hundred feet. They could get to the water and a good supply of grass growing along the bank. Next the men got out the tents, and the girls had theirs set up in no time with no help from the others.

"Let's have a celebration feast," Richard's wife said. "Poor Derick and his family are still badly shaken. We have plenty of food and only a few more days' travel before reaching Warren's."

The ferry tender overheard their conversation and chimed in. "If I can join you, I will bring a big salmon, a fresh one I just caught today. There is more than enough for everyone. I also have a couple bottles of fancy wine one of those prissy Frenchmen left as a tip for hauling them across the river the other day. Have a few fresh vegetables from the garden too. All ya have to do is the cooking—I'll furnish the food."

"Deal." Richard's wife laughed.

The fish was placed over the coals to bake. He had brought up fresh carrots and radishes as well as beets from the garden and collected some fresh greens, watercress from the creek running into the river by the ferry landing. Only a few steps away, the wild onions grew in abundance and were also added to a spectacular fresh salad. It was dark when the meal was finished, and they all sat around the campfire next to the river enjoying wine out of their metal camp cups.

"This is nearly as good as the wine from the Clay family vineyards in the Rhine Valley of Germany," Elizabeth said. With this, a tremendous flood of emotion moved through her. The day's experiences and the wine by the campfire alongside the river had brought on the memories of Thomas again. Elizabeth had lost track of the years that had passed since she had seen him.

Anne was busy entertaining the children, giggling with them one moment and holding another on her lap the next. They were still badly stunned from the sight of their father dangling over the cliff on hardly more than a thread. *These are tough little kids*, she thought. *Someday I'm going to have a bunch of them just like these.*

The next morning Willy, as the ferry operator eventually introduced himself, waited patiently for them to break camp and make ready for the crossing. He had relived Derick's frightful experience hanging over the cliff several times in the telling and retelling the previous night. He was in no hurry this morning to make the crossing—no one was waiting on the other side to cross, so he took full advantage of the morning to help the small group where he could.

He had taken a particular liking to Elizabeth. Anne had told him Elizabeth was a healer. She had relieved the level of discomfort from his gout to at least a tolerable level with some herbal tea and a horseradish-and-rhubarb poultice. The tea had put him soundly to sleep, the best night's sleep he'd had in months, he reported. The poultice probably accomplished no more than diminishing their food supply of some precious items that could have otherwise been baked into a pie, but nevertheless, Willy felt better.

Sitting on the bank and staring across the river, Elizabeth took in the full scene. The mountains rose sharply on both sides of the river but with very few trees, mostly grass and rocky outcroppings here and there. The sun would come over the peaks on the east side late in the morning and drop behind those on the west side midafternoon. She imagined the sun must beat down for the few hours it was overhead in the summer, and that the winter days must be shockingly short. Still, it was a beautiful scene, especially this morning with the light sparkling in the river water, the ferry platform docked on one side, and a small rowboat beached near the crossing on each side of the river.

As her eyes wandered, Elizabeth noticed a man slowly walking along the bank on the other side. He stood with his hands on his hips and his hat slid back on his head, looking right back at her. Never diverting her gaze, she stood up, placed her hands also on her hips, and stared back. This man at this distance was a striking individual. *Probably looks like a leper close up*, she thought then laughed at herself. *What a cynic*, she thought. *I've never even seen such a person in real life, only read about the disease in medical journals.* When he saw her laugh, the man took it as a smile for him, smiled back, and waved. She just stood there, *probably just gawking*, she thought later. She returned neither the wave nor the smile, just stood gazing with mild interest. What was it about this man that had stirred her? He appeared to be much older than her but still a striking figure.

She soon turned and strolled up the river bank to the wagons, paying him no further attention and soon forgetting him. With the team of horses pulling each wagon, they were too large to cross on the ferry at one time. Derick's wagon with his family and Anne would cross first. The ramp was laid out onto the bank, and the horses and wagon were soon loaded. The horses were very fidgety, no doubt remembering their experience on the narrow trail down the mountain yesterday, so were soon blindfolded to help calm them. When all were aboard, Willy started heaving on the rope and pullies that assisted the load across to the far shore. The horses stomped and snorted but presented no real threat, and soon they all arrived safely on the other side. After unloading, Willy returned back to the other side to get the other wagon.

The man Elizabeth had seen standing on the river bank earlier in the morning had strolled down the river a ways, removed his boots, and walked knee-deep out into the water on a tapering sandbar. *What is he doing?* Elizabeth thought. *He is just standing there with his hands on his hips watching.* Richard's wagon was now loaded with him and his family sitting in the front and Elizabeth perched on some supplies in the back. Willy had once again positioned himself to start heaving on the pulley rope, and they started across the river. The sun was noon high, with not a shadow anywhere in sight. The water flowing under the ferry made a pleasant gurgling noise, and the river was a beautiful faded blue. They picked up velocity the further they went toward the far shore, though the current did not seem so strong when they had first started.

Elizabeth was now sitting up with full attention—she had noticed a huge log floating downriver heading on a full collision course with the ferry. Willy noticed the log too and yelled for Richard to help him pull harder, as fast as possible on the crossing rope. Richard jumped down from the wagon to the ferry deck to help just as the log struck them full-on with a crashing blow. The ferry was suspended from each end by a rope tied to the main cable running across the river, and its full side was exposed to the smashing log. The rear rope snapped from the impact with the log, causing the rear of the ferry to swing downriver, leaving the whole structure now supported by the front guide only. The log hung only a moment then swung away from the ferry and floated lazily downstream.

The force of the gigantic tree slamming into the side of the ferry had thrown Elizabeth high into the air and overboard. One horse had staggered from the impact falling onto its side on the ferry floor, thrashing and threatening to kick the wagon to kindling. The scene was horrifying, and the small crowd standing on the approaching bank of the river was staring in a petrified trance.

Derick yelled at the top of his lungs to anyone listening, "Help me get this boat into the water."

Two men ran to help him launch the small rowboat beached near the ferry landing. Getting it into place, Derick grabbed a coil of rope left beside the boat for repairs and jumped in, shouting orders while the other two shoved the boat away from shore then jumped in at the last moment. Derick tossed the rope over the cable crossing the river that the heavily loaded ferry was still attached to by one end. With the rope looped over the cable and one of the other men rowing with the front of the boat pointed upstream, Derick would heave on the looped rope, helping to pull the boat up, relieving the pressure of the current, then quickly flip the slack out three feet on the cable to let the boat slip back. Then the man rowing would pull heavily on the oars, and Richard would pull the boat up a few feet then flip the looped rope again, gaining another three feet toward the stranded ferry swaying sickly in the current still a hundred feet from shore and threatening to break its one remaining line fastened to the main crossing cable at any moment. Derick repeated the process three feet at a time until they were in the middle of the river even with the ferry. They then worked franticly around the one rope still holding the ferry and for another twenty feet along the main support cable stretching across the river.

Now in a position above the trailing back end of the ferry, Derick dropped the end of the rope still hanging over the support cable into the water and let it float the twenty feet down to the back end of the ferry. Willy, seeing what they were trying to do, grabbed the floating rope, pulled it up, and quickly tethered it to the back of the ferry. With this done, Derick and the two other men let the small rowboat float down to the ferry, crashing into the side and nearly capsizing the small boat before they could climb aboard. With the rope still over the cable and now tied to the rear of the ferry, they all started to work the rear end of the ferry upstream, pulling and resting then pulling till they could pull no more, then resting a moment before pulling again. The ferry was heavy and loaded to capacity with the team and wagon. Some of the men's efforts would only gain a few inches, and then with a slight change in the current, the ferry would yield a few feet. Then only a few inches. It was a back-breaking, frantic effort.

A half hour later, they had the rear end of the ferry back to a position of being parallel to the main support cable across the river and were able to start pulling the rest of the way across. Richard had got the down horse untangled and back on his feet, and the terrified animal stood shaking. A few minutes later, the ferry was moored securely against the river bank with the loading ramp down, and the terrified horses were led ashore. Derick had brought the other team of horses down to help pull the wagon onto the bank.

"Well"—Willy perked up—"that was one hell of a ride, but everyone is okay and accounted for, and we never lost a thing."

"Where is Elizabeth?" screamed Anne.

During the chaos at the moment of impact with the log, Elizabeth had been thrown off the wagon and into the river, with no one hearing her frantic yell for help before she hit the water. She had struck the water flat on her back, knocking all the wind from her lungs, and had instantly begun to sink. Her cumbersome water-soaked dress was like an anchor, making it impossible to rise to the surface. Fully conscious and trying to get a gasp of air, she could only inhale water. From a depth of ten feet, she could look up at the brightly lit surface of the river with the sun shining down, creating a beautiful rainbow effect underwater. Her struggles to rise to the surface were to no effect, though, and she was sinking closer to the river bottom in a tranquil state of mind. It was as though her precious soul had left her body and was now watching from a distance thinking, *If my handsome Thomas has come to this beautiful place before me, I hope he is here to meet me*. Then she faded away into a peaceful bliss.

It seemed she was in this peaceful state for the longest time when suddenly she was aware of two powerful hands grabbing her and forcefully pulling her toward the surface. The light was getting brighter and brighter. *Leave me be now. I am ready for this*, she thought, but the hands kept pulling. She was steadily being pulled up from this abyss and broke the surface in a state of semiconsciousness.

William had noticed Elizabeth standing across the river earlier that morning. He had noticed the sun reflecting from her stunning golden hair, her perfect stance standing with a hand on each hip gazing right back at him with not a hint of bashfulness. He could see the way the slight breeze had ruffled the clothing around her tall, delicate, almost fragile physique and had even imagined a fading half smile as she had turned and walked back to the group. When she had broken her gaze from across the river, Willian felt a chill like he had never before experienced run up his spine, a foreboding feeling totally out of character for his more-than-confident personality. *Something dreadful is going to happen to that little angel*, he thought.

He then wandered aimlessly with no coherent reason down the river a short way and waited impatiently not knowing why. He removed his shoes, rolled up his pants legs, and was just wading aimlessly in the shallow water passing indolently over the sandbar. *I hate cold water*, he thought. *I don't even like to swim. What am I doing here?* He was just standing there nearly waist-deep in water a few feet from the shoreline, watching the ferry with only mild interest.

Then he saw the enormous log floating on a collision course with the ferry. The log crashed into the side of the ferry, the support rope holding the back end of the ferry parallel to the crossing cable snapped, and the stunning young lady he had seen earlier this morning was thrown overboard, immediately sinking and not surfacing.

Without thinking, William took several deep breaths, dove into the cold water, and swam deep under its surface. Though visibility was unobstructed, the water was cold and crystal clear, and as he swam he saw her floating along sluggishly with her eyes closed in a lifeless state. Her arms were hanging in a relaxed attitude to each side of her prone body. Her beautiful hair was floating like a halo lightly toward the surface. She was drifting leisurely only a few feet from the moss-covered, rocky bottom when he grabbed her and frantically kicked to the surface with

Elizabeth in tow. Time had stood still—he had swam down, located her, grabbed her, and resurfaced in one breath of air, a feat he would remember and question for the rest of his short life.

William now managed to delicately carry Elizabeth to the sandbar, turn her on her side, and press her back to expel the water from her lungs. Cupfuls ran freely out with each compression, but she would not breathe. *She is so delicate and fragile*, William was frantically thinking. *I'm afraid I will hurt her, but if I don't get her breathing, she will die. Please, God in heaven, let her breathe.* Rolling her to her other side, he tried again—more water purged out but no breathing. He gently rolled her to her back and placed his lips over hers, holding her nose closed, and gently blew air into her lungs. She coughed some water once but still did not breathe. Now in sheer panic, William covered her mouth again with his and blew with all his might. Her chest swelled, water boiled out in one tremendous cough, and she opened her eyes, staring straight into his eyes.

For only moment she lay there staring up at him but remembering him full well from the staring match across the river earlier in the morning. "Why did you have to do that?" she said. "I was prepared to meet my Thomas in the hereafter."

"Well, perhaps he was not prepared to meet you yet," William replied with a twinkle in his eye then helped her to a sitting position.

William had dived in to the water to rescue Elizabeth when she was thrown from the ferry, ultimately dragging her to the sandy beach and resuscitating her minutes before anyone even knew she was missing. Elizabeth was now shaking uncontrollably from the shock of drowning and the cold water. She was too weak to stand, so she just sat on the beach with William's shirt around her and him holding her close in an attempt to warm her up. They were huddled on the beach watching the last of the ferry rescue unfold when she heard Anne scream, "Where is Elizabeth?" She made a feeble attempt to stand and wave but slumped back nearing unconsciousness again. William stood and yelled, getting the attention of the group on the ferry landing and pointing down at Elizabeth now lying on the beach.

The entire group ran down the riverbank to where Elizabeth was lying, and William tried to recount the chain of events as best he could remember with all the questions coming from every direction. Seeing that Elizabeth was still alive but shaking uncontrollably, Richard's wife ran back to the wagons to grab some warm blankets and dry clothing. When she returned, Elizabeth was sitting up.

"Can you stand again, honey?"

"I think I can now." And with the help of the two women, Elizabeth was able to rise.

"Here, let's get you out of those wet clothes and into these dry ones."

The men politely turned their backs while the wet clothes were removed and the dry ones put into place, and then Elizabeth was wrapped in the warm blankets.

"I think I am too weak to walk," she stammered.

William was not a big man but was powerful with bulging muscles in his upper body as well as his legs. He was a miner from Warren's Diggins. Hastily—before one of the others could—but gently, he picked Elizabeth up in his arms and carried her back up the river bank to the wagons, placing her on a tailgate. The others had followed along closely behind and were now huddled around Elizabeth in constant chatter. Anne was still clinging to her and would not let go. This had been an earth-shattering experience that neither would ever forget.

William was a very soft-spoken, reserved, but attractive man and had been there to pick up mining equipment brought in on a freight wagon from Florence a few days earlier. Seeing that Elizabeth was now receiving the best of care and without anyone paying any attention to him, he walked to his wagon that was already loaded. After hitching his team, he climbed into the seat and slowly drove off up the road following French Creek toward Warren's. *If I am going to get back on time, I guess I better get on my way*, he thought and was gone.

His trip up the mountain was plagued with thoughts of Elizabeth and the recurring visions of her lifeless form floating in the river. *What a beautiful young woman*, he thought. And the thoughts haunted him. *Will I ever see her again? I think I did hear someone mention they were going to Warren's.*

Chapter 86

Salmon River Country,
Idaho Territory, United States

1866

"**E**lizabeth, I am so frightened." Anne was still hovering over Elizabeth on the tailgate of the wagon. "I don't want to leave here for at least a while, until you have your strength back."

"I am fine," Elizabeth kept saying even though she was not sure if she could even stand on her own yet.

Richard and Derick were fussing with torn harnesses and doing some repair work on the wagon that had been nearly kicked to pieces by the downed horse on the ferry. Looking over at Elizabeth, Richard shrugged. "It looks like it will take us at least the rest of today to do the necessary repairs. Maybe even part of tomorrow. There are two rooms available here at the crossing tonight. Anne and you can take one of the rooms, and Derick and family can have the other. I think Derick is still feeling the aftereffects of the beating he received when he was pitched out of the wagon over the cliff and could use a soft bed tonight. My wife and children would love to sleep out under the big full moon and stars on that sandy beach where that man drug you out of the river."

Suddenly Elizabeth sat up looking around. "Where is he? I never got a chance to thank him for saving my life."

"I think he has left," someone said. "He was going back to Warren's with a load of mining equipment."

"Anne, please look around and see if you can find him. I must see him again. What is his name?"

"I'm not sure," Anne said. "Maybe Willian or something like that—I don't know if he said. You're smiling, Elizabeth. Do you like him? After all, he did kiss you!"

"Anne!" she barely screeched, as her throat was still sore and sensitive from belching half of the river from her lungs. "He did not kiss me."

"He did. I saw him. He was leaning right over you kissing you smack on the lips."

"That was not kissing. He was giving me cardiopulmonary resuscitations, just in case you can comprehend more than single-syllable words."

"Did he give you chest compressions?" Anne smiled coyly.

"God, you are just ghastly, Anne."

"Well, do you think you like him? After all, he did save your life."

"He probably is a good man, I think, but how would I really know? Our time here was so fleeting, I don't even know his name and I didn't even thank him."

"You do like him, then."

"Don't be so persistent, Anne. I am still not ready to think of that yet. Thomas is still too close to me, and when I think of a man, I think of him. When I remember the good things, he was always a part of them. I want to keep those memories, for they were the richest and most beautiful part of my life."

"Well, it has been five years since you have heard from him, and I would suggest you start thinking, Elizabeth."

Maybe so, she thought. *And if I remember correctly, this William was quite strong and handsome. He did carry me up the sandbar to the wagon without stopping once.* He would not leave her mind. Was it just the fact that he had saved her life, or was it something more?

"If he did go on to Warren's, we will see him again, I'm sure, as well as a lot of other handsome miners," Anne chimed in. "And I will marry the most wealthy one there."

"Good heavens, Anne, you are already probably more wealthy than any miner in the country as it is. You have been socking away all that money from the theater and piling up tips that would fill a pillow case night after night. In Lewiston I helped you count $3,500 one night, and there were many more like that." Then she added with a grin, "There may have been some wealthy miners around but not anymore after they've given you all their money. Just how much do you have banked away?"

Anne thought a moment. "About $187,633 and some change in the bank in Lewiston."

"God, Anne, if Sister Mary knew that, she would revoke your trust account." And they both laughed again.

Anne looked at Elizabeth with a more serious expression. "I will pay her and Albert back if I ever see them again."

Elizabeth was feeling much better. She had warmed up considerably and had stopped shaking. Anne had pestered her into a better mood.

"Come on, Elizabeth, let's see if you are strong enough to walk over to the room we have for the night. Or do you want to try and con some other man into carrying you in his big strong arms while he gazes down into those pale-blue eyes?"

"If I did in fact feel better," she replied, "I would drop one of these bags of grain off the wagon onto your head."

The ferry landing on the French Creek side of the river had a store, a tavern that also served food, and a boarding house of sorts. It was a lovely setting, with the river only a few feet away. They had made it to their room while the rest of the group was busily making repairs to their equipment and getting ready to start the trip up the mountain to Warren's Diggins. The elevation here was only about two thousand feet above sea level, and Warren's was well over six thousand feet in elevation. It was slightly more than forty miles but up steep hills nearly all the way. They would have to climb nearly a mile higher. They had been advised the road was in good repair but very steep, limiting their travel to less than ten miles a day.

That evening the sisters met the rest of the group in the tavern for a dinner, a tasty meal of moose steak from the meadows up French Creek Canyon and fresh salmon from the river. The story was told again and again about Derick getting thrown over the cliff and surviving the ordeal by hanging on dangling bridle reins still attached to the horses then being pulled to safety. And the other story of the horrifying experience with the ferry line breaking and Elizabeth being pitched from the wagon into the Salmon River was recounted too.

"Elizabeth," Anne remarked at the table with a puzzled look, "just what was that man who saved you doing down on the beach?"

There was silence for a moment while she thought. "I don't know, Anne. I really don't know. I have been thinking of that a lot."

Willy ambled up and removed his hat. "Glad to see you're feelin' all right, miss. You know, they call this the River of No Return. I always thought it was for the scenery—once you see it, you never want to leave. But I reckon it's something to do with the fierceness of the waters too."

The general conversation picked up again among the group and turned to the logistics of the rest of the trip up the mountain to the boomtown of Warren's. The tavern was full now with the steady flow of miners both coming and going up the mountain. The ferry had been hastily repaired and seemed to be once again reasonably safe. This afternoon after its repairs, Willy had made fourteen trips back and forth across the river loaded with men going to the goldfields. Elizabeth's thoughts kept returning to William. Willy the ferry tender verified the man's name was William but knew little about him. He just seemed to show up, pick up his supplies at the ferry landing, mind his own business, and then leave again without a word.

Odd, Elizabeth thought. *I wonder if we will ever see him again.* She hoped so and smiled every time the thought crossed her mind. *What is wrong with me? That near-death experience was only that, but I do feel so different now. I can't get that man off of my mind.*

The sisters awoke early before daylight to the sound of a crowing rooster. Getting up to shut the window of their room against the outside noise, Anne noticed most of the others up and packing for an early start up the mountain. "Get up, Elizabeth. The others are nearly ready to go, and here we are still in bed."

They hurriedly dressed, packed, and started dragging their trunks outside. Anne had hers out the door and was busy helping Elizabeth with hers, noticing that she was still a little weak from her ordeal the day before. Richard walked over and offered to carry the trunks to the wagon, grabbing Elizabeth's first.

"Take special care of the one with the pink corner," she said. "It has my bird in it that Thomas gave me."

Richard just looked at her not sure he had heard her right but being very careful just in case he had. The wagons were loaded, and breakfast was served in the tavern. It was a more earnest mood and conversation this morning. In a few minutes they would be leaving this beautiful setting to start the forty-plus-mile trip up the mountain to Warren's.

Willy was telling Richard about the route, as he had made it many times over the years. "Just follow the road up French Creek until it switches back up the mountain. Before you leave the creek, make sure you water the stock and yourselves from the creek. The next water will be only a small spring pouring into an old wooden water trough on a wide spot along the steep road, and that will be up about seven miles. That's as far as you will make it in one day, given the steep climb.

"Spend the night there, and with an early start you can make on up another eight miles to the Fall Creek crossing, another wide spot in the road and a good camping spot right next to the creek. Day three should take you over the summit to the headwaters of Lake Creek. Day four will be an easy one, and you should make at least ten miles following along Lake Creek to its confluence with the Secesh River. There you will turn back to the east following the Secesh to the bottom of Long Gulch. That's a steep climb you'll have over Steamboat Summit, but you should be able to make it over the summit and down the other side to a stream. Probably should camp there.

"It's not but a few miles from there on to Warren's, but it would be better to approach that boomtown the next morning in daylight, not late at night. It's not as wild as Florence, but it is a boomtown, and you should take notice for your and the girls' safety. It does have its moments. There are now about ten thousand people there. Some are the Chinamen, most are miners, and there are a few families that operate different businesses, and of course the brothels. Not sure where you are going to stay, but the wagons will offer at least temporary shelter until something more permanent can be arranged."

"We are not staying in Warren's," Richard said. "We will just drop Elizabeth and Anne there then backtrack to the junction and continue out to the Payette Lakes, then down to what they call the Meadows. We plan to stay there a few days resting and making whatever repairs necessary to the wagons. Ultimately, we will follow the wagon trail on down the Weiser River and on to Boise."

"*What?* You're leaving the girls by themselves in that boomtown? That's a terrible idea."

"Well, it's not my idea!" Richard exclaimed. "It's theirs. And they're not changing their minds. We have been trying for weeks to get them to continue on with us to Boise, but they're staying, 'and that's that,' we were told."

Willy looked at them skeptically. "I will make a special trip to Warren's myself just to check up on them. I can make the trip in two days on horseback by myself, and I just love to stay over at that hot springs camp that that Burgdorf fellow maintains about halfway."

Elizabeth had been paying little attention to the conversation until Willy mentioned Burgdorf. Anne had heard also, and they were staring at each other in disbelief. *Could it be?* Elizabeth thought. *Not likely.* But it had them staring in disbelief at Willy.

"Let's get this show on the road," Richard said. "This first day is going to be a long haul to that spring at our first stop on the mountain."

"Wait!" Elizabeth said in a louder than normal voice, nearly panicky. "Just a minute, please," she continued excitedly. "Willy, what can you tell us about Burgdorf?"

"Well, not much. He just showed up here from the California goldfields about a year ago with his sidekick, Little Josh. Josh is, however, anything but little—he's a strapping big young man. Well over six feet tall, he is. Seems they came here all the way from Germany a-lookin' for some friends or something."

Elizabeth sat for a moment deep in thought. "It can't be," she said. "It just can't. It's surely not Fredrick C. Burgdorf that had lived and worked with Thomas's family in Darmstadt...but with little Josh, *the* Little Josh who Thomas had rescued from the slums there and taken him into the family—"

"Has to be the ones," Anne chimed in. "I knew a few years ago we would meet up with them sooner or later. Let's go."

"You two done delaying us now?" Richard asked then clucked to the team, getting them to move slowly away from the ferry landing.

This first day out was demanding, tiring, and dirty. They followed French Creek up a few miles, which offered plenty of water for the small group and plenty of water for the horses, but then the road switched back and left the creek for a barren, dry, and dusty hillside. They were climbing steadily up the hillside all day at a very steep slant. The road would take them into one canyon then out the other side time after time, with the dust from the horses filtering back onto the wagons and their passengers.

"Dusty it is, but quite beautiful," Anne said.

They had left the river at about six that morning, and twelve hours later were just arriving at the first spring alongside the road. Willy's directions had been good so far, but it had taken them several hours longer than what they had anticipated to reach this first campsite with the spring for stock water. Only one day out, and the entire group was exhausted and covered with dust. On several occasions, they'd had to lighten the wagons by getting out and walking. Even with the lighter load, the horses labored heavily and shaking with fatigue by the time they reached the campsite. They had met three wagons coming down the road in the afternoon, creating more of a delay, as they had to jockey all the wagons into a position on the road to pass. On most of the route, the road would prove to be no more than one wagon width wide. It was always a time-consuming challenge to position the oncoming wagons in such a manner to pass without one or the other getting too close the outer edge of the road and rolling over into the canyon bottom hundreds of feet below. It was obvious that this disastrous event had taken place for others. At more than one of the narrower sections of road, they could see the scattered remnants of a wagon far below, with the bleached and scattered bones of the horses that were pulled over the edge with the wagons.

Elizabeth and Anne had discussed the possibilities of Burgdorf at the hot springs being the same as their dear friend Fredrick from

Darmstadt in Germany. They knew from the previous letters from home that he and Little Josh had left Germany some three years ago, but no one had heard a word from them. Elizabeth was still tired and recovering from her near drowning, so she just sat on the tailgate of the wagon watching the others busily tend to the horses and prepare camp for the night. Anne was unusually quiet but hustled around helping here and there wherever she could. The impact of Elizabeth's accident had finally taken full effect on her.

During the night at their camping spot near the spring, several wagons passed on their way down to the Salmon River. The group had made camp away from the water so others could stop if necessary, but none did. It was an easy trip from here going down to the next water access.

No one slept well, and the mood the next morning was somber. The second day was much the same as the first. A very steep road, hot and dusty, with the constant challenge of passing wagons. The fourth day did find them going over the summit and heading down the other side into the headwaters of Lake Creek. The terrain had changed from steep, rocky, and barren canyon walls to a beautiful, heavily timbered valley with Lake Creek sparkling its way for as far as the eye could see.

This would be their first comfortable camp since leaving the river four days ago. The camp was set up, and they were all sitting around the fire when Richard announced, "We will be at your Burgdorf Hot Springs sometime late tomorrow afternoon."

"Can we stay there?" Anne asked. "I need a bath." The entire camp laughed, even the children. It had become a running joke as to the necessity of frequent baths for Anne.

Chapter 87

Burgdorf Hot Springs,
Idaho Territory, United States

1866

Late the following afternoon, Elizabeth was perched on top of the loaded wagon straining her eyes to get a glimpse of the hot springs, trembling with excitement. She and Anne had discussed the eventuality of meeting up with Fredrick and Little Josh, if it was truly them.

She first noticed the steam coming from the hot springs. Then as they got closer, she could make out the forms of several people milling around the buildings. A minute later a figure walked out from the buildings to the road to get a view of the wagons approaching.

Elizabeth shouted, "It's him! Anne, it's him."

The big, square-shouldered man standing in the road ahead was the old family friend from Darmstadt, Fredrick C. Burgdorf. He had been like a brother to Thomas as well as his best friend. He had fussed over Elizabeth every time she had visited the vineyards and the farm, making each of her stays there as pleasant as possible, and he had been as fond of her as Thomas was, however knowing full well that Thomas's attention was far more than a fondness. Thomas and Elizabeth had been deeply in love, obvious soul mates. It was a perfect match. Fredrick was to be the best man at their wedding—the wedding that never happened, due to Thomas's disappearance. Jumping from the moving wagon and running ahead, Elizabeth waving her arms and yelling like a banshee.

Seeing her, Fredrick stood in amazement at the approaching figure. *What the hell?* Then a slow feeling of recognition started over him. *It's Elizabeth.* She was nearly to him when she jumped, folding her arms around him in a hug that almost knocked him down. Anne was next, having also hopped from the slow-moving wagon joining Elizabeth in Fredrick's embrace. The Klein sisters clung to Fredrick, Elizabeth crying and Anne chattering like a magpie. He had hoped to locate them sometime but had no idea when, how, or where. He had failed to find their little farm in Hayes Valley near San Francisco and had not a clue as to their whereabouts.

"It has been years since I last saw you." He gasped.

Little Josh had also strolled out to meet them and was patiently standing off to one side, hands on his hips and a huge smile on his face.

Now noticing Josh, Elizabeth cried, "Look at you! No longer the little urchin we first met in Darmstadt years ago but nearly a grown—and quite handsome—young man."

"Yes, ma'am, I have grown a bit. It's so good to see you, Elizabeth." Then turning to Anne, he said, "Good to see you too. We were all so lonely after you left looking for Thomas. Any news of him?"

The wagons had arrived, and the other folks were sitting and watching this display of affection. Elizabeth and Anne had calmed and were now standing in the middle of the road just chatting about old times with Fredrick when he glanced up noticing the apprehensive looks on Richard's and Derick's faces. Fredrick walked the few steps over to the wagons then stuck his hand up and introduced himself.

"Fredrick C. Burgdorf," he said.

Both men shook his hand smiling. "It's a pleasure to meet you, Fredrick."

Elizabeth laughed at the introduction. "Sorry, gentlemen, I should have introduced you all sooner. Fredrick usually only answers to Fredrick C. Burgdorf. Is that still the case?"

"You all can call me whatever you want, Elizabeth. I outgrew that silly notion years ago. I'm just overwhelmed at your presence here, of all places. Please stay here tonight. I have so much to tell you, and I'm sure you have lots to share with me." Then turning to address Richard and Derick, he said, "Stay and camp here tonight. It's only about a mile from here to the usual scheduled stop at the confluence. As you can see, there's plenty of room, a big meadow for the horses to graze, the creek is running by just over there, and we have developed a big hot water pool over there behind that building." He pointed to the other side of the road. "It won't make much difference in your travel time staying here instead of where the road forks. I think quite soon this is going to be the scheduled stopping place anyway."

"Has my vote," Anne chimed in, smiling, "for the obvious reasons, and I never mentioned a bath."

Elizabeth just shook her head laughing. The decision was made.

"This looks incredible, Fredrick," Elizabeth said as they walked toward the cabins. "Is it all yours?"

"We just maintain it for now," Fredrick said, "but I plan to buy it proper soon. Just wait, this whole area will be called Burgdorf Hot Springs someday. Maybe I'll even have a sign."

Josh guided the two wagons over to the edge of the meadow near the buildings and the huge hot water pool that Fredrick had built. It was a good thirty feet wide and forty feet long. He and Josh had lined the edges of the pool with logs to separate it from the scalding hot springs that entered it on one end. It was deep enough to stand in and they had hauled several wagonloads of gravel from the nearby creek bed to line the bottom.

"What a beautiful setting," Richard's wife observed. "Can we swim in it?"

"You may, and please do. It is open to the public, and we do have many visitors from the mining town of Warren's over to the west about twenty miles."

Camp was being prepared, and one of the Chinese miners who had become disillusioned with the mines and was now working for Fredrick was busily running around preparing supper for everyone.

"Elizabeth, since you and Anne don't have a wagon to stay in or sleep under, why don't you let me help you put your things in the extra cabin over there by the pool?" Putting actions to words, he started unloading their trunks and moving them one at a time into the cabin. Coming to the trunk partially painted in pink, he raised an eyebrow.

"Don't even ask." Elizabeth smirked. "Just be very careful with that one. We'll talk about that one later."

Fredrick's cook had prepared a table long enough to seat the entire group of ten plus Fredrick and Josh. He had put clean white linens on the table with real matching plates, cups, and silverware resting on folded linen napkins. There were citronella candles burning at strategic places on the table for mosquito control, with other citronella torches placed around the table for light. "I have the citronella shipped in from Portland," Fredrick commented, "but I only use it for special guests. It's worth its weight in gold."

The full moon was in the process of rising over the trees in the meadow, and that, coupled with the torches, presented the perfect light. The meal was of mutton spiced perfectly with a side dish of onions, carrots, and turnips. "The root crops grow here very well," Fredrick commented.

"It is absolutely unbelievable, Fredrick," Anne whispered. "We haven't witnessed anything like this in years, since leaving San Francisco anyway. You have forgotten nothing."

Looking over the table with his guests now seated, Fredrick thought wistfully, *No, I have not forgotten anything, not even my dear old friend Thomas, but he is not here. Where is he?* he thought. *Is he even still alive?* With a very somber look, he tried to eat his meal.

"Why the long face, Fredrick?" Anne inquired looking up at the bright moonlit sky studded with millions of stars. "This is a four-star setting."

Fredrick chuckled at the pun, turning his head and looking at Elizabeth. He knew she was thinking his same thoughts. Where was Thomas? The four children were laughing and eating as rapidly as possible, all wanting to get into the pool. In fact, all of the adults were looking forward to the pool, too, but they also didn't want to leave this beautiful setting around the table. Fredrick had even opened a bottle of wine brought in from Portland with his last shipment of goods as well as soft drinks for the children. He was well on his plan to be prepared for guests and hoped they would be flocking to his facility as soon as they were official and the word got out about Burgdorf Hot Springs.

An hour later, the children had ran out of patience so they all relented to a plunge in the pool. There was a single dressing room, for which Fredrick apologized for the small size but promised to build another one soon—"If I can get this Josh to do something around here."

Laughing, Josh retorted, "You're the one sitting on his fanny all day drinking that wine stuff," which brought a roar from everyone.

Everyone took turns changing in the dressing room, and all were soon in the pool, with the children laughing and howling. *In the past few days, I have not seen them even smile, let alone laugh*, Elizabeth thought. *This is so good for everyone.* The children had witnessed Derick being thrown over the cliff as well as Elizabeth's near-drowning incident and had become very subdued.

"Fredrick, thank you so much for everything. We have so much to talk about."

"We do, and we will. You haven't mentioned your plans, Elizabeth. It will take weeks for us to catch up."

"We will talk in the morning, Fredrick. I would like to play now with the children. They are having so much fun, and I don't want to miss out on that."

When they were all tired an hour or so later, they all got out of the hot springs and made their way to their respective sleeping quarters. Elizabeth had just bid Fredrick goodnight, promising to talk again the next morning, when the most lonely but aggressive howl came rolling across the meadow.

"Good God, what is that?" she asked.

"The wolves. They start about this time every night, especially when we have a full moon like this one," Fredrick said, pointing over the trees at the full moon still rising. "We have brought in dogs on several occasions to help with the problem, but it's a dog-eat-dog world out there, and ours are the ones getting eaten. It just hasn't worked out very well yet. I think I will get Derick and Richard to help me move the horses in closer. We have lost several head of livestock lately. Don't know why, as there are herds of elk in the meadow most of the time."

Elizabeth instinctively reached her hand into her pocket, feeling for the derringer, then joined Anne in the dimly lit but warm little cabin. Sitting on the bed next to Anne, she asked, "Can you believe this? Fredrick here!"

"I can," she replied, "because it's for real—our dear friend Fredrick is here. His story will be an interesting one."

So is ours, Elizabeth thought, and with that they went to bed. The fatigue of the last few days' travel had exhausted them. That, coupled with a glass of wine and the hot springs, put them sound to sleep.

The wolves howled intermittently throughout the night, but the girls heard nothing. They awoke to the sound of someone chopping wood and a rooster crowing.

"Ohh," groaned Anne. "Who in their right mind would be up chopping wood before the chickens are even up?" Then she rolled over and went back to sleep. Elizabeth got up, dressing speedily. She wanted to talk with Fredrick before the others were up. *I would like to have his undivided attention for about a week*, she thought. Even then, it would be difficult to get caught up on everything that had happened in Germany since she left. She did know that people were fleeing there by the thousands, though, as she had met so many over the last several years on their way to the goldfields or the other areas conducive to farming and ranching. Stepping out of the door of the cozy cabin to see if it was Fredrick chopping wood, she gasped at the cold. It was midsummer, but a heavy coat of frost covered everything and the water bucket sitting just out the door had a thin layer of ice on its surface.

Fredrick noticed her standing there with her arms folded across her chest shivering. "Get your coat, Elizabeth! We are at over six thousand feet in elevation here, and it's like this nearly every morning."

Turning back into the cabin, she grabbed her jacket and returned outside with Fredrick. "Why are you chopping wood at this time of the morning?" she inquired.

"To warm up," he replied grinning. "When the sun comes up, it is too hot. This is the perfect time." She just stood shivering.

Fredrick stopped his wood splitting and piled more wood on the smoldering coals of the bonfire they had enjoyed the night before. Elizabeth sat down on the bench next to the fire with Fredrick next to her.

"It's been years, Elizabeth. We did get an occasional packet of letters once a year while I was still working Thomas's vineyards, but it was so unreliable."

"What happened there before you left Germany?" Elizabeth asked.

Fredrick filled her in on everything he could remember up to the time of his departure, mostly of the political turmoil leading to the mass exodus of Germans to the United States. Then Elizabeth interrupted him. "But Fredrick, when you got to San Francisco, why did you not contact Lolivey and her father? We have been in contact with her since we left, not often but she still forwards mail to us from the old country when it arrives, and our friend Timothy still does whatever it is he does in the wharf area to keep an eye out for news of Thomas."

"We did stop at your house in Hayes Valley, but no one was there. We inquired at the neighbors, and they had indicated Lolivey and her father had made a trip to town. Apparently it was their first since you and Anne left. It was reported that Timothy was with them, and everything was going well. Josh and I did leave a letter attached to the door informing them that we had made it that far and were heading on to the goldfields to the north. We soon tired of the grotesque conditions at Pierce, Florence, and Warren's just over the hill from here, so we picked this place by the hot springs, which as you can see is right next to the main road from the Salmon River going on to Warren's in one direction and Boise Basin the other."

Elizabeth was sitting in rapt attention. She leaned forward with one leg folded over the other and her elbow resting on her knee with her chin in one hand and a cup of coffee in the other. Fredrick had only touched on the highlights of the last few years when he asked Elizabeth about her and Anne's adventures in getting here to this place alongside the road with the hot springs in the middle of the mountains. The rest of the group was now up and strolling toward the fire. Fredrick had a large old two-gallon blackened coffee pot sitting next to the fire to warm.

"We will continue this later again," Elizabeth promised but was thinking, *We have only a short time before Richard and Derick take us on to Warren's. I know they are in a hurry to get on to Fort Boise.*

Josh had helped the cook with breakfast, and they all again sat at the large outdoor table. The sun had come up and was melting the frost—it would soon be very warm. They could see elk and deer in the meadow across the road, and the steam from the hot springs softly floated their direction with the light breeze.

"This is the most wonderful place," said Richard's wife. "Do we really have to go on to Boise Basin? I've heard it's a desert there. This is the most beautiful place I have ever seen."

Derick and his wife looked at each other. They had been discussing the beauty of this valley the night before. "We like it here too. The children love it, and perhaps we should reconsider going on further, at least this year."

Richard sat deep in thought. "You may be right. This mining business brings such a rough crowd, and I really don't want to be a part of that. I think I would like to go back down to the Salmon River and homestead there. Maybe start a small cattle ranch there, grow a garden. The weather down on the Salmon will be much milder, and we could always come up and visit here on occasion."

And it was decided—Derick and his family were to stay here helping to build a log cabin for themselves, Richard's family would homestead along the Salmon River, and Anne and Elizabeth would stay here with Fredrick in the little cabin for at least a few days or perhaps weeks. They were now less than twenty miles from the boomtown of Warren's Diggins, and could continue on over Steamboat Summit to Warren when Fredrick would have time to assist them. He was in no hurry to do that, he informed them. "It's a rough place with few accommodations."

Two days later they were saying goodbye to the Richard Rhett family heading back to the Salmon River, and Derick had already started dragging in the tall straight lodgepole pines for his family's cabin. They only had maybe two months until heavy snows. The Klein sisters spent every evening with Fredrick and Josh, living and reliving the years since leaving Germany, their experiences in Panama; in San Francisco, California; then in Portland, Oregon; their trip up the Columbia to Lewiston; then on to here with their chance meeting at the hot springs with Fredrick and Little Josh.

Anne pestered Fredrick daily about the conditions in the town of Warren—did it have a theater, a fine restaurant, hotels, boarding houses? "It is a rough place with all of the miners," he would reply.

"Occasionally in the summer, there will be a huge tent for a theater group traveling through but only the saloons for performances of any kind in the winter. The hotels are usually are full of miners, and there are no boarding houses." It had one main street lined with eleven saloons, two brothels, three hotels, a stable, two general stores, and a hardware store. The few side streets were packed with cabins for miners with families and other related services, he informed the girls. There was also a school at the east end of town with a volunteer teacher who tended classes when he was not working the mines.

"I want to perform," Anne would say. "I'm not getting any younger, you know."

Two weeks later Fredrick relented, hitched up the buggy, and agreed to take them to Warren's. They left early hoping to find accommodations for the night and not having to return late at night. That could be dangerous. There had been several robberies and murders along the road when miners or the weekly stage were taking a load of gold out. Fredrick was well acquainted with most of the business owners and some of the mine owners, so he was optimistic about finding accommodations, but they did take extra warm clothing in case they had to travel back to the hot springs in the night chill.

They arrived in Warren at noon on the mid-September day in 1866. Fredrick stopped just on the outskirts of the town for the girls to review their surroundings, and they were spellbound. This was a town high in the mountains of Idaho, nowhere near a sea or lake, just small ponds, yet there were huge boats that each had arms reaching out in front with big steel buckets. The buckets cycled around the arms, digging up rocks out of the ground and depositing them in piles behind. Each scoop of a bucket would dig the pond a little more and progress the boat forward slightly. It was a perpetual operation called dredging.

Elizabeth and Anne had never seen the likes of this or even imagined such a thing. They sat next to Fredrick on the buggy seat in total fascination. Everywhere they looked, there was activity. There were massive wagons being loaded with ore from the dredges, miners energetically working on the hillside portals, and logs being moved into town for firewood and the creation of new cabins. The street was lined with horse-drawn wagons. People were bustling up and down the street on the boardwalk in front of some of the businesses and then onto the dirt walks, which, Fredrick informed them, turned to knee-deep mud when it rained or the snow melted.

"This is absolutely the most exciting thing I have ever seen," Anne said, blinking with surprise.

Elizabeth just sat fascinated, even the streets along the piers in San Francisco did not match the activities surrounding this mining town. Slowly moving on toward town while dodging other wagons, men on horseback, pedestrians, and mudholes, they stopped in front of Jack Pickel's General Store. It was a beehive of activity. Fredrick helped them down from the buggy, and they weaved their way through the congested crowd into the store. Anne was ecstatic—she loved the activity. Before she'd stepped down from the seat of the buggy, she noted that the entire town was alive and seemingly moving with human bodies. Miners were laughing, swearing, and milling about.

"I really like this place." She laughed to Elizabeth. Looking at Fredrick, she asked, "Is there a tent theater set up now?"

"Yes, of course. You can see the top of it just sticking up over that building down the street to the right. It's next to the Mayflower Hotel and Saloon."

They toured the sizable store, and Elizabeth noted several items she wanted before they were to leave. Fredrick introduced them to Jack Pickel and inquired as to any vacant quarters that may be available for the girls to rent.

"There is not a vacant building in this town," he said, "nor a side of a building someone has not put up a lean-to for living quarters. My wife, Luci, and I do have two rooms above the store we used for overflow supplies that we could fix up for these two charming ladies, though. Nowadays we can't keep the shelves stocked, let alone worry about an area for backstock. Come, let's talk to my wife."

Weaving between the constant throng of people, they made their way to the back where Jack's wife was busy cutting material from a bolt of cloth for a miner's wife. "Luci, please come. I would like you to meet Anne and Elizabeth Klein. They are planning to spend time here and may be able to use the two rooms upstairs."

Eyeing them appraisingly then taking an instant liking to them, she replied, "Well, I certainly would rather have them here than any of those rowdy miners that would probably tear up the place. It will take some doing, though. Those two rooms haven't been cleaned out for a couple of years. They are still stacked high with empty flour sacks, gunny sacks, and other stuff. Don' know when I can even get to it."

Anne chimed in, "We will help if you wish."

"Have at it." Mrs. Pickel sighed then returned to cutting another piece of cloth from another bolt. When she'd finished, she said. "Come on, I'll show you the way. Don't expect too much, though. They will be hardly more than a warm place to lay your heads."

Chapter 88

Warren's Diggins,
Idaho Territory, United States

1866

Climbing a few steps up the stairs in the back of the store and now above the crowd, Elizabeth stopped to survey the crowd below. She was the last in line, and Fredrick and Anne had not missed her presence yet. *What an unconceivable group of people*, she thought. The store was full, and the streets were packed with milling people. It was almost hypnotic.

Turning to follow the rest up the stairs, she noticed a familiar figure walk in the front door. She gasped in shock, and her heart skipped a beat. It was him—it was the man who had saved her from drowning. *William*, she thought. The ferry operator on the Salmon River had said he thought his name was William. She stood there not sure what action she would take now. Should she ignore him and continue on upstairs? Should she go down and thank him for saving her life? After all, she had never had the opportunity to thank him.

The decision was made for her. William looked up, seeing her standing on the stairs, their eyes locked, and he smiled, tipping his hat and walking toward her through the crowd. She was trembling with emotion. *God*, she thought. *Get ahold of yourself, Elizabeth. He is just walking over for a casual greeting.* She was always the calm and collected one, and now she could hardly stand and was in a state of total indecision.

What will I say? How should I react? Ohhh, where is Anne when I need her? Elizabeth nearly turned and ran up the stairs, but William was now standing there one step below her but still eye-to-eye. He just stood there smiling, she speechless.

"Glad to see you have recovered," he finally said. "You gave me quite a scare. Sorry I didn't get a chance to talk to you before I left, but you appeared to be consumed with your friends, and I was running late after dragging you from the river." He chuckled.

The soothing sound of his voice and his casual manner had put Elizabeth totally at ease, and she took a gulp of air. She hadn't been breathing, she realized. "Well, I'm sorry you drug me from the river too—" She stammered, realizing what she had said. Regaining more of her composure by the second, she grinned. "Thank you, William. That is your name, isn't it? Willy at the ferry said he thought that was right."

He smiled and nodded.

"It did give me quite a scare too. I thought I had breathed my last breath."

"And that you did," he said chuckling. "When I got you to the shore, you were full of water."

"Well, all is well that ends well." Elizabeth exhaled, just standing there smiling, not knowing what else to say.

"Are you staying here in Warren's?" he finally asked awkwardly.

"I am. My sister and I are taking a room upstairs in this very building."

Standing for another minute in awkward silence, William replied, "I hope to see you around."

"I am quite sure you will, William," she said smiling then turned modestly and walked on up the stairs. She felt awkward, like everyone in the store was watching her, but no one had even noticed except William, whose eyes still followed her. She had an unexpected spring to her step and felt flustered. *He is older*, she thought, *but very handsome and considerate.* And then laughing at herself, she joined the others discussing what had to be done to the rooms to make them habitable.

"Where were you, Elizabeth? Did you get lost?"

Elizabeth stood there demurely with a sort of Mona Lisa smile. Anne turned, recognizing that look.

"Elizabeth," Anne snapped, bringing her sister back from gaga land to the here-and-now reality. "What were you doing that put you into that state of mind. Did you see a ghost?"

"Uh-huh." Elizabeth smiled then actively joined in the inspection of their new quarters-to-be by giving advice here about the color of fabric for a window shade or the color of the rug for the floor, and on and on it went.

Mrs. Pickel was thoroughly enjoying the girls' company. She normally had only the company of the miners that frequented the store or the ladies from the brothels—neither group did she find pleasing to talk with. Elizabeth and Anne were such a refreshing change.

Fredrick soon tired of this chatter and returned downstairs then across the street to a saloon. Taking his drink to a small table and chair next to the window, he sat watching for the girls to finish. From this vantage point, he could see the miners passing by, the multitudes of Chinese laborers coming from and going to work at the various mines, the horses toiling to pull heavily laden wagons full of ore up the street to the stamp mill on the outskirts of town, and some of the other more questionable personalities that worked at the brothels and saloons. Smiling to himself, he thought, *We do have a diverse group of inhabitants here*. Looking across the street again, he saw a tall, well-built, clean-cut older man standing off to one side of the covered porch. He had been there when Fredrick had come out of the general store and was now just standing, paying no apparent attention to anything. *Interesting*, Fredrick thought, keeping an eye on him.

Soon Anne and Elizabeth appeared in front of the store and Fredrick gulped down the last of his drink and crossed the street to meet them. He assisted each into the wagon, and they drove on down the road enjoying the activities of this thriving little boomtown. With the huge tent theater now in sight off to their right, Anne asked, "Fredrick, can we please stop for a moment? I would like to check out the theater. I may know someone here." Leaving Elizabeth to tend the wagon, Fredrick escorted Anne inside.

It was the typical boomtown tent theater with a rough wooden stage in one corner and the rest of the area filled with benches and a makeshift bar. The only person in the room was the manager of the performing group, and he recognized Anne immediately. Shouting from across the room, he said, "It's a miracle. Anne Klein, what are you doing here in this out-of-the-way place?"

"I might ask you the same." She laughed in reply. "I haven't seen this group since Portland."

"Anne, please tell me you are staying here. Our leading lady, Catalina Darottisy, came down with pneumonia a few days ago, and it is questionable if she will live let alone ever perform again."

"Where is she?" Anne asked with an alarmed expression.

"Why, she is just out back of the tent in one of the cabins reserved for the traveling theater groups."

"Has she seen a doctor?"

"No, there are no doctors here."

"My sister Elizabeth is a healer. Let me get her." Anne quickly ran outside and informed Elizabeth of the situation.

Hurrying back inside, Elizabeth was led to the tiny cabin and was soon administering to Catalina. The group had little in the line of medical supplies—some aspirin powder, salves, splints, and some bandages. Elizabeth put a piece of wood in the small stove then water in a pan, placing it on the stove to warm. Next she helped Catalina into a sitting position, causing her to cough deeply and severely from the bottom of her lungs pitifully.

"Let's get her up and walk a few steps, Anne."

After only a few steps around the small room, Catalina was exhausted. She was coughing a raspy, deep hack again and was flushed with a temperature. Elizabeth did not lay her down but assisted her to a sitting position in a chair next to the bed. By this time the water sitting on the stove was heated to boiling. She put a spoonful each of the Vicks mentholated salve and the aspirin powder into the boiling water, then placed the pan on a small end table next to Catalina. Taking the towel, she draped it over Catalina's head and the steaming pot, forcing the girl to breathe the steaming concoction. Within a few minutes, Catalina was breathing easier and the cough had diminished considerably.

"This has to be repeated hourly for the rest of today and the entire night," Elizabeth said. "Get one of the other ladies in the group over here immediately to assist this poor child."

"There are no other ladies in the group—she is the only one. All the rest are gentlemen." The stage manager sniffed.

Thinking for only a moment, Elizabeth responded, "Well then I'll stay and do what I can. If she is still breathing in the morning, she has a good chance of survival."

With that, she ushered the others from the shack, shutting the door then opening it again. "Anne will you get me another bucket of water? This poor girl needs to be cleaned up."

An hour later, the theater manager approached Anne on the street. "Anne, what are we to do? We have no second for Catalina to take her place."

"Well, I can't perform for her in a play with such short notice, having never seen her script. I can only sing and would be happy to do that."

"Deal!" the stage manager cried and hurried off to notify the others.

Fredrick had walked back down the street to the general store, and the Pickels had agreed to let him and Anne sleep on the bundles of sacks in the rooms upstairs for the night. The girls had rented the rooms on a long-term basis, but they were still cluttered and dusty. The girls were to help Mrs. Pickel clean, rearrange, and furnish the rooms soon, but for now they were still in a state of disarray.

Anne had told Mrs. Pickel of the sick girl from the theater group, and she had hurried down to assist Elizabeth. "We have far too few women in this town, and we can't afford to lose one to pneumonia if I can help it," she said.

Anne was an absolute smashing hit in her first performance at the theater that night. Elizabeth and Mrs. Pickel took turns nursing the pneumonia-ridden girl through the night, and she was showing great improvement the next morning. Fredrick and the sisters met in a small restaurant next to Pickel's General Store.

"I have to get back to the hot springs," Fredrick was saying. "Josh will be worried if I don't return today and may come looking for me."

"I can go with you," Elizabeth said. "Mrs. Pickel will keep an eye on Catalina—she is doing much better today."

"I think I will stay," Anne said. "Our room leaves a bit to be desired"—she chuckled—"but I will be okay for a couple of days. I am enjoying the theater, and Catalina will probably not be up and around for weeks. We haven't discussed this much with Fredrick yet, but I think I would like to move over here to Warren. I will help Mrs. Pickel get those rooms fixed up as soon as possible. I really like it here, Elizabeth, and I may find a rich miner to marry. You already have a noose, and I don't want to be left alone."

Fredrick chuckled but seemed confused, looking at Elizabeth in wonder but saying nothing. It was agreed Anne was to stay and help Mrs. Pickel tend to the sick girl and work on getting the rooms over the store ready for her and Elizabeth. When breakfast was finished, Anne walked across the street to help Mrs. Pickel. Fredrick and Elizabeth worked their way down the crowded street to the stable for the team and buggy.

"This is going to be different," Elizabeth stated to Fredrick. "There has not been a day since Anne and I left Germany years ago that we have not been together."

Fredrick glanced at her with understanding in his eyes. "It will be okay," he assured her. "I hate to see you two move on, but I will bring you back here as soon as you can make ready. We will only be a short trip over the summit away. You can come for a visit anytime you want to enjoy the hot springs, and Josh and I will come over to Warren's every other week or so just to see what is going on. We will be happy to help in any manner we can. Elizabeth, we never want to lose you and Anne again. Those years that we did not know where you were or if you were even alive were very sad ones. Things were never the same after Thomas left, then you and Anne."

Elizabeth just sat next to Fredrick on the wagon seat deep in thought, speaking little all the way back to the hot springs. She had not told Fredrick about William other than that he had pulled her from the river. She had not told him of her questionable feelings about this handsome, gentle man. *Why?* she thought. *Maybe there is nothing to tell. After all I have never really even had a conversation with this man, William. I will not mention him to Fredrick for now. I know Fredrick will be very upset. He was such an extraordinary friend to Thomas, and he feels in his heart that Thomas is still very much alive somewhere. I do not want to cause this dear man Fredrick any disquiet. I will wait to see where this goes.*

Elizabeth and Fredrick arrived at the hot springs late that night and were met by a smiling Josh. "I was starting to get worried," he said, amused. The Chinese cook was in the process of preparing another impressive meal, which Elizabeth enjoyed immensely knowing that when she and Anne were permanently moved over to Warren's Diggins, their accommodations were to be somewhat less desirable and the food probably deplorable. She busied herself in packing. Anne's worldly possessions were still neatly packed in her three trunks with the only thing missing being the clothes on her back, and they would be in need of a change soon. Elizabeth had unpacked very few items from her trunks earlier—the cabin was too small to accommodate anything more than just enough space for their trunks to sit. She had, however, hung the small glass hummingbird Thomas had given her in the window, and it reflected the sunlight merrily around the room as it gently moved with the slight breeze from the window.

Staring at the small glass figure swinging gently back and forth with its brilliant radiance, she felt her eyes start to mist with tears. There was no possibility of not suffering from the occasional tremors of hope that even now sometimes took her unaware when she found herself dreaming that she might yet see Thomas again. Her love for Thomas had begun so many years ago in Germany when she was hardly more than a child herself, and now she had come to accept the probability that she would never see him again. She might yearn for a time when they could be with one another again and rebuild their life together. She might tell herself that their love would survive and their dreams would come true, and try with all her heart to believe it. But then another voice deep inside her would ask, *How long do I wait? It's been years. What chance is there for that now?* Gently taking the small glass figurine from the window, she carefully wrapped it again with layer upon layer of cotton and replaced it gently into the trunk for the trip over the summit to Warren.

Chapter 89

Hmoy,
China

1866

Finally Thomas and Jason's time came in Hmoy, an island in southeastern Fujian China, on the Taiwan Strait. They had planned dozens of escapes over the years, but each time something would go amiss, and the attempt was aborted.

On this night, the captain and his bloodthirsty first mate, Hallo, along with some of his thugs had gone ashore in Hmoy. As usual Thomas and Jason had been chained in the dark and damp hold below deck with all of the others, who were now soundly asleep after another brutal day of work.

Jason, forever checking his irons, rolled over in total surprise. The manacle binding his wrist to the anchor in the wall had just fallen free. "Thomas," he whispered excitedly, so as not to awaken any of the others. "The fools were in such a hurry to get to shore, they did not get my manacles fastened securely, and it just fell off."

"What?" Thomas corked in disbelief.

Jason reached his hand out and whispered again, "I am free of the chains and will see if I can find a key for you."

Thomas spoke excitedly in a low voice, too excited to whisper, "I have seen them hanging just around the corner on a peg in the wall, at the bottom of the ladder leading to the upper deck."

Quietly, Jason rose and crept through the darkened room, desperately trying not to step on any of the sleeping crewmen. Making it to the ladder with no incidents, he retrieved the key ring hanging on the peg and slipped it around his wrist, not wishing to take a chance of dropping it on the way back into the dark hold to Thomas.

The light was better here at the bottom of the ladder, and as he turned to retrace his steps, he noticed a small closet next to the ladder. Quietly, out of curiosity, he opened the door and was rewarded with a trove of swords of all styles, sizes, and shapes stacked neatly on a shelf, to be passed out to the crew in case of an emergency, presumably if other pirates boarded their ship to attack. With the keys already hanging from his wrist, Jason secured two of the swords, one in each hand, then crept back into the dark room where Thomas and the others were chained. Carefully and as quietly as possible, he first slid the ring from his wrist and handed the keys to Thomas to unlock his bindings. When this was done and Thomas was free and standing, Jason handed him the sword.

"How in God's name did you manage that?" Thomas asked. "Keys and a sword. Is there no end to your surprises?"

"None." Jason grinned. "Now let's get out of here," he whispered.

Thomas stood a moment rubbing his wrists to get circulation back into his arms and hands. "Jason, we can't just leave these poor wretched soles here chained to the floor with never a better chance of escape."

"Give me the keys," Jason snapped in frustration. "As soon as you get up the ladder to stand watch, I will waken one and give him the key. From there on, they are on their own."

Jason watched Thomas silently climb the ladder with sword in hand then retreated back in the gloom to the nearest body chained to the floor still sound asleep. He placed his hand over the man's mouth, knowing he would cry out when wakened so soon, and the man began to struggle frantically.

"Quiet!" Jason snapped again. "I have a key that will get you all unlocked, understand."

The man on the floor stared at him through the semidarkness then nodded.

Jason went on. "When you free yourself, quietly pass the key on to another, then arm yourselves with the weapons in that closet by the ladder. But if any of you fools make a noise, it's all over. If the captain does not dispose of you, I will. Understood?"

The man nodded, and Jason turned and ran out of the hold and up the ladder carrying his own sword. Thomas helped him up the last step onto the deck whispering, "I have noticed only one guard. If we are quiet, we may make it overboard and to shore without being found out."

He had hardly released the words from his mouth when the guard turned and saw the two standing only a few feet behind him. He lunged at them, cutlass swinging, but Thomas had also jumped forward, and he fenced as his father and many of his diverse friends had taught him. The guard, with no apparent expertise, jumped back, repositioned himself, then came at Thomas again. Swinging the cutlass frantically, he seemed sure he would behead this black-haired beast in front of him. He cut sharply at Thomas and missed, but Thomas did not. His blade touched the point where the man's neck met his chest. He froze in place, not daring to move.

So did Thomas. He did not want to kill this man. He only wanted escape for himself and Jason.

From the wave action in the harbor, the ship gave a sudden lurch, throwing the guard forward and the point of Thomas's sword through his neck. Coughing, the guard slid to his knees, pulling the sword with him until he collapsed lifeless on the deck.

Shuddering, Thomas said, "I just killed that man, Jason."

"Don't flatter yourself, Thomas. You did not kill him. Your sword did with the sudden role of the ship throwing him onto its point. Now let's get out of here."

Rapidly regaining his composure, Thomas whispered, "No use in getting wet now. Let's lower one of the lifeboats and go ashore in style."

"What if one of them on shore sees us?" Jason anxiously replied.

"Well, they won't."

"How can you be sure? Let's just jump and swim for it, Thomas. This chance has been years in coming."

"It has," Thomas replied, "but I'm now in the mood for revenge." At Jason's shocked expression, Thomas retorted, "What! I want to make that monster of a first mate, Hallo, pay for the torture he and all the others like him inflicted on us. Join me if you want, but I will not be offended if you just get safely away from here."

"You know I'm with you." Jason sighed. "Although I should have my head examined."

Chapter 90

Burgdorf Hot Springs, Idaho Territory, United States

1866

Elizabeth had been at the springs two days again with Fredrick and Josh before they both accompanied her back to Warren. *It is so beautiful here,* she thought. *I never want to leave—or at least not go very far from this place. It has such a serenity that is equaled by no other place I have ever been.* Elizabeth returned to Warren and found Anne busily cleaning, painting, sewing new curtains, helping tend to Catalina, and performing a show every night at the theater.

"Glad you're back," Anne said. "Look at me! I'm a mess." Anne was disheveled. A long lock of hair hung in her face, and her dress looked as if she had slept in it for two days, and she had. "I'm afraid even that rough lot of miners at the theater will soon question my appearance." She laughed.

"How is Catalina?" asked Elizabeth.

"She is recuperating well and has asked about you often. Let's go check on her now. It's time to relieve Mrs. Pickel anyway."

Catalina was standing, with Mrs. Pickel's assistance, looking out the window when Elizabeth and Anne arrived. Opening the door for them, she beamed. "The Klein sisters, and Mrs. Pickel, my saviors." She chuckled weakly. "I have to get well enough to perform again soon. I hear Anne has been stealing the show night after night."

"I have, and you better get well soon or I will totally replace you." Anne smiled.

Mrs. Pickel returned to the store, leaving Catalina in the capable hands of the two girls.

Josh and Fredrick were busy moving the girls' trunks with all their worldly belongings to the upstairs rooms at the store, paying special attention to the pink-painted one, knowing about its delicate contents.

"Let's go across the street to the saloon now." Josh beamed.

"How many times do I have to tell ya, Josh? You're not old enough yet."

"Well, I think I am! How old were you when you first visited a saloon?"

"I was probably born in one," admitted Fredrick. "But first we have to check on Catalina."

She was in good spirits and enjoyed all the visitors in her tiny little room. "This is a bigger crowd than I had in the theater." She coughed. It would still be some time before she could really get up and around, but she didn't seem to mind all that much. *The journey from town to town with weeks in between in a covered wagon does take a toll on one*, she thought. *This is a needed rest. Besides the show will be dismantling and moving in another few days anyway, and I don't really care if I get on stage here or not. I hear tell that Anne Klein is a tough act to follow.* She sat down coughing miserably then smiled up weakly at the company.

Elizabeth stayed with her so Anne could go freshen up for the evening program, and Fredrick and Josh were soon on their way back to the springs, promising to return soon. Elizabeth sat with Catalina to bathe her face and arms frequently, trying to keep the fever under control. The actress was better, but it would take some time before she would be healthy enough to travel by the troupe's usual means again.

A few days later, the group had finished their time in Warren and rearranged the contents of the wagons so Catalina could have one to herself with a comfortable bed and a small stove for warmth if needed. They would be leaving Warren for a week's performance in Florence, taking the same route Elizabeth and Anne had taken weeks ago. They had been warned of the danger with the Salmon River ferry crossing and of the appallingly steep climb up out of the canyon to Florence. Catalina had become very attached to the sisters but was now well enough to travel, and the show must go on as they say. But it was a sad parting.

"Come with me now, Elizabeth," Anne said. "I want to show you all of the new things we have in our rooms. Mrs. Pickel was so kind as to give us each a bed she had stored out back as well as a small table each and a chair. I even have a full-length mirror. You have the short one," she said laughing.

Elizabeth only smiled. *I may have need for the full-length one*, she thought. *I have to start keeping up a better appearance just in case that William pays me a visit.*

Anne nearly dragged her up the stairs to get her approval of the work she and Mrs. Pickel had done. The rooms were magnificent. New freshly made curtains of a print unlike anything in town. Mrs. Pickel had reserved that specific bolt of material just for the sisters' use and no one else. From the curtains to the bedspreads to the floor rug, everything matched perfectly.

Elizabeth was stunned. "Here we are in a boomtown high in the mountains of Idaho, and we have the nicest accommodations we have had since leaving Hayes Valley in San Francisco. Anne, you are so precious."

Anne dimpled, smiling at the compliment. "Oh, I know," she said and wandered off to her room.

Chapter 91

Hmoy,
China

1866

Thomas and Jason found the captain and first mate in a waterfront dive filled with sailors. Thomas had heard all about the back room at these dives, the place reserved for officers and their shady ladies, and it was there he found the captain and, beside him, first mate Hallo. A giant of a man, Hallo had at least two drinks under his belt, and his meanness was riding him like a fiend on his shoulders. Thomas watched and waited, ever more bloodthirsty, until Hallo started toward a brothel room in the hallway. He saw Thomas, and Thomas grinned at him.

"What? How did you get here?" Hallo waved a hand. "You two were left chained below the deck in the hold like the mangy curs you are." Then the shock slid off as he shrugged and took a swig. "What difference does it make now? You can go no place no how, and I feel sorry for ya if you do. This here island hates plain old seamen, and that's what you are. Now get out," he slurred. "This room is for your betters only."

"You filthy slob," Thomas told him with total contempt. "Your time has finally come."

Hallo lunged toward Thomas in the hallway and learned for the first time the value of Thomas's straight left. It stabbed him in the mouth as though he had run into the butt end of a post, and stopped him in his tracks. Thomas went at him with fury and years of pent-up resentment. What followed was a deliberate, artistic, and enthusiastic beating. Thomas proceeded to drag Hallo from the back room and whip him unmercifully for the entertainment of the common sailors out front.

When it was over, Jason threw up his hands and sighed, "Now you've done it, Thomas. Can we get out of here now?! He will not be able to move for weeks, if he is still alive. We can go now, and we had better make it fast. If we're found, we'll be hung."

Chapter 92

Warren's Diggins,
Idaho Territory, United States

1866–1867

Anne was able to perform with all of the traveling theater groups that came to town. As a matter of fact, most groups had heard of Anne Klein and would make a request for her to perform with them long before they were to arrive. When winter came, the huge tent theater was taken down, and the presentations were held in the large lobby of the hotel. Every show was a sellout. The miners had nothing better to spend their gold on, and they loved the theater groups. Anne's portion of the program was always the most favored. Her voice was like no other, and it was not uncommon for a group of miners to travel over a hundred miles to hear her sing for just one night. Anne was quietly adding more and more to her already sizable fortune.

Anne and Elizabeth lived modestly in their small rooms above Pickel's General Store and had no lavish habits. Elizabeth would help Anne with her wardrobe, her hair, and other necessities during the time the traveling groups were there. Anne would in turn help Elizabeth caring for the injured or sick miners.

Elizabeth was sometimes overwhelmed with requests requiring her medical expertise. She established a relationship with the Chinese miners, some of whom she had been acquainted with in Portland's Chinatown. They would trade her various herbs and all kinds of medicinal goods for her services. The Chinese were not a popular group of people in any of the boomtowns at that time, and aid of any kind from any of the local residents was hard to be had. They all looked up to her with great respect, and once again she came to be known as the beautiful white woman who helped everyone. No person in Warren was ever denied medical attention by Elizabeth. If they were injured or sick and couldn't pay for her services, they or some of their friends would make it up in another manner. They might chop and bring in firewood for them. Or share some of their game from hunting. Others might shovel the snow around the store with their rooms upstairs—no easy chore, as at times that winter they had over twelve feet of snow. The girls could walk out of their second-story rooms onto the packed snow then down the steps hacked into the snowbank to the street below. In spite of the wild and sometimes ruthless behavior of many of the miners, times were good for the Klein sisters.

Anne had confided in Elizabeth on another occasion as to her accumulated wealth. "I have nearly $500,000 saved," she said.

Elizabeth blinked in surprise. "That's an unbelievable amount, Anne. Are you sure?"

"Sure, I'm sure. I have counted it on more than one occasion. What do you think I do on the long, lonely nights all alone in that little room? I *count my money*. I have gold nuggets that I have to guess as to the value, I have silver dollars, I have little pouches of gold dust the miners throw up onto the stage, and I have lots of those gold eagles and some of that paper money. I even have some of the Confederate bills that are probably worthless now that they lost that terrible war in the South!"

"How do you trust that dilapidated little log building here they refer to as a bank with all that money, Anne? I would be scared to death to have it there. I wouldn't trust that little log building with anything."

"It's all in one of the trunks in my room."

"You have got to be kidding. I had no idea that you had that much money, and I had no idea that you would keep it in your room."

"Well, where else could I keep it? In your room?"

"Anne, what if the building burns down?"

"Well, I'll have a big hunk of gold and silver laying on the ground when they get the fire out. Where else can I put it, Elizabeth? It's a hundred and fifty miles by stage back to a Wells Fargo office in Lewiston and over two hundred miles south to the same in Fort Boise. Besides, no one has any idea that a lowly little singer and stage performer has anything more than the roof over her head." She laughed.

"You better hope that no one ever knows any different, Anne." And the matter was dropped.

William came to visit Elizabeth on a regular basis that first winter in Warren. She grew fond of these visits and enjoyed his company and he hers. The next spring when the snow melted, Anne and Elizabeth bought a small tract of vacant land across the street from the store against the mountainside and had a beautiful little three-bedroom cabin built.

The business owners in town had employed the miners who had not returned to work in the mines yet to install a water line along the toe of the slope to service the buildings on the north side of the street with running water. The water supply was from a small stream up a canyon with no residences, so the water was fresh and pure with no possible contaminants—much different from the stream that flowed through town. The Klein sisters' new home was the first private residence to have fresh running water.

It was July 1, 1867, when the cabin was finished, and the Pickels helped them move their slight belongings across the street to their new log cabin. They had asked William and his friend Harry Mason to help move the heavy trunks across the street. It took Mr. Pickel, William, Harry, and both Elizabeth and Anne to lift and move the trunk with Anne's fortune concealed inside.

"What was in that trunk to make it so heavy? Rocks?" William asked.

"Not just any old rocks," Anne spoofed demurely. "They were those pretty little white ones from crystal mountain next to Fredrick Burgdorf's hot springs."

"We could have unloaded part of them and made that a lot easier to move across the street," Harry Mason commented.

"Well, we didn't, and they are here." Anne beamed. "And I just love them. Now go and get a drink or something while Elizabeth and I tidy up here." She couldn't stop smiling as the men walked away, shaking their heads.

"That was a crazy-insane stunt, Anne." Elizabeth gasped. "They just moved a half million dollars across the street in front of a thousand miners and no one the wiser."

"Yes, it was a crazy stunt, but it worked. Now let's get on with it. You have your glass hummingbird hanging in the window, and I have my trunk full of money stashed away in my room."

Not only did the Pickels help them move, but they helped them furnish their home with items from storage behind the store as well. It was the most pleasant and well-appointed private residence in town, and they were very grateful for it. The girls each had their own bedroom, and the third was to be used for an occasional patient, should necessity dictate, or a guest room for Fredrick and Josh when they visited Warren. There would be a Fourth of July celebration in a few days, and they were busy arranging their new cabin with its not-so-sparce furnishings thanks to the Pickels. Fredrick and Josh had made the trip from the hot springs over Steamboat Summit and down to Warren about a month prior for their first visit since the road had closed the winter before with the heavy, deep snow. They were planning to return again for the Fourth of July celebration and stay with Elizabeth and Anne in their new cabin.

Everyone in town was excited about the event. The first traveling theater group of the season would be there, and Anne had been asked to perform. There were to be horse races, a prize fight between some of the miners, and even Governor Ballard and family were to be there from Boise. It would be an event like no other.

Anne noticed Elizabeth standing in front of the window with a far-away look on her face. "What's wrong?"

"I haven't told Fredrick about William. I know how Fredrick feels about Thomas. I didn't want to alarm him or give him any cause to dislike me—he has been a friend since we were children, Anne."

"Fredrick is a good and understanding man," Anne replied. "But, please, do tell him before he sees you with William. That will soften the blow. Everything will work out just fine—I'm quite sure of that."

"How can you be so sure, Anne?"

"Because I am, Elizabeth. I know it. Now stop worrying and enjoy the festivities."

Elizabeth was still uncomfortable with worry. She felt a terrible guilt but no shame for what may happen between her and William. Her heart had been awoken by his gentle touch like a fairy-tale princess from a deep sleep. How could that be wrong? She had spent so much time denying herself the possibility of being with another man that it had become a way of life. Now William was definitely a part of her life, and she was worried sick about Fredrick's possible negative reaction. He had been a lifelong friend of her and her family, and she could never bear losing that friendship.

It was late and after dark on July 3 when Fredrick and Josh arrived at the Klein sisters' new little log cabin in Warren. They stabled the horses across the street from Elizabeth and Anne's and then came knocking on their door. The girls had prepared a light meal of cheese, cold cuts, and small slices of bread that Anne had trimmed the crust from. Along with her considerable skills in the theater, Anne was an accomplished cook. She had baked the bread and made fresh mayonnaise. They had plenty of eggs from some of the Chinese miners for the mayonnaise as well as for breakfast the next morning. The girls and their guests from the hot springs sat up late talking of old times again and of Fredrick's and Josh's travels from Germany to the Wild West of America.

During a lull in the conversation, Elizabeth questioned Fredrick about the beastly Horst back in Darmstadt. Horst had caused the family much discontent even after Thomas had beat him soundly with the sword and later when Fredrick had beat him senseless with his bare fists.

"Well, I had taken Josh with me to Darmstadt to get some supplies for the vineyards when Horst just happened to be outside the warehouse with two of his thugs. I think he was planning to do harm to Thomas's mother and sister when they arrived again, but seeing us, Horst was acting very belligerent again with his two cronies by his side. He recognized Josh and made some terrible threats. Ultimately, Josh and I followed the three of them into the warehouse hoping to settle the matter for good. I had spotted a shovel standing by the door, so I grabbed it as we went in. As soon as we stepped through the door into the dark warehouse, one of his thugs dove at me. I swung that shovel like a baseball bat and cracked him alongside the head. I nearly removed it from his neck. Horst immediately knew he was once again in trouble over his head and started limping as fast as he could toward the back door to get away when Little Josh sprinted across the room and tackled him. By then I had rendered the other man senseless with a broken arm and, I'm sure, a fractured skull.

"There were several crates there in the warehouse about the size of coffins loaded with shovels, rakes, picks, steel bars, and other hand implements labeled for shipment to the goldfields of South Africa near Johannesburg. We discreetly removed the contents of one of those crates and stuffed all three bodies in one, nailed the lid down, and sat it on the loading dock to be delivered to the shipping docks over on the Rhine River. I'm not sure if they ever reached their destination or not, but Darmstadt was well rid of them. It was not long after that, I took Josh and—with Thomas's mother's permission—we departed from Germany for the great American West. The rest you know."

Anne and Elizabeth had sat spellbound listening to the story in more detail. They had read a shortened version of this very incident in one of the letters from home, but the letter had not gone into any great detail.

Elizabeth had moved over to sit next to Josh after the story had unfolded. "I am so sorry you had to encounter that, Josh. You must have been terrified."

"Not at all," he replied, smiling. "Horst had not only nearly starved me to death but also beaten me on many occasions when I was just a small boy working around the warehouse district. That was about the time Thomas rescued me and took me home to the vineyards to live with his family. As a matter of fact, I loved every minute of getting revenge, and Fredrick even let me nail the lid on that coffin, so to speak, before we moved it to the loading dock, Africa bound."

Fredrick shrugged. "I probably haven't been the best influence on the boy," he said. "But the family is safe in Europe without Horst, and Josh and I are safe and sound here."

The girls looked at each other in skepticism but questioned the incident no further. Knowing Fredrick's history, they were sure it had happened just the way he told it. Eventually, they all tired and went to bed.

Elizabeth had just pulled the covers up over her head when the rooster a few blocks back in the Chinatown area started sounding off. *I wonder if those hens would lay eggs without his influence*, she thought. *He would go well in a pot full of noodles.*

Chapter 93

Warren's Diggins,
Idaho Territory, United States

1867

The Fourth of July celebration was going strong when Elizabeth and Anne finally got sleepily out of bed. Anne quickly dressed and groomed her hair, with Elizabeth's help, then rushed off to the theater. The huge tent had been erected again just a few days earlier and was ready for the evening's performance.

Even though it was July, it was cold in the mornings and evenings at this elevation in the mountains. Elizabeth started a small fire just big enough to take the chill off the room and boil a pot of coffee. She was sitting enjoying the coffee and watching the festivities out the front window when she heard a knock on the door. It was William. She sat there only a moment in indecision, then got up to open it.

"Come in, William," she said. "We need to talk." Grabbing him by the arm, she nearly yanked him into the room, insisting he sit. She poured him a cup of coffee and sat down across the small table to stare at him.

"William," she began. "I have been waiting for the right moment to discuss this present state of affairs with you, and I am sorry I have waited this long. We have been seeing each other for nearly a year."

"That we have." He nodded, watching her carefully.

"Well," she went on, "I once was in love with the most wonderful, kind, and generous man the world has ever known." With that, she unfolded the story of her and Thomas's life in its entirety up to that very moment. Then finishing, she added, "And Fredrick does not know about my involvement with you, if you can call us really involved."

William sat a few minutes sipping his coffee, glancing now and again at Elizabeth but not saying a word.

"Well!!" She finally said. "Are you not going to even make one comment?"

"Sure," he finally replied. "Your story is hardly a secret. A lot of the Chinese miners here in Warren knew you shortly after your arrival in San Francisco years ago. They knew of your search for Thomas. They all held you in high esteem. You were always referred to as the beautiful and kind white lady who cared for all, including the Chinese populace, even in San Francisco. Your reputation has seemed to precede you everyplace you went, Elizabeth. I had heard of you and Anne long before I met you at the ferry crossing on the Salmon River at French Creek.

"I just happened to be there upon your arrival at the river and saw you standing on the other side with your hands on your hips just staring back at me. Our lives became entwined at that moment. I had a strong foreboding that something was going to happen to you. I waited around for your crossing. I wandered a short way down the river to that sandbar for no apparent reason at the time. Just nervous energy. I had even removed my boots and socks and was just waiting—for what, I did not know. When you were thrown into the river from the wagon that was loaded on the ferry, I was all ready to swim out and retrieve you. I dove in deep and the sight of you floating near the bottom of the river with your beautiful hair fanned out around your head and gently rising toward the surface and the perfect serene look on your face will remain with me for as long as I live. I'm not sure how long that time will be, Elizabeth, but I hope it will be with you.

"I know Fredrick and Josh also. I had talked with them on occasion when passing by Fredrick's hot springs going down to the ferry crossing for supplies. And then after your arrival here, we have had many occasions to talk. I also knew this conversation was inevitable but did not want to pressure you for explanations until you were ready. I felt this moment would come in full force when you were ready, such as it has.

Fredrick also knows about our involvement. And yes, we are involved. I have talked with him on more than one occasion about this, and we do have his approval. He still believes in his heart and soul that Thomas is still alive. His presence may, however, never be known.

"So now, my dear, where do we go from here?"

The last hour of gut-wrenching conversation had totally drained Elizabeth of all emotion. "Let's sleep on it for now," she replied. "We have a huge weekend in front of us, and I would like everyone to have a good time." Then she added, "William, would you accompany me and Fredrick and Josh to the theater for Anne's performance tonight?"

"I will." Standing, he promised to return later.

William slid into his coat with his hat in hand and walked to the door, then turned to look at Elizabeth one last time before letting himself out. He could see that this was not something she could think further of this day.

Fredrick and Josh soon returned from roaming the town and enjoying the festivities.

"We just saw Willian leave," Fredrick said. "You okay now?"

"I am." Elizabeth smiled. "Thank you, Fredrick. Thank you. William will be joining us for Anne's performance tonight if that is okay with you."

"It is, and I am happy for it."

The three wandered aimlessly through town. They arrived at the boxing ring just as the first fight was starting. After a few minutes into the second round, Elizabeth asked Fredrick if they could leave this event and go watch the horse races. "I'm just not sport for watching these men beat each other to a pulp today, especially knowing I may have to stitch them up later this evening."

The horse races were exciting with many of the beautiful creatures brought in from the meadows south of Warren about fifty miles, and another two splendid animals had been brought all the way from Fort Boise. They watched the children's events. The sack race was a hoot, with each child enclosed in a gunny sack hopping across the field, stumbling and falling only to stagger up and continue on to the finish line.

Next they went to a wood-chopping event that Josh had entered. Every contestant was given a log roughly the same size. It was a timed event, with each man chopping as fast as possible to sever the log. Elizabeth was concerned for Josh—this had the possibility of being a very dangerous event with everyone's axes swinging fast and furious. *I hope this event does not render my first amputee patient*, she thought shuddering. *Any one of those men could easily chop off a toe, or even a foot, for that matter.* Josh only placed third in the event but was extremely pleased with his performance, and Elizabeth and Fredrick were impressed as well. Upon the completion of this event they went back to the girls' cabin for a bite to eat and to clean up before going to the theater to watch Anne.

William joined them just as they were starting across the street to the theater. Anne had promised them reserved front row-seats for this show, and they made their way to the roped-off area. It was the largest crowd Elizabeth had ever seen. They sat in anticipation. Anne would be the first with a beautiful song in French. She and Elizabeth had mastered that language when they were only children.

When Anne had finished, there was not a dry eye in the crowd of mostly men. At nearly twenty-one years old, she was such a rare and natural talent, and especially rare to be performing here in a mining town high in the mountains of Idaho.

Chapter 94

Warren's Diggins,
Idaho Territory, United States

1867

Elizabeth had an incredibly loyal following of miners who had been sick or injured patients. At times one would require attention who had absolutely nothing wrong. They were just lonely, and each of them loved her and her company, even if for no more than an hour at a time. She always somehow made time for each and every one of them and would make an elaborate, complicated diagnosis of some farfetched condition that could easily be cured with a drink from one of the many saloons.

Early fall crept in with Elizabeth and Anne in their spectacular little log cabin and William paying them a visit daily. Anne was glowing. During the summer, she had the opportunity to perform with all the traveling groups that came to town, and they always drew a huge crowd. The beginning of winter would see the road closed with deep snow, and even Fredrick and Josh made less frequent visits to Warren. Anne was not looking forward to that, but she tried to find some good in knowing her audience in the lobby of the hotel would diminish to just the local populace, still being plentiful when she sang. She often helped the miners chop wood and shovel snow. She would get at least one proposal a day and took none more seriously than intended. It was a game they all played for the joy of it. Every miner knew she had no intention of marrying but enjoyed the lengthy negotiating process of promising a big house on the hill, a covered and heated carriage, a maid and butler, a chef—and the list went hopelessly on and on, with her and the proposer eventually having a lengthy and entertaining laugh. They all loved and protected the Klein sisters.

As much as Anne adored the crowds, she craved time alone in the wilderness too. One fall afternoon, she quietly saddled her horse and climbed into the mountains above Warren. The aspen leaves had turned a brilliant yellow that looked like pockets of sunshine. The tamarack needles were turning golden, just a few of them already brown. The huckleberry leaves shone like garnets. And the pines and firs remained steadfast green. Anne took a deep breath of the loamy air and told herself she loved it here, ignoring the restlessness that niggled deep inside. *I need something exciting to look forward to, that's all*, she thought. Then she grinned and turned her mare back toward town.

The sun was setting when she was riding back into Warren. As she stopped at the stable, a young man came out to tend to the horse, and she walked the two blocks and across the street to the house. William and Elizabeth were sitting on the front porch enjoying the setting sun and each other's company.

She put one foot up on the second step and rested her elbow across her knee to look at them without saying a word. Her sister stared back with the faintest smile. Elizabeth recognized the glint in Anne's eyes and her mischievous mannerism as something that had to be dealt with now.

"*When are you two going to get married?*" Anne emphasized each word.

Neither Elizabeth nor William replied nor seemed uncomfortable with her question. They just returned the gaze with a faint smile.

"*Well?*"

"Well," William finally responded, "October 29!"

It was Anne's turn to be stunned, and she was. Standing there for a few more moments, she gasped, "Of what year?" and they laughed. She jumped the other step onto the porch and was hugging her sister and William. "I am so happy for you."

Chapter 95

Warren's Diggins,
Idaho Territory, United States

1867

The wedding day was soon upon them. Elizabeth and William had planned this to be just a simple, small ceremony performed by the minister of the town's only church. There were to be the bride and groom, Anne as the bridesmaid, Harry Mason as the best man, and Fredrick C. Burgdorf and Josh as lifelong friends of the Klein family. William was a very respected man in the mining community and at best kept a very low profile. He had on every occasion kept to himself but was a well-liked man, and Anne and Elizabeth were well-known by all and loved by everyone. Fredrick and Josh were also well-respected as they built up the little hot springs resort less than a day's ride from Warren. However, the wedding was attended by nearly one thousand miners, some with families but most alone and happy for any occasion to celebrate. There were even a few families from the south fork over the mountain to the east that had traveled a whole day for the wedding as well as the ladies from the three brothels. Elizabeth had treated each of the ladies with discretion, and they would be forever grateful for her kindness.

Three pigs and a whole beef had been placed into a cooking pit next to the hotel dining room, and the chef had worked all night preparing the meal. The south fork group had brought two dozen fried-up chickens, and Fredrick had brought over a whole elk that he and Josh had stripped and smoked. The few other women in town had prepared hundreds of pounds of potatoes dug up from the warm ground around Fredrick Burgdorf's hot springs. No one would be lacking of food, and if any was left over it would go home with many of the lonely miners.

The day of this special occasion was a Tuesday. Elizabeth and William were to spend the rest of the week honeymooning at Burgdorf Hot Springs, returning Monday to move William into the cabin.

"Well," said Anne when they were making the plans, "at least he can help with the cooking."

They all laughed, but it was clear that there was a hint of heartache in the air as well. It was a new chapter, and Elizabeth tried to embrace whatever life would be like with this gentle miner she had grown to love.

Chapter 96

Hmoy,
China

1867

Thomas and Jason stayed hidden in alleys and on the outskirts of the small community until the ship sailed without them. So that was the way of it.

There was no love in Hmoy for the white man since the Opium Wars, and for months Thomas and Jason lived a hand-to-mouth existence before they were able to sign on with a four-master sailing southwest for Africa. It was the Russian ship *Orel*, clumsy on deck and dirty below, but it appeared to be a sleek, fast ship. In fact it had been the only ship to pass through in months. Thomas and Jason were in hopes of gaining passage on a more friendly vessel bound for the Americas, but that didn't happen. They were to learn this one's cargo hold was filled with spices, tea, and silk.

Sailing in a southerly direction, they passed through the Indonesian islands safely and without incident, then weeks south by west heading for the central region of the east African continent. The oceans smiled on them. Though it was late in the season, Thomas and Jason could not remember an easier voyage. The ship was a mess of clutter and thoroughly dirty from top to bottom, but they were free men. The captain had immediately recognized them both for seasoned sailors and had assigned Thomas as his navigation officer, and Jason was in command of all ship repairs. It was only a few weeks until he had the ship cleaned and in excellent repair. The *Orel*, meaning "Eagle," lived up to her name, flying before the wind as if the sea beneath her keel were thin air.

Day after day, they sailed on, and the sea was beginning to change its character. The water took on a vivid indigo hue that stained the sky the same color. The water was so clear that, leaning over the bow, Thomas could see pods of porpoises four fathoms down, racing ahead of the bow and frolicking like a pack of rowdy spaniels until they rounded up to the surface. As they broke through, he could see the blowholes on the top of their heads open to breathe, and they looked up at him with a merry eye and a knowing grin. The flying fish were their outriders, sailing ahead of them on flashing silver wings, and mountains of towering cumulus clouds were the beacons that signaled them ever onward.

Thomas was living in a dream world. It was pleasing times like this that he would let his mind return to his former life in Germany with Elizabeth. *It has been so long*, he thought. *Where would she be now?* He questioned if she even remembered him, hoping she did. And hoping beyond hope he may find out soon. *Is any of my family still alive?* And of course Fredrick C. Burgdorf. Fredrick was always first in his thoughts every time there was a battle to be fought. He had learned well from him. "Oh Elizabeth." He sighed. "I will see you again, if from only a distance, but I will see you again."

Thomas and Jason had found some tranquility and contentment in their life now. The years in captivity had hardened them both physically and mentally, but now free men and on a ship that may someday return them to America, they were settling into their peaceful life and would look toward the next day with anxious wonder.

Chapter 97

Warren's Diggins,
Idaho Territory, United States

1870

William would be gone for a few weeks, and Elizabeth was concerned for his safety. There was much talk of Indian uprisings down on the Salmon River. There had been no issues with Indians here in the Warren area because of the large population here. There were just too many people here for the Indians to bother with. But the Salmon River between John Day Creek and White Bird Creek had been one of their winter hunting grounds, and there seemed to be much friction now between the few miners in that area and the Nez Perce tribe. In spite of possible trouble with the Indians, William and Harry Mason planned on going over to the Salmon River country to look for another gold claim. Mason was also a partner with Henry Elfers in a small ranch on John Day Creek and wanted to check on that as well as on Elfers's well-being.

"We will be gone for no more than three weeks," William was explaining to Elizabeth prior to their departure. "Our route will take us back down to the French Creek ferry crossing on the Salmon River then up the mountain to Florence. From there, we will go west on a trail over the mountain, then down into John Day Creek, where we will stay at Mason and Elfers's ranch and explore the possibilities of another mining claim from there."

"Well, why do you want another mining claim anyway?" Elizabeth asked in frustration. "You have one here that is paying you very well. I see no reason for another. And you being gone three weeks into Indian territory, William?"

"We are sounding like an old married couple." He chuckled.

Elizabeth cocked her head to one side with a smile forming on her face.

Mason and William left Warren two days later traveling horseback and leading a pack mule each loaded with mining equipment and gear for a small camp. They planned to spend the first night out with Fredrick at the hot springs then one night on the trail before reaching the ferry crossing on the Salmon for the third night. The next night would find them at Florence then a long day's ride on to Mason and Elfers's ranch at the mouth of John Day Creek on the Salmon. Mason wanted to help his partner, Elfers, with some work around the ranch, and William would spend a few days up and down the river prospecting for another mining claim. Mason and Elfers's ranch was an impressive two-story house with many extra rooms for overnight guests who sometimes traveled the wagon road up and down the river from White Bird to the wild little town of Gouge Eye some twenty miles upriver.

"Spend a couple of nights here at the ranch, William. Sleep in a soft bed for a change. We've been on the trail for days, and we have plenty of room here. It would be good to review the Injun troubles a bit too before going anywhere," Mason said.

William woke early the next morning before any of the others, and strolling quietly out to the barn, he saddled up a horse and rode with much awareness upriver a few miles. He was concerned about the recent trouble with the Nez Perce and didn't want to lose any of his hair this late in his life. At Carver Creek he saw the first settlers, a couple Frenchmen working a claim there.

Seeing him ride up, one of them said, "Have a cup of coffee. You're up early this morning. It's barely daylight. Where did you come from?"

"Staying with Elfers and Mason at the ranch for a few days." Getting down and tying his horse loosely to the front-porch rail, William followed the settlers inside the spacious log house for that cup of coffee.

"I'm living up in Warren," he said. "We heard you were having some issues with the Indians."

"Not much," one of the Frenchmen replied. "We leave them alone, and they in turn mostly leave us alone."

"Mostly?" William inquired.

"Yeah, mostly. There have been a few instances where one of them has stolen a horse or a chicken or something, but most of them are friendly enough, just different."

"I will be doing some prospecting up and down the river. You think I'll have any trouble?"

"Not unless you see one of 'em." The Frenchman who had been doing all the talking shrugged. "And if you do, you better be carrying a gun. Some of 'em can steal a horse right out from under you without you knowing it."

William chuckled, thanked them for the coffee, and continued another mile up the river to the next creek looking for likely places gold may be found. Finding nothing obvious in this area, he returned downriver again, hollering out a greeting as he passed by the Frenchmen's claim.

William was back at the ranch on John Day Creek by noon and had lunch with Mr. Elfers and his wife as well as Mason and some hired hands.

"This is quite a setup you have here."

"It is," Mason acknowledged. "We have panned some color from the creek here too. Not enough to matter, though, and seems we are always too busy with other chores to give it much thought."

"Mind if I look around some, maybe do a little panning here and there?"

"Not at all. Go right ahead," Mason replied.

After lunch Willian thanked Mrs. Elfers for the previous night's stay and the meal then walked down a short way to the mouth of John Day Creek with pan in hand. He found what he considered a likely spot, a small outcropping of bedrock just above the water line. The rock was riddled with seams filled with sand. He scooped a fistful of the sand from one of the many cracks and placed it into the pan. His interest increased considerably as he noticed some color in the sand even before he dipped the pan into the water and started swirling it around. This motion would leave the heavier ore scattered on the outer edges of the pan.

This is unbelievable, he thought. The bottom of the pan was filled with small chunks of gold, each the size of a kernel of wheat. *Wheat gold*, he thought. Taking his kerchief from his pocket, he placed the gold on it, then set it aside and filled the pan up again from the same crack in the rock. He saw the same result, another layer of the wheat gold glistening in the bottom of the pan. He washed three more pans with the same outcome, placing the gold in his kerchief each time. Folding the kerchief carefully so as not to lose any pieces, he walked back up the creek to the house. Mason and Elfers were repairing the front-yard fence when William walked up with his gold pan in one hand and the folded kerchief in the other.

"Any luck?" Mason asked.

"See for yourself," William replied, unfolding the cloth with approximately two ounces of the wheat gold gleaming brightly in the sunlight.

Elfers and Mason stood staring. "Where did you find that?" Elfers stammered. "That's a couple months' wages."

"I panned from a crack in the bedrock at the mouth of the creek. Most likely just a deposit in those many cracks of that bedrock but I have a feeling it will add up to plenty. It has probably washed down from not too far away. See how rough each kernel is? Likely the main lode is not far from here. You guys have a small fortune on your hands right here."

"You found it," Mason alleged.

"But it is on your land," William insisted, "consequently your mine."

Mason and Elfers followed William back down the creek to where he had found the gold. They each brought a pan this time, and they all saw the same results. The cracks laden with the gold-bearing sand—at least, the ones that were exposed with no digging involved—were roughly three inches wide and ten to twelve feet long. Elfers and Mason had a very valuable gold deposit here, and they would search for the main lode another time.

William was up before daylight again the next morning riding down-river this time. Ever watchful, he had seen no sign of Indians. He had traveled only a mile when he noticed what may be a good spot to try his luck panning. Tying his horse loosely to the limb of a nearby bush, he was able to pan some color. It wasn't much, but with a lot of work, one could pan a living. Mounting again, he rode farther, trying again in a six different locations with no luck.

It was getting late, and he did not want to return upriver in the dark with the threat of Indians. *I'm going to try just one more gulch*, he thought. *Should only take a minute.* Hastily he slid out of the saddle to the ground, not bothering to tie the horse, just holding the reins loosely in his hand as he bent and pushed away some top soil and scooped a pan of sand and gravel. Walking a few steps to the river's edge, still leading the horse, he bent to his knees to fill the pan with water and swirl it around for just a moment. Letting the water slowly run from the pan, he stood up in amazement. This was nearly as rich as the area at the mouth of John Day Creek!

Grinning, he dumped the sand-laden gold again into a fold of his kerchief, mounted, and rode back up the river toward the ranch. *This is a claim worth filing on*, he reasoned. If the boomtown of Warren ever slowed down, as all boomtowns eventually did, he and Elizabeth would have a place to come to—out of the snow and into the Indians.

He started up the wagon road toward the ranch, deep in thought but still very cognizant of the possibility of unfriendly Indians. *I will be glad to return to Warren*, he was thinking. *It may be a long cold winter there, but one does not have to worry about keeping his hair.*

William reached the ranch just as the moon was coming up over the mountain.

"Glad you made it okay." Mason greeted him in front of the barn then helped him with the horse. "Did you have any luck today?"

"I did." William smiled and again opened the cloth, exposing the gold still mixed with some sand.

Mason gazed at the gold. "You are a lucky man, William." He sighed. "A very lucky man."

William stood gazing down the moonlit canyon. A chill had run up his back. Was this feeling a sign of something to come? Was he really a lucky man? He thought so. He had another very rich claim by all outward appearances just in case the one in Warren ever ran out, and he was happily married to Elizabeth, and for that he was eternally grateful, but there was something about this canyon that was foreboding to him. Shaking the feeling, he walked back to the house with Mason.

"I would like to leave first thing in the morning," he advised Mason and Elfers at dinner. "I am anxious to get back."

"But you were going to stay a few more days prospecting." Mason frowned. "I'm not ready to return yet."

"I know," William admitted, "but I feel as though I must return now. Please stay, Mason, as long as you feel necessary. I have been traveling these hills alone for years and am quite comfortable making the journey back to Warren alone."

"Well, I'm not quite comfortable making the journey back to Warren alone with the Indian trouble and all. I'll be ready to leave with you in the morning at first light."

Five days later they were back in Warren, and William was sitting at the table with Elizabeth having a late dinner and relating the trip's events in detail to her. Anne had been wandering in and out of the cabin and had heard the part about Mason's ranch on the river and the discovery of gold there.

"I may just marry that man," she announced then flounced out on another errand.

Elizabeth stood shaking her long blond hair from the bun on the back of her head. "She can be so annoying at times, William."

"She can," he admitted, "but she is such a likable little creature."

"Well, don't be liking that little creature too much."

William only laughed at this. "I was just repeating the feelings of most of the miners in Warren." He grinned.

When he displays one of those rare grins, he radiates tremendous warmth, Elizabeth thought. *He just never seems to display them often enough.*

Later, after hours of conversation together, Elizabeth bid him a good evening then went to bed. William remained by the small fire. Even though it was only late August, it was cold. Shivering, he held his hands to the fire burning brightly.

It was late—he and Elizabeth had talked for hours. He'd had so much to tell her about the time he had spent on the trail with Mason in the Salmon River country. *And she is such an attentive listener,* he thought. Then he shook his head in irritation. *And I didn't even ask her how her day was today let alone what she did while I was away. Probably thinks I'm an inconsiderate fool,* he assumed as he rose and tiptoed to the bedroom. *I'll work on that.* Then undressing, he rolled into bed beside her.

As tired as he was, sleep would not come for hours. He lay there in the warming cabin thinking of his role in Elizabeth's life. *Never had much to do with women before her,* he thought. *Still don't know much about them. I'll have to keep working on that.* Then the mine. Most of the mines in and around Warren used a dredging operation. His mine was actually on the mountain across the canyon from Warren, a vein of high grade. At first it had been a shallow trench, and he was able to follow it, digging only a few feet deep, but the further he went, the richer it got and the deeper into the hillside it went. He'd had to sink a shaft, hiring Chinese laborers to cut timbers from the mountain side above the mine for shoring up the walls and ceiling, then more laborers to tunnel and remove the tailings on hand-drawn carts. He now had eight Chinamen working and would have more if more were available.

His mine was doing well, but some of the dredging operations were reporting diminishing returns. There was only so much area in the canyon bottom for the dredges to operate. In another year or two, they most likely would be out of room and out of business, and Warren would go the way of most other boomtowns. In a few years it would be a run-down ghost town with only a few rugged hanger-ons but most likely none at all. *It's a shame,* he thought. *This has the makings of a beautiful little town. It has a church and a school with more families that have moved in recently.* Florence had had several thousand people until recently and now was nearly empty with the residents moving on, some here to Warren and others on to the fabulously rich Boise Basin. The vacant buildings had collapsed under the unshoveled snow loads, and then the surrounding forest and other vegetation started reclaiming their territory. Soon nothing would be left but the scars of the dredging operations, and those, too, in time would ultimately vanish.

William was only somewhat confident as to the longevity of his mine. It still showed much promise, but he knew the rich vein he was now following would eventually run out. He had made a modest fortune and, unlike Anne, who had a trunkful of money under her bed, he had periodically taken the gold back to the Wells Fargo office in Lewiston for deposit. He had always kept a low profile here in Warren, and no one ever noticed his coming or going, hence his trips out with two or three mules loaded with gold went unnoticed. He would load each of the mules light, riding thirty hours straight to make the ferry crossing at French Creek without a stop. Resting there for a day in safety, he would change out his horse and mules, then ride another thirty hours or more, bypassing Florence, until making Mount Idaho, then another nonstop on to Lewiston. William had done this on several occasions over the last four years and no one the wiser. His return trip would be with supplies, and anyone taking notice only thought the trips were for those supplies.

Chapter 98

Warren's Diggins,
Idaho Territory, United States

1871

Spring came again as it always did high in these spectacular wild and rugged mountains: the wildflowers in abundance, the dogwood blooming in radiance, the delicate little yellow flowers called buttercups along the streambeds, and the beginning of the fireweed and Indian paintbrush that followed the melting snow slowly up the mountain sides. These implausible acts of nature with their repetitive occurrence from one year to the next had even failed to stimulate Anne's enthusiasm this spring.

On one bright sunshiny spring morning, she saddled her horse in the stable and rode a short distance out of Warren overlooking a mile-deep canyon with a tributary of the Salmon River rumbling down the bottom of that unfathomable gorge. Sliding from the horse, she stood by a burned, gnarled, ancient tree once struck by lightning. Standing there mesmerized by this spectacular view, she closed her eyes and enjoyed the faint breeze blowing through her hair and the sun warming her face. She was in need of something far greater than her existence here in this lonely mountaintop community called Warren. Something that could be impossible to fulfill here. Standing here alone in this vast untamed wilderness, looking across one majestic mountain range then on to another and another, she finally admitted to what she had felt deep inside for years.

I want to go home to Germany, she thought. *I am twenty-five years old. I miss the beautiful, centuries-old but well-maintained edifices in Darmstadt, the real theaters with huge stages overlooked by balconies. I miss the Perfumeries Douglas that Elizabeth once worked in with all of its latest fashions. I really want to see my father and older sister, Mary, again and Thomas's little sister, who will be a full-grown woman, and Thomas's mother, now my stepmother. I want to experience the old civilizations again and people, both men and women. I have seen only a few women in years, and they being the rough-and-tough frontier women, something I'm not and never will be. I have tried, but I don't want to do it anymore. We came here on a fool's errand searching for news of Thomas, and there is none. It has been years. Even Elizabeth has given up hope.* She blinked her eyes again to the splendor unfolding before her and wept. It had been forever since she had indulged in such a feminine act, and she wept until she could no more.

That night at dinner with her sister and William, Anne was somber. Choosing to leave was one thing, but actually leaving Elizabeth was another. Still, she knew she could not be happy here any longer.

In an effort to lighten the mood, she asked William, "So, do you have any rich miners for me to marry yet?"

"Actually, I do." William turned to her with a grin.

Anne's eyes grew wide—that was not the answer she was expecting. Elizabeth and William burst out laughing, Anne soon to follow, laughing so hard, tears welled in her eyes. "Good one." She dabbed her eyes with a kerchief, still chuckling.

Then more seriously, she added, "And it will make what I have to tell you much easier." Looking from her sister to William and back again, Anne finally said, "I have made up my mind to return to Darmstadt."

Elizabeth and William gazed at her with knowing eyes. "We felt this coming," Elizabeth acknowledged. "We will miss you immensely, Anne."

The three spent the first weekend of June 1871 at Burgdorf Hot Springs celebrating Fredrick's first year of smashing success with the resort officially up and running, soaking their worries away in the hot water, and enjoying each other's company as much as was humanly possible in the short time before Anne would be gone. On Monday, they would return to Warren to help Anne in her final preparation for the nearly yearlong journey she faced going back to Darmstadt in Germany.

A week later, Anne had completed her packing and had said her farewells to her multitudes of friends and was ready for William and Elizabeth to take her over the summit to the hot springs on the following morning. They would all spend the night there, and then Josh would accompany her to San Francisco, seeing her safely onto a ship bound for Germany. The biggest hurdle would be the trunk with Anne's fortune. Part of it was gold, part silver, and part currency of various denominations. It weighed nearly five hundred pounds—the weight was not so much the problem, but no one these days dared carry even a small poke of gold through the mountains, let alone nearly half a million dollars.

"Who is to know?" Anne said. "It has been perfectly safe for several years here under my bed. Why would that change now?"

"Things are different now, Anne. There are reported holdups all along the trails from here to the meadows the other side of the Payette Lakes, and there was even another robbery and killing over in the Florence area."

"That's not new," she retorted. "They have been robbing and killing people over there since that boomtown was started. Besides, I heard it was nearly a ghost town now with the mines played out and most of the miners coming here and on into Boise Basin."

"Nevertheless," William continued, "I have made arrangements for some of my most trusted mining friends to accompany you and Josh with another empty wagon all the way out through Mount Idaho and down to Lewiston, where you will be able to deposit your money safely in the Wells Fargo office. In this manner you will have a very capable entourage for protection, who will in turn bring back a badly needed load of supplies from Lewiston for my mine here. Josh will accompany you on to Hayes Valley and San Francisco. He hasn't been away from here since he and Fredrick settled here and wants to get out for a while too."

The two wagons left Warren that morning and were over the summit and down to the hot springs before dark. The group spent the night there. Elizabeth and William stayed in the honeymoon cabin they had stayed in the week before. Anne had her own little cabin, and the others stayed in other cabins Fredrick and Josh had recently built.

Anne woke early, dressed, and walked outside alone to enjoy the incredible setting of Fredrick's resort one last time. There were elk sounding off on the far side of the meadow, and she could hear the lonely cries of the loon too. Then she took a few moments to contemplate the trip ahead of her. *I know I am making the right decision*, she thought. *I just do not want to be here any longer, and Elizabeth will be fine with William. I will miss her immensely, and every one of my other friends too*, she thought.

The others were now coming out of the cabins and helping with the teams and two wagons, making final preparations for the long journey to Lewiston. Fredrick's cook had prepared breakfast for everyone and had packed a lunch for each. Josh had indicated they may try to travel all night, possibly reaching the Salmon River ferry crossing late tomorrow night and eliminating the necessity of camping alongside the trail. The other wagon master had agreed to this plan, and William's other guards traveling with the wagon were in agreement. If they were to travel thirty hours straight, it should be done this first day while everyone was still fresh.

Anne and Elizabeth had been preparing for this final goodbye for days so made no big deal of it now. After hugging Elizabeth then William and Fredrick in turn, Anne merely climbed into the wagon with Josh in the driver's seat, and they were off. Anne sat stiff-backed, not turning her head one way or the other, with tears rolling down her cheeks. Then at the last minute while the wagon was still in hearing distance, she heard Elizabeth shout, "Anne, I'll see you again one day." At these words, Anne stood up from her seat, turned, and waved frantically until she was out of sight around the first bend in the wagon road.

"Do you really think we will see her again?" Fredrick asked hopefully.

"I don't know about *we*, Fredrick," Elizabeth said with a chill running down her back, "but I do know I will see her again."

Fredrick and William pondered the remark but dared not question it.

Chapter 99

Indian Ocean

1871

The weather was changing for the worse, and the seas were getting rougher. The captain came to Thomas. "I fear we are in for a real blow tonight. Would you and Jason retire early? I will have the night watch warn us all should your presence on deck be required." It was only a suggestion, not a command. "I have seen these waters in this part of the world many times before, and they can present quite a challenge. I would like you both fresh for what I'm afraid will be a dreadfully wild day."

Conversing did not present much difficulty, the Russian captain could speak heavily accented English, and they were learning to speak Russian from him. They lingered with the captain for a while longer, and then, wishing him well, they retired to their quarters below deck. The weather was becoming severe—the wind was nearly gale-force—and Thomas and Jason were having a difficult time lying in their bunks as the ship pitched and groaned, sliding up one side of a giant wave then crashing down the other.

Finally Thomas gave up the pursuit of rest and swung his legs over the side of the bunk to stand and get dressed. Jason appeared to be in a fitful sleep as Thomas passed him on his way to the stairs up to the deck. He had just reached the last step before the deck when he felt a tremendous crash. They had hit something in the storm, and the ship had careened over to its side with water flooding the deck. Thomas hung on the doorframe watching in horror as he saw the captain and every man on deck get washed away by a giant wave. The ship did not right itself, and the masts were stretching out parallel to the water with each huge, smashing wave ripping them to shreds.

At that terrible moment, Thomas was startled by a loud metallic rumble below deck followed by a muffled crash of the mighty impact of the shifting cargo, torn away from its fastenings by the unusually heavy careening of the ship and its new attitude of lying on its side. The cargo had ruptured the bulkheads, and the seas had burst over her inclined deck. Thomas could see that the ship was rapidly foundering, and it appeared all was lost.

Chapter 100

Salmon River Country,
Idaho Territory, United States

1871

The road was mostly downhill all the way to the river crossing. Anne, Josh, and their entourage traveled all day, and at dark they stopped at Fall Creek for a hasty meal then continued on all night to reach the river late afternoon the following day. Finally, they would spend the night there. Most of the Florence mines had played out more than a year ago, and the miners had moved on to other boomtowns that had sprung up all over the west, thusly eliminating most of the traffic now on the narrow and often dangerous trail.

William and Elizabeth had brought saddle horses tied to the back of the wagon to the hot springs so they could ride with Anne in the wagon for that part. After they'd waved Anne off, the couple rode the horses back to Warren. Anticipating this ride, Elizabeth had donned a pair of men's britches. She rode a saddle like a man, refusing to ride side saddle. She and William rode side-by-side where the road would allow, talking continuously, and stopped at a small spring on the summit for a leisurely lunch. They were in a melancholy mood and in no hurry to get home.

On arriving back in Warren and passing their home, Elizabeth jumped off while William took the horses to the stable. Walking through the door, she stopped in the silence of the room. Something was missing. Without question, it was Anne. The house no longer had that bright, warm, cheery feeling that it once had. *I will light the lamp and start a fire in the stove—that will warm things up a bit*, she thought.

It didn't. It was still like being in a new and different place, foreign with no warm and cozy feeling! Like a new place moved into before you made it a home with your own personal touches. Would it ever be the same here without her?

William walked in after he had tended to the horses. They sat together with cups of coffee by the stove in silence, both trying to ease the tension but not knowing what to do or say. It was a tremendous adjustment for Elizabeth—Anne was gone for good.

Anne and Josh, with their entourage, spent a comfortable night in the inn at the ferry crossing on the river, sleeping in until after daylight the next morning. Willy would not be able to take them across the river for another two hours. They all had a leisurely breakfast waiting for Willy to make ready for the first wagon to cross. This crossing would require three trips—one wagon and team on each of the first two trips, then the last trip with the extra horses William had sent along in case of trouble. Josh was worried and fidgety while they waited.

"What is the matter with you, Josh?" Anne inquired. "I have never seen you like this before."

"I have never crossed a river like this on a rickety old ferry with a lady and a half million dollars before," he answered.

She laughed. "Relax, Josh. Everything will be okay."

And it was. The crossing went well with no mishaps, and they were soon all on the north side starting the lengthy pull up the mountain to Florence. Reaching the nearly abandoned town just before dark, they were not prepared for what they saw. On the trip through this town a few years ago on their way to Warren, they'd had a hard time finding a room to stay in. Now nearly every building was vacant, some falling in from the snow. They picked what appeared to be the most sound building and all just camped out with their bedrolls. There were a few miners left—some with families, some without. They were friendly enough but seemed somewhat intimidated by this heavily armed group. Anne, like her sister, had forgone the dress she usually wore for riding britches and also wore a belt gun strapped to her waist. It was not an uncomfortable night, but everyone was on edge, sleeping little and wanting to leave as soon as possible.

The next morning Josh was the first to get up and start saddling and harnessing the horses, with Anne right behind him, fixing breakfast for all. The road was now in far better condition than it had been a few years ago, and they were at Mount Idaho two days later with only having to spend one night on the trail. They rested there for two days then continued on to Lewiston, getting Anne's trunkful of money in deposit with the Wells Fargo, and were on the steamship heading down the Snake River the morning after that. Anne and Josh had bid William's crew goodbye, and that group was now en route back to Warren with a wagon load of badly needed supplies.

Going downriver was much faster than Anne and Elizabeth's trip had been a few years earlier coming up. A new railroad had been completed from just above Celilo Falls all the way downriver to a small port below Bonneville, requiring only one portage before catching a steam paddler that would take them all the way to Portland. The few days spent on the paddle wheeler were the most luxurious accommodations Josh had ever witnessed—he had no idea that such a lifestyle existed.

Anne bought Josh several suits of new clothes and a top hat from the ship's store. "If you're going to accompany me all the way to San Francisco, you need to look like a gentleman," she said laughing. And he did look and act the perfect gentleman.

Anne missed Elizabeth and William and Fredrick terribly but was becoming accustomed to life without them. She was also having an enjoyable time with Josh. He was so curious about everything. They both remembered that the Rhine River in Germany was every bit as large as the Columbia but totally different. The towering mountains that descended to the river's edge in the gorge with all the waterfalls and the incredible Mount Hood visible in the background were all spellbinding to him. His marvelous private stateroom continued to hold him in awe.

"I will have a most difficult time adjusting back to my humble lifestyle at Fredrick's hot springs," he told Anne one evening while they were dining in the fabulously appointed top-deck dining room filled with linen-covered tables and finely polished silverware.

"Oh, Josh, it was such a wonderful and beautiful life there. Everything is so new and rough with few regulations and rules, at least enforceable ones. It is a lifestyle like no other. Elizabeth and I have been very lucky there in those Idaho mountains. Sister Mary and her husband, Edward, had accumulated a tremendous fortune working the goldfields in California and left Elizabeth and me well off before they returned to Germany. We have never had to worry about making money being women in a rough-and-tumble man's world. But in spite of that we both have managed to accumulate more wealth without dipping into that assistance, at least in these later years. We have been truly blessed. And now I am going home, Josh."

They would have these conversations daily on the steamboat down the river, and soon they were docking in Portland, where they would be for three days staying in the nicest hotel until they could get passage on a larger ship going on to San Francisco. Anne was to spend this time showing Josh around Portland. When she and Elizabeth had been there a few years ago, it was barely a town, and now it was a thriving beautiful city with some brick-paved streets and real sidewalks and glass-fronted stores and fancy restaurants—the list went on and on. Josh had spent much time in Darmstadt, so being in a city was not new to him, but he loved the posh accommodations Anne had introduced him to.

They sat and talked at a quaint little coffee shop on the street near the hotel, and Anne told him about their stay in Panama with the Tribaldos family and their coffee plantations, and then about the rest of the trip on the sailing vessel to San Francisco and of their home in Hayes Valley there, and on and on.

At a break in the conversation, Josh asked, "Can we go to the theater here, Anne?"

"We can, and we will."

"I will see to tickets for this evening's performance. Will you perform?"

"I would if asked, but things have changed since I have been on a real stage. Things are different here, much more refined. There are rehearsals and wardrobes and managers and such, but I do plan on getting back into the business once back in Germany."

They sat and enjoyed every moment, Anne thinking she would never see him or Elizabeth or any of her friends in this country ever again. She knew she would miss this great free-spirited America. She was going home, though, home to the old country, the old ways.

Chapter 101

Indian Ocean

1871

Thomas was hurled across the sloping deck and was slowly making his way back to the hatch he had just exited. He crouched by the hatch and peered down. The ladder had torn away. Below, he saw deep water sluicing around the hold. It chilled his heart. Could anyone have survived down there? He doubted it. All he saw was black water.

"Jason!" he screamed.

No answer.

The ship lurched further over as more of her hull gave way. He knew he had little time before the ship would come completely apart. He braced himself against the opening and lowered himself through, into the water below. In the heeling ship, water filled the lower side to the ceiling, but there was still air on the upward side. Thomas crawled along, clinging to the ship's ribs and keeping his head just above water. *If it comes apart or she rolls, I'll be trapped,* Thomas thought, forcing himself not to panic. He put out his hand to steady himself and felt—flesh. Cold and wet, but unmistakably human flesh.

In the darkness, he could not even tell if it was Jason. He pulled the body toward him, feeling all around until he found the head. Putting his finger to the neck, he sensed a feeble pulse. The ship lurched again, settling deeper into the water. The last pockets of air disappeared. Thomas had just enough time to take a last breath before he was submerged. *Get to the hatch*, he told himself.

The water pushed him against the low ceiling. Holding the body under his arm, he dived, forcing his eyes open against the stinging saltwater to find his way to the hatch. He saw the dim light of the opening and kicked desperately for it. Flotsam banged into him. He almost caught his eye on an iron hook suspended from a beam. But he was there, and now, finally, the ocean helped him. The rising water lifted him through the hatch, over the broken ladder, and out onto the canted deck.

At least now he could see who he had rescued. It was Jason, though that would matter little if they did not make good their escape from this sinking ship. Thomas knew they had but seconds. The ship was going under. "We must get off this ship!" Thomas shouted at Jason's motionless form. But the water around the hull was thick with wreckage. If he tried to swim them both through it, they would most likely be dashed to pieces. But the mainmast had made a bridge across the debris, its rigging like roots tethering it in place. Jason stirred as he clung to Thomas desperately and opened his eyes. Thomas had slung him over his shoulder and now quickly set him down, thumping him on the back. Great streams of seawater spurted out of Jason's mouth.

"Can you move?"

Jason nodded. "I think so."

"Then let's get off this ship." Thomas heaved Jason onto the mast.

Without having to be told, Jason started crawling out along it, across the churning water. Thomas followed him. It was like riding a wild horse, an unbroken and unsaddled one. The mast was in constant motion, twisting and writhing with every wave that struck the ship. Thomas wrapped his arms and legs around the trunk, inching forward. Sometimes he crawled on top; other times he clung on upside down like a monkey dangling from a branch. Waves broke below him. Ahead he saw a huge bulk of canvas sail. He crouched against its side with Jason, cupped in its folds and protected a little from the storm, but they could not stay there. The wrecked ship was still shifting in the headwinds of the storm. At any moment the mast might roll over and trap them underwater. They were free of the worst of the debris, but any one of the waves was enough to dash them to pieces. Thomas looked out into the storm but could see nothing encouraging.

"Can you swim?" Thomas shouted at Jason.

He shook his head. Thomas did not hesitate. Grabbing his friend by the shirt, Thomas jumped into the raging sea only a few feet below. He used all his strength to stay afloat in the surging sea. Thomas had hooked his arm under Jason's shoulders to keep his head above water, letting the current take them, pulling them away from the broken ship until the wreckage thinned out. Then he started to swim with Jason in a semiconscious state.

After all Thomas had suffered, he barely noticed the waves. He didn't fight them. Instead as they curled over his head, he let them push him under, then kicked back to the surface to draw a breath when they released him. This had become totally exhausting, and he was near the brink of giving in to the thunderous sea when he felt his head strike something solid. When he looked, it was a broken fifty-foot section of the main mast with a huge swath of the canvas sail still entangled. Frantically grabbing for this flotsam, he managed to get a firm grip still hanging on to Jason. The portion of the sail still attached to the mast was balled up in a huge bundle with a portion sticking up out of the water. Thomas managed to climb up onto the pitching mass and drag Jason up, who had slipped into an unconscious state again. Securing him to the bulk sticking out of the water so his head would not slip back under, Thomas made an attempt to stand and survey their condition. They were free of the sinking ship. Neither it nor any more of its shattered debris were visible in the approaching dawn. They were alone and adrift, and there appeared to be no other survivors.

Chapter 102

Warren's Diggins,
Idaho Territory, United States

1871

William, sensing the tension at home, rose from his warm spot by the stove, coffee cup in hand. "I think I'll take a walk and check on things around town," he told Elizabeth.

She only nodded in agreement, and he set down his coffee cup, walked to the door, slipped into his coat and hat, and stepped out. Lingering a few minutes on the front porch, he thought about Elizabeth's reserved behavior. No doubt it was in part from missing her sister, but William could sense it was more than that. *I wonder if she will ever be at peace with Thomas*, he thought. *He must have been one dynamic man to have this kind of lingering impact on her life.* With that thought, he stepped off the porch and wandered aimlessly down the street. The town was unusually quiet. Anne had left for good, and there was a subtle change that seemed to have taken place and was reflected in the cool night air.

The next several days, William worked daylight till after dark at the mine, which was nothing new for him. The mine was easy walking distance from his and Elizabeth's home, and the mine portal was visible from their porch. Several times a day, he would step out and cast an eye in the direction of their cabin, hoping to catch sight of Elizabeth. On one of these days, he saw her walking across the street in the direction of the mine carrying a basket. He stood watching as she made her way up the trail cut into the hillside then onto the flattened tailing pile at the mine entrance.

"Brought you lunch," she said smiling.

"Hoped you would. Haven't eaten in three days." He chuckled, sitting down beside her on a blanket in the shade.

"Sorry for the cold shoulder," she said.

"Well, a cold shoulder is better than no shoulder." He grinned.

"It's very hard now, William. Anne leaving forever has finally hit home, and it will take a while to become accustomed to that change."

"It will," he agreed. "I've even noticed a change in the attitude of the miners hanging around town. She was a very popular fixture here." He knew that Anne had such a unique performing style and a voice that made every man in town's blood run cold with anticipation when she sang. She had nothing to do with any of them on a personal level, but she made each and every one of them feel special.

"Please leave the mine early, William. I would like your influence around the house for a while this afternoon." She smiled. Finishing their lunch, they made their way back down the mountainside then crossed the small meadow with Mayflower Creek running along its edge. She slipped her arm through his, and they walked blissfully back to their cabin.

Stepping through the door, the first thing that came to William's attention was the lack of pastel light flashing from the glass humming-bird that had been hanging in the window catching the sun's rays.

"He needed a rest, and so did I," Elizabeth commented. "I put him away."

Chapter 103

Indian Ocean

1871

All day long the two men drifted helplessly without sight or sign of a passing sail. The storm had subsided, leaving only the giant swells. Jason had drifted in and out of consciousness for hours but seemed to be improving steadily. They were both perched as high on the mass of floating mast and bunched-up sail as possible. A sudden swell would raise them up high, where they could get a good view of the vast unforgiving sea in all directions. Then they would rapidly slide into a trough with nothing but great walls of water on all sides.

As the day wore on, spasms of hunger and thirst began to assert themselves. The men had eaten nothing for nearly twenty-four hours. At length, darkness closed in over the troubled and merciless waters. During the night, Jason's condition improved considerably even though he and Thomas were even more thirsty and hungry. They both held on for their lives, one sleeping a short time while the other kept watch for any sign of light from a passing ship.

After a seemingly endless period of darkness, the gray morning broke again, and a blood-red sun arose slowly from the horizon and glowed feebly through a murky mist bank in the east. Thomas tried to stand in the soggy mess they were floating in to look in every direction for a hoped-for sail. But to the north and south and west, nothing was in sight except tumbling sea, depressing cloudy sky, and an occasional seafowl, the last of which was somewhat encouraging as it may indicate land not too far off.

But when Thomas again cast an eye eastward, he noticed a dark, jagged, irregular object strongly silhouetted against the sun, which was slowly rising from the water's edge. He gazed long and intently at the darkish looming object. *What could that be?* he thought then roused Jason, who had once again drifted into a coma-like, exhausted sleep. Staggering to his feet and wiping the salt-crusted hair from his face, Jason too gazed at the distant shape appearing on the far horizon. *Could this be a physical object, or was it a mere figment of an agitated imagination?*

"It has to be real," Jason mumbled to Thomas.

As the sun rose slowly and silently above the sullen sea, the dark object still remained outlined against the horizon.

"Yes," he muttered again through cracked lips. "No doubt about it. It is land. Unfruitful and unfriendly, perhaps, but land."

"If we can only reach it, we might yet be saved," Thomas added.

Once convinced that what they saw before their eyes was a physical object, they both gave way to their excitement in loud shouts and feeble laughter. "Land! Land! Land!" Their sudden yells startled the seabirds feeding among the waves. Jason had grabbed Thomas's arm, again pointing out the dark object far ahead on the horizon.

"Thomas, it's an island of some kind. There must be lots of them in this area, but how are we to get to that one? How do we know we are not drifting away from it?"

"Well," Thomas said, "I know we are drifting toward it. It wasn't there last night, and it was there this morning. Besides it's a good deal higher now than when we first sighted it. The wind here is steadily from the west, and I believe the current flows the same way to the east."

Jason tried hard to be convinced by the soundness of Thomas's reasoning, though God knows that except for the direction of the wind, there was but little substance for his trust.

"We will drift there by noon," Thomas said. "Let's watch how fast we gain." Thomas wanted to encourage his comrade and keep from being discouraged himself. So in spite of inward reservations, he sought to maintain an outward show of confident optimism. "We will drift there by noon," he told Jason again. "Now let's watch how fast we gain."

Thomas had of course heard of the great conflicting currents in the seas of this latitude but knew little of either their general trend, rate of motion, or extent. He could only trust to guesswork at best, and to luck. All they could do was watch that island and estimate the speed and course of drift. The wind was in their favor, and with the help of the sea, it could be depended upon to move them steadily onward. To their infinite joy, the island grew steadily larger and its rugged features grew constantly more distinct and clearly defined. Thomas reasoned they were drifting at a rate of about three knots per hour. *We should*, he thought, *pass the rock in about three or four hours. But how near?* That was troubling him now. Would they pass close enough to make a landing by swimming?

Then a horrible thought flashed across his mind. *Could either of us swim any distance in our weakened condition due to three days with no food or water?* They gradually approached closer to the island and could see that they were drifting in a roundabout way southward.

Thomas's mind was racing. "Jason, we may float past that island not close enough to even make an attempt at swimming."

Jason sat a moment surveying their precarious situation. "We are both weak," he squeaked through parched throat and salt-crusted lips. "But let's try hanging on to the tip of this floating mess of tangled canvas and mast and see if we can swim and pull it across the current so it may get us closer to the island."

They slipped out to the end of the mast, grasped a loose hanging rope, and began swimming as strongly as possible across the slow-moving current. Soon they felt their temporary shelter on the flotsam slowly coming along with them. Thomas would swim out in front of the mess pulling while Jason had moved back to the opposite end hanging on and kicking his legs, helping to propel them forward. When Thomas would get too tired to swim, they would swap places, and thus they continued hour after hour, slowly cutting diagonally across the unseen current in a direction that would very possibly put them ashore—or at least close enough for a short swim to the solid surface of the small island.

"We are getting very close," Thomas shouted. With the final energy of fatigued men, Jason kicking furiously and Thomas swimming and pulling with all his might, they brushed into the rocks on the edge of the island. They were both so weak from days of exhaustion, no food and little water except what they had been able to accumulate from an occasional rainstorm while floating in the slow-moving sea current, they were barely able to secure their makeshift raft to a nearby rock outcropping before both collapsed on the small area of sand and fell into a deep fatigued sleep.

Chapter 104

Pacific Ocean,
Off the Coast of America

1871

Anne and Josh's few days in Portland had passed quickly, and presently they were San Francisco bound. Again Anne had spared not a penny on lavish quarters and meals on this ocean-going ship. She pointed out many of the interesting sights going down the coast to Josh before going through the amazing Golden Gate into the San Francisco Bay. They would spend another night here onboard the ship waiting for a berth on the dock.

It was nearly noon the next day before they secured to the dock and the gangplank was dropped. Anne and Josh were two of the first to disembark and were standing off to one side of the dock waiting for Anne's trunks to offload.

"You two look as if you could use some help," a familiar voice said from behind them.

Josh jumped, crouching for action, and Anne turned.

"It can't be!" she exclaimed. "How on earth did you know we would be here, Timothy?" she shrieked as she ran and jumped into his arms.

When she had calmed a bit, he replied, "You spent three nights in Portland spending money like it was going out of style and living the life. I do have informers there too, you know. That's how I make a living, preying on unsuspecting and unprotected souls like you." He laughed.

"Hardly unprotected," Josh added in a sulk.

"Allow me to introduce myself," Anne's California friend said, holding out his hand. "I am Timothy, and who might you be?"

"I'm Josh," he stammered looking around at his totally unfamiliar surroundings and wondering what was to happen next.

"I have advised Lolivey of your return, and she is expecting you," Timothy announced. "She had planned on being here to greet you but needed to stay home to make ready for your arrival, and she hates to leave Hayes Valley. I was not able to tell her about your expected presence here until last night, and I'm quite sure she slept not a wink all night. She and her father are so thrilled to see you. He was in such a sorry state of mind when you and Elizabeth left for that Idaho country, he doesn't even remember you."

"Please tell me, Timothy, has there been any news of Thomas?"

"Nothing credible. As before, a drink at the pub will loosen a sailor's tongue, but as soon as the ale stops, so does the sketchy information."

"Elizabeth is married now, Timothy."

He stood in shocked silence. "Anne, I think Thomas is alive. I can't be sure, but I have heard of an incident in Hmoy, China, where a shanghaied sailor matching the description of Thomas and bearing that name was set ashore with a few of his shipmates for possible mutiny. That ship eventually arrived back here in San Francisco loaded with silk, spices, and other exotic goods. The story was told of a terrible fight on board led by a big black-haired moose with sparkling green eyes. When the battle was over, him and his friends were put ashore unharmed, not executed as usual, I was told, just stranded in some small island port."

Anne nearly collapsed. *It could only have been him*, she thought.

"Come," Timothy advised quickly. "We are starting to draw attention standing here jawing on the dock. I have a carriage waiting over there." He pointed over his shoulder to where the horse and buggy were tied. "We can carry on with this conversation on the way to Hayes Valley."

Two hours later after much discussion, they were pulling up in front of the house. It had been how long? Anne couldn't remember how many years it had been since she and Elizabeth had departed, ultimately taking up permanent residence in the boomtown of Warren, Idaho. *At least four—no, maybe five—years*, she thought. The place looked fresh with flowers growing everywhere, and the entire premises was impeccably neat and organized. Lolivey and her father were out front in the road to greet them.

Anne didn't wait for the carriage to stop before she had jumped from the seat nearly landing on Lolivey and her father. The two girls were laughing, hugging, and chattering endlessly with nothing making sense. Timothy pulled the wagon on a few more feet, stopping at the front gate with the two girls babbling along behind. They had a lot to catch up on and were wasting no time.

"Hey, you two!" shouted Timothy. "Can you stop talking long enough to help me unload this carriage? I have responsibilities, you know. I can't just hang around here listening to you two all day," he managed to say.

That did not faze the girls. Josh jumped down from the carriage to help Tim start the unloading process, and lengthy it was. Anne had all her worldly belongings in that carriage and was taking every one of them back to Germany with her. Tim had jumped back into the carriage and was turning the team around to leave when Anne finally stopped talking long enough to notice his apparent departure.

"Wait, Tim, we have much more to talk about," she shouted jubilantly.

"I will return tomorrow for dinner," he replied. "You all have many things to resolve, and I really do have to go for now. I promise I will be back tomorrow for dinner." Clucking to the horse and slapping the reins on his rump, Timothy bounced off back down the road to the city. The girls waved and continued the chitchat, stopping only long enough to introduce Josh to Lolivey and her father and find a room for Josh.

Two hours later it was nearly dark, and there was a lull in the conversation when Lolivey inquired quietly to Anne, "Who on earth is that gorgeous young man traveling with you?"

Anne filled her in on Josh's history, ending with, "And he will be returning to Fredrick Burgdorf's hot springs high in the mountains of Idaho soon."

"Not if I have my way about it," Lolivey said, laughing.

"You have all the charming young men in San Francisco to choose from," Anne said with a questioning look.

"Anne, I have not been to the city in all of the years since you left. Those wicked people there that caused me and my father so much grief have very long memories, Tim has advised me. We have been quite comfortable here in Hayes Valley. Whatever supplies we need that we can't get here, Timothy has very graciously gathered up for us and brought out. Thanks to the trust fund your very generous sister Mary and her husband set up for us when they returned to Germany, we have managed here most comfortably, but our social lives have suffered." She laughed. "Neither of us have left the area for years. Father busies himself here on the farm as well as with some random odd jobs, and we have done well." She beamed. "Now let's go in and prepare dinner. Father and Josh are probably starving."

"If they are so hungry, let them fix dinner." Anne chuckled.

"You haven't changed a bit, have you?" Lolivey smiled, and they laughed together and fixed a welcome meal.

Chapter 105

Uncharted Island,
Indian Ocean

1871

Thomas awakened first, not bothering to nudge his still sleeping and obviously fatigued companion. His first thought was of doing a quick survey of the tiny island. Upon standing he staggered, nearly collapsing, too weak to walk. Steadying himself with one hand on the shiny, smooth black rock outcropping, he slowly looked around and was delighted to see that all of the small beach below the high-water line was covered with large, white-and-pink conch shells. The tide appeared to be at its lowest flow, so he slowly, in an unsteady, faltering stance, half walked and crawled to the conch bed. He gathered up two of the larger ones then made his way back up the beach to where Jason still lay sleeping. Knocking off the bottom of the large shell with a rock, he was able to extract the thick meaty muscle inside.

The noise of smashing the shell awakened Jason, and he sat up looking around in a daze. Seeing Thomas with the shell in one hand and the meaty substance in the other, he wearily commented, "What are you doing?"

"Making breakfast, I hope," Thomas answered. "The first in four days if I'm right."

Connecting action to words, Thomas slowly turned to the rock wall to find a flat surface, picked up a smaller rock, and started methodically pounding the conch meat flat. After several minutes of pounding and hopefully tenderizing the meaty material totally flat and thin, he took a small bite then handed the rest of the raw conch steak to Jason, who eyed it closely for a moment then bit off a big mouthful. He chewed it only a few seconds before swallowing.

Raising a salt-crusted eyebrow, Thomas asked, "Well, what do you think?"

As Jason opened his mouth to reply, he gagged and the mouthful of conch flew out and onto the ground. The days with no food in his stomach had rendered it sensitive to any food, let alone a raw meaty mollusk steak.

"Try again," Thomas suggested. "Only this time take a small bite. We will need to get our systems accustomed to food in our bellies again."

Starving, Jason took another small bite and was able to keep it down without gagging. Between the two of them, they were able to consume Thomas's entire harvest of conch and immediately felt stronger and were able to at least stand and take a few steps.

"Now we need water," Jason choked and sluggishly climbed a few steps up the steep bluff to a slightly higher elevation. After a short search among the weather-smoothed rocks, he came upon a rounded dish-shaped basin approximately six feet across, probably worn into the rock bluff by eons of erosion by wind and rain. Excitedly turning back to Thomas, who was still sitting near their makeshift raft on the edge of the small sandy beach, Jason hollered, "Hey, I have found a basin of clean, clear, fresh rainwater."

By the time Thomas had climbed up the short distance to the basin, Jason had quenched his thirst and was leaning against a shelf in the rock. They sat there for hours resting, drinking small amounts of water, discussing what had happened over the last several days, resting, then drinking again until some semblance of questionable health returned to their very meager existence.

It was nearly dark when they made the short way back down the rock face to the beach where their raft was tied. The tide was rising, but Thomas was able to wade out a short distance and retrieve two more large conch shells, which the men cracked, pounded flat, and were successful in keeping in their stomachs. They were regaining their strength, but neither felt up to making any kind of a shelter against the weather. The clouds had thinned, and the night was warm, so they found a small hollow at the base of the rock bluff, grateful to spend the night on solid ground.

They had been subject to the pitching ship deck in the storms that had visited them over the last weeks, then the wreck and subsequent ordeal on the makeshift raft to this island. Tomorrow, they agreed, would be more exploring and a plan to make some signal to attract a passing ship, if any were to ever pass this very remote area of the world.

Chapter 106

Hayes Valley Homestead, California, United States

1871

Timothy did come for dinner the next night, and they all agreed to mention no more of Thomas until they had more reliable evidence of his existence, if that were ever to happen. Anne reported that Elizabeth and William were by all outward appearances happy with their new roles as husband and wife, and she did not want to do anything to discourage that unity.

The following days were frantic with last-minute preparations for her final departure from the great America homeward bound to Germany.

"I do not want to make that terrible trip again by ship around the horn with the brutal cold and waves taller than two-story buildings. It's horrifying. And besides, I have read that the new Panama railway crossing the Isthmus of Panama from Balboa to Colón on the Atlantic side has been graciously updated and is now very reliable. It will take only eight hours of comfortable travel to cross the Isthmus, saving months of travel around the southern tip of South America then all the way back up in those treacherous waters. I can also spend a bit of time there in Panama with our friends the Tribaldos family before making the isthmus crossing then continuing across the Atlantic to Germany. Any way I go, it will take about six months too long." She sighed.

Every day Lolivey would question Anne about Josh when he was not around, which was seldom, and in turn Josh would pester her about Lolivey when she was not in their presence, which was also very seldom. Josh was busy helping Anne make preparations and seemed to mysteriously have put his own plans to return to Idaho on hold for the time being. He and Lolivey had been enjoying casual strolls down the road and away from the house whenever possible, which was not as often as either would have preferred, but due to the frantic schedule Anne was wrapped up in, she required both of their attention constantly.

Catching Anne alone one morning, Josh said, "I really like her, Anne."

"Have you ever had a girlfriend before, Josh?"

"Sure, lots of them," he replied hastily, somewhat embarrassed by the question.

Noting his discomfort, Anne only smiled. "She is a lovely young woman, and you are a delightful young man. Are you sure you want to take that responsibility of a possible girlfriend now?"

"I do," he replied sincerely.

"Well, I think she is very fond of you also. Now let's let nature take its course here and see what we shall see, okay?"

Not entirely understanding what she had just said or what he had just agreed to, Josh simply responded with an "Okay."

Anne continued checking items off the list of things needed tending to prior to her departure, and Josh and Lolivey continued their not-so-discreet walks down the lane, with the trees on either side leaning over toward the middle, making it a lovely green tunnel.

Anne had been here at her home in Hayes Valley six days when it was time for her to leave to board the ship for Panama on the first sea leg of her long journey home. Timothy had arrived the night before and spent the night here with them, simplifying their departure for the docks. After a simple and light breakfast, as Anne knew she would be seasick for the first few days onboard the ship, they loaded Anne's trunks into the carriage.

"I can't stand long farewells and do not feel comfortable in the dock area. I am going to stay here with my father, Anne," Lolivey said.

Anne smiled in understanding. "Josh, why don't you wait here also? Timothy can handle my things fine, and he will not have to bring you back out to the valley after seeing me off."

"I love you, Anne. Will I ever see you again?"

"I love you too, Josh. Who knows if our paths will ever cross again?"

Noting his disappointment, she continued, "I'm sure we will meet again, Josh. And by the way, you two do make a handsome couple. I hope Lolivey's father approves. I do."

With that, Timothy started the carriage down the road toward the docks in San Francisco Bay. Like her sister Mary before her, Anne too was now on her way home, a wealthy woman at twenty-five.

Chapter 107

Uncharted Island,
Indian Ocean

1871

Thomas and Jason awoke to a cloudless sky with the sun well over an hour high. They'd been sleeping soundly each night on the island, still exhausted from the storm and shipwreck even after nearly a week. After another conch steak, they climbed the short distance up the rock wall to the hollow of invigorating clear water for a drink. Feeling wonderfully refreshed, they peeled off their scratchy, salt-crusted clothes, and plunged into the rain-filled cistern like frogs into a pond, scrubbing their salt-caked and itching skin and hair then thoroughly washing their threadbare clothes, giving no thought that this may be the only freshwater on this rock island.

"Our shelter can wait. Let's do some exploring and see what this island has to offer," Thomas proposed and pointed. "You go that way, Jason, and I'll go the opposite. Be careful not to fall and break a leg or, God forbid, something worse. We may be here some time or perhaps forever. Who knows?"

Making his way in a southerly direction on this huge rock outcropping in the ocean, Thomas guessed it to rise about one hundred feet above the water at its highest point. The top appeared to slope gradually toward the northerly end in great rugged terraces of jagged craigs and massive boulders of storm-blackened rock. Except for the cove they had miraculously landed in, the island appeared to be an upright pinnacle of somber, unfriendly rock heavily buttressed on all sides and practically inaccessible from the sea. As he climbed toward the summit, he saw thousands of seabirds had accumulated and filled the surrounding air with nonstop shrieking from being disturbed. In the distance he saw Jason working in his direction. Thomas sat on a rock, as if there were any other place to sit, and waited for Jason.

"What did you find?" Thomas hollered sarcastically, knowing full well the whole of the island was nothing but one big rock.

"About the same as you," Jason gasped, still not in the best of shape. "Nothing but thousands of birds with their nests scattered all over the rocks and tons of bird guano. The nests are all filled with eggs, though, if we had any way to cook them."

"Raw bird eggs and raw fish—what a great diet," Thomas replied. "I did notice many other small pools of fresh rainwater located on the outer edges of this solid-rock plateau. We may not starve to death, and we may have a bearable water supply."

Besides their staple diet of conches and eggs, they discovered a weed that hung in clusters from the rock ledges around the water's edge. The branches put forth little clusters of berries that were quite palatable.

Days after landing on the rock island, now being rested and somewhat nourished, they fell into a routine of climbing the rock wall a short distance for fresh water, gathering bird eggs from the nests under the swooping and screeching birds, and returning to their cove for conch and the edible seaweed. In order to keep track of time, they had found a flat ledge above high tide and placed a stone every morning before climbing the rock. They referred to this as their almanac.

The sky had become heavily overcast, reminding them of their lack of shelter. Jason had removed the remnants of the soggy canvas from the piece of shattered mast they had floated on to the island. After days of dragging pieces of the mast and other debris up the slope to a natural outcropping in the rock wall, they improvised a suitable lean-to that would keep them dry. They had no way to start a fire—even if they would have had any real supply of wood—but at least if not warm they could stay dry.

Hourly one or the other would climb to the top of the cliff and search the horizon in every direction in hopes of sighting a sail. On several occasions they did observe a passing ship at an extreme distance, but none were close enough to see them or their waving flag made from torn sail scraps.

Week after week of this frustrating routine slowly turned into month after month and ultimately, year after year.

Chapter 108

Warren's Diggins,
Idaho Territory, United States

1872

The boomtown of Warren was not booming anymore. One of the dredges had been shut down and dismantled to move on to Idaho City near the growing Boise Basin mining district. A few of the smaller placer claims had faded out of existence, with those miners leaving also.

"I'm afraid Warren will become like Florence in a short time," William told Elizabeth one day. "It will be just another ghost town. Dredges are stopping operations. And many of the miners are just leaving for no other reason than to just leave for another promising area. It's the way of the miner's life."

It had been over a year since Anne had left when they got the first packet of mail from her to the town of Warren. She had made it safely to Darmstadt in central Germany but stayed only a few months. The revolutions there were having a severe impact on the working-class people, and they were leaving by the hundreds to the less politically charged and more stable areas in Europe. And of course there was still the mass migration to the great western frontiers in America. After only a few months in Darmstadt, Anne had moved on to Copenhagen in Denmark with the rest of her family, which now included Thomas's mother and little sister. They all were living comfortably on the outskirts of

Copenhagen overlooking an inlet servicing the shipping lanes to the Baltic Sea. Anne Klein had become an accomplished actress in the very short time since her return, and the crowds loved the less formal entertainment she put forth, a style that she had in part picked up performing in the rough-and-tumble Idaho gold mining boomtowns.

After Elizabeth had read all of the letters from home several times over, William commented, "I think you miss them all tremendously, and the lifestyle."

"I do miss it very much but not enough to return, not now anyway."

William looked at her hesitantly for a moment but let the comment pass without further input.

Chapter 109

Warren's Diggins,
Idaho Territory, United States

1873

The town of Warren was slowly fading into nonentity. Elizabeth and William had stayed on another two years after Anne had left and watched the town come to its final demise with but a few full-time residents remaining. William's mine was still showing a good profit, but he and Elizabeth were becoming very restless in watching the town fade away to just a sliver of its once booming existence.

William had spent weeks at a time over the last three years on the Salmon River below John Day Creek starting a cabin there for them to move to. The mine there was proving very rich, and Elizabeth was ready to make the move. She had questioned William continuously about the Indian trouble down there on the Salmon River, and he had assured her that it was minimal.

Her old friends the Richard Rhett family, which she had traveled out from Lewiston to Burgdorf Hot Springs with on the way to Warren, had homesteaded on John Day Creek not far from the Henry Elfers family and Harry Mason's place. These were families she knew and was somewhat relieved with that. Mr. Devine, who was mining up the river from John Day Creek at Carver Creek, was also a friend of William's.

Over the many years she and William had lived in Warren, she had heard countless horror stories from the coming and going miners about the atrocious behavior of the plains Indians and was very concerned for her and William's soon-to-be presence on the Salmon River. It was said that it was only a matter of time until the situation there would reach a boiling point and if the army from the post on the Clearwater River near Lewiston did not intervene soon, it could turn violent.

It was the spring of 1873 when Elizabeth and William prepared to make the move to the Salmon River. William had sealed the entrance into the mine in Warren and had made several lengthy trips alone to the Salmon with wagonloads of mining equipment and household goods for their new home. He had started building it alone then required the assistance of Harry Mason and some of Elfers and Mason's hired hands from the John Day Creek ranch to finish before Elizabeth was to arrive on the river.

Upon William's return from the last trip to the river, he and Elizabeth spent three more weeks relaxing and enjoying the surrounding area, something they'd had little time to do in the past. They traveled over the mountain and down to the south fork to visit many old friends who had spent an entire day in travel just to get to their wedding. Then they returned to Warren for a day, going the next over to Fredrick Burgdorf's hot springs. Even though the town of Warren was no longer thriving, Fredrick's resort and waystation was booming. This place was located on the now-main road from the port at Lewiston all the way through the Idaho mountains to the Boise Basin, which was the new state capital. Fredrick was blessed with help. Josh had, after a rather lengthy delay in San Francisco, eventually returned to the hot springs with a new wife on his arm. Lolivey.

It was a wonderful and relaxing time for a few days there with the undivided attention of Fredrick's Chinese cook and Josh and the expecting Lolivey who was wobbling around now nine months pregnant. Fredrick was by far more excited about the possibility of the new baby, the first to be born at Burgdorf Hot Springs, than Josh, who was a complete panicky wreck.

"Calm down," Elizabeth would say several times a day. "You appear as though you will explode with all of this worry."

"But what will we do with no doctor, midwife, no nothing but you all telling me to just stay calm? Elizabeth, I just couldn't stand to see anything happen to her," he would say wringing his hands.

"*Calm down, Josh,*" she said again. "William has agreed that we will stay until the baby is born."

That evening Lolivey went into labor, and at seven thirty in the morning, Elizabeth opened the door of their small, cozy cabin holding a tiny beautiful little girl. Lolivey was the lovely, exhausted, young mother and Josh was the father to a beautiful new daughter. This was the thirty-seventh birth Elizabeth had assisted in since arriving in Warren.

"William, would it worry you to stay on here at the hot springs for a few more days? I would like to tend to Lolivey a few days before we leave. She is a young and very inexperienced new mother who has just experienced a difficult childbirth."

"Of course it's fine. Fredrick could use my help around here for a few days anyway. It really doesn't matter when we go over the mountain to the river mine, as long as we do it before snowfall."

Elizabeth smiled warmly at him. William had been an understanding and compassionate husband, never making any demands. *What more could I ask for?* she thought and sighed.

A week later Lolivey was up and around and was comfortable with Elizabeth and William leaving. They returned to their home in Warren for one night then packed the few remaining belongings into the wagon and finished boarding the house up securely. They both had agreed it would be a great getaway on occasion from the heat down at the river mine only a few days away.

It was Saturday, August 2 when they left Warren for their new life over on the Salmon. William was exuberant about the move and was busy taking care of the last-minute details, putting another board over a window, securing the door. Finally standing in front of the house with his hands on his hips and smiling jubilantly, he announced, "We're ready."

Elizabeth was already seated in the wagon in a grave mood. "William?" she asked quietly. "Are you sure this is the right move? We could stay on here. We have plenty of money—we really do not have to move on to the other mine at the river, and I do not feel good about it."

William climbed up beside her, draping his arm over her shoulder. "Let's at least give it a try. It's only a few days' journey, and it will be much nicer and warmer in the winter without all of the snow. I have heard that it doesn't even get cold enough to freeze down there in the winter, but I do have to question that. Imagine the garden we can grow. Mason and Elfers have both told me of growing cabbage heads as large as a bushel basket and all types of fruit trees. And, Elizabeth, I have just completed a beautiful home for you there. It, too, has water piped into it."

He was obviously very enthused, and Elizabeth did not want to disappoint him further, so she smiled, saying, "Let's go, Lord William."

They arrived at the beautiful small home overlooking the river just at dark on the fourth day after leaving Warren.

"Oh, William, it is such a wonderful setting."

The house sat just above the obvious highwater line of the river with a panorama view both up and down the canyon. Looking across, Elizabeth could see large meadows hundreds of acres in size and breathtaking mountains, some of which were heavily covered with timber. She could hear the crickets chirping and the deep throaty sound of the harmless bullbats as they swooped and dived for insects. The river here was two hundred feet across and ran lazily by the house.

"Let's just unpack enough of our things to be comfortable for the night," Elizabeth suggested. "You have totally worn me out, William." She laughed. "Maybe this will be a grand new adventure."

Putting actions to words, they took only a few blankets, a couple of pillows, and a tin of coffee for the night. William had already brought several loads of household goods over the mountain by wagon team, and the cabin was quite functional.

The following morning Elizabeth awoke to the sound of the river flowing by, the birds twittering in the nearby foliage, and the smell of freshly brewed coffee. William had risen before daylight to unpack the wagon.

"Aren't you the perfect gentleman?" she commented, smiling, as she strolled into the kitchen. William was sitting out on the front porch with a cup of steaming coffee but could hear her inside. Pouring herself the same, she joined him. She sat and stared at the river, mesmerized and not speaking.

Spectacular setting, she thought. *I never thought for a minute I could ever be happy in another place other than the little cabin Anne and I had built in Warren, but this is breathtaking. I don't know why William works so hard all the time. He certainly is not in need of anything and has a small fortune in gold stashed away, some of it we brought with us, but most buried securely and discreetly at the mine in Warren.*

Looking over at her, William said, "Do you like it, Elizabeth?"

"Yes, yes, I do very much. The view is breathtaking. The house is nearly perfect."

"Nearly?" he commented.

Elizabeth cocked one eyebrow over the cup she was holding. "I will sit and enjoy this beauty and this cup of coffee with you for a while then get my lazy fanny busy preparing some breakfast and arranging this household."

It was a wood-frame house with extra-heavy wood shutters that could be closed to protect the glass windows. It had two bedrooms and an open kitchen, dining and living all-in-one that looked out over the river. Later in the day Elizabeth, with William's help, had moved all of the wagon's contents into the cabin and had everything tidily arranged. The cabinets were full of dishes and cooking utensils, and the pantry was full of dry goods. It would be too late in the season to tend to a garden this year, but they could purchase their winter's supply of vegetables for canning from the Harry Mason and Henry Elfers ranch fourteen miles up the river from their mine and homestead. William could kill an elk for their winter meat supply, he had assured her, and there was a plentiful supply of salmon in the river.

Chapter 110

Salmon River Country,
Idaho Territory, United States

1873

The days passed quickly. While William was working the mine, Elizabeth would venture downriver to the new store that Harry Mason was building and then a couple of miles farther to HC Browns store already in existence. At times she would venture farther downriver to White Bird Creek to visit with a former patient, Mrs. Benedict, and her family. Elizabeth was already offering assistance to the sick and injured, and her services were becoming more in demand on a daily basis.

Harry Mason was in the process of selling his share of the ranch he owned with Elfers at John Day Creek back to Elfers, needing the proceeds to complete the new store and stock it with provisions for the ever-growing amount of settlers. There was much traffic up and down the river now with many new homestead families. These new families settling along the river presented a serious matter for the Indians, who had used the area for generations as a winter hunting and camping ground. Every year there were more conflicts, and the seriousness of the issue was increasing on a daily basis. Many of the new settlers had asked for more of an army influence in the area over and over, but none would come. Larry Ott had settled up the river on the south side of the horseshoe bend only a year ago on property the Indians had claimed as part of their winter camp. That issue was coming to a boiling point, and Elizabeth was much aware of the unrest between the settlers and the Indians.

"William," she questioned one evening over dinner. "I'm relatively new here in this great country. I have only been here ten years, and there is so much of your history I don't know. Who was here first—the white man or the Indians?"

"That's a good question, Elizabeth. They could have been here before the white man, but I think that may be debatable, according to a lot of new historical information coming to light. The Indian has never claimed any specific range. Usually only a wide area could be known as their hunting grounds. The hunting grounds of a certain tribe. But other tribes sometimes drove them away, as they had driven others away before them, and no boundary was ever recognized that could not be held by the strength of their specific tribe. Most often they fought among themselves over hunting grounds or areas where food plants grew. I've heard that sometimes they fought simply because they just enjoyed fighting. Often they fought for scalps. That's one of the troubles now. The older, wiser Indians have learned they cannot beat the continuous flow of the white man and they wish now to live in peace, but the young braves need scalps to impress the Indian girls, so sometimes they go raiding and get the whole tribe into trouble."

"You paint a gruesome picture, William." Elizabeth shivered. "I hear things from the other wives along the river, from other miners and ranchers about a pending war with these Indians. Am I safe traveling to and fro?" she questioned.

"I would hope so," William answered. "I have seen very little evidence of the Indians here."

"Little evidence?" Elizabeth inquired.

"Well, I have seen a few Indians on the other side of the river there"— he pointed to a flat meadow downriver a short ways—"but never on this side."

"What is to keep them from crossing the river?"

"There is nothing stopping them from crossing if they want," he replied. "I just haven't seen any. I think we are safe enough."

Elizabeth was forever worried about Indian trouble, even over the years.

"William, we have been here two years now," she stated one day after taking his lunch and joining him at the mine. "You work from daylight to dark nearly every day. Why?" she inquired for the umpteenth time. "I have a comfortable amount of money, and you have even more than I. We could take a lengthy leave from here. Maybe travel to Boise and take a train to—well, just anyplace, William. At least for a year or so until the Indian trouble is over."

Looking at her, he frowned. "I work because I can, and one can never have too much wealth. I do have a beautiful young wife to support now and maybe someday a family."

Elizabeth stood in silence digesting his words. They had been married almost eight years and no children. She was thirty years old, and William was twenty years her senior—how likely was it they would ever have a family? Leaving him with his lunch, she turned and walked back down to their house. She was extremely uneasy. Just the thought of William seeing Indians across the river upset her immensely.

William continued working the mine, and Elizabeth continued with her forays up the river to John Day Creek to visit the Elfers family. There she would help Mrs. Elfers in the garden then prepare and can foods for the coming winter and on occasion tend to an injured field hand or an ill child. Mrs. Elfers and her husband, Henry, had never been sick a day of their lives, it would seem. Elizabeth had even traveled farther up the river to Richard Devine's homestead and mining operation but only when William was away hunting and she could spend the night with the Elfers family before traveling all the way back downriver to their place during daylight hours. Mrs. Elfers liked to joke that any woman was fine anywhere, just so long as she remembered that anything was a weapon if she used it as such. Still, she encouraged Elizabeth to stay with them whenever William was away.

On one occasion when Elizabeth had ridden upriver to help Mrs. Elfers, Richard Devine was working his mine and had been in the path of a rolling rock coming down the mountainside. It struck him broadside, breaking his leg and two ribs. Hearing of the accident, Elizabeth rushed on farther up the river on her horse, finding him in terrible condition. He had managed to crawl into his cabin and was lying there unconscious when she arrived. She set and splinted the leg, bound his ribs, and made him as comfortable as possible. Then she returned to the Elfers ranch at John Day Creek. Elizabeth was frightened to travel the trail up and down the river alone after dark. One of the Elfers' hired hands went up to Devine's place to stay until Richard could get by alone.

Some of the Indians were becoming bolder on a daily basis and were now seen trading with the settlers up and down the river as well as stopping at Harry Mason's store and HC Browns store. Harry Mason did not like the Indians and had given two of them a sound beating when he caught them stealing from his store. The friction was steadily building. Some of the Indians were more plentiful, resentful, and impulsive as time went by.

Elizabeth would meet them on the river road randomly, never getting used to their presence. She had on several occasions, though, treated an Indian child for a broken bone, a cut, or another issue, and the Indians seemed to have a healthy respect for her. She had even treated some of the Indian women for one thing or another, but the men refused to let her touch them, no matter how severe their conditions were. No matter how hard she tried to overcome her fear of them, Elizabeth would always be uncomfortable in their presence.

Chapter 111

Salmon River Country,
Idaho Territory, United States

1877

Elizabeth had a foreboding feeling. Although a couple years had passed since the incident up the river at the Ott ranch, it played freshly in Elizabeth's mind: Two tribe members approached Mr. Ott at his ranch at the horseshoe bend in the river, still furious about his encroachment on their hunting ground. One of the Indians slid from his horse, stooped to pick up a stone, and threw it at Ott. It struck him full on the side of the head and knocked him semiconscious to the ground. They then walked over to where he lay still holding his horse's bridle reins. When one of the Indians grabbed for the horse, Ott sat up and shot him through the chest, killing him dead on the spot.

Elizabeth would discuss this and other incidents with William on a daily basis. "William, the situation is getting very tense between the Indians and settlers. The talk with the other women here along the river is that there will soon be a major uprising. We could all be slain, ravished, mutilated—God only knows what may happen. Can't we go back to Warren? Please, William. You yourself told me of a new gold strike there, and the town is steadily growing again. Even if it doesn't get as large and booming as it was a few years ago, it will at least be safe. We have only seen Fredrick Burgdorf and Josh with his new family twice in the years since leaving, and that was when they came here to call. William, I have not been back to Warren in three years. You have gone on occasion to check on our house and the mine there, but I haven't and, *William*, I'm frightened. I am going back, with or without you."

"Okay," William finally agreed. "The atmosphere here on the river is getting very edgy. It's even starting to wear on me. We can have Harry Mason watch the house for us. His sister and her family have relocated here from the east and are helping Harry with the store. Maybe they would stay here at our place and keep things up. I have discussed the stressful situation here with Mason, but he insists on staying and does not want to leave. He really doesn't believe the situation with the Indians is as serious as I do."

Once the decision was made, William and Elizabeth chatted non-stop every opportunity they had to make plans to return to Warren midsummer when the snow had melted enough to get over the high mountain pass. They decided to return to Warren on July 1, 1877, planning on being there for the Fourth of July celebration.

Elizabeth kept herself busy these early spring days trying not to think of the pending Indian trouble. *Maybe some soldiers from the fort at Lapwai over on the Clearwater will come and put an end to this before anything more serious happens*, she prayed.

She and William were sitting on the front porch one morning looking across the river having breakfast. "I love these mornings," she said. "We take the time to talk and plan and share thoughts, William."

"We do," he agreed. "Elizabeth, I am really looking forward to getting out of here. If we could get over the pass to Warren, we would leave tomorrow. I have checked with all of the miners up and down the river, and they all say last winter was most severe and the snowpack is still very deep. The only way we could make it over the summit now would be on snowshoes. We would have to leave the wagonload of goods there until the snow melted and I could return for it. I'm afraid that with all of the unrest here, we will be followed and the wagon and its contents would disappear if left unattended. If we can just wait another two or three weeks, we can make it with all of our belongings. I will be needing more implements for the mine in Warren to reopen it once we get there. If I go up to Mount Idaho now with the wagon, I can pick up the necessary supplies, saving me a trip later."

"The trip to Mount Idaho will require an overnight stay, will it not, William?"

"Yes, it will, and I will have Harry Mason's sister come spend the night with you."

Elizabeth thought on this for only a moment. "That will not be necessary. Their store is hardly more than a stone's throw from here, and I should be okay for one night, but please you be careful, William. There are Indians everywhere you look now, and the ones we see are less friendly by the day and more aggressive. I would almost be willing to walk over the pass into Warren on snowshoes with nothing more than the clothes on our backs than spend another two or three weeks here."

It was still early morning—the sun had not risen yet—when William had harnessed the team and was hooking up to the wagon. Elizabeth brought a basket of lunch items out and was waiting warily for him to finish and get on the road up to Mount Idaho.

"I will be fine," she reassured him. "But please be careful," she emphasized again.

He smiled, cracked the horses on the rump with the reins and turned to wave. Elizabeth walked the short distance down to Harry Mason's store, subconsciously sticking her hand through the fold in her dress to the hidden pocket holding her derringer. *Comforting*, she thought, *but what good will it do against a large group of Indians? There are more arriving here on the river daily.* The thought sent chills up her back.

Stepping into the store, she walked to the back room where Mason was lying on a cot. He had the curtains drawn, and the room was darkened. He had injured his eye two days prior while going through the brush to chase some of his straying cattle and was more comfortable in the darkened room.

"William just left for Mount Idaho to pick up some mining supplies to take back to Warren as soon as the road opens," she said. "We have decided to return to Warren at least until the Indian trouble here is over. He will have to stay the night there and will return late tomorrow. Could you please have someone keep an eye on me and my house tonight since you have injured yours?" She chuckled good-naturedly.

Mason laughed. It was good to hear a laugh now with all of the tension. The injury to his eye was not serious and was nearly healed. Elizabeth had been looking in on him from time to time to make sure he was okay.

Returning back to the house, Elizabeth fixed another cup of coffee and went out to sit on the porch looking over the river. As she let her eyes wander on the distant landscape, some slight movement caught her attention. Staring for a full moment, she saw nothing further and thought she was only imagining things. But as she turned her head slowly, she caught the movement again in her peripheral vision, recognizing it to be an Indian and a horse hidden in the brush across the river.

This is odd, she thought. *They have always been forthright, roaming freely in the open. Why would one be hiding in the brush across the river watching our house now?* Sitting and staring for another few minutes, she saw the Indian push through the underbrush and go out of sight into a cut in the distant hillside. *This is not good*, she thought then got up and once again walked down to Harry Mason's store.

Mason was up waiting on some of the other settlers. He had a patch over his eye to protect it from the bright sun. Elizabeth knew the other two women in the store—they were Mrs. Manual who lived up White Bird Creek three miles and Isabella Benedict who lived with her family near the mouth of White Bird Creek. They had come up to Mason's store for a few items and to check on any news as to the continuing decline in friendly relationships with the Indians.

Elizabeth immediately told them what she had just witnessed. Mason was apprehensive, and the two women hurriedly returned to the safety of their homes. "Why don't you spend the night here at the store with us, Elizabeth?" he asked. "With these circumstances, I don't like you staying alone, even if it is only a few hundred feet upriver."

"I will think about it, Harry. I am afraid."

Returning home again, she wandered aimlessly around the house ill at ease. *Nothing is right*, she thought. The Indians are up to something—we know that. And that one across the river watching me with William away. *Oh I miss you, Anne*, she thought. *I hope you are at least safe wherever you are.*

Night was rapidly approaching, Elizabeth had made the decision to stay at home. She had stayed at Mason's store on occasion when William had to be away all night, and she was grateful for his kindness, but he only had an uncomfortable cot in the corner of the store for her, and she wanted the comfort of her own bed tonight in spite of the unease. William had taken the rifle with him, and all she had was the small derringer in her pocket. Pacing the floor and looking out the window, she reconsidered.

She and William had been reasonably safe at this point and had had no real trouble with the Indians here. Even those around them seemed to have been safe except for the time two had tried to steal whiskey from Mason's store and he had beaten them both severely. *I will be okay for the night*, she reassured herself. *Mr. Mason is close by and can be here at a moment's notice.* With this thought in mind, she methodically went from room to room pulling all of the shutters in, latching each securely. They rarely ever closed them and usually left the windows open to catch the cooling night air from the river but not this night. With this being done, she went to bed and finally fell into a fitful sleep.

Chapter 112

Salmon River Country, Idaho Territory, United States

1877

Elizabeth awoke with a start. She knew not what time it was. What had awakened her? At first, there was no sound but the crackle of the woodstove. She squinted at it, noting the kettle was still on the back, releasing steam slowly and steadily, just as she'd left it. From where she lay, she could see, in the faint radiance from the turned-down lamp, the slightest movement of the front door latch. Ever so gently, it was lifted. There was a pressure on the door, which held firmly in place, then the latch eased down again. Elizabeth threw back the blankets and swung her feet to the floor, feeling for her slippers. She stood up and slipped into her robe. What was it Mrs. Elfers had told her? Anything was a weapon if you used it as such. The kettle, the stove poker, the heavy frying pan. Somebody was trying to get in. Was it the Indian she had seen earlier in the day? She waited, listening.

Noting again the shutters were all closed and latched, Elizabeth walked to the stove and added water to the kettle, then replaced the lid and edged it closer to the hottest spot. Boiling water thrown on an intruder may discourage a further attempt. She sat in total silence, not moving a muscle, only listening. She was tired, dead tired, but afraid to go back to sleep. From where she now sat, the door was in plain view. Her eyes slowly closed, but she was totally aware of the faintest of sounds.

Outside in the night, the wind stirred the dried leaves, and they skipped across the hard-packed soil of the yard. Again there was the faintest of noise. A whisper of sound, some coarse material brushing against something else. The edge of the house? Perhaps. She sat holding her small derringer in hand waiting for dawn. The house was secure, and nothing short of a fire could disturb her inside. Exhausted, she sat until the break of dawn.

Knowing Mason was an early riser, Elizabeth walked down to his store and told him of what had happened. He quickly slipped on his boots and walked up to the house with her. Checking the ground all around the house, he could see the confusing images of four and maybe five sets of moccasin prints. They appeared to have stopped at each window to test its security then on to the front door. With no easy access, they had moved on.

"William will be back late tonight," she told Mason. "If he is not here before dark, I will come and stay with you and Helen until he gets here." She shivered. It had been a horrifying night.

After the sun had gone down and it was nearly dark, Elizabeth was standing on the porch watching in anticipation for any sign of movement up the canyon on the road from Mount Idaho. *He should be here any minute, if he is coming tonight and did not get delayed*, she was thinking. *But what if something has happened to him?* She knew the Indians frequented the same road often.

Disappointed and frightened, she turned and started into the house when she saw something far up the canyon moving along at a steady pace. As it got closer, she made out the wagon and William's familiar form sitting in the seat. It would be at least half an hour before he would arrive, so she started walking up the road to meet him, then thought better of it. There were any number of places the Indians could be waiting to ambush, so she returned to the porch to just watch his progress down the mountain trail to their home on the river.

When William got closer, Elizabeth again stepped from the porch into the open road and waved. Seeing her, he waved back and continued steadily on. When he arrived in the yard of the cabin, she rushed to the wagon and jumped up to the seat with him.

"William," she said, holding him close. "I have been frightened sinless."

He put his arm around her and held her tight for a few moments. Then releasing her, he said, "Is everything okay, Elizabeth?"

"It is now." Still sitting in the wagon seat with him, she related the previous night's activities to him as he sat without moving, concentrating on every word she said.

When she had finished, he questioned her as to what she had seen across the river and what Mason had reasoned to have taken place with the moccasin tracks around the cabin. Finally, the horses moved impatiently, so William turned his attention. "Let's get down, and I'll put the animals and the wagon away," he said. "Go ahead inside, and I will join you in a few minutes. I have news to report too."

Elizabeth left his side, jumping down and walking across the yard to stand on the porch. She watched him tend to the animals then return back across the road in the dark to the house. She had an immense feeling of foreboding. *I have had many escapes from potentially life-threatening experiences since leaving Germany*, she thought, *but this one, none of us may survive*. She was oddly at peace with conditions now with William's return and was waiting patiently for his account of the journey and news from Mount Idaho.

Once they were both inside the cabin, they sat facing each other, and she asked, "Tell me, William, what is going on?"

"The people up there are also concerned as to the presence of all the Indians. It seems the majority of the tribes have moved peacefully to the newly established reservations, but the ones left here at this time on the Salmon have refused to join the rest and are ready to fight. The army may send a delegation here to help in arbitration, but no one knows when or if it will be soon enough. I was approached by six of them on my way down earlier this afternoon. They surrounded my wagon and wanted me to unload everything. I kept my rifle pointed at the one in charge at all times and only gave them some coffee and two slabs of bacon. Finally they left me alone but yelled threatening remarks as they rode away. I'm for loading up as much of our personal belongings as possible and returning up the hill to Mount Idaho tomorrow if you want, Elizabeth."

"I do," she hastily remarked. "We are in serious trouble here. It would be too risky to leave tonight, but we will leave tomorrow as soon as we can get things in order."

Chapter 113

Salmon River Country, Idaho Territory, United States

1877

In the dark of night as William and Elizabeth slept comfortably but fitfully, a group of six Indians used an old trail down the side of White Bird Hill. They had been camped in a high mountain valley and descended into the little valley watered by White Bird Creek where the Masons lived. Passing by the Masons' for now, they followed the creek down to its confluence with the Salmon then continued up the river to seek revenge on Larry Ott—but he was nowhere to be found. So the warriors decided to go on to another white man whom they hated.

He was Richard Devine, a miner who lived near the mouth of Carver Creek many miles upriver. Devine had been accused of murdering one of the tribe members a year earlier, and to the avenging warriors, he would be next in line. They recrossed the river, picking up the main trail going upriver to the Richard Devine mine, and reached his cabin after dark. They found him sitting in his cabin reading and unaware of their presence. They silently approached the cabin and entered all at once. Devine was no match for the warriors, and they killed him with a bullet from his own rifle.

Now filled with the lust for blood, they retraced their trail back down the river, passing the fort at Slate Creek quietly in the middle of the night to the Henry Elfers ranch. He had some fine horses, and his attitude toward the Indians had not always been favorable. He too was in line for their revenge.

Early in the morning of June 14, 1877, Elfers started with his horses for his hayfields a short distance from the house. He intended to try out his new mowing machine on the flourishing hay crop. His nephew working for him was already there with two other hired hands waiting. When the Indians had reached the ranch earlier in the dark, they had hidden near the path leading to the hayfield. When Elfers and the other three huddled for the demonstration of the new mowing machine, the warriors rose from concealment and shot each man down before they could move, some with Richard Devine's rifle they had stolen earlier. While the Indians were ambushing Elfers and his helpers, Mrs. Elfers was busily churning butter in the cool of the milk house perched over John Day Creek. The sound of the rushing water underneath and the noise of the churn drowned out the sound of the massacre less than a half mile away.

After rounding up all of the horses, the warriors stopped at the house, pillaging for guns and ammunition. Taking all the loot, they departed and continued down the trail leading to Slate Creek. Mrs. Elfers happened to look up and out of the window of the milk house to see the Indians leaving, but she suspected no wrongdoing. They had often stopped by, trying to trade for guns, ammunition, and horses, but Henry never had anything to do with them, and on more than one occasion, he had forcefully sent them scattering.

A neighbor, Whitfield, had been on the hillside a mile above the ranch hunting and witnessed the murders. He made his way back to John Day Creek to inform other neighbors along the way of the grisly happening he had just witnessed, then rushed on to where Elfers and the other lay bleeding on the ground. They were all dead, each shot several times.

Gathering the bodies, he returned to the Elfers' ranch house where other neighbors were starting to accumulate to console Mrs. Elfers. She could not believe what they were telling her and thought it all a horrible mistake until Whitfield came into the yard with the bodies in the back of the wagon. Not knowing if other Indians were lurking around waiting for another chance to ambush, many of the settlers hastily gathered their belongings and escorted Mrs. Elfers and her children up the river to the fort at Slate Creek.

Charlie Cone, a close neighbor and friend to the Elfers family, saddled his horse, not knowing which direction the Indians had gone but starting carefully downriver to warn the other settlers of the murders of four men so far—one the night before and three this morning.

The Indians had taken another trail around the mountainside high above the river and could see Charlie riding down the river road and stopping at each house. They were ahead of him up on the mountain trail and knew they would reach White Bird before he got there with his warning. About a mile above the mouth of White Bird Creek, the warriors came down off the mountain to a flat hayfield and pasture belonging to the Benedicts, who also were known to have no liking for the Indians. Two years ago, the Indians had been caught trying to steal liquor from the Benedicts' store, and Samuel had grabbed his rifle and started shooting, killing one Indian and wounding two more before the rest retreated to safety.

Seeing Benedict in the field alone, the angry men were ready to even the score. They rode up and, without warning, opened fire, wounding him. He dropped to the ground, and the Indians—thinking him dead—left him and returned to the top of White Bird Hill to their camp in the camas prairie. When they had left, Samuel dragged himself to his horse that was tied behind a haystack. The Indians had missed the horse and had not stolen it. Benedict had been shot through both legs but managed to get onto the horse and make his way home about a mile away over the ridge and down to White Bird Creek.

It was late afternoon on June 14 when the war party led by Yellow Bull made its way back to White Bird Creek, stopping first at the ranch of John Manuel. By now Charles Cone had managed to spread the word of the possibility of a pending attack, and the Manuels were aware of the situation, so they'd loaded their family on the horses to go downstream to another more defensible homestead. Manuel had put his six-year-old daughter on his horse, and their eleven-month-old son rode with his mother. They had traveled only a short distance when they came face-to-face with the Indians. Manuel was the next victim to fall when a bullet struck him in the hip, and he slid from the horse. Driving an arrow into the back of his neck, the warriors left him for dead. During the barrage, little Maggie suffered two arrow wounds, one in the arm and the second in the back of the neck, neither proving fatal. The attackers picked up the weapons Manuel had dropped and sent the woman and her two frightened and wounded children back to the ranch to be dealt with later.

Earlier that day, Isabella Benedict saw her husband approaching the house, sitting on his horse with difficulty. She ran to help him and found that he had been shot through both legs, bleeding profusely. Getting him into the house and into bed in the back room, she set about tending to the nasty wounds.

When she'd cut his pants off to expose his legs, she gasped in horror. The bullets had hit bones in his legs, and they were nearly severed, with bone fragments poking through the skin in various places. *This is more than I can handle*, she thought. *I will have to get Elizabeth here somehow to help me, if he lives long enough for help.*

She had just returned to the living room and closed the door to the bedroom when the attackers burst through the door. Finding only Mrs. Benedict and the children in the house, they ordered her and the children to leave and go to the Manuels' place with the other women and children. Hearing his wife and children leave by the front door, Mr. Benedict managed to crawl out the bedroom window and drag himself across the yard to the bridge crossing the creek, where he was spotted by the warriors and shot repeatedly until he fell into the creek.

The next neighbor down the creek, H. C. Brown, heard all of the shooting and came up the creek from the river to investigate but immediately saw the group of Indians and ran back down, yelling for his sister and her husband to get into the boat that was tied on the riverbank. He followed close behind. Brown cut the line holding the boat with his hunting knife as Benson, his brother-in-law, slid into the seat and took the oars.

They were not far from the bank when the Indians arrived and opened fire. One bullet smashed into Brown's shoulder, and a second nearly tore Benson's arm off. The boat soon glided out of range. Upon reaching the far side, the group disembarked at the Frenchmen's mine, safe for the moment. It would be an easy task for the warriors to swim their horses across the river and chase the small party farther, but they would be vulnerable to open fire from the four Frenchmen standing with rifles ready and waiting for such a move.

Later that afternoon, upon hearing of the slaughter of many families up and down the river, William rushed into the Mason store to tell him of the Nez Perce group on the rampage. Harry Mason lay on the cot in one corner of the store, still nursing his damaged eye. Mason accepted the news calmly. He had already whipped two of the Indians and shot one on another occasion two years ago and was not alarmed about them now. His sister, Helen Walsh, and her three children were also in the store when William brought the news. Elizabeth had accompanied William the short distance down to the store, and they all considered what the best plan would be to get through this night alive. There were so many in the raiding party of Indians that it would be nearly impossible for them to fight them off. They were finally able to convince Mason they should leave the confines of the store with a sack of food and go upstream to the boat ramp at William and Elizabeth's, then cross the river to hide for a couple of days on the other side. When the murdering was done, they could cross back to the east side of the river and make their way to Mount Idaho until the army had things under control again.

Just as they reached the bank of the river in front of William and Elizabeth's cabin, the war party appeared. They had no time to loosen the small boat but had to hurry back into the cabin. The refugees barricaded themselves inside. Mason went immediately to the room in the rear and poked his Winchester through an open window. He had a clear shot at some of the Indian group, but before he could fire one shot, the entire group opened up, firing shot after shot through the window. Mason dropped to the floor, but after the first volley, he rose, peeking over the sill to see a few of the Indians clustering no more than ten yards away. He snapped a shot into their midst then dropped to the floor again, not knowing if his shot had been effective or not.

"Mason, are you okay in there?" yelled William from the other room.

"I am," he casually replied. "You all doing okay in there?"

"So far, so good," William shouted back. "But without help, we don't stand a snowball's chance in hell of getting out of here alive."

They were now weathering fire from the concealed Indians. An occasional peek over the windowsill would bring on a volley of shots, and Mason could not see anything to fire back at.

"William, I think you had better crawl in here. This is the only window with open shutters, and I think they are getting ready to rush us."

Elizabeth cried out to Mrs. Walsh, "Helen, quick over here with the children while the firing has ceased. We can hide under the bed where it may be a bit safer." Helen quickly gathered the three children and crawled over to where Elizabeth was waiting. Together they coaxed the children under the bed then followed to shield the tiny bodies with their own. William had crawled across the floor on his hands and knees to the other side of the window from Mason.

"It's been nice knowing you, Mason," he said conversationally.

"It sure has," the man replied, "but let's make 'em pay for their gains here. You stand and fire a few rounds then drop back to the floor. I'll be standing when you drop out of sight, and when one of the buggers shows himself to retaliate with return fire, I'll nail him."

William stood to the side of the window then turned, firing three quick shots at the brush outside, then dropped to the floor. Mason was already standing when William fired, as planned, and he turned to fire at the first target that would present itself with return fire. One Indian rose from a rock pile across the road, and Mason, true to word, shot him. Things were quiet again for a few minutes, then another withering fire.

"They can't do that for long," Mason shouted. "They don't have much ammunition."

"I don't think they will have to," William shouted back. "They just set fire to the cabin."

Both Mason and William stood, one on either side of the window, peeking out. Whatever was to be done had to happen soon. They could hear the crackle of the flames as they increased in intensity. Suddenly, Mason turned and started firing at every spot that could conceal one of the attackers, only to be rewarded with a crashing blow to his right arm, knocking him to the floor.

He lay writhing on the floor with blood spurting from his wound. William dropped to Mason's side to offer assistance. Realizing how serious the wound was, he called out to Elizabeth.

"Mason is bad hit, and I can't cover the window and tend to his wound."

Suddenly two of the braves shoved their rifles through the window, emptying them into Mason's and William's bodies. Both men lay on the floor dead and bleeding. The rifle shots stopped, and the silence was deafening except for the faint crackle of the fire now engulfing one side of the building.

Concealed from what had happened, Elizabeth yelled, "William, are you okay? What is happening?"

There was no answer.

Chapter 114

Salmon River Country, Idaho Territory, United States

1877

When she heard a noise, Elizabeth peeked out from under the edge of the bed to see a set of leather leggings sprouting from moccasins. One of the Indians had crawled through the window and was now standing less than a foot from Elizabeth. The man in the moccasins walked to the door to open it to the rest of the group.

When they were all inside, one of them reached under the bed, grabbing Helen Walsh and yanking her out screaming and kicking. Elizabeth could hear Helen screaming and thought it would never end. She still lay shivering under the bed with the three children knowing they would soon come for her. *Oh merciful God in heaven*, she prayed, *give me the strength to endure what is about to happen.* Helen's screams had ceased, and the group of attackers returned inside to where Elizabeth and the children were concealed under the bed. Elizabeth's hand slid to the pocket in her dress that concealed her tiny derringer.

Another man reached under the bed and grabbed Elizabeth by the front of the dress, yanking her from her hiding place to her feet. Her dress was in threads as he jerked again, pulling the remnants from her body. As the dress was snatched away and she was left standing unclothed, she managed to hang on to the small derringer and had it pointed directly at the man, finally recognizing him as Yellow Bird. He stood there a moment staring at her shaking form holding the small gun pointed directly at his head.

"You have offered medicine to my sick child," he finally said when full recognition came to him as to who she was. "You are the white lady who heals. You even offer help to the Indians. You are a brave woman, Elizabeth," he said.

"I am not a brave woman. I am a desperate woman, and I will shoot you if you take one step closer, you beast," she screamed. "You and your group have just killed my husband, and you have just killed Mr. Mason. And God only knows what you have done to poor Helen Walsh. Now get out of here," she hissed.

The silence was broken only by the sound of the hammer being drawn back on the derringer. The click sounded like thunder.

"You take the children and go to the fort at Slate Creek," he said. "You will be allowed to pass safely."

"What about Mrs. Walsh?"

"No need." With this, he turned and walked out.

Elizabeth would never see him again.

She grabbed a dress hanging in the closet, put it on then walked out to treat Helen's wounds. She was dead. Realizing the cabin was now nearly completely engulfed in flame, Elizabeth rushed back inside and pulled the children from under the bed to get them to the safety of the wagon on the opposite side of the flaming building from where their mother lay. Elizabeth had no time to recover the bodies of William and Mason from the burning building.

Leaving the children in the wagon, she grabbed a blanket from under the seat and walked around the burning building to respectfully cover the body of Mrs. Walsh. She knew the fire and smoke would eventually draw some of the other neighbors over. Walking back around the charred building that was now nearly reduced to smoldering ruins, she decided to wait for neighbors and helped the children down from the wagon, took each by the hand, and walked them the few feet down to the river.

When the first neighbor arrived on the scene, they found her and the children quietly making a sand castle on the water's edge. Elizabeth had busied them with the technique of placing wet sand in their tiny little fists and letting the wet sand drizzle into a mound that could have been anything they desired, but they called it the magic castle.

What will become of these three beautiful tiny little children? And how much of this day will they remember? she thought. She prayed it would be nothing but the magic sand castle on the bank of the Salmon River.

The first arrivers stood around awkwardly waiting for Elizabeth to bring the children up from the water's edge and explain what had happened here at this devastating scene. With a tiny hand held in each of hers and the third clinging to her dress, Elizabeth walked back up the river bank to one of the wagons carrying a familiar face she knew to be a kindly woman by the name of Mrs. Sickles.

"Could you please care for the children for a few moments while I talk with the others of what happened here?"

"Glad to, hon," she said, smiling deeply and taking each child into her lap as Elizabeth lifted them up to her gently.

Elizabeth strolled to where the others were standing and gave a full account of what had just happened.

"Where would you like us to bury Mrs. Walsh?" one asked.

"Right here by the river will be fine. Please put a cross on the grave if you can. She was a respectable woman."

"And what about Harry Mason and William?"

"What about them? There's nothing left to bury." Elizabeth shrugged and walked back to the wagon, where the children immediately jumped to her clinging like limpets. She held them, looking down into their sparkling little faces. She had cleaned the soot and grime from them in the river after the fire, and they were perfectly beautiful.

The crowd gathered more around Elizabeth and the children, and all were busily reiterating the events of the day. Noting a lull in their conversations, she asked, "Would one of you be so kind as to assist us up to the fort at Slate Creek? I would like to be able to return to Warren as soon as the road opens in a few weeks."

"I would be obliged to," Mr. Titman volunteered and started to harness Elizabeth's team to the wagon.

One of the other women asked, "What about the children?"

"They are going with me!" Elizabeth replied, frowning indignantly, and not another word was said concerning the children.

Chapter 115

Salmon River Country, Idaho Territory, United States

1877

It was late evening when Elizabeth arrived at Slate Creek. The word of her horrendous experience had preceded her, and a place had been prepared for her and the children: little Cody and Dustin, twins nearly two years old, and Samantha, just four. The following days were tense. What was referred to as the fort at Slate Creek was no more than some big trees cut to length then stood on end in a trench that had been dug in sandy soil and filled back in to hold the trees securely in place. It was a strong fortification but was only manned by the refugee settlers who had taken shelter there as a result of the Indian uprising on the Salmon River. It was sixty feet square, making for cramped quarters, and its primary use was for the secure sleeping area of the settlers during the night. Once daylight would come to the canyon, the settlers would return to their close-by homes with guards posted on the higher points to sound a warning should any Indians approach aggressively.

Elizabeth and the three children were given permanent quarters inside the stockade but would wander out to Slate Creek or over to the river just to keep busy and keep the children active. Elizabeth felt that confinement in the fort would not be wise for the children. They needed activity now more than ever, and so did she. The reality of the horror they had experienced had an overwhelming impact on Elizabeth. The children did not once mention what had happened on that life-changing day and seemed content with their new life with Elizabeth. *What will they remember of this heartbreaking event?* she thought. *The mind has a mysterious way of intervening in the immediate awareness of some tragedies only to awaken at a later time to relive the horrors in their entirety.* If that were to happen, she hoped she would be there to help them through it.

So far no one had made any more attempt at even questioning her as to the future of the children, but she felt quite certain it would be an issue soon. She and the children seemed to be the center of attention. Many here had lost someone to Indian attacks over the last few days. But no one had experienced the revulsion and total disregard to human dignity and life that she had witnessed with the cremation of William and Mr. Mason and the ensuing murder and mutilation of Helen Walsh, the mother of these three beautiful children.

The days went by slowly, and the Indian raids had stopped. The army had experienced a devastating battle with the Indians on White Bird Creek and suffered a terrible loss, but with reinforcements the military had pushed them out of the area and were in pursuit of the entire tribe.

Elizabeth spent countless hours with the children playing in the sand by the river or reading stories borrowed from some of the other families with children. They seemed never totally happy but at least never in obvious grievance. She hoped as time went on, the children would settle into their happy-go-lucky attitudes again, and she hoped it would be her influence that helped them achieve this awareness.

They had been in the fort at Slate Creek for two weeks when word from Warren came that the road was now open for wagon traffic. Elizabeth was busy making plans to return as soon as possible—she was concerned here for her own well-being. She wanted the high-mountain community of Warren with many of her old acquaintances to help her in the healing process of the losses she had experienced. She also wanted to get the children to what she felt a healthier environment where they could roam somewhat freely without the shadowing threat of Indian trouble and the constant reminder of the heart-rending experiences they had suffered here. Little Cody and Dustin hardly let

Elizabeth more than an arm's length away, and Samantha insisted on being held continuously, a chore Elizabeth delighted in and never tired of. She'd had no children in all the years married to William but had desperately wanted them.

"How am I to get the wagon and these horses safely back to Warren's?" she mused aloud to no one, just speaking her mind, when a familiar voice from behind answered.

"Well, ma'am, I'd be happy to help."

Turning in surprise, she saw Josh standing right there behind her. "*How on Earth* did you get here?" she shrieked.

"Well, word of the massacre on the river got to us a few days after it happened. Fredrick and I immediately started making plans to get down here and see if you were still alive. We heard many stories from the passing miners about the tragedy, all of them conflicting—some said you were killed; others indicated you were alive. We just had to come down as soon as possible and find out for ourselves."

"Oh, Josh." And she was in his arms hugging him with tears running down her face, all with little Samantha resting on her hip and Cody and Dustin hanging on to her dress.

Josh held her quietly for a moment observing the children but making no mention of them now—that would come later.

Fredrick had taken care of the stock and now stepped up next Elizabeth and Josh. His face showed both relief and concern. "We were worried about you, Elizabeth."

"I'm fine now," she replied.

"We came to help you home, if you care to join us."

Elizabeth had turned loose of Josh with little Samantha still clutching to her and Cody staring at the two men from behind her dress and Dustin sticking his thumb in his mouth. "Can we leave today?" she said.

Fredrick looked at her questioningly, then at the children.

"That's another story for a later date," she said. Everyone at the fort had seen Elizabeth with the children hanging on her for weeks now, and it seemed perfectly normal with no questions asked.

Fredrick and Josh helped her get ready, taking only an hour, as she had but few belongings left. "What? Only one trunk?" one joked.

"Elizabeth, I remember the day you and Anne never even went across the street with less than three each," added the other.

Elizabeth smiled. "This is all I have now, and only this one by luck. William had placed it in the wagon to air out before we were to finish packing to return to Warren."

Fredrick started, "Did the pink one that always housed the hummingbird bur—" Then he caught himself and stopped, not wanting to say more in front of the children.

"No," she replied softly, "it did not. That trunk is still hidden away safely in a side shaft of the mine in Warren. It contains the majority of my wealth as well as other personal belongings I preferred not to bring down here, and I trust that trunk will be safe upon my return." William had left one there too containing the majority of his considerable wealth. At the time it seemed safer there than any bank in the area. Thinking of William, Elizabeth added, "When I have time, I will try to locate his inheritors, if any, to make sure they get his belongings. I need no more than I have amassed on my own. I never heard him mention any family. As a matter of fact, when it comes down to that, I knew very little of him. He was always very private about his past."

They were busy saying their final goodbyes to all the survivors still at the fort and making final preparations to leave Slate Creek with Josh and Fredrick when Mrs. Sickles, a dear friend, came to pay Elizabeth her respects and wish her a safe journey back to Warren.

"By the way, Elizabeth, I don't think I ever heard the children's names."

Without thinking, Elizabeth replied, "Why, they are those little Clay children." Then she stood there in total shock. *Why did I say that?* she thought. *I haven't allowed myself to think of Thomas for years.*

Fredrick and Josh overlooked the comment for now and were busily loading Elizabeth and "those little Clay children" into the wagon. The men had ridden saddle horses leading a pack string of two over the mountain. Josh was now securely astride one of the horses leading the others when Fredrick jumped into the wagon with Elizabeth, glancing at the children.

"I can't wait to hear about this," he said quietly with a questioning concern.

"You will hear it all on the way over the mountain," she replied.

Fredrick had prepared a comfortable little bed right behind the wagon seat for when the children were tired, but it appeared even when they were to sleep, they would be clutching Elizabeth.

The trip back to Warren was fortunately uneventful but tiring. They only stopped overnight at Fredrick C. Burgdorf's hot springs to see Lolivey, pushing on the next morning early over the summit to Warren with an entourage of Fredrick, Josh, Lolivey, Josh and Lolivey's daughter, and the three "little Clay children," as they had become known.

Chapter 116

Uncharted Island,
Indian Ocean

1877

One morning when it was Jason's turn to scale the cliff, raise their flag, and bring down the fresh bird eggs, Thomas remained below, set the almanac stone, then searched the beach for fresh mollusks for breakfast. The morning was thick and misty when Jason returned from the top of the cliff reporting there was nothing in sight.

"I can see no more than my hand at arm's length." He sighed in disappointment.

While they were busy with their repetitious breakfast, the mist slowly lifted. They paid little attention to this condition, as it was similar to nearly every other morning they had endured.

The observant Captain Justin of the large four-masted ship *Bestia Real* had noticed something out of the ordinary on top of the rock pile, what appeared to be a faded and ragged flag delicately flapping in the slight breeze. His curiosity now aroused, he maneuvered his ship closer to the island until he observed the small cove, which unbeknownst to him was harboring Thomas and Jason. Justin took up his glass and slowly swept the shoreline for any anomaly.

Passing over the men on the first sweep, he commented to the first mate, "Don't see a thing now. Probably saw nothing anyway."

Slowly moving the scope back for a second look, he suddenly stopped, stared at the cove, then whispered, "Holy Mary, mother of Jesus, will you look at that?" Handing the glass to his first mate, he instructed him to look closely at the distant cove surrounded by the black shiny rock stained with bird residue.

Thomas and Jason suddenly noticed the ship standing about a half mile out. They were completely stunned, not moving, just staring in disbelief.

"Must be two statues," the first mate said. "They're certainly not moving."

Then Thomas snapped out of his trance and waved frantically, running up and down the small beach and yelling at the top of his lungs.

The captain cautiously moved another four hundred yards closer to shore, then lowered a life boat. Electing two men to take with him to man the oars, Justin jumped aboard to personally investigate this unusual set of circumstances and retrieve the two souls that appeared to be stranded, should necessity dictate such action.

Seeing the smaller boat lowered and steering toward shore, Thomas stopped waving then turned to Jason. "They've seen us. We'll be rescued!"

Staring again closer at the ship anchored no more than a quarter mile off shore, then glancing toward the rescue boat approaching their cove, Thomas shouted at Jason only a few feet away, "That's the *Bestia Real*, the ship that brought me from Panama to California back in 1863!"

The moment the bow of the landing craft touched the gravelly shore, Thomas and Jason both jumped into the water and helped drag the bow high and dry. The ship's captain jumped ashore, firing all kinds of questions at the two castaways before a faint glimmer of recognition came to his mind. This man that stood in front of him with threadbare clothes covering hardly enough to matter and raven-black hair and piercing green eyes looked exactly like that young man Thomas Clay he had brought from Panama to San Francisco years ago.

"Aren't you..." he stammered.

"I am," Thomas answered, "and it is good to see a friendly face again. With your permission, we have a lot to talk about."

"We do." At that, Captain Justin smiled. "You have no idea what I have to share with you, lad." After learning Thomas and Jason were the only two survivors of a wrecked ship on its way to Australia returning from Madagascar, Captain Justin sympathetically questioned, "How long have you two been here?"

Jason took up the conversation at that point and said, "As of this morning, it must be around six years, give or take, according to our almanac."

"Almanac?" exclaimed the bewildered captain. "How did you manage to save an almanac?"

"Come," said Jason. "I'll show you." Leading the party the short distance to the almanac rock, where they found neat little rows of stones representing each day they had spent on the island.

Captain Justin was absolutely amazed. "Well, I guess this is one way to maintain some degree of sanity, but ah—but how did you two even wind up on a ship to Australia?" Then added, "Ah, never mind for now. We will get to all of that once aboard ship."

The men returned to the disheveled and seriously dilapidated shelter in the gravelly cove for a final inspection and then boarded the life boat and pulled off toward the ship waiting not far offshore. The life boat would take only a few minutes to reach the waiting ship, and no one said a word. Thomas and Jason were both too overwhelmed with a multitude of feelings to even try to talk. Justin was also consumed with opinions as to what kind of story this was to bring forth. Climbing the boarding ladder ahead of Thomas and Jason, Master Justin—as he was often called, and he preferred it over captain—was shouting orders to make way before all were aboard and the life raft secured back in its place. Thomas and Jason now stood on the deck of the *Bestia Real* watching the guano-covered island as it disappeared over the southern horizon.

Leaning over with elbows on the rail and one foot perched on a small keg, Thomas sighed. "When I get my feet on dry land again, I hope I will never have to get on another ship, fight another battle, or eat another egg—raw or otherwise."

"Not me," Jason replied. "This has been an astounding adventure, and we are both still alive. I do not ever want to eat another egg again either, but I may inquire about staying on the *Bestia Real* with Captain Justin. I do love the sea, in spite of what we have been through these last years."

Master Justin was busy getting the ship once again underway, heading to Melbourne, Australia, to offload goods that he had brought back from a lengthy voyage from South Africa. He left the two new souls aboard to their own devices for some time. Now finding them watching the island sink out of sight on the distant horizon, he said, "Would you two please join me in my quarters? I will outfit you in suitable attire before the wind blows what threads you are now wearing away at its whim."

Chuckling, they followed him to his quarters belowdecks, where they were both fitted with clothes, perhaps not the most stylish for the times but relatively new, clean, and suitably sized. After this, they were shown to their separate cabins, and then the captain invited them to dine with him so they could discuss the events that had taken place over the last fourteen years since he had delivered Thomas from Panama to California.

Thomas told of his first night in San Francisco after leaving Captain Justin's ship, of meeting up with Jason in a wharf-side tavern, and their subsequent Shanghai experience. He talked of never having the opportunity of looking for his long-lost love, Elizabeth, at her sister's home in Hayes Valley in San Francisco, of the horrors of being a captive slave for years on various ships, in the South Pacific and the South China Sea.

Jason's tales were mostly identical, as he and Thomas had been together throughout the last fourteen years. Prior to meeting up with Thomas in San Francisco, Jason had left Denmark for a better life in the great New World, America. He had planned to ultimately make his way to the fabulously rich goldfields in California, only to meet up with Thomas in San Francisco, and the rest was history, so to speak.

Over the weeks leading up to their arrival in Australia, as Thomas and Jason shared tale after tale, the captain listened tentatively, starting at times to interrupt with information of interest he had but then thinking differently for the time being. The two had been through a tormenting ordeal not uncommon for most shanghai victims, Justin was sure, but nonetheless an atrocious experience. He sat for hours listening, occasionally asking a question about a certain event or location at a given time. During Justin's voyages throughout the oceans of the world, he had narrowly missed meeting up with these two on more than one occasion and was regretful he had not been able to intervene in their miserable conditions.

Chapter 117

Warren's Diggins,
Idaho Territory, United States

1877

They only had one day to get Elizabeth's house in order before the Fourth of July celebration. Fredrick and the rest were busy removing boards from over windows and doors, making ready to get into the house that had been vacated four years ago when Elizabeth and William had moved on to the Salmon River.

"Fredrick, would you mind if I took a few minutes and walked over to the mine? I have a few things there and would like to retrieve some for the house. I really want to do it now and not wait until morning."

"Not at all, Elizabeth," he responded. "If you like, ask Lolivey to go with you. Josh and I can handle the children while you walk across the street and over to the mine."

"That will never work." She chuckled. "Little Samantha will not turn me loose for even a minute yet, will you?" She'd turned her attention to the girl and lightly pinched her cheek. "You little imp."

Lolivey was excited to go for a walk with Elizabeth, and they crossed the street with Elizabeth carrying Samantha on her hip, shifting her from side to side up the trail to the mine portal.

"Lolivey, if you could pry that one board loose, we could slip through the entrance. It's only a short distance to the side shaft holding the trunk with some of my very personal items."

Lolivey stepped in first, and then Elizabeth handed Samantha through the opening, squeezed through herself with the lantern, and took the girl back to walk the short distance to the side shaft. Finding everything exactly as she had left it, she opened the trunk and carefully rummaged through its contents until she found the little bundle of cotton protecting the glass hummingbird Thomas had given her some fifteen years ago. She hardly thought of him anymore, just an occasional flashing memory that would stop her breath then be gone. Tucking it securely into her dress pocket, they left, securing the entrance and returning to the house. Little Cody and Dustin were busy helping the guys as much as four-year-olds could, only looking up at Elizabeth and smiling when she walked through the door. Taking the humming-bird from her pocket, she once again hung it in the kitchen window to catch the first rays of light the morning would bring. They all worked until late in the night cleaning, dusting, washing dirty windows, and arranging then rearranging furniture.

Elizabeth was the first to rise the next morning and made a big pot of coffee and fried up a whole side of bacon. The fragrant odor of the bacon and coffee soon woke the rest, and after a hearty breakfast, they were at it again. By noon everything was in order, and they still had a half day before the Fourth of July celebration. Wandering about town enjoying the sights with little Samantha balanced on one hip and heading the twins down the street, they greeted old friends and just enjoyed the fresh cool mountain air—the safe cool mountain air.

Thank you, God, for this day, she uttered in a silent prayer as she let her eyes wander over the fresh and beautiful landscape then glanced down at the children. *Especially for these three*, she thought, hugging them all affectionately.

This Fourth of July celebration was just as exciting as the one she had attended three years ago with William before moving down to the Salmon River. *I am home and will not leave again*, she believed. *If the mines play out again and everyone moves on, I will stay even if I'm the only one in town, and I will raise these children right here in this fresh mountain air.*

Chapter 118

Indian Ocean

1877

After Master Justin had spent days and days tentatively listening, wanting Thomas and Jason to thoroughly purge themselves of the unhealthy and unwanted feelings and memories, the captain finally was ready to speak up with news he could share with them. Thomas had spoken many times of Elizabeth—the beautiful, young, spirited girl he had once known and loved and planned to marry in Germany. He was truly deeply saddened for the loss of Elizabeth.

"I have listened to your experiences for days now, actually nearly two weeks," Justin said. "I did not want to interrupt you in your recollection of the last many years of experiences, so I have waited until now to share some vital information with you both."

Captain Justin went on to tell of knowing Jason Klaus's relatives in Denmark. He had docked in Copenhagen to offload trade goods and had spoken with some of them not more than a year and a half ago. Some were warehouse owners, some merchants, and some dock workers, and they were all doing well.

"And for you, Thomas, I'm not sure where to begin." Justin tapped his fingers on the wooden table. "After your departure from my ship fifteen years ago in San Francisco, I did meet up with Captain Sawyer again in Panama while he was making a humanitarian effort in transporting the European emigrants who had made it to that country's Pacific shore but could not get on to California."

Thomas leaned forward, unsure what kind of news to expect.

"Your Elizabeth did in fact unite with her sister Mary in Hayes Valley near San Francisco," Justin explained, and Thomas exhaled. "From what I understand, she arrived there in the fall of 1863, about the same time you were shanghaied in San Francisco. Mary and her husband had struck the mother lode in the goldfields in California and returned to Germany enormously wealthy, going partway on Captain Sawyer's ship. It was his last voyage, as he retired from the sea, eventually settling in the new state of Idaho near a town called Gouge Eye. I heard from other sources that when Mary and Edward left California to return to Germany, your Elizabeth and her sister Anne also left California for Oregon then on to Idaho, where she ultimately met and married a miner in some boomtown called Warren's Diggins."

Noticing Thomas's intense dismay and disappointment with that last statement, Justin hastily changed the subject. "I have also learned over the years that your old friend Fredrick C. Burgdorf migrated to that area near Elizabeth and brought someone referred to as Little Josh with him—the boy you rescued from the Darmstadt slums, it's reported."

Thomas's heart pounded as he sat speechless.

"How do you know all this?" Jason asked.

Justin smiled. "We all have a mutual friend working the dock in San Francisco." He cocked his head. "His name is Timothy."

Thomas sat in stunned silence, his mind in turmoil and not thinking clearly. He had spoken with only Jason for years, with nothing new to discuss after their first few days stranded on the small, bare rock pile they had called home. Now, with so much new to take in, he wasn't sure if his overwhelm was because of information overload or the wine he had consumed with dinner, but he could hardly move.

The captain folded his hands under his chin and looked Thomas in the eye again before going on. "There is one more thing I should tell you."

Thomas only nodded.

Captain Justin continued, "Your mother married Elizabeth's father, and apparently they also have returned to Denmark."

Thomas looked up from the table to see Jason observing him thoughtfully then offering him not another glass of the captain's fine wine but the full bottle, which Thomas took and immediately consumed.

Chapter 119

Warren's Diggins,
Idaho Territory, United States

1877

The day after the Fourth celebration, Fredrick and Josh and Lolivey's family returned to the hot springs. Elizabeth was now alone in Warren with her children. She soon was busy again with tending to the ill and injured in town. Old friends were still periodically stopping by to check on her well-being and to inquire as to her three new children, who were a wonderful addition in the community.

The summer passed lazily, giving Elizabeth the opportunity to spend much time with the children. They would walk freely about town, and all of the traffic—either foot, wagon, or horse—was most courteous to their presence. She would sit for hours a day with the twins and Samantha when she was not tending to an injured miner, a sick child, or some other person requiring medical attention. As before, when an injured miner could not pay Elizabeth for her services, they would, when able, stop by to offer help with little things around the house needing repair or chopping wood.

The children were doing marvelously well. None had ever referenced the events of the massacre on the river, and they had even started to call her Mom or Mother, whichever their little minds decided to throw out. Elizabeth's disturbing thoughts and nightmares of the experiences during the massacre on the Salmon River were becoming less frequent, and life was returning to a normal routine. She once again was enjoying a wonderful life in this quaint little mountain community, and winter was soon upon them.

After dinner every evening when they were comfortably sitting in front of the radiant stove, with Cody or Dustin bouncing around, poking into everything in the house, dragging a pot out from under the kitchen cabinet and using a stick of kindling from the wood box for a stirring spoon to make whatever imaginary concoction they came up with to entertain themselves, Elizabeth would sit with Samantha at the kitchen table. She had just turned five years old, as well as Elizabeth could guess, and could do her basic arithmetic problems. She was reading at a very impressive level and could write. Elizabeth attributed much of this academic success to their previous livelihood but really had little idea what that was. Nevertheless, they had become brilliant children as well as very handsome and charming.

The winter was passing, and spring was in the air. It had been an interesting winter with only the children. Elizabeth had had few books to entertain herself and the children with, but Jack and Luci Pickel across the street at the general store were well stocked with hundreds of books. It was the largest collection of books Elizabeth had ever seen in one place.

Most of the snow had melted, leaving their front yard bare, and the first of the spring flowers poked their first shoots up through the earth. Elizabeth was sitting there on the front step of the cabin watching the children play. They were such a joy to watch romp about in the front yard. They each sprouted a head of beautiful snow-white hair and were not difficult to spot while playing outside.

Something flashing caught Elizabeth's eye. Turning her head slightly, she could see the little glass hummingbird swaying gently in the window, reflecting its radiance with each turn. A spasm of remembrance shot through her like a lightning bolt.

"He is alive," she said to the children, who just stared at her, not having any idea what she was talking about. "He is alive, and we all will be seeing him one day soon."

Chapter 120

Indian Ocean

1877–1878

Days at sea rolled on, and Thomas and Jason strolled the deck watching the water's changing color and mood as the *Bestia Real* gracefully tacked back and forth, battling her way steadily eastward to the lands beyond the horizon. Several weeks later they passed through the Bass Strait between Australia and Tasmania and were docking in Melbourne to offload goods brought from Africa then fill her cargo hold with wool for the continuing trip to the California coast of North America.

A dock worker flagged down Captain Justin. "This the *Bestia Real*?" he asked in a thick Aussie accent.

"Aye," confirmed the captain.

"Got this letter for ya. Special delivery from Timothy in America."

It had to be big news for Timothy to use his connections to send a message to him in Australia. Captain Justin unfolded the paper and read hastily before finding Thomas working in the hold. "Word from America." He waved the paper. "Apparently there was a war with the Nez Perce Indians someplace in Idaho."

Thomas's mind went straight to Elizabeth. *Was she hurt?*

"Elizabeth's husband was massacred." Justin paused with the weight of it. "Then she returned to Warren's Diggins with her three children—adopted children—where by all accounts she now lives."

Thomas stood breathless. His mind turned the statement *Elizabeth is alive* over and over, a drumbeat guiding him to her. He would do everything in his power to hold her again.

One hundred twelve days later, in the early spring of 1878, they were sailing through the Golden Gate and would be docking in San Francisco's harbor soon, depending on the number of ships in front of them. The trip had been unusually long—the weather had not been cooperative, and the ship had experienced days on end making little headway.

When they were finally anchored in the bay awaiting their turn to approach the dock, Captain Justin stood between Thomas and Jason in quiet conversation. "We have discussed this moment for the past three months, lads, but now we are here."

Thomas had gained back most of the weight he had shed on the small island months ago and was now fitting comfortably into the captain's clothes. The ship's barber—such as he was, just a crew member taking on that duty—had cut Thomas's long black hair to the stylish length of the day. Jason was also filled out and looking less destitute in the captain's clothes but refused the haircut.

Staring into Thomas's opaque green eyes then turning his head to meet Jason's gaze, Captain Justin broached the question on all their minds: Where would they each go now?

Neither spoke up immediately, both deep in thought. For months they had occasionally talked of the time they would be here, but the conversations were always vague, neither fully comprehending the impact this event would have on their lives. Elizabeth had been on Thomas's mind every waking moment. So many questions, and he had so few answers. Would she even remember him after all these years, let alone still have any feelings for him? At this moment in the harbor, it was very thought provoking for Thomas and Jason to face the decision of possibly parting company, probably never to see each other again.

After standing another few moments in thought, Captain Justin broke the silence. "Thomas," he said, "do you remember years ago when we sailed into this harbor from Panama?"

"I do," Thomas replied.

"Well, just as then, I am going to send a small boat into the docks and load up with fresh goods for a meal never to be forgotten before we dock the *Bestia Real*. And if the gods are with us, we will have a special guest brought back aboard: Timothy, who has been in constant touch with everyone you know here in America."

The boat returned shortly after noon the next day loaded with fresh goods, the likes of which Jason and Thomas had not seen in years. Timothy happened to have seen the *Bestia Real* enter the harbor the previous day while he was working, and he had kept a constant eye on its progress. He saved the crew of the landing craft the effort of trying to locate him as he happily met them on arrival at the dock.

The feast on the deck of the gently rocking ship was excellent. The introductions were made, and Timothy was soon recapping the events of Elizabeth, sister Anne, Fredrick, and others Thomas had known in Germany.

"You needn't worry about Elizabeth's feelings toward you, Thomas. I have not spoken to her personally for years, but every letter she has sent has inquired of any possible word from you. She has always believed you were alive."

Captain Justin excused himself and retired, but Jason and Thomas talked the night through with Timothy, and it was breaking daylight when he finally was able to get away from the two, promising to return later that evening if they did not make dock that day. After Timothy's departure, Thomas and Jason still sat on deck in quiet conversation enjoying the sun over America.

"I think I have decided what I wish to do, Thomas," Jason finally said. "You have strong ties here, with the possible reacquaintance with Elizabeth and other family members. I have on occasion discussed the possibility of staying on with Captain Justin. His first mate has expressed a desire to retire from the sea and hunt for gold in some of the Idaho boomtown areas. He has offered me that position and, with the good Lord willing, I will have my own ship one day soon. The captain says we will leave here with a hold of goods for Panama, then pick up a load of coffee to take around the horn up the North Atlantic to England, Denmark, and Sweden. Perhaps I shall also meet up with old family members. Anyway, that's my plan. And yours, Thomas? Have you made any decisions? What will you do now?"

"Not exactly sure yet," replied Thomas. "I will need more time with Timothy before I make any definite plans, but I am staying here." He rubbed his hands through his hair. "Will you do one thing for me, Jason?"

"Yes, yes, of course. What?"

"When you get to Panama, please stop in at the Tribaldos Coffee warehouses and tell Eladio of our adventures. Tell him of what has happened to Elizabeth and the others, and tell him I will see him again one day. Would you also please, upon arrival in Copenhagen, Denmark, try to find my mother if she is still alive? You will know what to do and say. I shall not try to convey any message now, but maybe I can compose a letter prior to your departure. It will be a hard thing to do."

"I can and will do that," Jason said.

Timothy returned later that evening, and again they talked the night through. He informed Thomas of Elizabeth and Anne's home not far away in Hayes Valley that they had let Lolivey and her father stay in. He went on to tell about Lolivey and her father—about Lolivey moving on to Warren's Diggins in Idaho with Josh. Thomas was amazed and overwhelmed.

Timothy went on. "You do not have to worry about working right away, Thomas. Elizabeth has left a substantial amount of funds with Hank, Lolivey's father, in case you were to turn up here in need of funds."

"How would anyone have known of my presence in that event?" Thomas inquired skeptically.

"I would have known as soon as you set foot on the dock," Timothy said. "For years I have been watching for a big black-haired moose with piercing green eyes, and you fit the description perfectly."

The *Bestia Real* was able to dock just before dark that night but could not start the offloading process until the next day. Captain Justin escorted Thomas and Jason onto the dock, discussing the departure date and times with Jason. The two men agreed to follow Timothy to Hayes Valley to meet Lolivey's father, still caretaking Elizabeth and Anne's home there, but Jason needed to be back in time for the ship's departure.

PART V

Chapter 121

Hayes Valley Homestead, California, United States

1878

As they pulled up to the Hayes Valley home, Thomas sat in astonishment. How had Elizabeth and Anne managed to acquire this beautiful setting? He still had so many unanswered questions.

Lolivey's father, Hank, seeing them approach, walked out to the front gate to greet them. "Please," he said, smiling, "come in, and I will fix refreshments."

With that, Timothy excused himself. "I have to get back to the wharf," he said, "but not to worry—I will be back tomorrow to check on you. We do not want the new first mate Jason to miss his ship."

Turning the small cart drawn by a spirited young pony back the way they had just come, he trotted off briskly, looking back over his shoulder and raising his hand in a wave. Thomas and Jason stood in awkward silence staring around at the beautiful well-kept home with the freshly painted white picket fence. There was a red barn off to the left with a pasture behind it. The pasture supported one horse that was used only rarely. Hank never went into the city, so the horse was totally content to graze the small pasture in peace.

Hank noticed their bewilderment and invited them into the house. "Come in, please," he said again. "Let us get you comfortable for the evening."

"I have not been in a setting such as this since leaving Germany so long ago," Thomas said. "We have been confined to ship life so long, I'm having trouble standing in one place without swaying and compensating for the movement of the ship."

"Come, come," Hank said smiling.

Jason and Thomas both took up their small sea bags and followed Hank into the beautifully appointed home. Passing through the door, Thomas stopped once again in total amazement. The interior and furnishings were something of which he had not seen since his visit to the Tribaldos Coffee plantation in Panama some fifteen years ago.

Jason was equally overwhelmed. "This is a lot to digest all in one day." He sighed, looking around at the modern furnishings.

Hank hastily prepared a pot of coffee and put cups on the table. "I am quite sure you have many questions to be answered. I know much about you, Thomas, but not you, Jason."

Staring at Thomas, Jason stretched out one arm palm up and smiled. "You first."

Hank chuckled. "Let me start. You know nothing of me. Let me tell my tale for the last fifteen years, and then we will fill in the blanks." For hours, he told of his own kidnapping and subsequent rescue, of the girls' adventures there in San Francisco, of their trip on to the boomtowns in Idaho, and the stories went on and on. He had been informed by regular mail of Elizabeth and her three children now living in Warren's Diggins in Idaho. He went into great detail of Elizabeth's misfortunes in the Nez Perce War. He said he received packages occasionally from Anne, now back in Denmark. Then he told his favorite part—of his daughter Lolivey marrying Josh and settling in an area with Fredrick C. Burgdorf not far from Elizabeth. He finished, "I am a proud grandfather."

Thomas sat in stunned silence. Little Josh married and with a child. Elizabeth with children living in a boomtown in Idaho. Slowly his conscious mind fully comprehended the gravity of the existing situation. "I am going on to find them," he said at last.

Jason sat across the table with his arms folded across his chest. Grinning, he prodded, "Figured you would. What's keeping you?"

"You," Thomas said. "I want to see you and Master Justin off before I leave."

They had once again talked away the night, and the sun was poking its way through the mist in the valley.

"It is six a.m. Let's get a bit of sleep," Hank suggested. "Then I will fix us breakfast."

Chapter 122

Hayes Valley Homestead, California, United States

1878

Timothy returned late afternoon to announce the *Bestia Real* would be sailing in two days. Thomas and Jason would have one more day in Hayes Valley to take advantage of Hank's wisdom before Jason would be off with Captain Justin. The route was planned, but God only knew where they'd actually end up. Meanwhile, Thomas would start his journey to Warren's Diggins and Elizabeth.

On the date of the ship's departure, Thomas went back to the San Francisco harbor with Jason to say their goodbyes. The two stood on the dock looking up at the ship. The conversation was light, both deep in their own private thoughts. Finally Captain Justin yelled down, "Get up here and earn your keep! We can't sit here all day, ya know." Then he walked down the loading ramp, all smiles. Placing a hand on the shoulder of each man, he said, "We will all reunite again one day." Then he and first mate Jason walked up the ramp, pulling it up behind them. They both turned to lean over the rail for one final wave.

Looking up seeing them standing there, Thomas smiled. *They look so much alike*, he thought, *they could be brothers.*

Thomas's first major stop after leaving California was Portland, Oregon. He would trace Elizabeth's route all the way until he found her. Spending only a day in Portland, he continued up the Columbia River, and three days later, he was in Lewiston, Idaho. The trip up the Columbia Gorge was magnificent. He had witnessed many inspiring places in the South China Sea, Australia, and Africa in his many years on the sea but nothing as inspiring as this trip up the gorge.

Upon arriving in the Port of Lewiston, Thomas would find and stay in the Luna Hotel if a room was available—the same hotel Elizabeth and Anne had stayed in, he knew from one of the many conversations he had with Hank. Thomas checked into an upstairs room with a balcony looking over the Clearwater River on the north end of town, while the Snake River made the town's western boundary.

I am absolutely captivated by this town, he thought. Barren and rugged but nevertheless attractive in its own way. He was to stay there a week, and he was tired and filled with apprehension. *What will Elizabeth be like now after all these years?* He knew she had never forgotten him. Hank had informed him of all the letters she had sent inquiring of any news of him. But still, his mind was a blur with unsettling thoughts. How could he ever explain his absence of fifteen years? Maybe she wouldn't even want to see him. Maybe she had only inquired as a matter of curiosity.

Thomas wandered the few streets of Lewiston daily, striking up a conversation here and there, always casually asking about Elizabeth and Anne. Did anyone remember them passing through? Did anyone remember them living here for a year? On one occasion, he happened to meet a manager of the theater who did remember Anne. She had been an amazing hit, and her sister Elizabeth had been seen in the audience of each and every one of Anne's performances, the stage manager remembered.

Thomas also wandered the street paralleling the river, enjoying the relaxed attitude of the local population. This was what he had dreamed of as a child—to be in the great American West. Now here he was, not searching for gold but something far more valuable: Elizabeth. He paused a moment and corrected his thoughts. He was not searching for Elizabeth—he knew where she was, or at least where she had been only a few months ago. He was just trying to adjust himself from the constant fighting and turmoil he had endured during his life at sea.

"I hope never to lift another weapon in anger or harm another man as long as I live," he said to no one in particular as he walked with hands in pockets, alone along the river on the edge of town, enjoying the serenity. Chuckling to himself, he commented again to no one, "Everything is going to work out just fine."

Realizing he was thirsty, he noticed a sign across the street: *Jim Brown Saloon*. He thought he'd have a beer. Strolling across the street to the tavern, he opened the door and stepped in, where he was promptly greeted by the friendly bartender. The man waved before popping a morsel of bread in his mouth. Thomas realized the bartender possessed not a single tooth in his head, so when he chewed, his weathered old face folded like the leather bellows of a blacksmith forge. It was well-known that he was the strongest man in town and quite friendly and a wealth of information, as most bartenders are.

The next thing Thomas noticed walking into the saloon was a man with tremendous bulk heading straight to the back wall, where he stood and scowled at him. The man's hands were the size of small hams, and Thomas could tell he was a tough one and probably no stranger to a brawl. A good one to avoid. Thomas wanted no trouble, just a glass of beer and a bite to eat.

Luther noticed the black-haired man at once from his stance at the end of the plank bar in Jim Brown Saloon. He made it a point to saunter in Thomas's direction, stopping next to him.

Looking at the hulking man again, Thomas thought, *This man is huge, a good three inches taller than my six feet, and fifty pounds heavier. From the looks of those hands, he is most definitely no stranger to fighting, and he is missing one thumb,* Thomas noticed. *I do not want any trouble with this brute.*

Luther gave him an appraising glance then asked, "Where ya from? I don't remember seeing you around before."

"I haven't been around before!" Thomas told the truth—the part he wanted to tell.

Frowning at him a moment, Luther said, "A real cocky one, aren't ya? How would you like me to beat you to a pulp right here in front of everyone in this room? I have a reputation for doing just that," he claimed. "And I've never lost a fight."

He looked the type that would fight for sheer pleasure, enjoying the utter brutality of it, Thomas guessed. "Sure, it can be here and now in front of everyone, as it will be you who takes the beating and I would like everyone in this room to witness such an event. But first," Thomas added, "can I buy you a drink?"

"A drink? I came over here to give you a whoopin'."

"Why me?" Thomas smiled.

"Because you're the only one around I haven't whooped. But on second thought, let's have that drink you offered. I hate fighting when I'm thirsty."

The bartender hastily set up two glasses and a bottle of whiskey. Thomas poured, his glass with but a little and Luther's to the top. Thomas picked up his glass with his left hand, leaving his right ready for action. Luther did the same with a slight twist to his lip. They clanked glasses in a toast, Thomas never taking his eyes from Luther, and said, "May the best man win."

"And I will," the bigger man said with a lopsided grin. "Always have, always will."

Again giving him the once-over, Thomas thought, *I have been in some brawls over the last many years while sailing the South Pacific, but this one may be more than a handful.* Feeling he was not going to be able to talk his way out of this, but stalling for time to hope for some intervention, he said, "Now, you started to tell me about the missing thumb."

"I never did such a thing."

"You did, just before you drank that glass of whiskey." Thomas quietly set his shot glass atop the bar.

Luther stared at him with amusement. "I didn't start to tell you any-thing, but I will before I beat you sinless, 'cause when I'm finished with you, you won't remember anything ever again. I was taking advantage of a couple of unwilling girls a few years back over on the Columbia River one night, and one of them shot my thumb off." He cackled.

Thomas chuckled. "Pity that's not all they shot off."

"That's what that one named Elizabeth said." Luther sneered.

A chill ran up the back of Thomas's neck. *A couple of girls? And one of their names was Elizabeth?* "The other wouldn't have been Anne, would it?"

"Doesn't matter," Luther replied. "Just doesn't matter."

"Does to me. I would like to know their names before I give you the beating you said you have never had."

Luther's eyelids dropped slightly over his eyes like a lizard's, and his face was turning red with anger. "They were those two from Germany. The Klein sisters."

Luther's glass was left hanging in midair as Thomas's left fist smashed into Luther's huge, hardened midsection. His eyes flew open, and he backed up a step, only slightly stunned. Thomas fired his right fist in a straight jab that smashed the big man's nose like raspberry jam all over his face and then another speeding left to the torso. The years of hard labor aboard the many ships he had served on had honed every muscled in Thomas's body to perfection, and he had gained tremendous power in his thick chest and arms. He had taken all the wind from Luther with this blow, and the big ugly man stood there in complete bewilderment with arms only half raised when another right smashed him again in the windpipe. Luther's arms dropped to his sides like heavy anchors, and then Thomas hooked him again on the right cheek, splitting it to the bone and splintering his jaw. Luther's mouth hung open at an unnatural angle. He stood teetering. Thomas grabbed him by the shirtfront and held him up. "That was my fiancée, my bride-to-be and her little sister."

Then Thomas turned Luther loose to fall toward the floor, snapping the big man's head back on his way down, wrenching his neck at an angle that should have broken it. It would be a long time before he would ever regain consciousness, and that would not be a very pleasant experience. Thomas left a coin on the bar for the drinks and started out the door.

"That was the most amazin' thing I ever seen," the toothless old bartender garbled. "That brutal beast had that coming for a long time."

"Well he got it," Thomas answered.

He immediately walked down the street and around the corner to the stable. *I think I have had enough of this town*, he thought. He had planned on staying a few more days, relaxing and enjoying the lazy atmosphere of this lovely little community by the river, but now he wanted only to continue on and find Elizabeth.

Walking into the stable, he saw an old man with unkempt white hair, baggy pants held up by one suspender, and boots so ragged they were hard to tell the bottom from the top. Looking at him sitting there half asleep, Thomas said, "You run this place? I am in the market for a horse and saddle."

Slowly looking up and smiling, the old man replied, "Want a bridle too? Might come in handy, ya know."

Chuckling, Thomas answered, "Yes, sir, I'll take one of those too."

"When do you need this outfit?"

"Right now. What do you have?"

The old man had yet to move, just sitting there eyeing Thomas. "All the horses I have are good uns and expensive."

Glancing around, Thomas noticed the corral full of horses behind the barn. "All things are valued according to their scarcity." Thomas balked. "And you have a corral full of them."

"Now, that may be, where you are from." The old man grinned, slowly rising. "But that corral full of horses are all mine, and they are like I just said: ex-pen-sive." He exaggerated the syllables.

Two hours later they had made a deal for a beautiful Appaloosa with a saddle, a bridle, and the blanket the old man said he would throw in for the sake of the horse. Leading the horse a block to the hotel, Thomas tied him outside and retrieved his meager belongings, rolling them into a bundle and tying them behind the saddle. It was getting late in the afternoon, but he was anxious to get started again. He wanted to make it at least partway on to the next stop that would have a hotel.

Chapter 123

Salmon River Country,
Idaho Territory, United States

1878

In two days he was in Mount Idaho, having had to spend only one night sleeping on the ground on the banks of a small stream where his horse could feed and water. After tending his horse at the stable, he crossed the street to the hotel and checked into a room—a nice room with a bed, a small table, and a chair with a window looking over the heavily forested area behind the hotel. The bathroom was just three doors down the hall. The clerk had told him his evening meal and breakfast were included in the price of the room. What luxury!

Thomas cleaned up and lay down on the comfortable bed, planning to rest a few minutes before joining the other guests for dinner in the hotel's dining room. The conversation was casual but interesting. Deadwood, South Dakota, had experienced a horrific fire, burning three hundred buildings and leaving two thousand people homeless. An inventor named Thomas Edison had effectively created a new lightbulb, and something called Madison Square Garden had opened in New York.

As the meal was nearing completion and the conversation was waning, Thomas casually brought up a group traveling through about ten or twelve years ago with two delightfully young ladies in attendance, the Klein sisters.

Without hesitation, the owner of the hotel—Mrs. Brown, who had joined the guests—spoke up. "I do remember them. They were with that Richard Rhett group. They stayed several days before moving on, heading for Warren's Diggins. A delightful group. Anne was an instant hit with the singing act she gave every evening while here, and it was that Elizabeth who was thrown into the Salmon River and drowned."

Thomas sat looking horrified. "But I thought—" he started, then was interrupted.

"Well, not really drowned dead. Some miner saved her, and the last I heard, she was back living in Warren's Diggins with her three children after that awful Indian massacre that killed her husband down on the Salmon River."

Thomas sat in confused silence while the conversation faded away as the other guests slowly retired to their rooms. He was the only remaining guest at the table, deep in troubled thought, when the proprietor spoke up.

"That Rhett group with the Klein sisters, did you know any of them?"

Hesitating a moment, Thomas shrugged. "I did. I once knew Elizabeth in the old country."

Looking over at Thomas with a sudden new interest, Mrs. Brown inquired, "What is your name?"

"Thomas Clay."

Her eyes searched the ceiling, obviously trying to recall some connection. "From Germany?"

"Yes, originally from Germany." Thomas felt a pitter-patter thrum up through his exhaustion and worry.

Looking at him with understanding in her eyes, Mrs. Brown asked, "Are you the one, Elizabeth's lover from her childhood days? The one she calls 'my Thomas'?"

"I would like to believe that," he whispered hoarsely.

"My God, after all these years. What are you doing here?"

Thomas sat with Mrs. Brown at the hotel's kitchen table for hours as he related his adventures since leaving Germany until his presence here and now. The proprietress sat in amazed silence then whispered in a kindly voice, "You will see her again soon, son." Her eyes grew misty, and she told Thomas all she remembered of the Rhett group traveling through those many years ago. Then she patiently answered all of his questions about Elizabeth and the Rhett group, as best she could.

"Thomas, it is after midnight. Come, now, let's get you to bed. You will need your rest for the journey before you. You only have a few more days' travel before reaching Warren's Diggins, but they will be difficult ones. We will talk more of this in the morning. Now off with you for this night."

The night passed in troubled sleep for Thomas. He knew he was only a few days' travel to where Elizabeth was last reported to be living, and he was more anxious than ever before in his life.

At breakfast, after Mrs. Brown had finished making all the guests comfortable, she sat down beside Thomas as he ate. "You have but two days in reaching Florence. There is not much left there now, a few old buildings and only four families still living in the area. After the gold played out, it seems most went on to other boomtowns, including Warren's Diggins. I don't think there is even a hotel there anymore—not a standing one, anyway. You may wish to push on to the ferry crossing the Salmon River at French Creek. That is only one or possibly two days past Florence. They still have very nice accommodations there, I've heard." She nodded decisively and made to clean up a guest's plate.

"One more thing before I leave," Thomas spoke up, "and then I will stop pestering you about the past. Have you heard of Fredrick Burgdorf, who I think also lives over in the area near Elizabeth?"

"Heavens, yes, I do know him. I know him very well." Mrs. Brown stacked another guest's empty plate on her palm. "I try to visit there every spring when the road opens over the pass. Fredrick has a delightful hot springs resort in a stunning valley in the area where Lake Creek runs in to the Secesh River. He has an incredible Chinese cook working for him, and his establishment is known for a hundred miles around. He and his pardner, Josh, have accomplished a tremendous degree of success."

Thomas had been informed of Josh immigrating with Fredrick from Lolivey's father in Hayes Valley but still pictured him as the skinny little urchin he had brought home from the slums in Darmstadt. More indecisions raced through his mind. *What will Fredrick be like now? And as a matter of fact, what will Little Josh be like now?* Married with at least one child and maybe two, it had been rumored.

Thomas and Mrs. Brown talked nonstop for another several hours, and he was finally ready to leave as the sun was positioned directly overhead. His big Appaloosa was nervous and a handful as they left Mount Idaho.

"You better conserve some of that energy, old boy," Thomas told the horse prancing sideways down the wagon road. "You will be needing it soon."

The road rose steadily toward the mountaintop, and again Thomas found himself traveling through some of the most breathtaking countryside he had ever seen anyplace in the world. He spent one night on the trail, reaching Florence after dark the following night. After finding an empty building to shelter in, he tended the horse and spread his bedroll out on the floor. He ate a meal that Mrs. Brown had carefully packed away for him and he had tied in his roll behind his saddle.

Once sated, he lay on the floor of the old abandoned building looking up between the missing shingles. His eyes traced a shooting star, and he drifted off to a sound sleep for the first time in weeks.

Despite the peaceful sleep, Thomas woke up long before daylight cold and stiff. He saddled the Appy and headed out again on the wagon road leading down the mountainside to the ferry crossing. *It's cold up here in these mountains. I'm going to have to invest in warmer clothes before winter*, he reasoned. For the last many years, he had been no higher in elevation than the top of the ship's mast. Now at about six thousand feet in elevation, he was shivering.

He made his way down the mountain into the canyon and finally came to the infamous Salmon River he had heard so much about. He'd even read about it in some of the books in his family library in Germany.

It was just coming on twilight when Willy, the ferry tender, sitting on the opposite side of the river, noticed Thomas sitting on his horse and waving to request to come across.

"It's nearly dark!" Willy shouted. "Do you want to camp there tonight and cross tomorrow morning or come across in the dark?"

"I'll come across in the dark!" Thomas shouted back. "I would like a comfortable bed and a warm meal."

Willy waved his hat and moved down to the ferry. Crossing in the dark was certainly nothing that he had not done many times in the past, and there would be the added revenue of another guest for the night.

The crossing went without incident. Thomas had already heard of the horrifying crossing experienced by the Rhett group where Elizabeth was thrown into the river and nearly drowned so did not question Willy about it now. His accommodations were more than satisfactory, and he lounged around the landing and hotel all day, soaking up the beauty of the canyon and the wildlife wandering in its depths.

Finally that night at dinner, Thomas decided to question Willy about the road to Burgdorf Hot Springs resort. He was informed it was in excellent repair and far improved from its original route of years ago when Milner had first built it.

"If you push that big Appy hard, you will make it in one day. A long, hard one, but it can be done."

"If it can be done, I will do it," Thomas responded.

And he did, riding into the meadows with the breathtaking hot springs the following night just at twilight. The road up over the mountain then down into these meadows along Lake Creek had been another sight that he would remember forever—its beauty surpassed by only a few sights he had ever witnessed. The steam rising from the hot spring was totally mesmerizing. He sat on the big Appaloosa in silence, enjoying the sheer beauty of it all. The only noise was the creaking of the saddle leather as the big horse shifted his weight from foot to foot. There was a faint star becoming visible in the night sky just as some light-pink tails of fog drifted off to the south.

Suddenly an atrocious howl broke the silence, harkening Thomas's memory back to the wolf packs in Germany. It was very close and had frightened the big Appy, which now stampeded, nearly unseating Thomas. Once he got the horse under control, Thomas directed him to the edge of the outbuildings surrounding the lodge.

Chapter 124

Burgdorf Hot Springs,
Idaho Territory, United States

1878

Josh heard a commotion outside and wandered out to the road to see what was happening. There was some light left in the night sky, and he squinted into it to see a man sitting on a big Appaloosa. "You okay, mister?" he said. Without waiting for an answer, he added, "Looking for a night's lodging? It gets pretty cold here at this elevation, and we do have some bunks available."

"I would love a room with a bed and a warm meal," the man said. "I have come a far piece from the ferry crossing on the river this morning, and me and my horse are both worn out."

It was too dark to see the man's face, but Josh recognized the voice even after all these years. He said nothing but cautiously walked forward a few steps. Josh looked up into the green eyes of the big black-haired man sitting on the horse and stuttered, "Holy shit, Thomas. It's you!" and collapsed in a heap on the ground.

Thomas sat just a moment then jumped from the saddle to assist this young man who had just spoken his name then collapsed.

Fredrick, hearing the ruckus, came out of the lodge with a lazily swinging lantern. They often had travelers arriving after dark, so he was not concerned. But when he got closer, he saw Josh sitting on the ground with a large man kneeling beside him, still holding the reins of a big Appaloosa. "What in tarnation is going on?" he shouted, holding the lantern higher for a better view.

Thomas stood and faced Fredrick, who immediately stared back into those piercing green eyes then to the head of coal-black, wavy hair and said, "Holy shit, Thomas. It's you," and dropped the lantern.

The lantern burst and seeped oil on the dirt road, flaming brightly under the night sky. With the surge of flame, the big horse flared his nostrils and swung his whole weight, eyes huge with fright. Thomas held tight to the bridle reins. Fredrick, regaining some composure, collected up Josh before he could get run over and moved back to the side of the building until Thomas got the horse under control. Although Josh was back on his feet, his mind was stuck in total bewilderment as Fredrick stood there with a most stunned look on his face.

Finally Thomas quietly said, "I am so sorry to have created such difficulties. Please forgive me."

Fredrick had now totally regained his composure. "I knew you were alive, Thomas. I always knew it, but this is going to take a lot of explaining, and we better get inside where it's warm with a bite of good food from that cook of mine and a few bottles of good wine."

"Can't wait," said Thomas, untying his bed roll with all his worldly belongings from behind his saddle.

Josh stammered, "Thomas, I will tend to and stable the horse. Come into the lodge now, and let's get this reunion underway. I gotta hear this."

Thomas couldn't believe he was now in a high mountain valley in Idaho at a place called Burgdorf Hot Springs. It would be an easy day's ride over Steamboat Summit to the mining community of Warren's Diggins, where Fredrick had just confirmed Elizabeth was now living. He and Fredrick sat at the table overlooking the hot spring pool, deep in conversation. The cook had brought them each a plate of enjoyable food, and they ate as they talked. They both were notorious for their habitual way of talking with their hands, and their combined gesticulations gave the appearance of a rapidly spinning windmill.

Josh had tended to the big Appaloosa and hurried into his cabin to inform Lolivey of the appearance of Thomas Clay, whom he had presumed dead for years. After bundling their two small children, they crossed the small meadow to the lodge and, on entering, stood a moment in wonder watching the wild conversation in progress.

Soon noticing Josh and Lolivey standing there, each holding a small child, Thomas stood and was introduced to Josh's wife and children. After a lengthy introduction, Thomas commented, "The last time I saw you before leaving Germany, Josh, you were hardly bigger than your children here."

Thomas was called upon to relate his adventures and how he'd managed to find this place high in the Idaho mountains. He was constantly interrupted with a question here or a comment there, and he talked and reiterated his tale for hours, at times asked to repeat a portion time and time again. Long after midnight they all agreed to call it a night and continue the next day. Thomas was shown to a small cabin the cook had made ready for him hours ago. A fire was going in the little wood-burning stove, and Thomas noted a window that would look out over the hot springs and meadow when daylight came. The bed looked unconditionally inviting.

As tired as he was, he could not help but walk out the door and submerge in the log-lined, steaming-hot pool. *I haven't had a soak like this in years*, he thought. Upon returning to the cabin, he fell into bed and did not stir until the sun was at its zenith the following day.

Fredrick could wait no longer and was pounding on Thomas's door when he sleepily rose, slipped on his pants, and opened it, nearly getting a rap on the forehead from Fredrick's hand knocking.

For days, Thomas helped beside his old friend around the hot springs in every way possible. The conversation never stopped and always ended in questions about Elizabeth, her life, her children, her home, and on and on.

Finally Fredrick turned to face Thomas. "You are worrying yourself sick, my old friend. Relax, she still thinks of you continually, actually has never stopped. Like you, she has also had a tough and traumatic life since arriving in San Francisco years ago, but she is a stayer, Thomas.

She is as beautiful and sensitive as ever, but she is tough, probably not exactly the beautiful young bride-to-be you remember in Germany but real close. We have not talked of you much over the years, me thinking you probably dead but her never wavering in her faith that you were alive, hoping beyond belief she would someday see you again.

"You have been here with me now for six days stalling in making the one-day trip over the summit to meet Elizabeth after all these years. Do you want me to go with you?"

Thinking on this a few moments, Thomas looked up. "Would you?" Thomas sucked in a gulp of the fresh air. "I would like you and Josh both to go."

Overhearing the conversation, Josh chimed in, "We can do that."

"I have been fighting many battles all over the world." Thomas sighed. "But never have I been as terrified as this moment."

Chapter 125

Burgdorf Hot Springs,
Idaho Territory, United States

1878

Lolivey saw them off early the next morning for the trip over the summit to Warren. She had managed the hot springs and the stage stop alone on various occasions before.

"Give my best regards to Elizabeth and the children, will you, Thomas?"

"I will." He smiled. "Certainly, I will."

Josh had harnessed a team to the buggy so the three of them could ride side by side and continue with their conversation covering the events of the last many years. The wagon road on to Warren's Diggins followed the lazily flowing stream, Lake Creek, for a couple of miles before merging with the Secesh River. Hearing a faint far-off noise, Thomas looked up.

"Look at the flock of geese flying overhead migrating south for the winter," Thomas said. "I haven't seen this since our life on the farm in Germany."

Fredrick also noticed the geese. "Well, it's getting that time of the year. The leaves are changing colors, and we have a heavy frost every morning. Probably won't be long till we are butt deep in snow."

Thomas laughed. "I haven't seen frost or snow for years."

The road wandered along the river for several miles. The changing colors of red and gold on the underbrush and aspen trees were in stark contrast to the pine trees mixed amongst them, making it a peaceful and lovely sight. All of a sudden, they heard a tremendous splash in the river and watched a moose—with horns extending longer than a man could reach—jump into the river and wade to the other side. For Thomas it was a sight he had never before witnessed. *I think I will adjust to this life very easily*, he thought.

The road climbed around the mountainside, leaving the river to lead up and over Steamboat Summit. It then made its way down the other side and on to Warren's. Every turn offered a different mesmerizing view. They had seen a moose, then many deer, and on one occasion a small herd of elk that crossed the road in front of them.

They were now riding along beside huge piles of moss-covered boulders in neat rows. Seeing the puzzled look on Thomas's face, Josh explained their existence as tailings from the huge floating dredges. "We will see one in operation in a few minutes," he said. "We are now in the bottom of the canyon where the streams flow, filling the ponds that float the dredges."

When they rounded the next corner, they saw a huge floating barge affair with a long neck of buckets on a continuous conveyor belt, dipping into the water, churning up buckets of sand and gravel, then dumping them into washing bins on deck for the process of removing much gold.

Continuing on across a small bridge, they could see the edge of the town ahead. The scene was shockingly busy with horses, laboring men with picks and shovels, and wagons heavily laden with ore.

"Unbelievable," Thomas said.

Once they were in town, Fredrick suggested, "Perhaps we should stop and tie our horses here in front of the saloon. When Elizabeth sees you, I wouldn't want her to screech and frighten the horses, causing a stampede down the street."

After wrapping the reins around the hitching post about a block away, they turned and walked abreast the final few steps up the street. It was a balmy warm fall day. The trees and brush with their changing colors in the hills on each side of the town looked like an artist's fine painting. *What a magnificent setting*, Thomas thought.

Chapter 126

Warren's Diggins,
Idaho Territory, United States

1878

As was her routine, Elizabeth was sitting on her front porch enjoying the fall sun and watching the children play in the yard. Taking her eyes away from the children for a moment, she noticed three men ambling up the street in her direction. She recognized Josh and Fredrick and immediately rose to her full height to wave a hand.

"What brings you two vagabonds to town this day?" she shouted over the noise of the passing ore wagons.

Thomas noticed the twinkling pastel light of an object hanging in the window behind Elizabeth. *It can't be*, he thought. *It's the hummingbird I gave her before leaving Germany. That's really Elizabeth.* His heart pounded in his chest, and he could hardly walk the remaining few steps to where Elizabeth stood with the children now at her side.

From where she stood, Fredrick and Josh were shorter than her by a half a foot, but this other man between them, the one with the green eyes and wavy coal-black hair was looking at her straight in the eyes, not blinking nor diverting his gaze, just staring. She stood a moment returning the gaze before her breath caught and she nearly fainted when full recognition hit her like a mule's kick to the stomach.

"Thomas!" she shrieked so loudly, it got the attention of everyone within a hundred feet. "It's you." Then she jumped off the step into his arms, burying her face in his shoulder.

They stood clinging to each other in that manner with at least a hundred miners watching.

Then Elizabeth looked up into those green eyes. "You had better not be a shy boy this time, Thomas."

Their lips met in a lingering kiss.

Finally breaking the kiss, she said, "How I have missed you, you brute." She gasped. "You have a lot of explaining to do. I'm a good listener, and we have a lifetime ahead to hear this story," she said with one eyebrow cocked but a smile on her lips. "And it had better be good."

Thomas held her tightly to the applause of all the miners on the street. All knew her story and of the unending search for her Thomas.

"Well," Fredrick finally said, breaking the spell, "I guess you won't be needing us any longer, and I'm sure you two have a lot to talk about. I think Josh and I will return back to the hot springs."

Beaming with delight, Thomas answered, "We will be in touch soon." He clutched Elizabeth even tighter. "Thank you, Fredrick. Thank you, Josh."

Then relinquishing the tight embrace he had on Elizabeth, Thomas stepped back to look at the three children. "And what do we have here?" he asked, smiling.

"Your three children," Elizabeth replied. "And I know you are going to help me give them the best of care for the rest of our lives." Then she added, amused, "That is, if your story is a good one."

His story was good, and they spent a lifetime together—with Thomas retelling the events that took place during all the years he was held captive working as a slave laborer on merchant ships in the South Pacific and China Seas, and Elizabeth in turn telling of her adventures during the same time frame.

Thomas Clay and Elizabeth Klein were married a few months later in January of 1879. The ceremony was attended by their three children and everyone within a day's ride of Warren's Diggins, high in the mountains of Idaho. They were to honeymoon with their children on a ship that visited Eladio Tribaldos's coffee plantations in Panama then on to Denmark to visit their entire family before returning to live out their lives not far from Warren's Diggins.

About the Author

Dorian Clay was raised in the Salmon River Valley and Hells Canyon. From childhood, he helped his family work one of the larger cattle ranches in the Pacific Northwest, primarily located on the Idaho side of the Snake River in Hells Canyon. After completing school, he worked in heavy industrial construction, in the telecom industry, and on high-voltage electrical transmission towers. He was also a diver for the installation of underwater fiber optic cables on his South American project. His work has taken him throughout the Oceania area, Southeast Asia, Central and South America, and the Caribbean Islands. Dorian now lives near Riggins, Idaho, and enjoys frequent trips to Burgdorf Hot Springs and Warren with his wife, Marie.